The Black Consciousness Reader

Written and compiled by Baldwin Ndaba, Therese Owen, Masego Panyane, Rabbie Serumula, Janet Smith and Paballo Thekiso

With photography and videography by Paballo Thekiso

First published by Jacana in 2017
Second edition, 2021

10 Orange Street
Sunnyside
Auckland Park 2092
South Africa
+2711 628 3200
www.jacana.co.za

© Text: Baldwin Ndaba, Therese Owen, Masego Panyane, Rabbie Serumula, Janet Smith and Paballo Thekiso, 2021
© Photography and videography: Paballo Thekiso, 2021

The financial assistance of the National Institute for the Humanities and Social Sciences (NIHSS) towards this publication is hereby acknowledged. Opinions expressed and those arrived at are those of the author and are not necessarily to be attributed to the NIHSS.

All rights reserved.

ISBN 978-1-4314-3066-6

Also available as an ebook

Cover design by Trevor Paul
Editing by Megan Mance
Proofreading by Lara Jacob
Indexing by Janet Smith and Megan Mance
Set in 11,5/15pt
Printed by ABC Press, Cape Town
Job no. 17456

For a complete list of Jacana titles, visit www.jacana.co.za

For Ntsiki Biko, whose story is mostly untold. It was her political strength, her meagre nursing salary and her love that supported her husband Steve as he helped lead the country to Black Consciousness. We honour you.

Baldwin Ndaba: *To my family — for allowing me the opportunity to document the contributions of Black Consciousness adherents to the liberation struggle in Azania.*

Therese Owen: *Thank you, dear father — for teaching me that racism is an evil invention of humankind and must be fought with courage and a true heart.*

Masego Panyane: *For my mother — I'm glad you still have the eyesight to read this. For young Blacks, may this book begin the process of liberating your mind as it has mine.*

Rabbie Serumula: *For my father, who left me lessons from beyond the grave. He scribbled them down at the back of his books. I understand, Papa, how heavy it was. Keep resting.*

Janet Smith: *For Deb, on the river between silence and noise.*

Paballo Thekiso: *Ho mosadi wa ka o tsotehang, Refilwe, ho baradi baka Atlegang le Rorisang. To my Heavenly Father, thank you for the strength and wisdom; I'm humbled, grateful and forever thankful.*

Contents

List of Abbreviations ix
Foreword xiii
Introduction 1

1 Steve Biko and the Rise of Black Consciousness
   Written and compiled by Baldwin Ndaba and Janet Smith 23
2 Africa, the Intellectuals and Black Solidarity
   Written and compiled by Janet Smith 78
3 Black Consciousness and Christianity
   Written and compiled by Janet Smith and Paballo Thekiso 166
4 The Soweto Massacre and the Growth of a New Black Consciousness
   Written and compiled by Baldwin Ndaba and Janet Smith 204
5 The Art of Black Consciousness
   Compiled by Rabbie Serumula, Therese Owen and Janet Smith 246
6 The Conscious Women
   Compiled by Masego Panyane 319
7 Land: The Continuing Revolution of Black Consciousness
   Compiled by Janet Smith 377

Appendix 399
About the Authors 409
References 410
QR Codes 424
Index 425

List of Abbreviations

ANC	African National Congress
ANCYL	ANC Youth League
ARM	African Resistance Movement
AZANLA	Azanian National Liberation Army
AZAPO	Azanian People's Organisation
AZASO	Azanian Students Organisation
BAWU	Black Allied Workers' Union
BC	Black Consciousness
BCM	Black Consciousness Movement
BCMA	Black Consciousness Movement of Azania
BCP	Black Consciousness Programmes
BLF	Black First Land First movement
BOSS	Bureau of State Security
BPC	Black People's Convention
BSS	Black Students Society
BWF	Black Women's Federation
CERT	Centre for Education Rights and Transformation
CI	Christian Institute
CODESA	Convention for a Democratic South Africa
COSAS	Congress of South African Students
DRC	Democratic Republic of Congo
EFF	Economic Freedom Fighters
Frelimo	Mozambique Liberation Front
IFP	Inkatha Freedom Party

IMF	International Monetary Fund
IUEF	International University Exchange Fund
LACOM	Labour and Community Resource Project
MAGA	Make America Great Again
MK	Umkhonto we Sizwe
MPLA	People's Movement for the Liberation of Angola
MRI	Medical Rescue International
NAACP	National Association for the Advancement of Colored People
NBA	National Basketball Association
NEUM	Non-European Unity Movement
NFL	National Football League
NGO	Non-governmental Organisation
NLF	National Liberation Front
NUSAS	National Union of South African Students
OAU	Organisation of African Unity
PAC	Pan Africanist Congress
PASMA	Pan African Student Movement of Azania
PET	People's Experimental Group
PFI-SA	South African Paulo Freire Institute
PLO	Palestinian Liberation Organisation
Poqo	military wing of the PAC
PYA	Progressive Youth Alliance
SACC	South African Council of Churches
SACHED	South African Council for Higher Education
SAIRR	South African Institute of Race Relations
SAPA	South African Press Association
SASM	South African Students' Movement
SASCO	South African Students Congress
SASO	South African Students' Organisation
SOPA	Socialist Party of Azania
SPCC	Soweto Parents Crisis Committee
SPRO-CAS	Study Project for Christianity in Apartheid South Africa

List of Abbreviations

SRC	Students Representative Council
SSRC	Soweto Students Representative Committee
Swapo	South West Africa People's Organisation
TANU	Tanganyika African National Union
TECON	Theatre Council of Natal
TRC	Truth and Reconciliation Commission
TUCSA	Trade Union Council of South Africa
UBJ	Union of Black Journalists
UCM	University Christian Movement
UCT	University of Cape Town
UDF	United Democratic Front
UM	Unity Movement
UNIA-ACL	Universal Negro Improvement Association and African Communities League
Unisa	University of South Africa
UWC	University of the Western Cape
WARC	World Alliance of Reformed Churches
Wits	University of the Witwatersrand
WNBA	Women's National Basketball Association
YCCC	Yu Chin Chan Club
YCL	Young Communists' League

Foreword

Questions swirl and grow about the relevance of Black Consciousness in post-apartheid South Africa. But my response to those questions comes with one of my own: Why do commentators, analysts, academics and activists seem confused when Black students of today mobilise?

What is it that inspires their radicalism and, for some, their militancy?

My contribution to an answer is informed by my development as a student activist, national leader and, later, professional community organiser. And that, as it is for so many other people, begins and ends with Black Consciousness – a resistance and an interrogation of centuries-long shared experiences lived through domination.

The fact is that the role, relevance and contribution of the BC philosophy is more warranted now than ever. Black Consciousness does not die. It remains vibrant even when it is apparently dormant. Its approach and method are always readily available to be used by the oppressed when the need arises to confront particular and universal challenges posed by institutionalised racism and violence.

Black Consciousness emerged because Black people's social and economic status, our potential for development and advancement and our meaningful contribution to society were often, if not always, ignored, devalued and frustrated. Meanwhile, the relationships between Black and white people were and are institutionally defined as that between the 'inferior' and the 'superior'.

In South Africa, persistent high rates of unemployment, deepening inequality, grinding poverty, an unacceptable provision of public services, the plague of untamed greed and corruption among the elite, and unaccountable and patronising political leadership is the story of post-democratic life. And that story is a horror.

Deep reflection on race relationships between people in the diaspora and colonies such as South Africa raised awareness of the painful position of Black people. It reminds us that the only response was a justifiable programme against the entrenched socio-economic order. But the relatively unchanged state of that order in a post-democratic South Africa has left Black people, workers and students restless, and increasingly protesters, as they seek a re-examination of what was demanded of a new establishment's institutions and policies.

More and not less was what was expected from a Black-dominated administration.

It is startling that the issues that lie behind our current public discontent are primarily the same as those that have long marginalised and disadvantaged Black people. While it is true that established political and economic systems do not easily submit to change, this becomes more entrenched when the authors and beneficiaries of a new system believe in, work for and use culture, history, misinformation, corruption, law and force as tools.

A new system becomes a threat when any rebellious impulse is condemned as counter-revolutionary and unpatriotic, if not seditious. How is the ANC likely to deal with the growing tide of Black protest against the perceived betrayal of Black aspirations by its government – one that was essentially installed by the Black vote?

It could use covert force, not to mention its internal party structures and processes, as a 'legitimate' means of dealing with growing dissent. It might – as it has in the past, out of desperation – resort to a vulgar and distorted version of Black Consciousness that relies on caricature.

It may be laughable but it is also dangerous when Black aspirations, Black image and Black dignity are displayed as grave ignorance. This is the worst form of racism. But we know that genuine Black resistance is costly, and rare indeed is sincere support for Black initiatives towards fundamental systemic change.

Why shouldn't the subjugated be suspicious? Their lived experience, instincts and discernment are reliable guides in choosing allies and strategies. Trust and mutual recognition must be earned.

South Africa is one of the most informative case studies of militant radical Black social and economic action for change. Afrikaner administrations failed because they assumed they 'knew' Black people. And Black resistance was aimed at frustrating those imposed symbols, leaders and institutions, and that political and social engineering. But it was also a struggle against a clear dramatisation of power used to abuse, dehumanise and degrade.

Above all, it was the students and the youth of the 1960s and 1970s who promoted, intensified and sustained an all-embracing programme to end economic and social injustice in our wounded and fragmented country, well-endowed in natural resources as it was.

We were not surprised that the second-last apartheid president, PW Botha, described the war that white South Africa waged against Black people as 'a total onslaught'. The society that racism created was abnormal and inhumane, despite its righteous Christian proclamations.

Black people's initiatives against domination, dispossession and oppression had to be nuanced and sophisticated. The philosophy maintained a mission to be simple, relevant and clear, and a defensive, constructive and life-enhancing ideology emerged, nourished in the Black soil by grief and blood.

Black Consciousness bloomed as it bravely assaulted and ultimately defeated the 'rationale' of a racist ideology. How did it do that? We believed that critical dialogue, reading, exposure to real situations and carrying out corrective actions served awareness.

Combative and rigorous questioning was an essential element in our peer and participatory education. A deepening of knowledge and personal agency in the advancement of self and community were at the centre of our endeavour, and Black Consciousness became a way of life. This was a deliberate process in which each individual was expected to commit, to show personal responsibility, in order to be truly free while striving to expand broader human potential.

One had to be consciously self-critical and ceaselessly engage in education and radical social analysis. At the same time, to remain relevant, one had to be effective, helpful and astute towards others, whether this was in the family, a trade union, a club, a choir, a church or a political or student organisation.

It has to be emphasised that we never saw ourselves as the exclusive custodians of truth and wisdom. The act of raising consciousness was properly considered a two-way process. We all benefitted. We affirmed ourselves and each other as we utterly rejected the notion that Black people were inferior.

Our free thinking directly challenged the racially and tribally engineered plans of colonialism and apartheid. I thank my friends and close associates as well as some teachers, lawyers, health workers, youth club members and theologians that we walked together. Our shared life stories increasingly compelled us to take drastic action for change.

Hope was aroused and fear banished. Ours was a spiritual and mental awakening. That stage in my life equipped me for the long haul. Theory was particularly tested in fierce rural land disputes in areas like Mgwali near Stutterheim, Driefontein in Mpumalanga, Tshikota and Madimbo in Limpopo and Mogopa in the North West. Yet, some paid the ultimate price in their fight for safe and affordable housing.

Although conversations about these kinds of issues have to be approached with extreme circumspection, our political education would have been meaningless if it had remained disinterested, impartial or aloof from society. That is how I found myself living, thinking and practising Black Consciousness among people subjected to harsh lives, especially on the mines, in factories, on farms, in hostels, in townships and in discarded rural areas.

Conscious and motivated, we could not resist grasping every available strategic opportunity to work for change also in hospitals, places of worship, and social and sports clubs. We resisted tribal authorities and the bantustans.

Racially and tribally segregated universities became hotbeds of activism, and we must remember that it was not only Black students who were affected. Black staff and tutors were not sheltered from the indignities of the Group Areas Act, 'influx' control and the enforcement of the pass laws either. All these served to fuel discontent and nurtured a peculiarly powerful Black liberation movement that was irrevocably changing minds, bodies and souls – from the inside.

Black Consciousness was at first dubbed a platform for misguided Black malcontents, deviants, misfits and dropouts. We were also confused with the Black Power and civil rights movements in the United States. Others claimed we were communists, thus creating a social shield around police brutality and the state-sanctioned murders of people who included some of our role models such as Onkgopotse Abram Tiro.

But it was not only the apartheid state which opposed us.

The deaths of Pan Africanist Congress (PAC) leaders like Robert Sobukwe and Zeph Mothopeng were celebrated even among sections of the rest of the anti-apartheid movement who knew we, as Black Consciousness adherents, recognised and supported them.

I still believe their premature deaths were intended. They were too dangerous to too many people on different sides of ourselves.

Despite all attacks on us, we maintained our independence of thought and operations. We spoke openly about the shortcomings of established nationalist, capitalist or communist orders. We supported wars of independence, resistance to military conscription, and resistance to the increased production and spread of weapons of mass destruction. We supported peace campaigns.

But while acts of heroism at that time are often credited for shaping the direction antiracist movements are taking today, rigorous study and application of the history and philosophy of Black Consciousness are always needed. This affords other legitimate voices being heard, and useful lessons persistently being gleaned to keep making valuable challenges on the past.

Ishmael Mkhabela
Chairperson of the Steve Biko Foundation and The Johannesburg Inner City Partnership

Introduction

'Beware those who think liberation comes/ through noisy discussion:/ we must prepare ourselves,' wrote Karen Press[1] in her 1990 poem, 'Priorities'.

A signal to the new nation, the words circle, then wrap themselves around and hoist up the meaning of Black Consciousness (BC).

In 1990, when liberation movements were unbanned in South Africa and Nelson Mandela released from prison, 'priorities' were everything. What were the priorities of BC? Through love, it said Black people had to redefine their entire outlook.

Steve Biko said it was 'the realisation of the need to rally together around the cause of oppression, to rid ourselves of the shackles that bind us to perpetual servitude.

'It is a manifestation of a new realisation that by seeking to run away from themselves and to emulate the white man, Blacks are insulting the intelligence of whoever created them Black.

'Black Consciousness, therefore ... seeks to infuse the Black community with a newfound pride in themselves, their efforts, their value systems, their culture, religion and outlook to life.'

So much politics has happened since Biko spoke those words in the 1970s. Indeed, laws have changed to lay the groundsheet of equality in South Africa, and there have been five Black presidents. But do we know the history sufficiently to reach radical and intrinsic liberation?

In this book, we examine that history and also the culture,

---

[1] Karen Press founded the South African publishing collective, Buchu Books. She is the author of eight poetry collections and writes children's books. She has been published in South Africa, Britain, the United States, Australia and Canada and her work has been translated into French, Italian, Turkish and Tamil.

philosophy and meaning of BC through voices, art, religion, music, writing, politics, solidarity and dreams.

Since it is not an ideology like its enemy, capitalism, but a state of mind, the way its history is approached will be subjective – as Karen Press said, a way to prepare ourselves. Many created it. Many are still moving its shining particles in patterns in the sand. The revolution is unfolding, it is beautiful and it is Black.

Baldwin Ndaba
Therese Owen
Masego Panyane
Rabbie Serumula
Janet Smith
Paballo Thekiso

Johannesburg, 2020

[Biko, 1978: 53]

A South African timeline

1652 Regarded as the beginning of the history of the Black struggle against slavery, colonialism and apartheid as white settlers began to arrive in the Cape.

1946 Stephen (Steve) Bantu Biko is born in Tylden, near Queenstown, in the Eastern Cape province, South Africa.

1948 Apartheid is institutionalised.

1951 The racist National Party government of Daniel François (DF) Malan introduces the Bantu Authorities Act to establish 'homelands', pejoratively known as 'bantustans', to corral Black South Africans. The bantustans – which amounted to 13% of the land, with the rest technically reserved for whites – would be run by puppet leaders.

1958 Led by Inkosi Albert Luthuli, with Johannesburg attorney Oliver Reginald (OR) Tambo the deputy president and Johannesburg advocate Duma Nokwe the secretary-general, the African National Congress (ANC) is deeply divided. Its constitution is rewritten and there are divisions in the movement over its adoption of the Freedom Charter, signed in Kliptown, Soweto, in 1955.

The Freedom Charter has as its first clause that 'the land belongs to all who live in it, Black and white'. This clause not only helps split the ANC into 'Charterists' and 'Africanists', but also later becomes central to the land argument within the Black Consciousness Movement (BCM).

Editor of *The Africanist* newspaper Robert Mangaliso Sobukwe, who was a member of the ANC Youth League (ANCYL) and an ANC branch secretary, leads a breakaway of fellow Pan-Africanists from the ANC. They oppose the liberal, multiracial ideological slant of the 'Charterists'.

1959 The Pan Africanist Congress (PAC) is formed in Soweto with Sobukwe as its founding president. The PAC supports the international intellectual movement of Pan-Africanism that seeks solidarity among those of African descent.

The Extension of University Education Act is passed, making it illegal for traditionally white universities to allow Black students to freely enrol.

1960 The PAC's Positive Action campaign against the notorious pass laws, under which the racist government regulates Black lives, ends in bloodshed when apartheid police open fire on marchers in Sharpeville outside Johannesburg. Sixty-nine people are killed and dozens injured in the massacre.

A State of Emergency is imposed and the apartheid government introduces even more punitive measures to stem activism, including detention without trial and the 'banning' of individuals.

Three main liberation movements – the ANC, the PAC and the Non-European Unity Movement (NEUM), a Trotskyist organisation established in 1943 – are banned.

1963 Biko is enrolled at the liberal Catholic institution for Black scholars, St Francis College, at Mariannhill in Natal.

A number of the multiracial Liberal Party's leadership are detained or banned. Others go underground.

1964 The Rivonia Trial of the ANC's top leaders, including Nelson Mandela, Walter Sisulu and Ahmed Kathrada, concludes at the Supreme Court in Pretoria. Lengthy sentences of imprisonment on Robben Island are imposed.

The National Union of South African Students (NUSAS) begins a period of decline in the wake of Black students' increasing antipathy towards white liberals. About a quarter of NUSAS' membership is Black.

Martin Legassick – later an influential Marxist historian – represents NUSAS at an international students' congress in Dar es Salaam, Tanzania, and brings home the discussion about it not being representative enough of the South African reality. Its moderate base triumphs against its more radical members, despite an agreement at a NUSAS conference that Black students should lead and that there should be a more outspoken approach against repression.

A small group of white former NUSAS students is associated with the renegade African Resistance Movement (ARM). But there is widespread condemnation after one of them, John Frederick Harris, places a bomb in the whites-only waiting room at Johannesburg's Park Station. It explodes, killing a woman and injuring 23 other people. Harris was later hanged by the apartheid state.

1966 Biko starts his medical studies at the Non-European Section of the University of Natal in Durban, and through his election into the leadership of the Students Representative Council (SRC), publicly questions NUSAS' white liberal control.

1967 In an act of BC, the University Christian Movement (UCM) is founded at a congress in Grahamstown. Rhodes University theologian Basil Moore is elected president, and 30 branches are established over the next two years.

Biko and other Black students plot their rebellion against NUSAS at a congress at Rhodes after they are excluded from 'white' accommodation and dining facilities.

1968 Black students continue to caucus about forming an all-Black student organisation.

The UCM holds its second national conference at Stutterheim, Eastern Cape.

The apartheid regime interferes in the appointment of Black anthropologist Archie Mafeje at the University of Cape Town (UCT), leading to solidarity action by Fort Hare students in the Eastern Cape, who then boycott the appointment of Afrikaner principal JM de Wet.

More than 300 students are suspended at Fort Hare, with BC proponents Nyameko Barney Pityana, Kenneth Rachidi, Justice Moloto and Chris Mokoditoa being excluded entirely, and the UCM prevented from holding meetings at the university. The management at other 'bush' campuses – Turfloop in Pietersburg in what was then called the northern Transvaal, but is now Limpopo province, Ngoye in Zululand and the University of the Western Cape (UWC) – does the same.

Black student leaders meet at Mariannhill, where Biko leads a discussion about the formation of the South African Students' Organisation (SASO).

1969 A SASO constitution is adopted and Biko is elected president of the organisation. Other leaders include Pityana, Harry Nengwekhulu, Hendrick Musi, Petrus Machaka and Strini Moodley. It takes a BC direction.

1969 The South African Council of Churches (SACC), in collaboration with renegade Afrikaner church leader Beyers Naudé's Christian Institute (CI), launches the Study Project for Christianity in Apartheid South Africa (SPRO-CAS), which studies issues of Black liberation.

Catholic priests Smangaliso Mkhatshwa, David Moetapele, John Louwfant, Clement Mokoka and Anthony Mabona – exponents of Black Liberation Theology – express concerns about discriminatory treatment towards Black clergy in the Black Priests' Manifesto. Published in a Johannesburg newspaper, the *Rand Daily Mail*, it made a public call for the Catholic Church in South Africa to be Africanised.

1971 SASO releases its policy manifesto, describing BC as 'a way of life'. It endorses its relationship with the UCM, as well as with the South African Institute of Race Relations (SAIRR) but withdraws its support for NUSAS.

Black Theology starts to take hold within the UCM.
Biko delivers a speech at the Abe Bailey Institute in Cape Town, in which he openly criticises the ANC.
SASO backs the launch of the Black Consciousness Programmes (BCP), and Biko, Pityana and other BC leaders caucus widely across Black theological organisations to promote the BCM.

1972 Moore and BC activist Sabelo Stanley Ntwasa of the UCM are banned and Moore goes into exile.

Churches abroad start to fund the BCP through the intervention of SPRO-CAS and Naudé. Social worker Ben Khoapa becomes the BCP director.

Onkgopotse Abram Tiro gives a speech highly critical of

apartheid at the Turfloop graduation ceremony and is expelled, sparking a student boycott on that campus that results in the expulsion of more than a thousand supporters.

The South African Students' Movement (SASM) gains prominence. Formed out of the ashes of the African Students Movement, it is predominantly based within Soweto schools Orlando West High, Orlando High and Diepkloof High. Although SASM is later associated with BC and has some contact with the UCM as a mentor, it is essentially non-aligned.

SASO holds its first 'formation school' at the Federal Theological Seminary in Alice, Eastern Cape, producing the Alice Declaration, which resolves that students around the country should shut down apartheid universities in protest against the action against Tiro and others.

'Bush' campus students endorse the strike, and SASO is widely banned, leading to solidarity action by some white students at UCT, who are then baton-charged outside St George's Cathedral in Cape Town – an event which leads to coverage of the repression of students in the white-controlled media.

Themba Sono, who was SASO president between 1971 and 1973, gives a speech during SASO's third general council in Hammanskraal outside Pretoria in which he suggests SASO should find a way to cooperate with white liberals and some bantustan leaders, particularly Chief Mangosuthu Gatsha Buthelezi of Zululand. Sono is compelled to resign from the organisation after that speech[2] at the meeting from which some white journalists are also excluded for refusing to call Blacks 'Blacks' in their reports. The newspaper style 'rule' at the time was to call Blacks 'non-whites'.

Some SASO members go into exile after the Hammanskraal gathering.

BC ideologues Strini Moodley and Saths Cooper, who are

---

2   A quote from Sono's speech, 'In search of a free and new society', is included in Robert Fatton Jr's book *Black Consciousness in South Africa: The Dialectics of Ideological Resistance to White Supremacy*. Fatton notes that, as far as he knows, Sono's speech was never published, but that a copy exists at the Melville J Herskovits Library of African Studies at Northwestern University [Fatton, 1986].

students at University College in Durban, add their weight to the BCM by saying their increasingly popular Theatre Council of Natal (TECON) will only perform for Black audiences.

The Black People's Convention (BPC) is launched in Edendale, near Pietermaritzburg, with Reverend Mashwabada Mayatula as interim head and Drake Koka as interim secretary-general.

The apartheid regime's Schlebusch Commission begins to investigate BC and anti-apartheid organisations, including the UCM, the SAIRR and NUSAS, finding the UCM to be 'a danger' and denying it overseas funding. It is forced to disband and gives its assets to SASO and its Johannesburg offices to the BPC.

The BPC establishes the Black Allied Workers' Union (BAWU) out of interim secretary-general Koka's Sales and Allied Workers' Association. It faces off against the now all-white Trade Union Council of South Africa.

Biko quits his medical studies and joins the BCP on a full-time basis.

Journalist Bokwe Mafuna, who joins SASO through registering as a first-year student at the University of South Africa (Unisa), is tasked with drawing up a plan for a Black workers' council.

UWC's management is accused of working with the apartheid regime to undermine SASO.

The BPC holds its first congress, also in Hammanskraal. There are 25 branches, and Limpopo-based activist Winnie Kgware is elected president.

BCM activist and writer Mthuli ka Shezi is murdered after being pushed in front of a train at Germiston Station. This was after he had stood up for the dignity of Black women cleaners being abused by their white colleague.

Black workers go on strike in Durban, and this creates the opportunity for a closer allegiance between the BCM and the working class, which the BCM has not yet been able to properly access or recruit from.

The apartheid regime bans Biko, Pityana, Nengwekhulu and other BCM leaders including Jerry Modisane, Moodley (then SASO president), Koka, Cooper and Mafuna. Henry Isaacs, a law student at UWC, is elected acting president of SASO. Tiro becomes permanent organiser.

Biko is banned to King William's Town in the Eastern Cape and continues building the BCP in that area.

BPC national organiser Mosibudi Mangena is detained and convicted on charges under the Terrorism Act, allegedly in a sting operation in which it was said he attempted to recruit two apartheid policemen.

The state's rage against BC continues as printers of BC material are raided and intimidated and activists are detained around the country.

Despite the repression, the BCP forms an umbrella body, the National Youth Organisation.

With Isaacs as a leader, the SRC at UWC issues the unprecedented *Geel Dokument* ('yellow document'), which exhorts the university's management to accede to demands for reform. A mass meeting is held and Isaacs is detained.

Students stage a major protest action and UWC is shut down. As happened at Fort Hare when Pityana and others were entirely excluded, the university says all students will have to apply for re-admission. Another mass meeting is held at which the re-admission policy is rejected, followed by more protests and a huge rally in Athlone on the Cape Flats.

Mafuna, Nengwekhulu, Tiro and other BC activists go into exile in Botswana, but it's not a smooth process as the ANC and PAC are deeply embattled in their different camps there. The BCM is targeted as a potential 'Third Force'.

Khoapa is banned and put under house arrest.

Mangena is convicted of terrorism.

1974 Tiro is killed by a parcel bomb in Botswana.

Mozambique and Angola are put on the path to independence from Portugal, their colonial occupier.

The Union of Black Journalists (UBJ) is formed.

SASO organises pro-Frelimo (the Mozambique liberation movement) rallies at Curries Fountain in Durban and on the Turfloop campus. The regime bans rallies and manages to shut down Turfloop, but Durban's BC showpiece goes ahead. Dogs and general violence are set upon thousands of SASO supporters there, and soon activists – including Mapetla Mohapi and Malusi Mpumlwana – have to be sent to Natal from the Eastern Cape to keep SASO running in Durban. Through force of circumstance, bonds are forged with the ANC in the province.

More activists from SASO, the BCP, BAWU and TECON are banned.

Hundreds of representatives of Black organisations around the country attend a Black Renaissance Convention in Hammanskraal, but SASO and the BPC are disappointed by the lack of militancy and support for forming alliances with the working class and trade unions.

1975 Nine SASO activists arrested for organising the pro-Frelimo rallies go on trial, as Turfloop suspends all SASO activities.

BCM doctor Mamphela Ramphele founds the Zanempilo Community Health Centre in Zinyoka, outside King William's Town.

Biko and Sobukwe meet, and their discussions are apparently around the reunification of the ANC and PAC. Biko is said to be speaking also underground to ANC lawyer Griffiths Mxenge and Natal leader Harry Gwala, as well as the PAC's second president, Zephania Mothopeng.

Mozambique gains independence under Frelimo.

The ANC starts recruiting top BC activists, creating a concern within the BCM that it needs to hold onto its membership through the BCP. The BCM tries to deflect its supporters from finding an ideological home within the ANC, whose second national consultative conference, the Kabwe Conference in Zambia, had seen a shift towards mass mobilisation and armed struggle.

The BPC holds its fourth national conference in King William's Town, where attempts are made to align it with the non-racialism of the ANC. It is at this conference that the name 'Azania' is first used, and the BCM discusses Black communalism.

BCM's economic policy is debated at a fiery consultation in

Mafikeng. Biko and others draw up papers on this topic, calling these the Mafikeng Manifesto.

1976 Biko testifies for five days at the 'SASO 9' trial, using the stand as a platform to promote BC.

A decision to protest on 16 June is ratified. The Soweto Students Representative Committee (SSRC) is included in plans for building the underground from within the PAC and the Black Left.

About 20 000 mostly school children rise up against Afrikaans being given dominance in some Black schools, and against Bantu Education and repression. Hundreds are shot by the regime's police, and many are killed in the ensuing massacre.

The regime bans more than 120 people, while the death toll is officially given as 174 Blacks and two whites, the number of wounded as 1 222 Blacks and six whites, and the number of people arrested as more than a thousand. A nationwide prohibition is declared on public meetings under the Riotous Assemblies Act as uprisings spread. The regime then says teaching in Afrikaans is no longer compulsory, leaving the choice of the medium of instruction in Black schools largely to principals.

More activists are arrested, including members of the Soweto Black Parents' Organisation, which was dedicated to BC.

BCM leader Mapetla Mohapi dies in detention. Apartheid police say he hanged himself with a pair of jeans.

Two massive strikes cripple Johannesburg, and there's more violence in Soweto and other Black communities around the country.

The SAIRR says more than 400 people, including more than 50 children, are still in custody. A hundred were in 'preventative detention', which meant that there were no charges pending. Many activists are banned or detained, including Ramphele, under the notorious Section 10 of the Internal Security Act.

The SASO 9 trial ends with the conviction of all defendants, who are sent to Robben Island with five- to six-year sentences.

Free compulsory education is declared by the regime in what amounts to the fifth agreement with Black demands after the

Soweto uprising.

A Black home-ownership scheme is drawn up, and more than 100 detainees are freed, even though Winnie Mandela and five others are banned or restricted.

Biko is detained.

1977 Leaders of the SSRC are arrested.

The Southern African Catholic Bishops' Conference makes a Declaration of Commitment to promote BC together with other organisations.

As the number of those who have died in police detention grows to 18 – and a figure of more than 600, including at least 50 children, is released of Black people who died violently after the massacre – Biko is released. He is then re-arrested.

Soweto rent protests see violent clashes with police.

The BC-driven Committee of 10, formed by prominent Soweto residents, including Dr Nthato Motlana, wants autonomy to be given to Soweto. It wants powers to levy taxes and control education, police and elections.

Biko dies in police custody on 12 September, with the presiding magistrate saying the 'likely cause of death' was a 'head injury with associated extensive brain injury, followed by contusion of the blood circulation, disseminated intravascular coagulation as well as renal failure with uraemia'. The magistrate's view was that 'the head injury was probably sustained (when) the deceased was involved in a scuffle with members of the Security Branch of the South African Police at Port Elizabeth'.

Winnie Mandela is banished to Brandfort in the Free State.

Ramphele is banished to the rural northern part of the Transvaal where she forms the Isutheng Community Health Programme.

Thousands, including a dozen western diplomats of whom one is the United States (US) ambassador, attend Biko's funeral in King William's Town.

Members of the US Congress send a written request to the South African ambassador in Washington urging the apartheid government to 'invite an appropriate international body to examine South Africa's laws and practices relating to detention and to make recommendations, with special reference to the death of Biko'.

The regime is unperturbed. It proclaims, under the all-encompassing Internal Security Act, that 18 organisations are now unlawful, and arrests some 70, mostly BC, leaders. Others – including Donald Woods, editor of the *Daily Dispatch* newspaper in East London, and once an associate of Biko – are restricted, as is the daily newspaper *The World* and its *Weekend World* and their editor, Percy Qoboza.

Beyers Naudé is also banned.

Apartheid Justice Minister Jimmy Kruger, who had told a gathering of National Party stalwarts that '[Biko's death] leaves me cold', bans all movements affiliated with the BCM. These include SASO, the BPC, the Black Parents Association, the Black Women's Federation, Naudé's CI, the Medupe Writers' Association and the UBJ.

The US, under Democrat Jimmy Carter, declares it will 're-examine' its relationship with the apartheid regime, while a United Nations (UN) Security Council debate on South Africa is held in New York.

1978 A police investigation into Biko's death and a post-mortem report make unanimous findings: extensive brain damage, due to at least a dozen injuries.

Attorney-general of the Transvaal Jacobus E Nothling announces that an inquest into Biko's death will be held, but that he will not institute criminal proceedings. Counsel for the Biko family Sydney Kentridge calls for a verdict that Biko died as the result of a criminal assault by members of the Security Police.

The inquest results in presiding magistrate Marthinus Prins finding no one can be found criminally responsible even as Sir David Napley – a leader of the Law Society of England, who attended the Biko inquest as an independent observer at the invitation of the Association of Law Societies of South Africa – gives a 25-page report on the inquest in which he criticises police procedure.

Sobukwe dies of lung cancer at 53, and is buried in his home town of Graaff-Reinet in the Cape at a ceremony attended by a number of high-profile individuals, including Buthelezi and Anglican bishop and activist Desmond Tutu.

Qoboza is released from detention, together with nine other Black leaders, including Motlana and Soweto-based journalist Aggrey Klaaste.

The Azanian People's Organisation (AZAPO) is formed at an inaugural conference at Roodepoort outside Johannesburg and adopts the same slogan as the banned BPC of 'One Azania, One People'.

AZAPO's leaders Ishmael Mkhabela and Tiyani Lybon Mabasa are arrested in Soweto, and Tutu comes to their defence, describing them as 'authentic Black leaders'.

The trial of 11 Soweto students charged under the Terrorism Act begins.

1979 Black trade unions are recognised under the Industrial Relations Act for the first time.

Six executive members of the newly formed Congress of South African Students (COSAS) are held by police.

AZAPO elects new leaders at its first congress near Johannesburg, choosing former Soweto school teacher Curtis Nkondo as its president. He had resigned from his job as a protest against Bantu Education.

The Azanian Students Organisation (AZASO) is formed.

1980 The London-based Black Consciousness Movement of South Africa changes its name to the Black Consciousness Movement of Azania (BCMA).

A Coloured schools boycott is joined by a number of Indian schools.

1983 The National Forum, which represents 170 Black organisations across political, religious, labour and student movements, holds its first conference at Hammanskraal. Delegates unanimously adopt a manifesto, which says 'racial capitalism' is 'the real enemy'. They pledge to establish a socialist republic.

The South African Medical and Dental Council is ordered to

Introduction

hold an inquiry into the conduct of doctors who treated Biko. Two are found guilty of misconduct, and Dr Benjamin Tucker is struck off the roll for disgraceful conduct.

COSAS is banned. The Soweto Parents Crisis Committee (SPCC) is formed to address the critical situation in education.

1988 AZAPO and the Azanian Youth Organisation are banned.

Some BCM activists join the ANC in exile and undergo military training.

1990 Bans on all liberation movements are lifted.

1991 The Harare Commonwealth Declaration acknowledges preconditions for negotiations between former liberation movements, other interest groups and the National Party government. This will be a first step on the way to the negotiating forum, the Convention for a Democratic South Africa (CODESA).

The Azanian Student Convention is launched at the Medical University of South Africa outside Pretoria.

1994 The ANC and AZAPO talk about land repossession and Black empowerment, but AZAPO launches an anti-election campaign as it believes that BC has not been addressed.

Democratic elections are held, and ANC leader Mandela is elected president, with National Party leader FW de Klerk and Buthelezi, leader of the Inkatha Freedom Party (IFP), declared second deputy in a three-year Government of National Unity under an interim constitution.

The BCMA merges with AZAPO, with BCMA chairman Mangena elected president.

1997 The TRC confirms reports that five former security police officers have confessed to the murder of Biko in 1977.

1998 The Socialist Party of Azania (SOPA), a breakaway from AZAPO, lays claim to BC under leader Mabasa.

2001 Mangena is made deputy minister of education by ANC President Thabo Mbeki. Mangena becomes minister of science and technology in 2004.

2008 Mbeki is recalled, and AZAPO announces that it is withdrawing Mangena from his ministerial position.

2009 AZAPO earns a seat in the National Assembly after national elections are held.

[Baldwin-Ragaven, London & De Gruchy, 1999; Kalley, Schoeman & Andor, 1999]

Conscious concepts

Emancipation

The word comes from the Latin *exmanuscapere*, or 'detach from the hand'. This meant 'a setting free'. It's the act of liberating an individual or social group or making citizens equal after slavery, bondage, servitude or serfdom.

When discussing emancipation, history often directs us to the Proclamation issued by Abraham Lincoln during the American Civil War, on 1 January 1863. This purported to change the federal legal status of millions of enslaved people in the South, then under the control of the Confederate Government, but was also a war measure to suppress rebellion.

About 20 years before the ratification of the Thirteenth Amendment to the US Constitution, which abolished slavery and involuntary servitude, the German philosopher and revolutionary socialist Karl Marx discussed emancipation in his 1844 essay, *On the Jewish Question*.

He presented emancipation as the rendering of equal status to individuals in relation to the state. Marx made it clear, however, that while individuals could be politically free, their freedom could still be curtailed through economic inequality.

Philosophers continue to critically grapple with the nature of emancipation.

In *The Three Concepts of Politics*, French Marxist philosopher Étienne Balibar writes that 'the whole history of emancipation is not so much the history of the demanding of unknown rights as of the real struggle to enjoy rights which have already been declared'.

Many African writers and philosophers have also expressed the view that emancipation requires more than just a change in the law.

Poet, politician and cultural theorist Léopold Senghor, who served as the first president of Senegal for two decades, wrote extensively about Négritude – the consciousness of the value of Black identity.

He believed emancipation could be prevented by people's inability to create unique cultural values for themselves and live according to those.

Perhaps the thoughts most pertinent to the South African situation in terms of emancipation came from Biko: 'It becomes more necessary to see the truth as it is if you realise that the only vehicle for change are these people who have lost their personality.

'The first step therefore is to make the Black man come to himself; to pump back life into his empty shell; to infuse him with pride and dignity, to remind him of his complicity in the crime of allowing himself to be misused and therefore letting evil reign supreme in the country of his birth.'

[www.marxists.org/archive; Balibar, 2002b; Biko, 1978]

Restoring Black culture

Speaking on New York's *Democracy Now!* TV news show during the US Social Forum in Atlanta in 2007, Zimbabwe-born activist and writer Dennis Brutus – then 83 – said 'there is this insistence on trying to discover the humane values, not to despair, not to resort to violence, if you can avoid it, and achieve a kind of social justice by persuasion, by organisation, mobilising'.

Other Black writers developed this. For instance, Senegal's Fatou Diome, interviewed about her bestselling book, *The Belly of the Atlantic*, which explored immigrant life in France, was quoted: 'I wrote this book, thinking also of the Africans who say that they have lost everything because there is racism.

'In any field, when you continue to struggle, when you prove yourself, even racists at some point can no longer do anything against you.'

Afro-Caribbean psychiatrist, philosopher and revolutionary Frantz Fanon's view, given during a statement he made at the Second

Congress of Black Artists and Writers in Rome in 1959, was that 'a struggle which mobilises all classes of the people and which expresses their aims and their impatience, which is not afraid to count almost exclusively on the people's support, will of necessity triumph. The liberation of [a] nation is one thing; the methods and popular content of the fight are another... The future of... culture and its riches are... part and parcel of the values which have ordained the struggle for freedom'.

Fulbright scholar and foremost poet of BC, Mongane Wally Serote, issued a warning around the need for the restoration of culture: '... So you keep looking back/ if you did not listen when the past was breathing/ the present erases your name...' – from his 1975 poem 'Heat and Sweat, for sisters and brothers who may be weary'.

Like African-American writer and political activist Amiri Baraka – born LeRoi Jones in 1934 – and Maulana Ndabezitha Karenga, Biko was something of a 'cultural separatist', who believed that the liberal tendency of 'multiracialism' was a tactic to, among other things, remove the desire to promote and live their own culture among Black people.

Karenga – born Ronald McKinley Everett in 1941 – is an African-American professor of Africana Studies, activist and author, best known as the creator of the pan-African and African-American holiday of Kwanzaa.

[Fanon, 1963; Serote, 1975; Diome, 2008]

Freedom from white liberalism and anti-Black racism

BC neither trusts nor places value in white liberalism. The antipathy on the part of BC is, in part, based around the 'progressive assimilation' or integrationist ideas of liberals – the belief that there can be stasis while conditions 'gradually' improve.

Many within the BCM felt that this was, in fact, 'a dialectic of terrorism', which, at its core, was a fear among white liberals that if Black people started to lead the fight against apartheid or racism, they would be able to shake off white liberals and develop a militancy liberals couldn't control.

Biko's view in *I Write What I Like* was that 'the idea of everything being done for the Blacks is an old one and all liberals take pride in it, but once the Black [students] want to do things for themselves, suddenly they are regarded as becoming militant'.

Some within the contemporary BCM have identified a similar tendency within South Africa's ruling party, the ANC.

The BCM's position is that Blackness is a positive value in itself, as it seeks to undo the colonial mentality that promotes white superiority. It is a philosophy of liberation, not about what the white liberal is expecting the Black person to do. Rather, Black people do not have to prove themselves to anybody.

'You have to be very careful introducing the truth to the Black man, who has never previously heard the truth about himself,' wrote Malcolm X. 'The Black brother is so brainwashed that he may reject the truth when he first hears it. You have to drop a little bit on him at a time and wait a while to let that sink in before advancing to the next step.'

There is a view within BC that reciprocal recognition by many whites, whose minority rights were, for instance, guaranteed in the South African Constitution, is minimal, and that their communication with Blacks can be inauthentic. This doesn't make the BCM anti-white. As Biko said: 'As we proceed further towards the achievement of our goals, let us talk more about ourselves and our struggle and less about whites'.

Instead, its task and purpose has more intellectual, political and social energy: to fight the intention among Black people themselves to have them feel inferior. It's about total Black emancipation: psychological, intellectual, emotional, social and physical.

Even Mandela reflected this. In paying tribute to Biko in 2002, he said: 'Black is beautiful! Be proud of your Blackness! [Biko] inspired our youth to shed themselves of the sense of inferiority they were born into as a result of more than 300 years of white rule.'

[Biko, 1978; Haley & Malcolm X, 1965; Nelson Mandela quoted in Mangcu, 2012: This quote from Nelson Mandela appears in 'A Tribute to Stephen Bantu Biko by Nelson Mandela'. Xolela Mangcu reprinted it with permission from the Nelson Mandela Foundation. An edited version was published in 2002 as part of a Steve Biko supplement that Mangcu edited for the Steve Biko Foundation.]

The battle against neo-liberalism and capitalism

The intention of BC was not only to undo a capitalist society supported by the oppression of Blacks, but to entirely disentangle society from the white value system upon which it was built.

Race and class were not initially seen as intertwined in the BC paradigm, but by the mid-1970s, BC and organisations aligned with it had begun to embrace either a Marxist ethic or one which situated the Black person, the poor and workers first.

There was, however, a clear view throughout that capitalism was anti-Black and that it could not be adjusted, altered, watered down or reformed to be in the interests of all Black people.

Azania

A word first used by the ancient Greeks to describe the part of an ancient continent believed to be south-east Africa.

Pliny the Elder documented the 'Azanian Sea', which, he wrote, ran around the Neoproterozoic Ocean on the south-east coast of Africa, while the *Periplus of the Erythraean Sea*, a travelogue of the 1st century AD, also described 'Azania' as an area south of what is now Somalia. A copy of the *Periplus* is housed in the Robarts Collection at the University of Toronto.

A reference to 'darker-skinned' people appears in Ptolemy's *Geographia*, referring to an area even further south, likely northern Mozambique. Historian Cosmas Indicopleustes also made reference in the 6th century AD, while the Chinese referred to 'Azania' as Zésàn in the 3rd century AD.

Modern historians believe the 'Azania' to which ancient historians refer as a continent in itself consisted of central Madagascar, southern India, parts of Somalia and east Ethiopia, and Yemen. This likely rifted off, suggested African Studies pioneers, the British academics JD Fage (1921–2002) and Roland Oliver (1923–2014), in their influential book, *A Short History of Africa*.

It was when the PAC and then AZAPO used 'Azania' to refer to South Africa that it entered contemporary South African history. These parties described South Africa as the Pan-Africanist Republic of Azania, but the ANC rejected that title.

Today as Black communities, students and workers rise up against an elitist Black hegemonic class, there is talk again of an 'occupied Azania' – a phrase not in use since the late 1960s.

[Oliver & Fage, 1986; *Periplus of the Erythraean Sea* was referred to in William H Schoff's *Travel and Trade in the Indian Ocean by a Merchant of the First Century*. It was first published in New York by Longmans, Green and Co in 1912; *Geographia* referred to in Shalev & Burnett, 2012.]

The commandments of Black Consciousness

An actional, not a reactional, racial moral identity;
a psychological freedom from racism, including anti-Black racism within Black communities;
developing an interrelationship between culture and politics;
freedom from the internalisation of white superiority and from the institutionalisation of white privilege;
a delinking from the western bourgeois;
the realisation of self-determination.

One

Steve Biko and the Rise of Black Consciousness

Written and compiled by Baldwin Ndaba and Janet Smith

Every crusade needs a hero. Venezuela's Admirable Campaign against the Spanish in the early 1800s had Simón Bolívar. Anti-imperialism in 1980s Burkina Faso had Thomas Sankara. Fidel Castro's 26th of July Movement in Cuba had Argentine Marxist Che Guevara; Palestine's liberation fighters, Leila Khaled; literacy, Paulo Freire; jazz, Miles Davis; philosophy, Simone de Beauvoir; Black Consciousness in South Africa, Steve Biko.

The man who grew up in Ginsberg, Eastern Cape, has retained an extraordinary charisma that regenerates through the decades. A thinker, writer and orator of considerable prowess and persuasion, Biko's devotion to total liberation – mind, body and spirit – out of Blackness is today perfectly in sync with a young global consciousness that increasingly sees no borders between people.

Naturally, there is controversy. Biko was as imperfect as the society out of which he emerged. Yet, we can never know what his singular drive for self-determination would have achieved had he not been murdered by the barbarians of the racist apartheid state.

Here, we uncover more of his history, recapture his influence and decry the supremacist hatred that not only removed Biko from South Africa's future, but also sought to destroy Black Consciousness.

~

'You will call us Blacks at gunpoint'

Baldwin Ndaba talks to Professor Ranwedzi Harry Nengwekhulu, a founder member of SASO with Biko, Barney Pityana and Hendrick Musi. (Musi would later become Free State Judge President, and Pityana – who, like Musi, became a lawyer – would later be elected President of the Convocation of the University of Cape Town.) The interview was done in March 2017 at the School of Governance at the University of South Africa of which Nengwekhulu was the director.

Ranwedzi Nengwekhulu was a student at the 'bush college' of Turfloop[3] in what is now Limpopo when he threw down the gauntlet. It was 1968, and the rest of the world seemed to be afire with popular rebellion, if not outright revolution. The US civil rights movement had brought the Black Panthers to the fore, while Americans were protesting in growing numbers against the Vietnam War.

This, after the Tet Offensive of January that year showed that the US government's propaganda about the North Vietnamese, its enemy, being defeated was not yet true. Many ordinary Americans were appalled by South Vietnam general, Nguyen Ngoc Loan, shooting dead suspected Vietcong guerrilla Nguyen Van Lem (Bay Lop), execution-style on a violent Saigon street in February 1968. His action was captured by NBC TV cameras and, now legendarily, by Associated Press photographer Eddie Adams.

In 1968, socialism was the ideology of the Europe of the moment, in particular in France where millions of students and workers threatened the government with massive protests in May. Workers, who made up nearly a quarter of the population, went on strike

---

3   'Turfloop' was so named after its location – a farm about 40 kilometres from the formerly whites-only town Pietersburg, now Polokwane. Formally the University of the North, it was established in 1959 under the regime's policy of separating institutions of higher learning not only by race, but also ethnicity. Nicknamed a 'bush college' it was designed for inferior and unequal education.

and occupied factories, while students occupied universities to rail against capitalism and the classical Gaullist 'order'. They didn't succeed in making political revolution, such was the violence, but France undeniably experienced a social revolution, which remarkably changed it as a nation.

Meanwhile, the Troubles were just getting underway in Northern Ireland and there was the dark to the light of the remarkable Prague Spring in Czechoslovakia.

At the same time, there were often deadly student protests in Sweden, Brazil, Spain, Mexico, Poland, Italy and Yugoslavia. In Czechoslovakia, this was not a demonstration against their government but rather one in favour of it. It was a heightened contrast to France, as ordinary citizens staged a passive resistance campaign against invading Soviet troops.

In Sweden, there was a surprisingly little-known but powerful event taking place, too. Activists in the quaint Scania town of Båstad were protesting against apartheid South Africa's and Rhodesia's participation in an international tennis competition, and their demonstration turned bloody when police and protesters clashed in what was to be the most violent incident of its kind in Scandinavian country. There was more conflict over the admission of the South African team at the 1968 Summer Olympics in Mexico City when more than 40 teams threatened to boycott. In the end, South Africa was banned.

By October 1968, when the Rodney Riots unfolded in Kingston, Jamaica – inspired by the fury of students and others when their government banned Black Power leader and Guyanese historian Dr Walter Rodney from returning to teach at the University of the West Indies – it was clear the mood in the world was turning Left.

Rodney provoked outrage against capital and the middle class, raising political consciousness about the poor. And so, it wasn't surprising that Nengwekhulu and others among the militant young Black intelligentsia of southern Africa were affected by this, becoming increasingly restive around their own liberation.

Nengwekhulu says it was, in fact, 'an apartheid-compliant student body, a docile student body', which prompted him and the like-minded law scholar Hendrick Musi to form a radical, Black issues-driven organisation for universities. Nengwekhulu was on the SRC, which was made up of junior students in their second year at Turfloop, when he met Musi and found they 'shared common political beliefs'.

Nengwekhulu's political trajectory started while he was still at high school in a village in the bantustan of Venda close to the border with Zimbabwe: 'Half of the teachers at the high school were white and other black. The white teachers were very racist. Steve Biko was at Healdtown in the Eastern Cape, and he had experienced the same thing.'

'But Biko's history', says Nengwekhulu, was 'never sufficiently traced back to his youth.'

'We had no political activity at Turfloop. The concept "Black" did not exist. We were called non-whites or Bantu. We wanted to trace the student bodies which (had once) belonged to the PAC and ANC at Fort Hare. We wanted to revive them. There wasn't much information and people's lives were at risk when they spoke about it.'

It was at a NUSAS congress in Grahamstown that April that Nengwekhulu and those who shared his views found a way forward. 'That's where we met Steve Biko and Pityana and other students who came from the Transvaal College of Education, which was for Indians. Others came from different seminaries,' he explains. 'These were also views shared in the UCM.

'At the NUSAS conference, a debate arose about where should all the delegates sleep, and we suggested that we should all go to the township, but there was a strong resistance to that. In the past NUSAS conferences, Black students slept in white campuses and white suburbs. They resisted now to go to the township, and that bolstered our conviction.

'We agreed to meet at St Francis College in Mariannhill in December. It was a Catholic school, and the Catholics were very supportive – unlike other churches. Other churches, like the Lutheran and Anglican Church, opted to take a back seat at the time.'

It was at Mariannhill that the discussion was had as to whether SASO, the proposed Black students' organisation, should operate underground or above ground. A unanimous decision was taken to operate above ground, with the aspirant membership accepting that the organisation probably had 'a life-span of only five years', if that, before the National Party government banned it.

Despite the backlash from and defensiveness of some white liberal students in NUSAS, SASO was never formed to be anti-white. It was, quite simply, pro-Black. This was articulated by Biko, who said: 'Let us first organise ourselves, and we will accept white members if we are a unified group.'

Nengwekhulu says that to demonstrate this, the South African Students' Movement (SASM) was formed. It embraced even students from Botswana and Swaziland 'to show that our struggle was the struggle for the region'.

It was at Mariannhill that we had a discussion as to whether Biko would lead SASO, but the official conference to formally establish it was at Turfloop in 1969 where Biko was indeed officially elected president. Pityana became secretary.

Nengwekhulu says SASO was immediately influential at Turfloop and the Non-European Section at Natal University because of existing links between Black activists within those two institutions. Both had a strongly militant grouping, unlike other universities where SASO was initially received with some reluctance, particularly at the University of Zululand.

Nengwekhulu recalls Biko and Pityana going to Zululand to address students there, suspecting that Chief Minister Buthelezi[4] had 'something up his sleeve'. Biko and Pityana openly attacked Buthelezi, even as some students objected, asking why the pair chose to attack Buthelezi 'and not Matanzima'. Kaiser Matanzima was the chief minister of the bantustan of Transkei.

Biko said the attack on Buthelezi was based on the fact that an impression had been created that Buthelezi was not pro-bantustans. After all, he had been a member of the ANC, having joined the ANC Youth League at Fort Hare in 1948. He was also given the support of

---

4   Mangosuthu Buthelezi's Inkatha yeSizwe – later the Inkatha Freedom Party, IFP, which has MPs in the post-apartheid government – was founded in March 1975 at KwaNzimela outside the town of Melmoth in Zululand. The IFP was cited as a collaborator with the apartheid regime, and in massacres and killings of political rivals and enemies of the apartheid state, especially in the early 1990s.

the ANC when he was elected to lead the Zulu Territorial Authority, an apartheid construct, in 1970 in the belief that he could work for liberation from within.

But Biko and Pityana were able to demonstrate that despite earlier synchronicity with the ANC, Buthelezi was a beneficiary of the apartheid government. They put him in the category of 'sell-outs'. Although there was a degree of deep-seated antagonism from students at the University of Zululand, a few – including Mthuli ka Shezi, who would become a leading intellectual and cultural activist, and Deborah Matshoba, who would later be a political prisoner and banned by the state – were drawn to the BCM.

There were also 'pockets of resistance' at Fort Hare, where attacks on SASO were partly marshalled by *Daily Dispatch* editor Donald Woods,[5] who would later have a change of conscience, and Rhodes University NUSAS leader Clive Keegan, says Nengwekhulu.

He reflects on how Woods initially disparaged SASO members as 'the children of apartheid' because of the insistence among a growing number of Black students to be called 'Black'.

Partly as a result of these kinds of white public rebukes, 'Biko told us that we should develop a strategy to attack liberals'.

'He said Black people did not think that the English were also the oppressors because their children, if they graduate, immediately went to the corporate world. Our people saw Afrikaners as oppressors because they saw them in the police, pass offices, home affairs.'

Nengwekhulu says the 'arrogance' of white liberals particularly affected him when he led a SASO delegation to a NUSAS conference in Cape Town in 1969. The delegation wanted NUSAS 'to realise that they – SASO – were a force to be reckoned with', but 'a lot of them were reluctant'.

'They had to accept it after two days of ongoing attacks on [their union].'

Biko was 'the brains behind the formation of a Black student

---

[5] Donald Woods (1933–2001) was initially critical of BC, later writing editorials supporting Biko. Woods photographed Biko's battered body, helping to expose how he died. Woods's six-year-old daughter was injured when her clothing was poisoned, leading to the Woods family fleeing South Africa and Woods becoming an activist abroad in 1978, following his banning in South Africa.

organisation', but Nengwekhulu reflects on how 'we also realised that it was a mistake to elect him... because we actually exposed him to the regime'.

'He was a deep thinker and creator of ideas and so we had no choice [but to elect him]. There was a shortage of leadership.

'We had a strategy to infiltrate other organisations. We supported Black Theology in the churches and we had a number of pastors who supported us like Zionist priest [Mashwabada] Mayatula.[6] We called him "Castro".

'Steve was the president. He had to travel the country to convince the people to support.'

Nengwekhulu says that although he and Musi got backing from fellow students at Turfloop, when they later tried to organise a solidarity action after Pityana and others were expelled from Fort Hare, Turfloop management denied them that right. So they drew up a petition that they hoped would result in an official grievance being raised with Fort Hare: 'But our rector [instead] chose to visit the Kruger National Park and our petition expired without him signing. So the registrar told us that we could not strike.

'It was only in 1969 when one of the male students was found in the women's hostel and charged with misconduct that we organised a protest march, and members of the media came to attend, that there was some impact.

'I had contact with [renowned photographer] Peter Magubane[7] who came, and we made it necessary for the media to also join the march. We really wanted sympathetic Black reporters. Even the [largely anti-apartheid] *Rand Daily Mail* editor Allister Sparks[8] did not want to call us "Blacks".

---

6   Mashwabada Mayatula (1921–1980) was a pastor in the Bantu Bethlehem Christian Apostolic Church of Africa, an affiliate of the Christian Institute. He was interim president of the BPC and president of AICA; named 'Castro' for his revolutionary speeches. Mayatula was detained for refusing to testify for the state in the SASO 9 trial. A founding member of the Soweto Committee of 10, he was loved by ANC and AZAPO supporters.

7   Peter Magubane (1932–) went on to become an award-winning photographer whose work was published around the world. He covered many important events, including the 1956 Women's March on the Union Buildings, the 1960 Sharpeville Massacre, the Rivonia Trial of the 1960s and the 1976 uprisings.

8   Allister Sparks (1933–2016) gained world attention in 1977 when, as editor of the *Rand Daily Mail*, he published a story by then-reporter Helen Zille that Biko had been

'I remember Stan Ntwasa and I visited the newspaper's offices in Commissioner Street, Johannesburg, and confronted Sparks about his refusal. He told us the word "Black" was emotive, and so we told him that white people were initially called "Europeans" when they came here, and now they were called "white".

'Sparks told us that they [the newspaper's management] were "trying" to "get a name" for us, and the Institute for Race Relations was doing that. You know the name they were proposing was "Afrocolosians"! A combination of "African, Coloureds and Indians [Asians].

'I remember telling Allister Sparks: "You will call us Blacks at gunpoint!".'

'We were not anti-white, but we were pro-Black'

In 1970, SASO had a leadership change when Pityana took over from Biko as president, and Nengwekhulu was elected national organiser.

He says Biko remained very important as he had become 'a central figure in the formulation of strategy' for SASO.

'We discussed strategy, and Biko was the author of [that]. We called ourselves the "Broederbond" [in irony, after the secret, exclusively male, Calvinist organisation dedicated to the advancement of Afrikaner interests]. It was Biko, Pityana, myself, Strini Moodley and Bokwe Mafuna.

'Mafuna was not a student. He was a freelance journalist at the *Rand Daily Mail*. I was attracted to him by a picture he took which was published [in the newspaper]. It was a picture of a Black man's arrest and I was [drawn to] a caption below which said this man was arrested for a crime which was committed because of poverty.'

Nengwekhulu says the two of them met 'by chance' at a welcome party organised for Winnie Mandela after she, writer and poet Mongane Wally Serote and other activists had been released following their arrests during an anti-apartheid protest outside the American Information Centre.

---

beaten to death by the police. This, after the regime's minister of justice, Jimmy Kruger, said Biko had died during a hunger strike. Sparks also edited the *Sunday Express* and was correspondent for the *Washington Post*, the *Observer* and *The Economist*.

The welcome party was at 2nd Avenue, Alexandra, opposite the local Catholic church.

'I noticed a man complaining about the dominance of white media and the promotion of white privilege outside the party. It turned out it was Bokwe Mafuna.'

They spoke, and ultimately it was agreed that Mafuna should register at the University of South Africa [Unisa], which would allow him to join SASO as only students could be admitted to the organisation. This intervention was aimed at getting positive reports about SASO activities into the press, Mafuna then being well-placed to do that.

As a result of this insider status, Mafuna also gained somewhat privileged access to the SASO leadership and was roped into the 'Broederbond'. He later admitted that his SASO membership greatly enhanced his journalistic skills.

Nengwekhulu says Biko remained key within the 'Broederbond' in terms of developing its thought and tactics around how SASO could infiltrate other organisations. Literacy projects were developed, and major targets were migrant mineworkers filtering in and out of Park Station in central Johannesburg.

Nengwekhulu himself visited the mines with the aim of politicising and empowering labour. Meanwhile, particularly good progress was made on a literacy project in the impoverished area of Phoenix, outside Durban. SASO was, in any event, finally growing in strength on Durban campuses.

'We had a slogan: We are Blacks first before we are students.' But there was always the threat from the state.

Nengwekhulu reiterates: 'We knew we were going to be banned. We had initially given ourselves five years to mobilise people.' And then he explains: 'During that process, we had six layers of leaders in SASO. This was to allow those below to take over if we were banned.

'I was tasked to befriend Abram Tiro who was a class below me. Pityana befriended Ben Langa, who was later killed by the ANC after the apartheid government manufactured information that he was an informer.

'He was not a spy. The ANC later saw the mistake.'

Langa and Tiro were indeed part of the group of people who took over the leadership of SASO after banning orders were imposed on Biko, Nengwekhulu, Pityana, Mafuna and others in February 1973. Nengwekhulu says high school pupils were also recruited, with this part of the programme championed by the author Mandla Langa, who was Ben's brother.

The decision thereafter to form the BPC was not designed to oppose the ANC and PAC, although some said SASO was 'closer' to the PAC. 'It was not,' Nengwekhulu emphasises. 'We did not believe in the "Africa for Africans" of the PAC. We believed in "Africa for Africans", which should include white people.'

SASO was however opposed to a 'pre-fabricated multi-racialism', the word 'Black' not referring to the pigmentation of a person, but their socio-economic situation: 'You can't say a donkey is a non-horse.'

Yet, there was serious concern from some SASO members over Indians and Coloureds being referred to as 'Blacks'. Nengwekhulu says this came from the apartheid 'fact' that if you drew a pyramid, white people would be at the top, followed by a layer of Indians, then Coloureds. At the base would be 'the Africans'.

'Steve was always a good communicator. He spoke to those who were opposed to Indians and Coloureds being referred to as "Blacks" and urged them not to repeat what the National Party did. We remained friends with whoever we liked, even though some among us were opposed to Black people having love affairs with whites. But Biko emphasised that the struggle was not against individuals: It was against the system. SASO members were allowed to have relationships of their choice.'

At the same time, Biko and other SASO members were 'a group of angry people' who couldn't see a way forward for white liberals who 'determined how Black people should react to their own suffering'.

Nengwekhulu recalls an incident when he was invited to the home of the staunch liberal and Progressive Party MP, Helen Suzman. Among others at the gathering were editor of *The World* newspaper MT Moerane, physician and businessman Nthato Motlana and *Rand Daily Mail* reporter Helen Zille [who, at the time of writing this book, was a leader in the post-apartheid liberal Democratic Alliance party, which was the official opposition].

'In welcoming us,' Nengwekhulu says, 'Suzman told us that we were "all family in her house". During the party, I approached one of [her] employees – a Black man. I asked him to show me the toilet. He led me to an outside toilet, which he was expected to use along with other Black employees. As I walked back to the house, I came across Helen Suzman who asked me where am I from. I replied, I am from a "family" bathroom. She was completely shocked.'

Nengwekhulu says Suzman's reaction was simply an example of how white liberals treated Black people in reality. This incident caused him to reflect on how, during his high school and university days, Black students 'were inclined to verify each and every thing they were told by their white teachers'.

'If they said "2 + 2 = 4", we had to verify that. So that's exactly what I did.'

'In SASO, we never said "if". We always said "when" we take over.'

Biko was 'the most diplomatic person in the leadership of SASO', says Nengwekhulu. 'He could talk to anybody. If we wanted to deal with someone who had to be dealt with abruptly, we used to refer them to Strini Moodley. [Strini] would just tell them, "you are talking shit".

'But Steve never showed any emotions. I never saw him angry. Barney, on the other hand, could be very arrogant. I remember one day me and Barney went to Anglo American. We were looking for funds, and there we met Mr Harry Oppenheimer. As we sat down, I remember Barney asking Oppenheimer: "Are you the clown called Harry Oppenheimer?"

'It shocked Oppenheimer. He did know how to address it.

'Oppenheimer knew me through my father, as my father worked [at Anglo]. And so Oppenheimer asked us why are we asking for money [from him] when we are attacking liberals. We told him that when we take over, we will nationalise your company, but if he decided to give us money, we might think twice on the matter.

'In SASO, we never said "if". We always said "when" we take over. We were aware that it was going to be such a big struggle.

'Oppenheimer gave us the money.'

Explaining the SASO decision to focus on liberals, Nengwekhulu is quick to point out Biko's meticulous retort: 'Steve always said liberals determine the leadership of the struggle. They determine how you react to a kick. They said we should not be violent, but the violence came from the other side.'

Nengwekhulu says the apartheid government was also afraid of SASO: 'I remember when I was arrested in the Free State, I was with Stanley [Ntwasa]. We were arrested by a police officer whose name I remember. It was Dippenaar. He said to us: "I know you are going to take over, but that will not happen, not in my lifetime. My children will have to deal with you".'

Demonstrating how the fear among apartheid's rulers was deepening, Nengwekhulu says that during that year, 1971, the then minister of the interior, Theo Gerdener, addressed a public meeting in Brakpan in which he said: 'This Black Consciousness is the head of an ugly snake.'

'They were not comfortable with the fact that we had Indian and Coloured members in SASO. I remember Dippenaar also saying to me, "but why can't Africans and Afrikaners join forces because we both eat pap en vleis?".'

Nengwekhulu reflects on Woods's petulance, who 'became very popular for the attacks on SASO': 'He was preaching multi-racialism. And that was the reason that it became very difficult for SASO to have a strong membership at Fort Hare University.

'Later on, Steve Biko and Donald Woods became friends, and, as a result of that friendship, the media started to define Biko in terms of Woods. But Biko was recreated by the media into a different Steve Biko. He was written out of the context of the group of angry young people whom he worked with. Biko was defined in the media in terms of his personal life. He was defined in terms of Mamphela Ramphele. Even the media created their own Steve Biko like they did with Nelson Mandela. The media recreated Nelson Mandela as different to the ANC.'

Nengwekhulu says Mandela was portrayed in the media as 'a Mandela who is serving the interests and guarantees of the minorities, but the ANC was different to that Mandela'.

'I lived with Biko and his wife Ntsiki, and Pityana and his wife Dimza in the same house in Umlazi township (south of Durban).

Dimza was a nurse at McCord Hospital while Ntsiki was also a nurse, at King Edward Hospital. That part of Steve Biko's life is not written about. We lived off those women. They were feeding us. We were not working. I was receiving R50 from my brother, monthly. Those women fed us.'

There were members of the PAC and the ANC who also belonged to SASO. Many in their ranks were defended in legal conflicts by lawyers who came from the ANC and the PAC, including Griffiths Mxenge, who was a neighbour of Biko's in Umlazi.

Mxenge, an activist and Robben Island detainee, was assassinated by four members of the regime's death squad, the Vlakplaas askari (turncoat) unit, in November 1981. Having represented many political activists, he was abducted, stabbed and then hammered to death. His mutilated body was found next to the Umlazi Stadium.

Other activist lawyers who represented SASO students for free were Thembile Skweyiya (who became a Constitutional Court Justice) and Pius Langa (who would become Chief Justice). Meanwhile, when SASO students were in Johannesburg, Motlana, a physician, gave them free medical treatment, saying 'all of them' acknowledged that 'SASO was a movement of the people'.

'There is a perception that he loved Mamphela more than Ntsiki. This is not the Steve I know.'

Nengwekhulu is an angry man, especially outspoken about his emotions when he talks about Richard Attenborough's 1987 epic film *Cry Freedom,* which premiered in South Africa in 1990. Although many South Africans went to see Denzel Washington playing Biko (Washington received an Oscar nomination for his performance), Nengwekhulu was not one of them.

Even when the film aired on TV, he wouldn't watch it. In his own words: 'I did not want to destroy my television set.' What troubles him is the story of Biko's extramarital relationship with Ramphele, which was depicted in the media for years, as it was in the film. Yet, says Nengwekhulu, 'nothing in the media or in that film depicted the commitment of Steve Biko to his family, and, particularly, his wife, Ntsiki'.

He said there are 'weaknesses' in the 'public' story about the life of Biko which he believes is 'one-sided'. For instance, stories that Biko wanted to divorce his wife were 'not true'. Nengwekhulu says it was, on the other hand, 'a conscious decision' on the part of fellow activists to make the relationship between Biko and Ramphele open, because 'hiding it was going to become a weapon in the hands of the regime'.

The other reason, says Nengwekhulu, was that Ntsiki Biko had indeed come to know about the affair. Yet, while the media reported extensively on this, as if it was Biko's Achilles heel, 'that was never counter-balanced with his deep attachment to his family'.

'He was a principled man. He was very careful. We cannot assume that his family had collapsed. Ntsiki knew about Steve and Mamphela's relationship. She did not want to act to give the regime an excuse to act against Steve. Steve was taken out of his family and defined and analysed according to Mamphela. Ntsiki was made to feel that she did not exist. She was made to feel that she was a second-hand wife of Steve.'

Nengwekhulu believes that all these 'negative depictions of Ntsiki and Steve's love life' could have prompted her to shy away from taking public platforms.

'There is already a public perception that he loved Mamphela more than her. I feel angry. This is not the Steve Biko I know. If Ntsiki said Steve had no plans to divorce her, no one will believe her. Barney and I know that Steve loved his wife, but Steve was defined in an environment which was not his.'

He believes 'what made the situation worse, was that Ntsiki Biko was never approached' for her comment. No one interviewed Ntsiki in the same way they interviewed Mamphela. [And so] we took a decision that we are not going to talk about Steve and Mamphela Ramphele's relationship.'

Equally, Nengwekhulu says reports of Biko as having 'failed his [medical] exams' were not accurate: 'Steve Biko was a brilliant student. He did not fail his exams. He was failed in his exams. Steve came to dislike medicine, and he then decided to commit himself to the Struggle.

'Part of the problem that I say the story of Biko is "one-sided" is that nothing is mentioned [for instance] that he passed his Matric first class in the Joint Matriculation Board. Other people took more than five years to pass their Matric.

'It is difficult for Ntsiki. She was and has continued to be made to defend her marriage, which is something that she is not supposed to do. But a platform was created which was already polluted, and so people are not going to believe her.'

'Very few people could contradict Steve Biko'

Nengwekhulu revealed how SASO made plans for Biko to leave South Africa, and that it could have been those very plans which led to Biko's cruel death. Himself in exile after skipping the country in September 1973, Nengwekhulu says he continued to have regular telephonic contact with Biko. He gave him updates, he says, even on efforts to facilitate unity talks between the BCM, the ANC and the PAC. 'My main contact in the ANC was Thabo Mbeki, and it was the late David Sibeko in the PAC.'

'The ANC guys always asked me what the PAC was talking about because the PAC always had factions within themselves, also in exile. Factions are not a new thing in the PAC.'

Nengwekhulu says he usually spoke to Biko on Wednesdays at 8pm. The appointment was routine. At that time, part of their discussions involved preparations to secure a passport for Biko who had been designated a "banned" person by the regime and was therefore unable to officially obtain or use documents. The idea was to facilitate Biko travelling legally to Botswana to join the proposed unity talks.

Nengwekhulu says that failed.

He and Pityana, who was by then also in exile, consequently made plans to visit ANC President Oliver Tambo in Lesotho, but that also failed as neither could secure a passport either. Yet that did not dampen their mission regarding Biko.

They engaged the Swedish government for assistance and there was agreement around support for an invitation to Biko to attend a meeting in another country via the International University Exchange Fund (IUEF).

The Fund was to identify an organisation in the Netherlands –

suitably conservative – which would invite Biko in a formal capacity. But Nengwekhulu says he thinks the apartheid government became aware of their intentions, with the possibility that 'superspy' Craig Williamson communicated the plot to the regime.

Williamson – who had masqueraded as a white liberal member of NUSAS, among other 'fronts' – would soon start working undercover for the IUEF. He also had contacts among people who were close to Nengwekhulu in Botswana.

Nengwekhulu says his first impression of Williamson – who 'shaved his beard like a policeman and liked to wear safari suits' – was that 'he was a policeman or spy'. But Williamson also embodied everything Black South Africans felt in their gut about apartheid's handlers.

Nengwekhulu was once asked to drop Williamson – with whom activists sometimes worked, ostensibly as liberal 'logistical support' – at a spot where those who exited Botswana to return to South Africa could do so without using an official passport.

This was known as 'the people's border'.

'I had my suspicions about this man, [and so] I never dropped him at the people's border. I told him I did not know where the people's border was, and he told me to drop him anywhere. I dropped him at the American embassy.'

Williamson joined the IUEF in Botswana as a deputy director before leaving for the Fund's headquarters in Geneva.

'I later met him again there,' Nengwekhulu explains. 'He still had the behavioural patterns of a cop. He lost his temper easily with the secretarial staff at the Exchange Fund. I [once] found him reading literature about the [South African] Air Force and asked him what was interesting him about it. He gave me a convincing explanation saying, if you want to fight against your enemy, you needed to know it better.'

Nengwekhulu says Williamson discouraged him from contact with the ANC and said there were 'white people who were keen on joining the BCM'.

Nengwekhulu's qualms about Williamson were confirmed when he asked Williamson directly 'if he was a cop' while they were having tea outside the house of a family, the Erikssons, who were Nengwekhulu's hosts in Geneva.

'Alison Eriksson replied. She said he was a cop before. I then phoned Pityana and told him that I think this man is BOSS (Bureau of State Security) or CIA. Pityana dismissed this. He said I "always had suspicions" of people.'

But Nengwekhulu's misgivings grew when Williamson gave him a detailed account of a trip Biko had taken to Cape Town, and of how Biko was 'betrayed by his own comrades'. 'Williamson also knew who was in love with whom in the BCM in the Western Cape. He told me that BCM members in the Western Cape were sleeping with their comrades' girlfriends and wives. [But perhaps more serious was that] he said Neville Alexander refused to meet with Steve because the police were aware that Steve was in Cape Town. At the time, Steve was banned and travelling incognito. All this proved my suspicions about Williamson. He told me that when Steve and Peter Jones drove back from Cape Town to King William's Town, they were stopped by the police at a roadblock. He said the roadblock was meant for Steve, but Williamson never gave me any explanation beyond [that].

'Remember in Geneva while we were having tea, I asked Williamson whether he was a cop and he did not reply? Instead Allison Eriksson confirmed it? A few minutes after asking him that question, Williamson approached me. It was only the two of us.

'He asked: "How do Black people identify a cop?" In reply, I said: "I don't know. It is not only me. In the past, railway police always wore overalls, but Black people would say this is a cop. Some of the police officers would wear suits; the Black people would always say these are cops. It has something with the behaviour of how you dress. I've never seen Black people making a mistake about a cop." He was very surprised. He knew I never trusted him.'

Another suspicious incident came when Williamson gave Nengwekhulu a detailed account of how the BCM-aligned Black Allied Workers' Union (BAWU) was getting money from New Zealand.

'A strange thing happened when I left Geneva for Botswana. On my arrival in Botswana, I bought the *Financial Times* and the story about [Kalushi] Drake Koka's BAWU was splashed on the front page. It was the exact story, word by word, I got from Craig Williamson. I then phoned Drake and informed him about this betrayal.'

Nengwekhulu links Williamson to other spy activities, saying he was instrumental in sending money to South Africa to support BCM activities 'and SASM, the student organisation led by Tsietsi Mashinini'.

Funds would be sent directly to the account of Father Aelred Stubbs who had a parish in Lesotho.

'Father Stubbs was a friend of Pityana and Steve. We sent the cash to [him] using the code-name "Bob". [At that time] there was a musician known as Zakes Mofokeng… I wish I can meet him… who I always contacted and asked to go and see "Bob". Mofokeng knew that the instruction meant he had to go to Lesotho and collect money from Father Stubbs.'

Nengwekhulu believes Williamson knew about the 'code' he was using with Mofokeng.

'[One day] Zakes Mofokeng was stopped by the police and they asked him: Are you going to see Bob? It was clear [then] that this code was broken. And I suspect it was broken by Craig Williamson.

'Mofokeng informed me about it. I then contacted the director of the IUEF, Lars Eriksson, and told him that "the water-pipe" was broken.'

In 1980, Williamson was exposed as a spy and Nengwekhulu believes that led to him giving an interview to the *Sunday Times* in which he said Nengwekhulu had 'bribed Desmond Tutu to participate in the struggle'.

'The story, I think, was in 1980 or '81. It was on the front page. It was not about me but it was about Tutu. Partly, the story was true.

'Bishop Tutu's daughter [Mpho], who is a priest, was studying for her BSc in Botswana and she ran short of money. Bishop Tutu was in Lesotho. So I spoke to Steve that we should assist Bishop Tutu's daughter. But at the time, we wanted someone for the BPC who would be like [nationalist leader and United Methodist Church] Bishop Abel Muzorewa [who served as Prime Minister of Zimbabwe/Rhodesia from the Internal Settlement to the Lancaster House Agreement in 1979, holding office for only a few months before Zimbabwe achieved majority rule in 1980].

'We approached the BCM in South Africa to talk to Bishop Tutu. That's how he became involved in politics, although he is seen as a revolutionary. I do not feel guilty about it. I raised money for his daughter from the All Africa Conference of Churches and the World Council of Churches to study. We wanted a figurehead for the BPC.'

Nengwekhulu is unconflicted about one thing: 'I still don't think the police wanted to kill Steve. They were under immense pressure on the basis of information they got from Craig Williamson. They wanted to know why [Biko] was leaving the country.'

Nengwekhulu says he only came to know about Biko's death a few days afterwards: 'I had phoned Steve on our usual Wednesday. Ntsiki picked up the phone and said Steve was sleeping. I did not believe it because Steve never slept before 10 pm. [But] I accepted Ntsiki's explanation. I suspected something might have happened. Maybe he was betrayed. The next day, I was told I must go to the President Hotel in Botswana to receive a telephone call. I knew he was dead.

'I think the police assaulted him beyond the limits of endurance. [Steve] was not a pushover. It makes me angry. I feel like crying. People are preaching reconciliation. We got misled by the TRC.'

Nengwekhulu also questions the decision by the Swedish Academy to share the Nobel Peace Prize in 1993 between the last white apartheid president, FW de Klerk, and Mandela. He's of the view that De Klerk and Buthelezi should have been criminally prosecuted.

'Chief Buthelezi was a "Mr X" in various cases against ANC members. De Klerk was not prosecuted. Instead, foot soldiers like Eugene de Kock [a colonel in the apartheid security police and a former mass assassin for the regime] were prosecuted. De Klerk did not change. People changed the struggle in the country. It became too strong and had gone out of hand.'

Nengwekhulu feels the shared Nobel prize devalued Mandela, who was a commanding leader: 'He took decisions which people could not oppose. When Mandela said no, it was no. He was not a vindictive person. He talked like a king. You needed a commanding leader. Mandela went to Braamfontein when the Communist Party continued to attack the ANC and told them to stop or they were out. Steve Biko was just as much a commanding person as Mandela – even physically. He spoke with authority and conviction, like Mandela. Very few people could contradict Steve Biko.'

The main points of the SASO Policy Manifesto

Black Consciousness is an attitude of mind, a way of life;

the basic tenet of BC is that the Black man must reject all value systems that seek to make him a foreigner in the country of his birth and reduce his basic dignity;

the Black man must build up his own value systems, see himself as self-defined and not as defined by others.

Nontsikelelo (Ntsiki) Biko: 'It doesn't bring the man back'

Born Nontsikelelo Mashalaba, this hero of BC grew up in Mthatha in the Transkei. She met Biko when she was training to be a nurse at King Edward Hospital in Durban, and Biko was a medical student at the University of Natal. Biko's eldest sister Bukelwa was a student nurse at the same institution as Ntsiki.

Ntsiki told historians compiling the story of BC and Biko for the Apartheid Museum that Biko 'used to tell his friends, "Meet my lady… she is the actual embodiment of Blackness – Black is beautiful".'

With their shared belief in BC as an ideological and lived position, Ntsiki and Steve Biko's relationship and marriage are prized, if largely undocumented. Ntsiki offered some insights into the independent nature of their bond for the museum's exhibition, noting for instance that 'Steve being Steve, really, he wouldn't take the banning order seriously because he would do things done by everybody else. I mean, if he feels like a party, he would go to a party'.

Yet, her own story, of her own history, is rarely told. We were unable to gain an interview for this book. Ntsiki thus remains an enigmatic icon inextricably linked to Steve Biko, her past as painful as it is inspiring.

It was only after significant and sustained 'domestic and international pressure' that she and her children with Steve, Nkosinathi (8 at the time) and Samora (3 at the time), received compensation for his death – two years after a 15-day inquest.

Although 'legal authorities' told *The Washington Post* in 1979 that the out-of-court settlement was 'the largest amount ever awarded a family by the Pretoria government for a death in police detention', it was clear this was 'an attempt to stave off any future legal proceedings that would attract the kind of international publicity that accompanied the official inquest into Biko's death'.

The inquest ruled there that the police officers who had detained Biko could not be charged with murder as there were 'no eyewitnesses'.

The Washington Post reported that the settlement amounted to $76 700 (the rand/dollar exchange rate at the time was R0.84), which Ntsiki dubbed 'blood money' and 'an admission of guilt' by the apartheid regime.

'(An amount of) $35,400 awarded to (Nontsikelelo) Biko (would) be donated to a community project in memory of her husband and of "the great struggle Steve was engaged in towards liberation of the Black people",' the newspaper reported. 'Under the terms of the settlement, Biko's two sons received $15,340 and $10,620 respectively and Biko's mother, Nokuzola, $15,340.'

The Washington Post quoted Ntsiki as saying, 'It doesn't bring the man back… The most important thing was the man's life, not the money'. The regime told the paper it had made the payment to the family 'without admission of liability', and that it had also paid the legal costs of the family. The Bikos had originally made a civil claim of $106 008 against the government.

'Minister of police Louis le Grange (said) that the settlement meant "the file on the Biko case has now been finally closed".' Ntsiki was in turn reported as having 'rebutted this': 'As far as we are concerned it is only the beginning. The Black people of South Africa will not rest until such time as we get to know how Steve Biko came to meet his untimely death'

More than 20 other Black people had been killed in detention in the 18 months prior to Biko's murder in September 1977.

And there still has not been justice for Ntsiki, or the family – or indeed Black South Africans.

When Biko's family sought prosecution again in 2003 of those responsible for his death, the National Prosecuting Authority concluded there was 'insufficient evidence' for a murder trial two and a half decades later. The time frame for prosecution 'had lapsed'.

The *Los Angeles Times* reported that even the ANC 'took issue with the decision, saying it might give the impression that the post-apartheid democratic government tolerated such "evil"'. It quoted the ruling party's then-spokesperson Smuts Ngonyama, lamenting: 'We believe that it is unfortunate that the killers of Steve Biko are not being prosecuted. It would have been necessary for such a thing to take place because it was going to set our country on a direct course of reconciliation.'

Five apartheid-era policemen were denied amnesty for Biko's murder at the Truth and Reconciliation Commission (TRC), as they could not prove a political motive for their involvement. But perhaps the whole matter of Biko's killers being free to continue with their lives, in spite of that, is more of a BC issue than the world has been made to understand. Ntsiki is at the heart of that global debate.

AZAPO joined with her in taking the President of the Republic of South Africa and Others to court to challenge the constitutionality of the amnesty provision of the National Unity and Reconciliation Act, which established the TRC, in 1996.

They argued the Act 'violated international law, in particular the four Geneva Conventions of 1949 on the laws of war, which South Africa had signed and ratified in 1952'.

Further, they argued that the Act was unconstitutional in that 'anyone who receives amnesty is exempt from all liability', stating this effectively violated a citizen such as Ntsiki's right to 'possess the right to have disputes settled in a court of law'.

The Constitutional Court's final decision in this matter was that while it 'recognized the pain behind the applicants' court case, it upheld' the Act. Bizarrely, it took the official position of 'ubuntu' ('universal bond of shared humanity'), saying that the post-apartheid South African Constitution was a 'historic bridge' between the country's past and future, and that there (was) a 'need for reparation but not for retaliation, a need for ubuntu but not for victimization'; that 'in order to advance such reconciliation and reconstruction, amnesty (should) be granted in respect of acts, omissions and offences associated with political objectives and committed in the course of the conflicts of the past'.

Reading it afresh in 2020, it suggests that Black deaths at the hands of white supremacists and agents of the racist regime were considered 'sacrificial' in what we now know was the broader intention to secure investors in a post-apartheid South Africa.

Investors from the Western world especially demanded the peaceful, 'rainbow nation' which Tutu, Mandela and others agreed to present as an alternative to civil war.

Ntsiki Biko and the BCM would be required to collaborate in that travesty, which the court had the anti-Black audacity to say would offer 'the incentive of amnesty'. Ntsiki and others like her and their families, not to mention greater Black society, would be offered 'the healing power of finding out the truth through amnesty from criminal liability'.

Patronising and harmful, the court has been proved wrong as not one such apartheid-era criminal had been prosecuted by 2020, even as cases have come before other courts or inquests reopened.

The court shamed itself by stating that 'the families of those unlawfully tortured, maimed or traumatised (would) become more empowered to discover the truth (and) the perpetrators (would) become exposed to opportunities to obtain relief from the burden of guilt or an anxiety they might be living with for many long years'.

Anti-Blackness is not corrected through white killers being allowed to walk free. Anti-Blackness is a state of mind; it is interwoven in the core. BC is the only truth, and the only healing mechanism.

It now seems improbable that a post-apartheid Constitutional Court could tell Ntsiki Biko, her children, AZAPO, other supporters of BC and Black South Africans in the main, that South Africa needed to begin 'the long and necessary process of healing the wounds of the past, transforming anger and grief into a mature understanding and creating the emotional and structural climate essential for "reconciliation and reconstruction"'.

Using Western methods of law-giving, and a then-Interim Constitution which has, two decades later, been shown to be wanting in certain key areas, the court told the Bikos *et al* that it wished to lift 'the burden' on 'perpetrators of human rights abuses (who would otherwise) remain on the outskirts of society, filled with guilt and uncertainty'.

If this is a reason Ntsiki remains distant from going on the public record with her own history, it should be respected.

[https://www.apartheidmuseum.org/uploads/files/BIKO-2b.pdf; Murphy, 1979: https://www.washingtonpost.com/archive/politics/1979/07/29/s-africa-pays-biko-family-76700-in-compensation/bfbac904-4d31-4bf4-b01b-340cf767692a/; Business Tech, 2016: https://businesstech.co.za/news/finance/116372/rand-vs-the-dollar-1978-2016/; Associated Press, 2003: https://www.latimes.com/archives/la-xpm-2003-oct-08-fg-safrica8-story.html; Martin, 2015: University of Pennsylvania]

Bokwe Mafuna: 'I knew there were going to be casualties'

Baldwin Ndaba engages the former journalist and BC activist. They met at Mafuna's house in Roodepoort, a city in the greater Johannesburg area, in early 2017.

At 33, journalist Bokwe Mafuna was the most senior student to join SASO. Not that being a student was what Mafuna had envisaged for himself, his membership was 'manufactured' as he'd had to register as a first year at Unisa to qualify. That being the 1970s, most SASO members were born after 1940. Biko was born on 18 December 1946. Mafuna was born in 1937 and was married with children when he signed up.

Prior to enlisting, Mafuna worked as a freelance journalist for *The World* and the *Rand Daily Mail*. His life would change irrevocably once he was a SASO member, because that deepened his allegiance to the BCM. He would also later help establish AZAPO's Azanian National Liberation Army (AZANLA) while in exile.

Before he devoted himself to working for the BCM, and before he was banned along with Biko, Nengwekhulu and Pityana – driving him to flee the country in 1973 – Mafuna had made a living capturing stories about Black township life. He knew the streets of Soweto, Alexandra and Sophiatown intimately, remembering them even before the forced removals of the 1950s and 1960s.

'I grew up in Sophiatown… Soweto… I knew Eldorado Park, and I later lived in Alexandra,' Mafuna tells. 'I saw Nelson Mandela in the 1950s before he was jailed on Robben Island in 1964. I think it was in 1953. Mandela was initially scheduled to address people at the Square in Sophiatown, but the police came there before his arrival.

The crowds were waiting for him. He had to change the venue. He then addressed the crowd from the balcony of a flat at Bremmer Court in Victoria Road which belonged to the parents of (former South African TV talk show host) Felicia Mabuza-Suttle.

Mafuna was recruited after SASO's leadership strategised around finding a way into the predominantly white media. According to Nengwekhulu, the way most Black journalists would report was dangerously passive: 'They might say: "The situation was calm in the township: only 12 people died"[1]... These stories used to annoy me.'

Mafuna never lost his taste for journalism and was instrumental in the formation of the UBJ. Although the union's constitution was drafted in Natal, the UBJ was founded in 1973 at the Planet Hotel in downtown Fordsburg, Johannesburg. Mafuna was banned when the UBJ met for the first time at the Planet, being under house arrest in Alexandra.

Certainly, there were political allegiances at play within the BCM, but Mafuna says he never regarded the ANC as his 'preferred political home'. Rather, it was the NEUM, which later became the New Unity Movement under Neville Alexander and others, which had 'a great influence' on his thought.

The Sophiatown leadership of the NEUM was very critical of the ANC and would gather at the Digger's Hall, a popular community space also in downtown Johannesburg, to analyse public statements and publications issued by the Charterists.

'My conditions of oppression and apartheid allowed me to question the state of affairs in the country,' says Mafuna. 'I witnessed the formation of the PAC in Orlando Communal Hall in Soweto in 1959. There was a lot of discussion and debate and the PAC had emphasised the issue of the land.' He was 22 at that time, but decided not to join the PAC.

Mafuna moved to Alexandra – a township outside Johannesburg first laid out in 1912 – in the early 1960s and joined a Catholic seminary to train as a priest. But this was a career choice he cut short as he quickly grew unhappy with the 'sitting on the fence' of the church leadership while the country was in turmoil. He was fortunate, though, that while in the seminary, he discovered trade unionism and this made his entry into the multi-racial Trade Union Council of South Africa (TUCSA) easier when he was later an ordinary working man and a member of the Engineering Workers Union, an affiliate.

Mafuna's unionism was disrupted when TUCSA was ordered by the regime to get rid of its Black members, but Mafuna and some white fellow workers resisted. Due to his defiance, Mafuna was, however, among those expelled from the union. This led to him venturing into journalism and Mafuna's relatively meagre income helped raise his family.

He was conscientised as much in the township streets as he was in the newspaper buildings where he worked, and where he was as much exposed to the lived reality of Black people in the white workplace, as he was to their lives in their homes. Black journalists were separated from white journalists while most of the editors were white, and their role, says Mafuna, was 'gatekeeping to prevent Black journalists from writing anything that could threaten – or annoy – the National Party'. There was no union to look after freelancers like him, which is why when Mafuna was introduced to the idea of SASO, he 'knew [they shared] my perspective'.

'I got more acquainted with the SASO leadership and their thinking. We discussed policies in the BCP. We read about [American activists] Eldridge Cleaver, Stokely Carmichael and Malcolm X. [They] had a great influence on me. SASO was trying to reach out to Black people. I, in turn, introduced SASO's leaders to a lot of people like [Dr Nthato] Motlana. I made them understand the plight of Black doctors, nurses and teachers and other people I'd met and interviewed through my job.'

Mafuna was part of SASO in 1971 when Biko started a literacy programme and, eager for it to succeed, Mafuna even went back to the nuns and priests he'd met at the seminary and encouraged them to get involved in sourcing learning materials.

'It was my birthright to be a member of SASO,' says Mafuna. 'I did not need permission from any editors. [Anyway] we were not in the habit of asking permission to be members of a political party.'

He would part ways acrimoniously with the *Rand Daily Mail* in 1972 after he was assigned to cover the SASO congress in Hammanskraal – a story which he had to dictate to his news desk from a telephone at the venue.

The newspaper had a policy of describing Blacks as 'non-whites', which irritated BC members, and so when Mafuna dictated his article, he wrote about 'Blacks' and his editors changed this for publication.

That led to him cutting ties with that paper, but before doing so, he warned the editors that sooner or later they would have to recognise Black people as Black. 'The *Rand Daily Mail* had no choice. It was *The Star*, the most liberal newspaper, which first started calling us Blacks. More people [then] started reading *The Star* and the *Rand Daily Mail* was forced to call us Black.'

Mafuna then joined Biko and Ben Khoapa, a professional social worker, on the BCP. The men visited Black communities and set up organisations to complement programmes of the BCM.

In January 1973, Cape recruitment had started, but apartheid security agents pounced on Mafuna, Pityana and others while they were canvassing for support in Port Elizabeth. 'They were shouting at Steve Biko and he stood up to them,' recalls Mafuna. 'He was defying them. He was standing his ground. It was the first time I saw defiance like that.

'He lived up to what he preached about a Black man standing his ground. He was not afraid.' Mafuna says the verbal interrogation was so intense that he told himself that 'these white people would kill Steve'.

Despised regime agent Gideon Nieuwoudt was among the security agents. He was denied amnesty in 1999 after he failed to make a full disclosure to the TRC about Biko's murder. The Commission recommended Nieuwoudt and his co-conspirators be criminally prosecuted, but Nieuwoudt died in 2005 without facing any charges.

Mafuna last saw Biko at that interrogation in Port Elizabeth. 'I was ordered to leave PE. I was driving a BCP car and the security branch escorted me until I reached Cradock. I drove to Joburg. Two days [later], I was served with banning orders and placed under house arrest.'

Mafuna broke his banning orders and served three months at Leeuwkop Prison: 'It was where I met PAC guys like Dikgang Moseneke,

Mark Shinners and others who were from Robben Island and were about to be released from jail.' Mafuna was released in August and, in September, went into exile in Botswana using the popular 'Dinokana' route through the North West province town of Zeerust.

Nengwekhulu left the country the same day, and both remained active in the BCM. Mafuna later went to France, where he was joined by his wife and children, resuming his journalism there on international newspapers and radio stations. He spent exactly 20 years in exile, returning in September 1993.

Mafuna says he found out about Biko's murder in a French newspaper but that 'did not surprise' him: 'I knew there were going to be casualties. I cannot describe my feeling at the time. I knew it was going to happen. I saw his character when we were arrested in 1973. I saw how the police behaved then, that they were going to kill him.

'Other comrades were also killed in a similar manner, [although] I could not believe it when Mapetla Mohapi was killed. Mohapi was as humble as a sheep.

'Mthuli ka Shezi was killed after being pushed in front of a moving train in Germiston. He left me in Joburg saying he was rushing to buy a sewing machine for his mother but he was killed at a railway station.'

The murder of Shezi became an unexpected focus of attention during the SASO 9 trial in 1975, where the accused included Muntu Myeza, Strini Moodley, Pandelani Nefolovhodwe, Mosiuoa Lekota and others. Biko was the main defence witness, and he used the platform to condemn the barbaric manner in which Shezi was killed. Mafuna concedes: 'Steve Biko's death had an impact on all of [us].'

Biko, Rick Turner and the Durban Moment

On 9 January 1973, a powerful shift took place in the Black workers' struggle.

The late 1950s had been an extraordinary period for labour disquiet, but by the 1960s a slew of new apartheid laws had dramatically curtailed this action. These included the Bantu Labour

Act and the Bantu Labour Relations Regulation Act, which added further imperialistic controls to the lives of working people. There was now stricter regulation through labour bureaux, and bargaining procedures were more onerous than ever.

Most Black people were still not recognised as actual employees, and although liaison committees were designed to manage settlements in disputes, few – however racist – were ever set up. Meanwhile, ever more townships were being built to service burgeoning white monopoly capital's needs at a time of intense industrialisation. But these were places of increasingly dreadful circumstance. The apartheid regime then saw fit to also resettle hundreds of thousands of Black people who had been living in the urban areas, in the bantustans.

So the memory of the 1955–60 period, when there had been more than 70 strikes a year, was a stinging rebuke to the class struggle. There was also the painful irony that although the level of industrialisation should have afforded Black workers greater bargaining power, the 1960s were a period of ever-greater repression. Then came the 1970s – a different political moment altogether.

There was no recovery from the violence of the apartheid state through the previous decade, but now Black people were at a stage in the struggle where immediate action was imperative, and the workers struck back. History collective the Labour and Community Resource Project (LACOM), an offshoot of the South African Council for Higher Education (SACHED), as well as South African academics like Darcy du Toit and Jeremy Baskin, have described this in detail in their research.

Bus drivers in Johannesburg and stevedores in Cape Town would have reward for their resistance in 1971 and 1972, and then factory workers in Durban downed tools. But it was what began as a strike at Coronation Brick and Tile outside Durban for an extra R2 per week on 9 January 1973 that turned the tide. A nearly 100 000-strong force of workers engaged in public shows of force.

Mass, even militant, struggle seemed possible again as trade unionists and theorists alike in the BC movement began to accept they would finally have to identify a clear ideological direction, which understood the axis between race and class. As growth in the unions offered unparalleled opportunities for Black leadership, with political assertion surely more easily steered out of those, change in how the struggle would be fought was possible.

It also swung the struggle in another, unexpected direction – one still debated in BC, on the issue of white liberalism. Although the birth of SASO had successfully marginalised student neo-liberal intentions, it offered the white intelligentsia a chance to regroup, and some saw how they could reinvent themselves from inside a left-wing labour movement.

They could be radicals, but not really have to address burning race issues as they would be dealing with class. And while this was indeed problematic for BC – which was becoming more radical itself as it grappled with working-class support – it soon presented real, personal dangers.

This was the Durban Moment– or at least, a conflicted part of it. In the paper 'Steve Biko, Richard Turner and the politics of Black Consciousness, 1970–1974', Ian Macqueen of the Society, Work and Development Institute at Wits contends that activist and academic Tony Morphet coined the term the 'Durban Moment' in the 1990 Rick Turner Memorial Lecture to the University of Natal in Durban 'to describe four simultaneous intellectual projects that took place [there] between 1970 and 1974'.

'These were the philosophical and political work of the intellectual Richard [Rick] Turner; the elaboration of the philosophy and political discourse of BC by Biko and the development of its community development projects; South African sociologist Dunbar Moodie's historical re-evaluation of Afrikaner history, and Mike Kirkwood's challenge to the English literature canon from a South African perspective.'

Macqueen recorded that this signalled a 'structural shift in... intellectual patterns', which were matched by 'stirrings in the Black working class'. The shift happened against the backdrop of those 1973 Durban strikes.

Macqueen's paper is so richly detailed in emotional, personal and ideological context for political players of that time in BC history that it is vital to revisit his research.

The history is that Turner met Biko in Durban in 1970 when Turner was appointed a lecturer in political science at the University of Natal, Howard College campus. Biko was a medical student at the Non-European Section, and Durban was effectively the headquarters of SASO. According to Morphet, Turner and Biko were introduced to each other by Foszia Fisher, a philosophy honours student who would later marry Turner.

Macqueen boldly states: 'Biko and Turner stood most prominent in their breadth and force of intellect.'

Described as 'a disturber of the peace' by a colleague when he was at Rhodes University, Turner, wrote Macqueen, was famous for hosting weekend seminars at his mother's farm outside Stellenbosch, attracting 'a large number of students who took the opportunity to study and discuss more deeply New Left ideas and thinkers'.

In the early 1970s, Turner – who taught radical political philosophy with a grounding in Western, albeit humanist, Marxism – was an advisor to NUSAS and a 'facilitator' between students and activists in Durban.

This was a critical role as NUSAS and SASO were deeply divided from each other, and many white student activists were flailing as they tried to find a new role for themselves in the struggle.

'He had close contacts with members of SASO, as well as members of the Natal Indian Congress, the Coloured Labour Party and Chief [Gatsha] Buthelezi.' While there was 'an active search for intellectual resources, from thinkers from the African Diaspora, such as [Amilcar] Cabral, [Léopold] Senghor, and especially Frantz Fanon', Biko and Turner also shared an admiration for French Marxist philosopher Jean-Paul Sartre.

Turner earned a doctorate in 1965 at the Sorbonne in Paris for his dissertation on Sartre.

According to Ramphele, the men would argue over socialist perspectives within BC. Macqueen records Ramphele as saying: 'Steve... pointed out to Rick... [the dangers of] an economic class analysis which ignored the racist nature of capitalist exploitation in South Africa.' The pair would discuss 'the false consciousness of white workers, ending with Steve challenging Rick to go out and conscientise white workers'.

Peter Randall, director of SPRO-CAS, invited Turner to join the group's economics and politics commissions. While there, Turner produced *The Eye of the Needle*, a 1972 book which Macqueen describes as 'a provocative projection of a utopian future South African society'.

Biko had meanwhile been forced to abandon his medical studies in 1970 due to his political activities. Although then a law student at Unisa, he dedicated himself to the BCP in Durban. Biko's friend, the insurgent writer Hugh Lewin, would comment that Biko always maintained good personal relationships with certain white NUSAS leaders even as he 'remained clear on the need to relegate the white liberal to a secondary position'.

Macqueen records how Biko described the role of the liberal, that they needed to serve as 'a lubricating material so that as we change gears in trying to find a better direction for South Africa, there should be no grinding noises of metal against metal but a free and flowing movement which will be characteristic of a well-looked-after vehicle'.

When Pityana replaced Biko as SASO president, and Biko was elected chair of SASO publications, there was 'an outpouring of scholarship [on subjects like poetry, aesthetics, culture, politics, economics, and theology] within the movement'.

This importantly included *Black Review*, which Biko produced with fellow BC exponents Malusi Mpumlwana, Tomeka Mafole and Welile Nhlapo, but when Biko was banned in 1973 after the Schlebusch Commission, his name famously had to be omitted and fellow BC scholar Khoapa cited as editor.

Turner too was banned along with NUSAS leaders Neville Curtis, Paul Pretorius, Paula Ensor, Philippe le Roux, Sheila Lapinsky, Clive Keegan and Chris Wood, and had to remain in his home in Bellair, Durban.

Biko was then banished to King William's Town, and while Biko built Black self-reliance projects under the banner of the BCP, Turner used his banning for further study, learning how to speak and read Portuguese to follow the path to liberation in Angola and Mozambique, and German to study the transcendental idealist Georg Hegel, as well as Immanuel Kant and Karl Marx.

Turner also helped found the Institute for Industrial Education at the University of Natal and its publication, the *South African Labour Bulletin*, which assisted the 're-emergence of African trade unions, one of the most salient features of the Durban Moment'. Turner worked with Fisher (his wife) and left-wing intellectuals like Lawrence Schlemmer, John Copelyn, Alec Erwin, Omar Badsha and Hilton Cheadle at the institute.

The forced separation of Turner and Biko through their bannings would mark the 'last direct encounter' between them. But Macqueen's contention is that their interaction during the Durban Moment 'helped develop a critical political awareness'.

Morphet says that Turner's 'shift away from the confusions of the liberal position were evinced by his contacts with the BC movement, most notably Biko'. 'As such, it was friendship which helped steer liberals towards a more radical outlook.'

Turner would, however, appeal to Biko that BC activists see different 'categories' of white South Africans, said Macqueen – namely 'racist, liberal and radical', concerned that SASO's analysis 'was confused by a very loose grasp of the concept "liberal"'. Turner argued that there were Black and white racists, and Black and white radicals. 'He emphasised that, rather than demonising white liberals, the aim should be the creation of a new culture.'

Macqueen feels that both Biko and Turner 'were committed to the quest for a true humanity'.

Using the pseudonym Frank Talk in *Black Review*, Biko said: 'True integration is the provision for each man, each group, to rise and attain the envisioned self.' He felt 'each group must be able to attain its style of existence without encroaching on or being thwarted by the other' and urged 'mutual respect' and 'complete freedom of self-determination'.

There were problems between SASO and the nascent white radicals, a powerful example being liberal intervention in a Black-run community at New Farm, Phoenix, outside Durban. BC activists there were working at building a self-reliant community when Turner and other white activists arrived to supply resources.

'This', said Ramphele, who was active in the BCP in that area, 'was an overt sign of white arrogance', and a discomfiting example of that quality of 'wanting to take over', which the BCP found so antithetical to developing communities.

In the end, Biko and Turner were linked through the human and political tragedy of their murders by the state within four months of each other in 1977 and 1978. Biko died at the age of 30 on 12 September 1977 after being savagely assaulted in police detention. Turner was murdered at the age of 36 at his home on 8 January 1978, shot through the window in the chest by an unknown assassin after he opened a curtain in his front room, having heard a noise outside. It was around midnight. He died minutes later in the arms of his 13-year-old daughter Jann. His other daughter, Kim, was also in the house when he was killed.

[Macqueen, 2014; Biko, 1978]

What the TRC revealed on Rick Turner's assassination

Journalist Ivor Powell of the *Weekend Argus* reported in June 2015 on the release of the Section 29 hearings of the TRC: 'No amnesty applications were received by the TRC in respect of Turner's murder,' he wrote, 'but TRC investigators engaged in a series of hearings in 1997 aimed at uncovering what happened'.

Among the witnesses called to testify were murder and robbery captain Chris Earle, his commanding officer Major (later Colonel) Christoffel Gert Groenewald and BOSS operative Martin Dolinschek, later a senior manager in the National Intelligence Agency.

Earle said he came to suspect 'early on, in the absence of any apparent motive' that government's security forces could have been behind the murder. But Powell mentions in his piece that an anonymous phone tip-off had also been received at the time 'to the effect that the ANC had had the outspoken BC intellectual eliminated'.

Jann Turner made the film, *My Father, Rick Turner*, about the murder but, said Powell, 'could not definitively unmask his killer'.

The murder remains unresolved.

[Powell, 2015]

What the TRC revealed on Steve Biko's murder

On 16 February 1999, the TRC released a statement on its amnesty decision on the death of Biko. It said: 'Four former officers of the security branch in Port Elizabeth who applied for amnesty for the murder of Black Consciousness leader Steve Bantu Biko in September 1977 were this week refused amnesty by the Amnesty Committee of the TRC and their applications were dismissed.'

The officers were: Major Harold Snyman, who led the investigation team that interrogated Biko; Daniel Petrus Siebert, a former bodyguard to apartheid Prime Minister BJ Vorster; Jacobus Johannes Oosthuysen Beneke; and the 76-year-old Rubin Marx. Their accomplice and the fifth applicant, notorious agent Gideon Nieuwoudt, had his application heard by a different amnesty panel, and was refused in December 1998.

The Amnesty Committee said it had based its decision on the facts that the killing of Biko was 'not an act associated with a political objective' as required by the Amnesty Act. The committee was also not satisfied that the applicants had made 'a full disclosure' as further required by the Act.

It was not satisfied that the applicants testified truthfully to the events leading to the injury of Biko, and further concluded that the applicants' version of how Biko sustained the fatal head injury was 'so improbable and contradictory, that it had to be rejected as false'.

'Instead,' said the TRC's release, 'the committee concluded that the attack on Biko appeared to have been actuated by ill-will or spite towards him.' The Amnesty Committee said it was satisfied that the killing of Biko was 'wholly disproportionate to any possible objective pursued by the applicants, particularly the stated one of extracting information or admission from Biko with a view to a possible criminal prosecution'.

The three-member panel that refused amnesty on the Biko matter was made up of judges Hassan Mall and Denzil Potgieter, and advocate Ntsiki Sandi. The panel also officially declared Biko's next-of-kin to be victims of gross human rights violations in relation to his killing, and said they were therefore entitled to 'appropriate reparation'.

It is still shocking that apartheid minister of justice Jimmy Kruger lodged a complaint against the *Rand Daily Mail* at the South African Press Council after Biko's murder, when the newspaper published a front-page story claiming Biko had suffered extensive brain damage.

The Star came out in support of the *Rand Daily Mail*, and *The World* and *Weekend World* continued to cover Biko's murder, as did the *Sunday Express* in Johannesburg. Kruger brazenly denied that Biko was even so much as 'beaten' by his police officers.

There was, however, a clear upswelling of fear within the apartheid government and, not long after Biko's murder, those 18 BC-linked organisations, individuals and sympathetic newspapers were banned. Then Vorster and the National Party won an election, which strengthened racism in the face of a UN Security Council vote to ban mandatory arms sales to South Africa in 1977, and Western capital came under fire for profiting off the oppression of Blacks. Vorster forged ahead even as the US Congress expressed its outrage at Biko's death and demanded an investigation.

It was, therefore, entirely unsurprising that BC would reassert itself the following year, when AZAPO was formed.

[www.justice.gov.za/trc/media]

The timeline of Biko's murder

19 August 1977: Biko is detained in Port Elizabeth under Section 6 of the Terrorism Act, which allows for him to be held indefinitely.

6 September 1977: Biko is taken to security police headquarters for interrogation. Interrogator Harold Snyman tells Pieter Goosen, head of the Eastern Cape security police, that Biko is 'acting strangely'. Dr Ivor Lang, district surgeon in Port Elizabeth, is called to examine Biko who is lying on a mat, manacled to a metal grille. Biko cannot co-ordinate his muscles and his speech is slurred.

8 September 1977: Lang is called again as Biko has not urinated and cannot eat. He examines Biko in the presence of Dr Benjamin Tucker, chief district surgeon, who sees signs of brain damage. Biko indicates he is in pain. Private specialist neurologist Colin Hersch examines Biko. Lang says there is no evidence of any abnormality.

9 September 1977: Hersch says Biko has a speech defect, left-side weakness and signs of brain damage. Biko cannot turn over and walks with a limp. Hersch performs a lumbar puncture, where he finds evidence of either a brain injury and/or the piercing of a blood vessel. Lang visits but does not examine Biko. A warder tells him Biko has eaten but 'was found in a bath fully clothed'. Tucker does not act on indications of brain injury in Biko.

10 September 1977: Dr R Keely, a neurosurgeon, is consulted on the phone and suggests brain damage. Lang examines Biko but finds 'no pathology'. Biko is returned to the cells where he is left on a mat on the cement floor.

11 September 1977: Goosen calls Tucker to the police station where Biko is found 'collapsed, glassy-eyed, hyperventilating and frothing at the mouth'. Tucker conducts a five-minute examination and concludes there is no change, but that Biko be transferred to the provincial hospital in Port Elizabeth. Goosen refuses. Police are instead told to 'transfer' Biko to Pretoria, 1 100 kilometres away, in a semi-comatose state, naked and handcuffed on cell mats on the floor of a Land Rover, without medical personnel. Hours after arrival, district surgeon Dr A van Zyl gives Biko an intravenous drip and vitamin injection.

12 September 1977: Biko dies alone and unattended, on a mat on a stone floor.

[The Apartheid Museum, 2020: https://www.apartheidmuseum.org/uploads/files/BIKO-2b.pdf]

The mystery of the Biko autopsy documents

In December 2014, Biko's family and the Steve Biko Foundation took legal action to gain access to what they believed were Biko's post-mortem report and other autopsy documents. This was widely reported by the South African Press Association (SAPA), News24 and Independent Online. Nkosinathi Biko, Biko's son, had been alerted by email to the fact that such documents were to be auctioned off with an opening bid of about R70 000 by Westgate Walding Auctioneers in Johannesburg.

The South Gauteng High Court in Johannesburg, however, ordered that Biko's autopsy report could not be auctioned, about an hour before the documents were due to go under the hammer, and ruled that unauthorised access to health records was unlawful. The post-mortem, claimed Westgate Walding Auctioneers on its website, elicited certificates from pathologists, a certificate in terms of the Criminal Procedure Act and a 43-page report, had allegedly been in the possession of siblings Clive Anthony Steele and Susan Elizabeth Sey. They claimed the document was given to their mother, Maureen Steele, former PA to Dr Jonathan Gluckman, the independent pathologist originally appointed by the Biko family in 1977 – for safekeeping.

After Maureen Steele died, the documents were apparently passed down to her children, who were also in possession of Ahmed Timol's post-mortem report which had, in the same way, been held by Maureen for safekeeping on behalf of Gluckman. The High Court also ordered that Timol's reports could not be sold on auction.

Timol died in police custody in 1972. He was alone with a policeman when police claimed he 'fell out of a window' at John Vorster Square police station in central Johannesburg. A new inquest into Timol's death was held at the High Court in Pretoria before Judge Billy Mothle in 2017, as an inquest held in 1972 had found that Timol had committed suicide. The Timol family had fought for justice for 45 years. Mothle found that Timol was murdered.

Michele Pickover, a principal curator at the Wits Historical Papers department, came forward in 2014 to say that the original Biko autopsy files had been stolen in the early 1990s. She doubted that the Steele siblings had the originals and suggested the documents they hoped to auction were likely to be copies.

Pickover revealed that Wits had been in possession of Gluckman's files since 1995 when these were given to the university by Medical Rescue International (MRI). Pickover said she had been told there had been a break-in at the Historical Papers department and the Biko file had been removed from a cabinet. This allegedly happened shortly before the TRC was due to start its hearings in 1996. It's believed the Biko file contained photographs when it was stored at MRI's Braamfontein offices. MRI had asked Wits to hold the files on its behalf, but it is not known how the company first gained possession of the papers.

Nkosinathi Biko said in his founding affidavit that his family and the Steve Biko Foundation were not aware of the report until the day of the auction. Westgate Auctioneers told *Sowetan Live* that 'Dr Gluckman was very concerned about the safety of such documents as his offices had been bugged and he had received numerous death threats. He therefore asked Mrs Steele to keep the copies of such documents.'

Nkosinathi Biko said Gluckman had indeed been appointed at the time by the Biko family 'because we wanted an independent report as the police had claimed that [my father] died as a result of an extended hunger strike – a claim which later proved to be false'.

Biko was reported by the *Sowetan* as saying the report 'belonged to the Biko family, and that the Foundation wanted it for preservation purposes. At the very least the report is emotionally sensitive and of familial significance to the Biko family. It is a report that the Biko family wished to preserve and display to all South Africans to further the legacy of my late father.'

Initially, the court ruled that the auctioneers would be able to remain the owners of the documents. But, in February 2015, the legal wrangle continued after Biko's family filed papers for the Steele siblings to hand over the file.

The Star reported that the Biko family was wanting the court to declare that the two siblings were not owners of the copy in their possession; direct Westgate Walding Auctioneers to deliver it to Nkosinathi Biko with immediate effect, or, alternatively, the Steeles and the auctioneers should be barred from selling, copying, alienating, destroying or damaging the report; and ensure that the report could not be circulated in the media or the public domain, as free availability would drive other people to try to auction it off.

'The report belongs to the Biko family. The public auction of the late Steve Biko's autopsy report is an undignified affront to the late Steve Biko.'

Meanwhile, the Steele siblings, in opposing the application, said they intended to bring a counter-claim for damages and defamation, although they were yet to file their responding papers. The auctioneers' advertising poster had read: 'Autopsy of Biko's brain… a unique document of the struggle era of great historical importance that gives full details of the autopsy/post-mortem.'

Joining the Bikos in their application were Gluckman's three children.

[SAPA, 2014a; www.sbf.org.za, 2015: 'Update on the Steve Biko autopsy report on auction response to the Steeles']

⁓

Other assassinations of BC heroes

Mthuli ka Shezi (1947–1972)

A playwright and political activist, Shezi was a student at the University of Zululand when he was elected the first vice-president of the BCP in 1972. His writing reflected the struggle of recovering African identity in colonial and post-colonial societies, a theme close to BC and Fanonism.

'I am Black/ Black like my mother/ Black like the sufferers/ Black like the continent,' he wrote in his play *Shanti*, which was published in 1972 and later banned.

Not long after his election as vice-president of the BPC, Shezi was pushed in front of a moving train and killed. He posthumously received the Order of Luthuli for his 'political leadership, outstanding contribution to the performing arts, and activism against apartheid'. *Shanti* was performed in Durban and the Transvaal by the People's Experimental Theatre (PET) troupe. They also staged *Requiem for Brother X*, a play inspired by Malcolm X.

Mapetla Mohapi (1947–1976)

The BC activist's wife, Nonhle, employed ANC attorney Griffiths Mxenge to represent her at the Grahamstown Supreme Court when she sued the minister of police in 1979 for R35 000 for claiming her husband, Mapetla Mohapi, had written a suicide note. Nonhle Mohapi argued that neither the note nor the signature was in Mapetla's handwriting, while further claiming he had died after being assaulted by the Security Branch while being held under Section 6 of the Terrorism Act.

Social worker Mohapi – who was born in Sterkspruit in the Eastern

Cape – certainly died in detention. He was a mere 28 years old. He had become a BCM activist after he joined SASO when he was a student at Turfloop, serving as SASO's permanent secretary and the administrator of a trust that cared for ex-political prisoners and their families. He was detained along with other SASO leaders in 1974 after he was involved in organising the Frelimo rallies in support of Mozambican independence. And although Mohapi was released without charge in 1975, he was then banned under the Suppression of Communism Act and confined to Zwelitsha near King William's Town.

Mohapi was detained again in July 1976, not long after the Soweto massacre, this time under the Terrorism Act. He was dead only three weeks later in police custody, found hanging from his trousers from the bars in his cell. The police claimed a suicide note had been found. In the end, however, no one was held responsible for his death.

Onkgopotse Abram Tiro (1947–1974)

A brilliant SASO leader and resistance teacher, Tiro was killed while handling a parcel bomb at a safe house near Gaborone. He was in Botswana at the time to raise support for the BCM.

Tiro had been completing a Unisa application form when a man he believed was a fellow student handed him a parcel said to have been sent by the IUEF, where Williamson would later become a deputy director. The bomb exploded, and Tiro was killed instantly. Later it was revealed that the Z-Squad, a unit of BOSS, had planned and effected his assassination, although the TRC controversially did not pursue its testimony. The exposé came in the 1981 book, *Inside BOSS*, written by apartheid spy Gordon Winter who masqueraded as a journalist while employed by the regime's intelligence agency.

Tiro's murder was a great loss to the BCM. Born in Dinokana near Zeerust, he worked as a dishwasher and did manual labour to save money in order to study. He enrolled at Turfloop to study humanities, and his leadership abilities were quickly recognised, seeing him elected SRC president in his final year.

He gave an unforgettable speech at the 1972 graduation ceremony, which was dubbed the Turfloop Testimony for its trenchant criticism of Bantu Education. This got him expelled, but so popular was Tiro within the student body that protests and strikes spread around campuses in solidarity.

He only got involved with the BCM the following year when he was immediately elected as SASO's permanent organiser. SASO was by now a banned organisation. Tiro was then also elected president of SASM, and when the courageous headmaster Lekgau Mathabathe gave him a job teaching history at the now-famous Morris Isaacson School in Soweto, he began to conscientise his students through BC. Members of SASM at Morris Isaacson were deeply inspired, and Tiro's reputation of being a danger to the state was entrenched. Among those scholars influenced by Tiro was young Tsietsi Mashinini, who would later lead the children onto the streets of the township in the Soweto 1976 uprising.

When Tiro left teaching after unbearable pressure was put on Mathabathe, he began a journey through southern Africa in support of BC, but threats to his life saw him having to base himself in Botswana at a Roman Catholic Mission in Khale outside Gaborone.

An internationalist, Tiro began reaching out to empathic revolutionary organisations in other parts of the world on behalf of the BCM. These included the Palestinian Liberation Organisation (PLO), engaged in its own struggle against the settler colonialism of Israel.

Tiro was assassinated in February 1974 and buried in Botswana as the apartheid regime denied his family the right to bring his body home. It took 24 years for his remains to finally return to his village, after intervention by the TRC and the president of AZAPO, Mosibudi Mangena.

The SASO founders, 50 years later: 'BC was a movement without compromise'

The Zoo Lake park in Johannesburg has an unusual history in a country that endured white settler colonialism for nearly 350 years. It was donated to the people of the city in 1902 by British gold and diamond magnate Alfred Beit's company to mark 10 years since one of its partners, Hermann Eckstein, a German-born British Randlord,[9] died.

'To the people of the city' meant all the people – Black and white.

This might not have been lost on an historic gathering of the SASO founders on 10 April 2019, when they met at the Zoo Lake Bowling Club and officially founded the 70s Group. That the Bowling Club had been at the centre of a controversial lease agreement involving one of the members of that group might also have been in the background. Yet the history of the venue is incidental in comparison to the weight of the delegation.

Notable in attendance was Pityana, the former SASO president, with others including stalwarts Ramphele and Cooper, who was involved in the leasing debacle.

As Nengwekhulu explained, the BCM consisted of members of the ANC and PAC as both of these two major liberation movements had been banned after the 1960 Sharpeville Massacre, leaving supporters of both equally at risk and many needing a common political home. They found this in BC.

Some SASO members – including Cooper and Pandelani Nefolovhodwe – who were imprisoned on Robben Island for organising the 1974 Frelimo Rallies, would also expand support for the BCM among other political prisoners of the same ideological persuasion.

This was a powerful quality of the BCM: the respect for and love of Blackness and Black life, whose intensity and commitment could negate loyalties to either the ANC or the PAC.

After the assassination of Biko in 1977 and the increasing brutality of the regime towards Black people and even some white allies, BC was driven ever deeper underground. Without its exceptional human qualities and communalism being brought to bear upon public spaces and in the public imagination, the late 1980s and early 1990s saw fierce internecine violence in Black communities.

Stoked and funded by the apartheid regime, the bloody hostilities were designed to divide Black people so as to bear out the National

---

9   The mostly British freebooters who exploited the discovery of gold from 1886 on the South African highveld.

Party's propaganda of 'Black-on-Black violence'. This was highly antithetical to BC, the quashing of which was an essential aspect of the regime's plan. It couldn't allow the BCM to continue. It couldn't allow Biko to thrive, or the movement could have overtaken the very ANC and PAC which it had banned.

The reunion at the Bowling Club in 2019 regenerated friendships among Black comrades. They embraced each other as if they were coming from the same belly. The music that serenaded the event echoed the spirit, and everyone was on the dance floor when Sibongile Khumalo, Sipho 'Hotstix' Mabuse and Mara Louw took to the stage.

All consciousness was raised when Ingoapele Madingoane rendered his protest poetry, reciting his work which had been the embodiment of South African liberation from the 1970s. No one had forgotten his words.

Their role in the liberation struggle was affirmed by former South African President Kgalema Motlanthe, who was the guest of honour at the event. That the 1970s was a watershed in our politics, a period of cruel, unrelenting repression, was moot. Yet the role of the BCM had not been given its due, often suppressed within the ANC and even the PAC, each of which sought dominance of the people.

Motlanthe spoke of how the emergence of young Black activists inspired by the philosophy of BC across university campuses at the time was at once an eloquent response to the divide-and-rule tactics of the regime, and a solid affirmation of the dignity of the oppressed.

'We gather here to celebrate the 50th anniversary of the founding of SASO, the silver jubilee of our democracy,[10] the 60th birthday of the PAC and to commemorate the assassination of comrade Chris Hani[11] as well as other martyrs whose lives were cut short by the apartheid hangmen,' Motlanthe reminded the assembly before he endorsed the '70s Group'.

He described it as 'a rebuttal of the current narrative that regards

---

10   In 2019, it was 25 years since the first democratic, non-racial elections in South Africa.

11   Chris Hani (1942–1993) was a former commander of Umkhonto we Sizwe, a leader of the ANC, and secretary-general of the South African Communist Party. He was gunned down in his driveway in April 1993 by supremacist Janusz Waluś acting in concert with Clive Derby-Lewis, a member of the apartheid government.

and treats everyone who was involved in the liberation struggle as corrupt'.

'Given the intellectual luminance and erudition that radiates from [you all], I believe you are qualified and better placed to help our nation define our national course.'

This endorsement of BC came at a moment in South African history when the ANC had been discredited for its internal breakdowns and inherent amorality, which had allowed the election of Jacob Zuma as its president and, thereafter, president of the country.

Over Zuma's decadent and destructive 10-year administration, South Africa collapsed into economic ruin through a toxic mix of patronage, policy failure and the worst effects of capitalism upon Black lives. This cemented the devastating effects of neo-colonialism and apartheid.

Motlanthe remarked upon the 70s Group's anti-sectarianism and 'quest for our common humanity'.

The outgoing president of the South African Council of Churches (SACC), Bishop Ziphozihle Siwa, delivered a sermon on the occasion, saying that 'before the invention of the mirror, human beings could not see themselves and therefore could only see beauty in others'.

'Today the mirror has turned all of us into actors. We look into the mirror and we fall in love with what we see. We even deliver moving speeches in front of the mirror and so we substitute ourselves for the people.

'The struggle for liberation was waged on behalf of and in the name of the people.'

The role of the 70s Group would be to 'inject new energy and ideas'.

'Let us imbue them with the determination to attain political attitude in their world outlook and never to become politicians,' said Ziwa, echoing one of the guiding principles of BC. 'As elders, we tend to adapt to circumstances and therefore lose the will to continue struggling for... progress. The notion, "as it was, so shall it be for ever and ever, amen" is a barrier.'

Ziwa noted as serious omissions upon the silver jubilee that democratic South Africa had 'failed to establish a Chapter 9 commission [referring to the chapter within the Constitution which guards human rights] to write and document our history' and that it had not properly calculated the enduring effects of Bantu education.

'In fact, all excesses, brutalities and crimes of apartheid pale into insignificance relative to the ravages of Bantu education.'[12]

'We must resist the inclination to romanticise the past and to suffer from false consciousness. History is important because it gives us context. In 1992 Ali Mazrui[13] said, "You were victims of colonialism and racial oppression. Now you are victors over colonialism and oppression, you must guard against becoming the next villains".'

Yet a South Africa without an overtly antiracist policy of governing, and a governing party which fails to assert BC, in favour of the neo-liberal ideology of non-racialism, has seen xenophobia towards fellow Black Africans, corruption and state capture.

Ziwa spoke of how, without BC, 'the fruits of our liberation have not filtered down'.

'People feel left behind, marginalised and crushed by… poverty and… In fact, to some, living means "not dying". They are vulnerable and hopeless.'

In a remarkable letter written in defence of Black civil rights in the US,[14] Martin Luther King Jr stated, in part, 'When you are forever fighting a degenerating sense of "nobodyness", then you will understand why we find it difficult to wait.'

Referring to this, Motlanthe reiterated: 'Many of our people are forever fighting a degenerating sense of "nobodyness", and therefore we have no right to ask them to be patient.'

Pityana spoke at the event about the need for an 'organisational

---

12   The Bantu Education Act of 1953 legalised separate education. 'Bantu' is a family of languages spoken by millions of Black people in sub-Saharan Africa, but apartheid used it as a kind of racial slur. The act was repealed in 1979 although schools remained largely segregated until this became unconstitutional after 1994.

13   Ali Al'amin Mazrui (1933–2014) was a Kenyan-born American academic and political writer, director of the Institute of Global Cultural Studies in New York, and director of the Center for Afro-American and African Studies at the University of Michigan.

14   'The Letter from Birmingham' or 'The Negro Is Your Brother' was an open letter written by Martin Luther King Jr on 16 April 1963 during the civil rights movement.

entity' that could 'consolidate, mobilise ideas and focus attention on the continuous transformation project of liberation'.

'This could become the means by which to marshal creativity and ensure that as we grow old we never become grumpy armchair critics but remain engaged, thinking, walking the talk, soiling our hands as a patriotic duty.

'The 70s Group is made up of comrades and compatriots who seek to claim their right and duty to become a resource for good, for human development, for social advancement.'

Pityana described the 1970s as signifying 'a new intensity of struggle, a resolve and a purpose that could not be vanquished. It was the youth and children who went to war against the system… who made the ultimate sacrifice.'

'For me, it was [Mthuli ka] Shezi, a young graduate who deeply desired to make a difference in his mother's life, who was instead murdered at Germiston Station' by being pushed onto train tracks in December 1972.

'It was [Mapetla] Mohapi, a graduate social worker, husband and father of two beautiful young girls, whose life was extinguished in police custody at Kei Road. It was the women who were wrenched from their children in the prime of their lives to be subjected to humiliation and violence by security police.

'I could go on and tell about [Onkgopotse] Tiro, [Tsietsi] Mashinini and many others whose names are not recognisable to ordinary South Africans today. Their stories must be told. Their visionary aspirations lay the foundations… We must never be shy to recall the pioneers of our movement.

'Yes, the 1970s was a struggle by young South Africans in defence of their future. But it was also something… born out of an existential experience of oppression… It was a system of values that sought to have the humanity of all God's people recognised.

'This revolutionary ideal emphasised a long history of struggle and resistance' from the time first the Portuguese set foot at what is now Mossel Bay and then 'the Cape of Storms' (also called 'the Cape of Good Hope') in the 14th century, before Dutch settlers docked at Table Bay in the 16th century, followed by the English. Indigenous Khoi and

San communities were robbed of their freedom and hunting lands, and white settlers warred viciously against Black pioneers moving into the region from East Central Africa.

Speaking of BC in the 1970s, Pityana said its values 'were meant to seek to achieve a humane society... to serve others rather than ourselves'.

'But it was never meant to deny what previous generations had put into the struggle, rather to establish a new phase in the same continuous rejection of white supremacy, and to hasten the dawn of freedom...'

Pityana distinguished the BCM from the ANC and the PAC, explaining that its 'activism... was not simply a regurgitation of the historic struggle of the oppressed people of our country'.

'It was also a time of strategic thinking and of innovation. For example, BC took its commitment to... unity... to a higher level by redefining the nature of the struggle. It named the essential participants in that struggle. It was BC that had the sagacity to name who the oppressed were and as such who and what Blackness was.

'It was BC that dared to define the theory for action as a philosophy and a way of life. It generated a philosophy of total infusion in the culture of resistance. BC defied simple definition by the white power structure, or a total systemic regime of total oppression.

'BC was a movement without compromise, radical in outlook and engaged with the communities it sought to serve.'

Pityana described the essence of BC.

'[It did not] prescribe the specifics of a future for South Africa. That was... a matter for all South Africans to construct... [but] We must take our freedom seriously... We must never become so fascinated by the backward glance that we forget our duty to move into the future. Freedom is not and was never designed to be the mere breaking of the chains... Freedom is a continuous process, the making of the human in us and to overcome the legacy of oppression that made non-humans of us.

'... Frankly, South Africa owes us nothing. South Africa is and has always been the occasion for us to realise our ambitions, our dreams and to strive for human fulfilment. That is as true today as it was under apartheid.

'Freedom comes with responsibility. For me that… is best expressed in this poem by Alice Walker.[15] "Try to think bigger than you ever have/ or had courage enough to do:/ that Blackness is not where whiteness/ wanders off to die: but it is/ like the dark matter/ between stars and galaxies in/ the Universe/ that ultimately/ holds all/ together."

'Our responsibility is to make this country something that it has never been: to "hold together" its multiple gifts… Tribalism and ethnic chauvinism is a denial… Racism is an insult… Blackness is an indictment to all that denies the humanity of others. Blackness is not a triumphalistic graveyard for "whiteness", but rather the glue that holds society in all its diversity together.

'… We need to give confidence back to the people of this country. What has been lost must be recovered.'

Whites and Black Consciousness: 'You are on your own'

American journalist and writer Julie Frederikse once questioned Reverend Beyers Naudé as to whether or not there was a role for white people. He said: 'A white person should learn that the contribution he can make to the struggle for liberation can only be a complementary one. A white should be willing to offer his skills, experience and knowledge but the initiative for change, the real steps to be taken, must come from the Black community.'

Where some white liberals dubbed Biko and his associates 'Black racists', Naudé and more radical white students within NUSAS leadership 'did not see it that way'.

'We saw the reasons why the traditional *modus* of the liberal organisations had become unacceptable to Black people,' wrote former NUSAS activist and campaigner Horst Kleinschmidt in his 2013

---

15   Pulitzer Prize-winning and National Book Award-winning writer Alice Walker's *Taking the Arrow Out of the Heart* (Simon & Schuster, 2018) is a collection of nearly 70 works. Walker won a NAACP (National Association for the Advancement of Colored People) Award for this collection [simonandschuster.com, 2018: https://www.simonandschuster.com/books/Taking-the-Arrow-Out-of-the-Heart/Alice-Walker/9781501179525]

'personal reflection', *Roots and Journeys Linking the Christian Institute and Wider Community to the Re-ignition of Resistance to Apartheid in the early 70s* . 'If [Biko] and BC had a case for withdrawing from the liberal organisations, then white folk who opposed apartheid needed to acknowledge that there was good reason for criticism, and thus, that we had to ask ourselves fundamental questions and take a fresh look at our organisations, if our response to apartheid was to be credible and to have impact.'

'We had to question in which way our contribution to a free and open society would be part of the emerging, much bigger national effort for liberation. The spotlight had fallen on the divide between pontificating about the wrongs apartheid created versus a more radical activism. Specifically, we realised that verbal condemnation was the stance of privileged well-to-do people, unwilling to entertain material discomfort as a consequence of their stance.'

The relationship between NUSAS and many Black members imploded in Grahamstown during a union congress there in 1967. The apartheid regime would not allow Black students attending from universities around the country to be accommodated in Rhodes University's residences or in the white town. So the university instead allocated church-based accommodation in the surrounding townships.

Black students were outraged. Many demanded, but were outvoted, that the congress be suspended until this issue was resolved, and expressed their anger that fellow white students were not prepared to either join them in the township accommodation in a show of solidarity, or engage in any other form of public protest.

Despite this, a number of white students were aggrieved when a Blacks-only caucus was held in the segregated accommodation. It is there that a Black student association was discussed in earnest.

The following December, a consultative gathering happened at Mariannhill, Natal with the background being that only a quarter of NUSAS membership was Black at that time, and many of those members felt ostracised or ignored when they expressed discomfort with the traditional white activities.

Many Black students saw those as being neither non-racial nor aware of the political strife outside the campuses.

In July 1969, the Black students' split from NUSAS was a *fait accompli*. SASO held an inaugural conference at Turfloop, and Biko was elected the first president. This happened against the backdrop of the founding of the UCM after that fateful NUSAS congress in Grahamstown.

Powerful ideologies emanating out of Black Theology and the work of Brazilian education theorist Paulo Freire were used to invigorate a sense of Black Power. SASO leveraged off the UCM's 'formation schools', where Freire's theories of pedagogy were employed to conscientise. His position was that 'oppressed people needed to develop their own critical faculties rather than have [a] vanguard force an ideology upon them'.

Although solidarity was also sought for SASO with the Black working class, its bond with the UCM – which helped to resuscitate Black politics after the bloodshed and brutal crackdowns of 1960 – was critical.

There was only the possibility of a relationship between the BCM and the ANC at that point, with the impact on prospects for imminent liberation having diminished after the Rivonia Trial in 1963 and 1964. Eight of the ANC's top leaders were given life sentences and jailed on Robben Island: Mandela, Walter Sisulu, Denis Goldberg, Govan Mbeki, Ahmed Kathrada, Raymond Mhlaba, Elias Motsoaledi and Andrew Mlangeni. (Mandela was already in Johannesburg's Fort serving a five-year sentence for inciting workers to strike, and for leaving South Africa illegally.)

That trial put the ANC into the political doldrums, not only internally – with the apartheid regime having introduced ever-more draconian legislation – but also in exile. There it was embattled over non-racialism, the question of re-entry into the country and its ideological stance.

The Morogoro Conference in Tanzania in 1969 dramatically exposed these organisational fault lines, with Tambo having to intervene as comrade went up against comrade, at times violently.

Meanwhile, the PAC was dealing with its own internal crises. Talismanic leader Sobukwe would be held on Robben Island till 1969 and it was experiencing a leadership crisis on the ground as its armed wing, Poqo, embarked on a destabilising series of attacks and murders. SASO policy was anti-colonial and anti-imperialist, although some of its members would turn to socialism and others to Pan-Africanism.

The intersection between the intellectuals in a radical UCM and SASO meant that there was a vigorous exchange of ideas. The UCM was most valuable as 'an inconspicuous, but vital organisational backstop', wrote Africanist historians Thomas Karis and Gwendolen M Carter in their 1993 collection, *Protest to Challenge: A Documentary History of African Politics in South Africa*.

There was reflection on the UCM again in their 1997 *Protest to Challenge* collection, *Nadir and Resurgence, 1964–1979*. '[It provided] financial and logistical support, contacts with potential overseas backers, and an expanded network through which political literature could be obtained and circulated among student activists.'

It was when that very prohibited literature was disseminated and the UCM barred from holding meetings at 'bush' universities like Turfloop, Fort Hare, Ngoye and the University of the Western Cape that SASO finally had to come into its own.

The apartheid regime's Schlebusch Commission of Inquiry in 1973 ensured that the UCM had to close when it barred it from receiving foreign funding. It then transferred its assets to SASO. This propelled some among the leadership of NUSAS – which was finding itself increasingly out in the cold in terms of being part of a future 'solution' – to reconsider their options. Some made an ideological switch, although there remains a debate as to whether this was in order to remain relevant. (There were some white students – including Wits SRC members Glenn Moss and Cedric de Beer, who went on trial in 1976 – who were untarnished campaigners.)

Just as BC had to take necessary steps within its movement in the 1970s to find an ideological identity that would add class to the race analytic, so too did NUSAS have to urgently examine itself.

Inasmuch as BC was battling to cross over into nuts-and-bolts organisational work, the more so with NUSAS. The Schlebusch Commission ironically gave it a certain credence, depicting it as perhaps more dangerous than it was in reality by declaring that NUSAS was 'encouraging arms boycotts and economic boycotts against South

Africa as part of an attempt to bring about radical change in the existing political order'.

The commission described this as 'a form of subversion of the state'.

But whether or not this exaggerated the power NUSAS held, it was not the irony that mattered in the end, but the immediate, extreme and demobilising impact its report had on many members.

Support for the union waned, particularly as the commission barred any further foreign funding. Some leaders were detained. Worse, some were banned and had their passports removed. Others, where this was possible for the apartheid state, were deported.

This strike-back was vicious enough to expose a paucity in what it meant to be in the white Left in contrast to BC, which understood itself still to be steeped in community.

Where Biko's immortal words, 'Black man, you are on your own', referred to the essence of BC – that Black communities had to band together to build themselves up from the inside – for the white Left, a slogan like, 'white man, you are on your own' might as well have applied.

NUSAS activist Gerhard Maré recorded some of this while writing his UCT Master's thesis on the literature of dissident Afrikaner Breyten Breytenbach in 1975. Breytenbach's frustration at being treated like a verraaier (traitor) was intense, but so was the void into which white 'lefties', for so long personified by NUSAS, stepped once excluded from the Black frame which had been their *sine qua non*.

'I don't know whether it was the correct perception or not, but that came out for me – that I was in detention as an individual,' said Breytenbach.

There was a morass until 1976, when the Soweto massacre happened. But the moral *imbroglio* was that, on the surface at least, it took another round of state-sanctioned slaughter of Black people for the white Left to find some meaning. After the massacre, NUSAS attempted a revival under an 'Africanisation' banner: a visceral link which its compatriots in SASO had been advocating since the late 1960s. But in 1977, when Biko was murdered and there was a fresh wave of bannings, the pressure was on NUSAS to locate a more militant consciousness.

Fink Haysom – a NUSAS Wages Commission member in Durban

in 1973–75, the UCT SRC president in 1976 and NUSAS president in 1977 – has alluded to its efforts to define an authentic role, saying 'the white Left has always been perceived as a greater threat than it actually is'. Only a small number decided to take every risk imaginable with their privilege and join the MK.

Afrikaner activist Marius Schoon (1937–99) was one. He fled to Botswana in 1977, having been imprisoned for 12 years for his activities with the (white) Congress of Democrats, an ally of the ANC, while doing postgraduate studies at Wits. In the early 1960s, he had been part of an MK plan to bomb a police station in Hillbrow, Johannesburg. Entrapped, Schoon was then arrested and convicted. Once released, he was banned.

In an interview with Frederikse, Schoon's view was that 'the SASO breakaway' had been 'misinterpreted' by some whites who believed they had no role left to play. He pointed to the fact that a number within the white Left then turned to workerist politics. But Schoon identified a truth: 'The real political work is going to have to be done with Black people, and the real political change is actually going to be brought about by Black people.'

Support for the white Left was to shift again. Craig Williamson was exposed internally to the ANC by Schoon and his wife Jeanette while they were working for the movement in 1980. But they could not be saved even by this warning as Jeanette and their young daughter, Katryn, were murdered upon Williamson's orders in Angola in 1984 when Jeanette opened a parcel bomb. The white Left endured another aspect of this as a particularly harrowing reminder of the injustice of history.

Despite his part in the Schoons' deaths – and those of fellow Black activists – Williamson was given amnesty by the TRC in 2000. It was just a year after Schoon died at the age of 61.

Those activists were different to some of the more prominent 'global' white 'allies' of 2020, who have made international careers off ideas of BC.

Perhaps the most well-known is American education professor and diversity consultant Robin DiAngelo, whose book, *White Fragility*, dismisses whites who deny or resist that there is a racist bias afforded them by a supremacist society.

First published in 2018, DiAngelo's book would have its second life in 2020 after the murder of George Floyd as especially Americans sought guides on how to navigate race. Her book was a *New York Times* bestseller, but some Black academics and activists believe it 'infantilises' Black people. This syncs with the necessary peripheralising of liberal whites on race and other issues that directly affect Black people.

Columbia University linguistics professor John McWhorter believes DiAngelo's book is 'a racist tract' which 'diminishes Black people in the name of dignifying us'. McWhorter's view is that the writer's 'hyper-awareness' of 'unintentional racism ever lurking inside of her that was inculcated from birth by the white supremacy on which America was founded' has resulted in DiAngelo 'endlessly exploring, acknowledging, and seeking to undo whites' "complicity with and investment in" racism' as 'the bearer of an exalted wisdom'.

McWhorter's position is that this is in itself 'an ideological bias' as DiAngelo presents 'some sort' of racism as being at the core of 'all disparities between white and Black people'. He labels DiAngelo's approach as 'a cult' in which 'white Americans [are] muzzled, straitjacketed, tied down, and chloroformed for good measure'.

'[What does this] gloomy, knit-browed... self-mortification... glum recitations of white perfidy... serve?... [This is] a book about how to make certain educated white readers feel better about themselves [with its] depiction of Black people as endlessly delicate poster children... [in a] blinkered, self-satisfied, punitive stunt of a primer.'

[Frederikse, 2015: The Schlebusch Commission Report on NUSAS is referred to in Frederikse's essay; Kleinschmidt, 2013; Magaziner, 2010: 28; Karis & Gerhart, 1993: 74; Karis & Gerhart, 1997; Maré, 1975; McWhorter, 2020]

Two

Africa, the Intellectuals and Black Solidarity

Written and compiled by Janet Smith

No movement takes place in isolation, or it cannot succeed. Black Consciousness in South Africa was seeded and flowered at a time when Black Power was putting Malcolm X and the Black Panthers into the rhetoric of a white United States. Socialist students and workers were shutting down France, Spain, Mexico and Yugoslavia. Young Czechs delivered a Prague Spring, and across our continent Africans anticipated the end of colonialism from Cape to Cairo.

What did they have in common? The thought of the great philosophers, revolutionaries and intellectuals who were read, studied and discussed in every part of the world where there was a will for liberation. And the sense of a much wider community, which would support and encourage – sometimes with a shotgun and a fist, and sometimes with placards and speeches.

That is not only true of the 1960s and 1970s. Not much has changed. We're still made more alive and are propelled by the possibilities in the great thought and powerful solidarity of others.

These include Frantz Fanon, who was born a colonial subject but remains forever a free international mind; Julius Nyerere, the foremost mwalimu of Africa; Robert Sobukwe, who was regarded as the most dangerous man in South Africa; the contemporary feminists bell hooks and Pumla Dineo Gqola; Négritude; the brazen Assata Shakur; the accelerating global organisation of Black Lives Matter; and the quiet radical brilliance of writer and broadcaster Farrukh Dhondy.

Here, a light is shone on only a few astounding individuals and conscious philosophies.

'A leader must have total commitment to the struggle of the African people'

Dr Motsoko Pheko[16] delivered the Robert Sobukwe Memorial Lecture in July 2014 at the Methodist Black Consultation held in Springs, near Johannesburg. Launched in 2003, the annual lecture is an initiative of the Steve Biko Foundation and the University of Fort Hare. 'It commemorates the legacy of the late Pan-Africanist, who early on articulated the importance of African unity and the need for an African Renaissance. Accordingly, the gatherings focus on developments in Africa that have a bearing on the realisation of Sobukwe's vision.' A 'national ritual of collective remembrance', the lecture has been given by, among others, Professor E'skia Mphahlele, advocate Dumisa Ntsebeza, former President of Burundi Pierre Buyoya, and languages and culture specialist Adama Samassékou, who is a minister in Mali.

Mangaliso Robert Sobukwe is a leader who walked the political talk to the finish. In biblical language, he ran the race and kept the faith. He went through a glorious contest with distinction. This is a man that the apartheid colonialist regime so silenced that even his closing speech in Court Case Number 173/60 was expunged from court

---

[16] Motsoko Pheko (1933–) is an expert in indigenous African knowledge. He joined the PAC in 1960, and served as an MP, representative to the UN and president of the party until he was expelled in 2006. He founded liberal arts college Daystar University in Kenya. He has qualifications in law, political science and systematic theology.

records. Researchers and filmmakers thirsty to find his voice in radio stations have searched in vain. The enemy destroyed anything he ever said audibly. He was a banned person to his grave.

As a young man... Sobukwe was an omnivorous reader. At school, right up to the University of Fort Hare, he was an outstandingly brilliant student and a great thinker. He grew up to be a person endowed with profound intellect, revolutionary vigour and deep spirituality. He had exceptionally disarming humility towards everybody, friend and foe alike. Unashamed of his humble beginnings from which he came, he declared, 'I am the son of Sobukwe, born in Graaff-Reinet – that land of goats'.

Leadership is [the] responsibility and duty to serve the people. Leaders who are servants of the people defend the poor and the powerless and work in their interest. They are not afraid to stand against the mighty.

They reject the false philosophy that 'might is right'. Might has been found wrong many times.

In the politics of South Africa, Sobukwe introduced a new style of leadership. On leadership, he declared (in the first version of the Programme of Action adopted by the ANC in 1949): 'True leadership demands complete subjugation of self, absolute honesty, integrity and uprightness of character, courage and fearlessness, above all a consuming love for one's people.'

He refused to compromise the birthright of his people – land repossession.

After the Sharpeville uprising exploded like a huge bomb on apartheid South Africa, Lewis Nkosi, a highly respected journalist, described Sobukwe as... 'a tall, distinguished African prisoner, a university lecturer and political leader who at the age of 36 has a rare distinction of having scared the South African government out of its wits.'

AP Mda, who was the President of the ANCYL after the death of Anton Muziwakhe Lembede, and then a prominent lawyer, said: 'I found that Sobukwe believed that a leader must have total commitment to the struggle of the African people for national emancipation, no matter what hardships may be or what the obstacles may be.'

When the University of Ahmadu Bello in Nigeria conferred an honorary degree of Doctor of Laws on Sobukwe posthumously, the dean of the university chanted: 'Honourable Chancellor, I present to you this courageous African revolutionary, this strong believer in the principles of Pan-Africanism, this great fighter for the liberation and unity of all African peoples, this symbol of the struggle against apartheid and colonialism; for the posthumous conferment of the honorary degree of Doctor of Law.'

Sobukwe understood that the struggle in South Africa was fundamentally an anti-colonial struggle, not a mere civil rights struggle against apartheid. Apartheid was the symptom of the disease brought about by the Berlin Congress of 1885 which enabled Europe to partition Africa into its colonies, robbed African people of their countries and used the riches of Africa to develop Europe and underdevelop Africa. He knew how land dispossession of the African people came about in South Africa and that a doctor who treats the symptoms of a disease and not the disease itself is bound to fail.

He recognised all African kings who fought against the colonial land dispossession of the African people in South Africa. King Cetshwayo was the architect of the Battle of Isandlwana, where African spears triumphed over the guns of a well-armed British army. In today's Eastern Cape, King Hintsa fell in the Sixth War of National Resistance against British colonialism in 1834. The colonial soldiers were commanded by a British colonel, Harry Smith. He still has a town in the 'new South Africa' named after him. Another one called Ladysmith is named after his wife.

In July 1959, Sobukwe paid tribute to all African kings. They were the first freedom fighters in this country against colonialism. Among other things, Sobukwe said: 'Sons and daughters of Afrika, we are going down the corridor of time renewing our acquaintance with the heroes of Africa's past – those men and women who nourished the tree of African freedom and independence with their blood, those great sons and daughters of Afrika who died in order that we may be free in the land of our birth.

'We meet here today, to rededicate ourselves to the cause of Afrika, to establish contact beyond the grave with the great African heroes and assure them that their struggle was not in vain.

'We meet here, sons and daughters of the beloved land, to drink from the fountain of African achievement, to remember the men and women who begot us, to remind ourselves of where we come from and restate our goals.

'We are here to draw inspiration from the heroes of Thaba Bosiu,[17] Isandlwana, Sandile's Kop[18] and numerous other battlefields where our forefathers fell before the bullets of the foreign invader.'

A generation that is ignorant of its past has no past and no future. A generation that does not know its past does not know even its present. It, therefore, cannot understand its present and plan its future intelligently. The past has determined how the present must be handled. Sobukwe got his politics and his history correct. He did not forget that if a realistic and just society is to be created in South Africa, the facts of the political history of this country must not be swept under the carpet.

Have you ever read the Union of South Africa Act 1909 and the Natives Land Act 1913? These are two pieces of legislation that created South Africa. The Natives Land Act legalised the unjust distribution of land and its riches. It created massive poverty and alarming economic inequalities affecting the African people today. This same law is today hidden in Section 25(7) of the South African constitution under a new name – 'property clause' – while the country's majority people are propertyless. Millions live in filthy shacks not fit even for pigs.

The rulers dangle before the dispossessed of this country 'land claims' from the crumbs of 13% allocated to the African people in 1913 and 1936. They are now offered to buy back the property of their ancestors through a dismally failed policy of 'willing seller and willing buyer'. But even this is merely their land, which was further seized

---

17   The birthplace of the Sotho people, this mountain fortress lies about 23 kilometres south-east of the capital of Lesotho, Maseru. It was the bastion of Sotho nation founder Chief Moshoeshoe, and has never fallen to an enemy [http://samilitaryhistory.org/vol163ds.html]

18   A hill with commanding views of the Tyume Valley and Amathole Mountains near Lovedale in the Eastern Cape, which takes its name from Chief Mgolombane Sandile kaNgqika who took a strong stand against British colonial conquest [http://centenary.ufh.ac.za/sandiles-kop/].

from 13% through the Group Areas Act of 1950.

Indeed, the country Sobukwe fought for is like the one which Prophet Isaiah described in Chapter 1 verse 7 of his biblical book, when he wrote, 'Your land is desolate... Your land, strangers devour in your presence.'

Sobukwe knew that this would happen if some liberation struggle leaders in this country would confuse the symptoms – apartheid – for the disease of colonialism itself. The apartheid colonialist regime feared Sobukwe. Balthazar Johannes Vorster, the regime's minister of justice, called Sobukwe a 'heavyweight boxer' when compared to his political opponents in South Africa.

Sobukwe was a Pan-Africanist visionary. He preached Africanism and Pan-Africanism in South Africa when these concepts were frowned upon by his political opponents as 'anti-white'. But of course, today there is the Pan-African Parliament.[19] There has been the Organisation of African Unity (OAU), which has been succeeded by the African Union.

It is very clear that if Africa does not unite, she will not defeat the onslaughts of a new form of colonialism threatening Africa's people. Situations such as Libya, the Central African Republic, Somalia, Mali, South Sudan, and Boko Haram in Nigeria show that no African state can go it alone.

Sobukwe was an ideological brother and comrade of Pan-Africanist luminaries such as Kwame Nkrumah, Julius Nyerere, Modibo Keïta,[20] Ahmed Sékou Touré and Patrice Lumumba. He was a strong advocate of a 'United States of Africa'. He declared: 'Besides the sense of a common historical fate that we share with other [African] countries, it is imperative for purely practical reasons that the whole of Africa unite into a single unit... Only in that way can be solved the immense problems that face the continent.'

The official slogans of the PAC have always been 'Izwe Lethu!' or

---

19   The Pan-African Parliament (PAP) is an organ of the African Union as set out by the Treaty Establishing the African Economic Community (Abuja Treaty) for discussions affecting the continent. The first Parliament was inaugurated in Ethiopia. It sits in Midrand, near Johannesburg in South Africa.

20   African socialist Modibo Keïta (1915–1977) was first president of Mali and prime minister of the Mali Federation.

'Africa for Africans, Africans for humanity and humanity for God!'

... This is what Sobukwe wrote in *Drum* in March 1959: 'Nobody disputes our contention that Africa will be free from foreign rule. What is disputed by many, particularly the ruling white minorities, is that she will be free within our lifetime or by 1963 or even by 1973 or 1984.

'However, the African nationalist movements which met in Accra in 1958 put 1963 as the target for freedom for all of Africa.'

There were only eight African states when Sobukwe said this. But by 1963, there were 32 and the formation of the OAU happened on 25 May 1963.[21] By 1984, only South Africa remained an apartheid colony.

Sobukwe was never naive about the hardships of the liberation struggle he led. Long before the Sharpeville uprising, [there was the] armed struggle that was initiated by him and his colleagues such as PK Leballo,[22] Zephania Mothopeng and Nyathi Pokela.[23]

Sobukwe had warned: 'There is plenty of suffering ahead. The oppressor will not take this lying down. But we are ready, come what may.'

Without Sobukwe's leadership, the UN would never have been seized with 'the problem of South Africa' for over 30 years. As Frantz Fanon, the author of *The Wretched of the Earth*, writes, it was the Sharpeville uprising, led by Sobukwe, which made the vile system of apartheid known internationally. Without this uprising, there would never have been a UN Special Committee Against Apartheid.[24] This world body

---

21 The OAU created a reasonable unity between the Casablanca Group comprising Algeria, Egypt, Ghana, Tanzania, Guinea, Libya, Mali and Morocco which had anti-colonial leaders and sought political 'federation', and the Monrovia Group comprising Liberia, Nigeria and most of Francophone Africa, including Senegal and Cameroon, which favoured autonomous states.

22 Potlako Kitchener Leballo (1915–1986) was an Africanist who led the PAC until 1979. Leballo was co-founder of the Basutoland African Congress in 1952 and a World War 2 veteran and headmaster.

23 John Nyathi 'Poks' Pokela (1922–1985) was educated at Fort Hare. He was a member of the ANCYL, but left the ANC and helped found the PAC in the late 1950s. In 1966, he was sentenced to 13 years on Robben Island on charges of sabotage related to the Azanian People's Liberation Army which he founded as Poqo ('pure') in 1961.

24 The UN Special Committee Against Apartheid was established by the General Assembly under Resolution 1761 (XVII) of 6 November 1962 to keep apartheid under review throughout the year.

would never have declared apartheid a crime against humanity.[25]

As a result of Sobukwe's leadership, the UN – in honour of the martyrs of the Sharpeville uprising – declared 21 March International Day for the Elimination of Racial Discrimination.

Without Sobukwe's actions, there would never have been Robben Island. Robben Island was primarily meant for Sobukwe and PAC members. That is why they were the first to be imprisoned on Robben Island from 12 October 1962.

Was Sobukwe a 'racist'? In a court of law in which he and his 23 colleagues were convicted of leading the Sharpeville uprising, he stated that he believed in one race only. Asked: 'Do you imply that the Africans ... and the whites of this country belong to this race?' He replied: 'Correct.'

It is Sobukwe's organisation that coined the phrase 'non-racial' in South Africa. The others were multi-racialists. Sobukwe said there was enough racism in South Africa to multiply it. The experts of the English language those days said there was no such word in English. Today the constitution of this country talks of a non-racial society. Unfortunately, no English experts ever afterwards came forward to thank Sobukwe and his movement for giving the English language a new word: non-racialism. They just quietly put it in their dictionaries.

Sobukwe was a pace-setter in the politics of South Africa. When he formed a military wing of his party, others did the same. When he went to Robben Island, they followed him there. Let me give one example.

When he appeared in court in April 1960, he reminded the magistrate: 'Your Worship, it will be remembered that when this court began we refused to plead because we felt no moral obligation whatsoever to obey laws which are made exclusively by a white minority...

'But I would like to quote what was said by someone before, that an unjust law cannot be justly applied... We stand for equal rights for all individuals... We are not afraid of the consequences for our actions

---

25   Apartheid was declared a crime against humanity in 1973, but this was not ratified by any country in the industrialised West [Lingaas, 2015: Oslo Law Review].

and it is not our intention to plead for mercy.

'Thank you, Your Worship.'

Two years, six months after Sobukwe had addressed a colonial court in this mood, a rival political leader in 1962 followed on the pace that Sobukwe had set. He said: 'I challenge the right of this court to hear my case. Firstly, I fear that I will not be given a fair trial. Secondly, I consider myself neither legally nor morally bound to obey laws made by a parliament in which I have no representation.'[26]

Sobukwe was far ahead of his political opponents. His revolution began with the destruction of the enslaving pass laws, which had conditioned the African people to regard their colonial masters as demi-gods. They suffered the terrible disease of the inferiority complex.

For Sobukwe, the 'dompas' symbolised men who could never become owners of products and masters of their destiny. They were mentally damaged by the system of apartheid and colonialism and had helplessly accepted their inferior status in the land of their ancestors. Sobukwe worked on distinct fronts as a thought leader. These were:

- Africans must be owners of the means of production;
- Africans must be owners of land and minerals; and
- Africans must declare their freedom from mental slavery by thinking, working and behaving like free men and women without the continuing mental chains of the 'dompas' that Sobukwe and his colleagues paid a high price to destroy through the Sharpeville uprising.

These are still the biggest challenges faced by our country. Without attainment of these three objectives, there will be worse Marikanas.[27]

At some stage, the slave conditions of employment, especially in mines and farms, and unjust distribution of land and its resources according to population numbers, will create more uprisings.

26　The person to whom Pheko refers is Nelson Mandela.

27　'Marikanas' refers to the Marikana massacre near Rustenburg, two hours from Johannesburg, where 34 striking miners were killed presumably by the South African Police Service on 16 August 2012 in the most lethal use of force by security forces against civilians since the Soweto uprising of 1976. The massacre was widely compared to the 1960 Sharpeville massacre.

Sobukwe became the main target for the racist colonial regime because of these objectives. They knew just how the economic consequences would be for their colonial paradise that economically excluded the indigenous African population.

Sobukwe defied the demi-gods of white supremacy who wanted to destroy the image of God in Black people.

Freedom is not free. Its price is sacrifice. Sobukwe walked the political talk against fearful odds, with extraordinary patriotism and consuming love for Africa.

God bless Africa and her sons and daughters.

[www.drmotsokopheko.co.za; Mandela's speech can be read at www.mandela.gov.za]

'He left deep footprints of our uprising': Sobukwe's zeal lives on at Wits

Wits officially renamed its Central Block (the main administration and reception area) the Robert Sobukwe Block in September 2017. A plaque was unveiled by his son, Dinilesizwe Sobukwe, and Wits Chancellor Justice Dikgang Moseneke. The renaming commemorated Sobukwe's service to the university and his contribution to fighting apartheid.

Wits Vice-Principal Professor Tawana Kupe, who presided over the ceremony with Justice Moseneke, said the renaming was befitting for Sobukwe, who was 'a noble individual with an unrelenting spirit'.

'Robert Mangaliso Sobukwe is one of the most illustrious Africans ever to be born on our continent,' said Kupe. 'He was an academic, a thinker, a philosopher and a tireless, selfless, dedicated and resilient fighter for freedom of the African people. For all the injustices and calculated, sustained and cruel assaults on his human dignity, he responded by affirming the humanity of all in everything he did.'

Sobukwe was, among other achievements, a lecturer in African studies at Wits.

Dinilesizwe Sobukwe said his father had 'had a lot of fun here and there are a lot of people who still call, who were his students'.

'They write letters to say he was a friend, a teacher and a mentor.

I would like to say most of his students were white and they still write and say he was a man who made a great contribution in their lives, for them to see this country in a different way.

'This place energised him, it made him know what it is that he had wanted to do with his life.'

In his keynote address, Moseneke paid tribute to Sobukwe for his tenacity and selflessness, and described him as a compatriot who 'left deep footprints of our uprising'.

'Every nation, every people, from time to time, yields from amongst its very own a truly courageous, selfless and visionary patriot who stands tall and apart from the rest. As she or he passes on, the rest of us would know that it was a life... worthy of celebration.'

David Manabile, Wits SRC president, said the students were 'very honoured... that the Pan African Student Movement of Azania (PASMA) tabled such a motion for the celebration and renaming of a building after an icon such as Mangaliso Robert Sobukwe.

'We must learn and embody what Sobukwe stood for.'

PASMA representative Phyllia Ngoatje said Sobukwe was 'the most formidable opponent to the apartheid system': 'Without his revolutionary zeal, unshakeable dedication to the struggle, and the conviction of his beliefs, it is unlikely that apartheid would have ended and collapsed like it did.'

[University of the Witwatersrand, 2017: This university's website carries the press release from the university about its decision to change the name of its Central Block]

African and diasporic influencers
Samora Machel, Frelimo and the SASO 9

Tambo issued a statement from the ANC's headquarters in Lusaka, Zambia, to the Frelimo (Mozambique Liberation Front) Central Committee on 22 October 1986 when news came through that Mozambican revolutionary leader Samora Machel had been killed along with 24 others in the Tupolev 134A-3 presidential plane.

The party was on its way home from the Lusaka Summit when the aircraft thundered to the ground around the Lebombo mountain range near Mbuzini, Komatipoort, where the borders of Swaziland, South Africa and Mozambique meet.

In his statement, Tambo, 'on behalf of the masses of South Africa', said: 'Our leader, comrade-in-arms and brother, Samora Moisés Machel, one of the most outstanding leaders of our continent, one of its best brains, an unsurpassed fighter... has been killed by the only enemy who stands to gain by his death: the apartheid regime of Pretoria and its agents'.

There was an unbreakably robust link between Machel – ideologically, a Marxist-Leninist and a socialist – and BC in South Africa as it struggled to find its own ideological *modus* in the 1970s.

There were 59 witnesses in the apartheid regime's case against nine members of SASO who had defied it by organising rallies in support of Frelimo's triumph over Portuguese colonial rule in 1975. Posters and placards held aloft at the rallies are today much sought after, displaying the cogent sentiments of South African students in solidarity with their brothers and sisters in another African country: 'Frelimo fought and regained our soil'; 'Change the name and the story applies to YOU'; 'Revolution!'; 'Machel will help!'

The nine who appeared before Justice Johan Boshoff in the Pretoria Supreme Court, amid clenched fists and freedom songs, were Saths Cooper, Mosiuoa Patrick 'Terror' Lekota, Muntu Myeza, Aubrey Mokoape, Nkwenkwe Vincent Nkomo, Pandelani Vincent Nefolovhodwe, Strini Moodley, Zithulele Cindi and Kaborane Gilbert Sedibe. The prosecution's expert witness was Stoffel van der Merwe, a senior lecturer in politics at the Rand-Afrikaans University and later apartheid minister of education.[28]

Cooper retained his reputation as a firebrand after initiating trial proceedings by insisting he would not plead. That led to a 'not guilty' plea being entered for the nine defendants. Found guilty of terrorism and incitement to insurrection, the 'SASO 9' served their sentences

---

28   He was the National Party's secretary-general for 13 months during the time of De Klerk with the task of helping to spin-doctor a 'moderate' swing during the transition process.)

on Robben Island alongside ANC stalwarts, including Mandela and Sisulu.

As planned within the BCM, a 'second layer' of leadership had been nurtured who would continue in the event others were banned or imprisoned. This would unfold by 1973, when all too many BCM leaders – including Biko – had been 'prohibited' by the state.

Fearless young people like Muntu Myeza, SASO's secretary-general at the time, caucused to stage the BCM's most public demonstration of resistance yet by holding the rallies in support of Frelimo's transitional government and Mozambique's imminent independence. Curries Fountain was the appointed site in Durban, and Myeza defied the regime by addressing 5 000 people.

Turfloop students were immediately at war with the regime's uniforms. Within hours, 200 activists in the fold of SASO and the BCP had been raided, 37 detained and nine ultimately charged.

Although it has been written that Biko was not comfortable with the rallies, he was nonetheless subpoenaed as a defence witness. He testified for a week in May 1976, with a particularly complicated brief. Although it was an explicit intention of the BCM to use the podium to promote BC, he could not portray it as 'a terrorist body' or this would seriously compromise the nine. In the end, Biko was a scintillating advocate for the movement and his fellow activists, although it would be impossible to save them from prison, and analysts seem to agree that Justice Boshoff lowered his original expectations for the defendants on the basis of Biko's testimony, which broke his enforced silence.

That was the impetus for editor Millard Arnold's 1978 book, *The Testimony of Steve Biko: BC in South Africa*.

Others important to the defence included Rick Turner, who took on Van der Merwe on technical details around SASO's 'insurgence', and one of the accused, Nkwenkwe Nkomo, whose devotion to his church was used to stress that the nine were not necessarily 'revolutionaries' in the classic sense.

Boshoff would concede the point that 'revolutionary' and 'protest' strategy were different models, and that a violent overthrow of the state was not what was being proposed by the 'SASO 9'. Boshoff, however, convicted them partly on the basis of the 'revolutionary potential' of their ideas. While the freedom of Mozambique remained at the core of the trial, being the raison d'être for the nine's incarceration, it drew muscular attention to BC among South Africans, and to the struggle for liberation in our neighbouring state.

Thirty years later, no one has yet been identified, charged or found guilty of Machel's murder. The 1987 Margo Commission declared the plane was 'in good order' and that it was therefore pilot error – a finding which the International Civil Aviation Organisation accepted, although it was rejected by Mozambique. Among the witnesses at the commission were Military Intelligence operatives; Machel's widow Graça Machel; the former honorary secretary of the British Anti-Apartheid Movement, Dr Abdul Minty; and apartheid 'superspy' Williamson.

The Soviet Union under Communist Party leader Leonid Brezhnev claimed the Russian-piloted Tupolev had been 'deliberately lured off course' by the South Africans. Both the Soviet Union and a Mozambican medical investigation later also disputed the Margo Commission's finding that there was no interference with the aircraft or any evidence of sabotage.

[Tambo, 1987]

Frantz Omar Fanon (1925–1961)

Speaking at the Congress of Black African Writers in 1959, Fanon said: 'Colonial domination, because it is total and tends to oversimplify, very soon manages to disrupt in spectacular fashion the cultural life of a conquered people. This cultural obliteration is made possible by the negation of national reality by the occupying power.'

Decolonisation was a central topic for Fanon, born a colonial subject in what was then the colony of Martinique, a region of France in the Antilles in the eastern Caribbean Sea. As he developed his chosen field – psychiatry – around revolutionary philosophy, Fanon would be as misunderstood as he was influential.

A strong description comes via *The Guardian* writer Bhakti Shringarpure in 2014, on the subject of Swedish filmmaker Göran Hugo Olsson's documentary *Concerning Violence: Nine Scenes from the Anti-Imperialistic Self-Defense*, which is mostly about Fanon.

Shringarpure writes that decolonisation is 'that short yet potent moment at the tail end of an anti-colonial war followed by the transfer of power when the new nation comes into being.

'This has often proven to be one of the most violent episodes in post-colonial history, and Fanon is its most articulate philosopher.'

A supporter of the Algerian War of Independence, Fanon remains a dominant inspiration for those seeking liberation, advocating as a central aspect the self-awareness of anti-Back racism.

[Shringarpure, 2014]

Ngũgĩ wa Thiong'o (1938-)

The activist Kenyan author and post-colonial theorist's *Decolonising the Mind: The Politics of Language in African Literature* (1986) is an exposé of cultural imperialism unlike any other. Not only examining the complete undermining of Black life by British missionaries and colonial instruments, it revealed the intention of the Western education system to assume total power over the Black mind.

This unravelling of how the British schooling system, the ultimate reach of the 'empire', was intended to psychologically conquer children, is one of the reasons why Ngũgĩ is such an important writer. *Decolonising the Mind* is indeed a theoretical publication, yet its strength is in how perfectly it reads as a devastating indictment of white will.

Ngũgĩ's vision flies the anti-colonial flag, the 'civilisation' of Black people under white domination affecting not only Africans.

It may be that the Nobel Prize for Literature eluded him for too long because he went further than theory when he decided to stop writing in English and continue only in indigenous sub-Saharan African languages Gĩkũyũ and Swahili.[29]

Among Ngũgĩ's greatest works are *Weep Not Child* (1964), *The River Between* (1965), *A Grain of Wheat* (1967), *Petals of Blood* (1977), *Caitaani Mutharaba-Ini* (1980, *Devil on the Cross*), *Matigari ma Njiruungi* (1986, *The Patriots Who Survived the Bullets*) and *Mũrogi wa Kagogo* (2004, *Wizard of the Crow*).

A distinguished professor of English and comparative literature at

---

29   There are a number of major African language families, with Gĩkũyũ, Swahili and the indigenous languages of southern and South Africa, such as isiZulu, Sesotho, Setswana and isiXhosa, emanating from the Niger-Congo regions and falling largely into the Bantu family.

UC Irvine, Ngũgĩ's latest work, *The Perfect Nine: The Epic of Gĩkũyũ and Mũmbi* (2020) 'remains engaged with his homeland in new and perhaps unexpected ways', says the *Los Angeles Times*' Anderson Tepper.

'A recounting of the creation myth of the Gikuyu people of Kenya, [this is] a quest novel-in-verse that explores folklore, myth and allegory through a decidedly feminist and pan-African lens. It is Ngũgĩ writing in oracular mode, looking back at his country as if from a great distance of space and time.'

[Tepper, 2020: https://www.latimes.com/entertainment-arts/books/ story/2020-10-12/ngugi-wa-thiongo-kenyan-epic-the-perfect-nine]

Carlos A Cooks (1913–1966)

Founder of nationalist organisation the African Pioneer Movement, Cooks was described by writer Robert Acemendeces Harris as 'the ideological son of Marcus Mosiah Garvey'. Writing for the key African and Caribbean social network, *BN Village*, Harris's tribute to Cooks appears under the headline 'A true Blackman'.

The writer also allies Cooks to the substantial BC heritage of West Indian-born educator-diplomat-politician Edward Wilmot Blyden (1832–1912), a so-called 'father of pan-Africanism'. Blyden was among those Blacks freed from slavery in the US who agreed to migrate to Sierra Leone, then a British West African colony. He developed his thought on Pan-Africanism in that time, creating 'Ethiopianism', based on a form of Zionism, which Blyden envisaged would attract African Americans back to Africa to fight colonialism and neo-colonialism.

'Carlos Cooks was to Black Nationalism what John Coltrane was to... jazz, and what Aretha is to soul music,' writes Harris.

Cooks, who was born in the Dominican Republic and died in Harlem, New York, is regarded by many within the diaspora as a major figure. He set up and sustained the African Nationalist Legion, which he hoped would one day be able to join the African liberation struggle. A protagonist of street oratory, Cooks fought against 'ghetto minds' along with other heroes of Garvey's 'red, black and green' movement (red for blood, black for the hopes of Black people, and green for their growth potential). These included Betty Shabazz, who would go on to marry Malcolm X in 1958.

Cooks argued against the word 'negroes', preferring 'Black' or 'African', and found particular brotherhood with the South West Africa People's Organisation (Swapo) and the People's Movement for the Liberation of Angola (MPLA).

Charles V Hamilton (1929–)

A political scientist and civil rights leader, Hamilton was the WS Sayre Professor Emeritus of Government and Political Science at Columbia University. He earned a PhD at the University of Chicago in 1964 and held faculty positions at Rutgers University, Lincoln University and Roosevelt University. Hamilton joined Columbia in 1969.

Hamilton co-wrote *Black Power: The Politics of Liberation* with Stokely Carmichael. Both are credited with using 'institutional racism' as a term which would then fall into popular use.

Hamilton believed Blacks were taught to hate themselves with the clear intention of holding them back from decision-making and all social and political processes in favour of the dominance of the white middle class. He never wavered from his belief in Black pride and Black Power.

CLR James (1901–1989)

Although radical historians like Robert Hill (UCLA), Paul Buhle (Brown) and Kent Worcester (Marymount Manhattan College), editor Anna Grimshaw and Africana studies expert Paget Henry (Brown) have compiled erudite scholarship on Trinidadian revolutionary James, his own, more accessible writing is found in *CLR James and Revolutionary Marxism: Selected Writings 1939–1949* by Paul le Blanc (La Roche College, Pittsburgh) and Scott McLemee (Intellectual Affairs columnist for *Inside Higher Ed*, a Washington DC-based media company).

Le Blanc explores how Cyril Lionel Robert James 'has begun to enjoy a revival among [American] and European intellectuals' in a fine report on *www.solidarity-us.org*.

Best known for his 'magnificent history' of the Haitian revolution, *Black Jacobins* (1938, and in reprint, *The Black Jacobins: Toussaint L'Ouverture and the San Domingo Revolution*), and the 1937 classic *World Revolution*,

1917–1936: The Rise and Fall of the Communist International, James is 'generally acknowledged to have been one of the most original Marxist thinkers to emerge from the [West], yet essential aspects of his identity came from the other side of the Atlantic, from Europe and Africa'.

James called himself 'a Black European', bringing to intersectional analyses ahead of his time the subjects of anti-colonialism, the French Revolution, the socialist movements of Europe and North America, and Bolshevism. He believed in 'the mass popular response in which... people creatively transform reality', helping to found the Fourth International, a global organisation of revolutionary socialists.

James – who wanted to see an Americanised Marxism and Bolshevism, placing Blacks and oppressed nationalities at the centre – had a marked influence on Africa's anti-imperialist leaders, in particular his protégé Kwame Nkrumah in Ghana.

He advocated the rights of the African-American proletariat, which he believed should challenge the bourgeoisie and capital in order to produce working-class leadership and ultimately socialism.

But it was primarily James's belief in Black self-determination – both in terms of 'setting up a politically distinct nation', if they so wished, and the right of oppressed people to define their own future – which he put at the core of his revolutionary Marxism.

In terms of BC, James saw that 'the awakening political consciousness of the "negro" not unnaturally takes the form of independent action uncontrolled by whites'.

James distinguished between 'Black chauvinism in America... merely the natural excess of the desire for equality and essentially progressive' and 'white American chauvinism, the expression of racial domination, [which] is essentially reactionary'.

Le Blanc (and others) have a central criticism of James, in his belief in socialism being 'inevitable'. Rather, these critics advanced, Blacks and the working class would need to be mobilised 'to work collectively – [to become] an integral part of the reality around us'.

James was expelled from the US in 1951.

[Le Blanc's essay, 'The Marxism of CLR James', can be read on www.solidarity-us.org]

Arturo Alfonso Schomburg (1874-1938)

Beloved as 'a bibliophile, collector, writer and key intellectual figure in the Harlem Renaissance', Schomburg spent his life 'championing Black history'.

The Zinn Education Project, which teaches people's history in American classrooms, tells how, when Schomburg was at primary (grade) school, he was struck by a teacher claiming 'Blacks had no history, heroes or accomplishments'. He determined to find these from the African continent and in the diaspora and compile an archive for the world.

Schomburg's vast collection of literature, documents, manuscripts, and art and artifacts from and about the Black world is held at the Schomburg Center at the New York Public Library, New York.

Born in Puerto Rico, he was also a co-founder of Las Dos Antillas (The Two Islands), which assisted the independence cause in his home country and Cuba.

George Padmore (1903–1959)

Arch anti-colonialist and internationalist, Padmore was a Trinidad-born journalist and Pan-Africanist who later became an adviser to Ghana's first post-colonial leader Kwame Nkrumah. Padmore had an optimistic political outlook, which explored hope, solidarity and equality through connections between the Caribbean, Africa, Europe, North America and Asia.

WEB du Bois (1868–1963)

William Edward Burghardt du Bois, 'a harbinger of Black nationalism and Pan-Africanism', was described by Martin Luther King Jr as 'a tireless explorer and a gifted discoverer of social truths'. King commended him for his 'honest study of the Black man', and Du Bois has undoubtedly been an enduring influence in the social science of race and racism and therefore on BC.

Top contemporary Black intellectual Professor Achille Mbembe of the Wits Institute of Social and Economic Research (WiSER) was a visiting research professor in history and politics at Harvard University's WEB Du Bois Institute for African and African-American

Research. Cameroon-born Mbembe – a foremost scholar on decolonisation, among other subjects – was elected to the prestigious American Academy of Arts and Sciences in April 2017.

The WEB Du Bois Learning Centre in Kansas City, Missouri writes in its biography of its mentor that Du Bois studied Blacks 'as a social system certain that the race problem was one of ignorance' and wanting to find 'a cure for colour prejudice'.

Du Bois's key work, *The Philadelphia Negro*, 'revealed the Negro group as a symptom, not a cause, as a striving, palpitating group, and not an inert, sick body of crime; as a long historic development and not a transient occurrence'.

An ideological controversy later grew between Du Bois and respected orator and educator Booker T Washington, whose Tuskegee Institute in Alabama for African-Americans became a powerful resource for Washington. Writes the Du Bois Centre in Kansas City: 'Du Bois was not opposed to Washington's power, but rather he was against his ideology of handling the power. On the one hand, Washington decried political activities among Negroes, and on the other hand dictated Negro political objectives from Tuskegee.' Washington wanted to see the 'American Negro' emerge 'into a higher civilisation'.

When Du Bois's *The Souls of Black Folks* included a critical discourse on Washington's philosophy, the battle was on. It reached a crescendo in the establishment in 1906 of the Niagara Movement, which advocated civil justice and the end of 'caste discrimination'. Together with a group of white liberals, his associate William Trotter and members of the Niagara Movement (named for the 'mighty current' of change which they trusted would come), Du Bois was a somewhat reluctant inspiration for the National Association for the Advancement of Colored People (NAACP). He would become the controversial – and, later, effective and outspoken – editor-in-chief of the NAACP's successful *Crisis* magazine. Throughout, Du Bois objected to the involvement of the white liberals, feeling Blacks should lead.

It was, however, only upon his travelling to Africa and finding an association with Black nationalists that Du Bois unlocked his true calling.

He died at the grand age of 95 in Accra, Ghana where he had settled a few years before, having been attracted there by his acolyte, Nkrumah, who would invite him to Ghana's independence celebrations in 1957. The WEB Du Bois Memorial Centre for Pan-African Culture was established in his honour in 1985 in Accra.

[www.duboislc.org]

Garveyism

'Up you mighty race, you can accomplish what you will.' — Marcus Mosiah Garvey

Jamaican politician and journalist Marcus Mosiah Garvey Jr founded the Universal Negro Improvement Association and African Communities League (UNIA-ACL) in support of Pan-Africanism. His Black Star shipping and passenger line, which promoted the return of Africans in the diaspora to 'ancestral lands', was material to Garveyism in promoting itself as a 'global mass movement' focusing on Africa.

Rastafarians and members of the Nation of Islam were strong adherents of Garvey's philosophies, while some, like Jamaican educator Valerie Dixon, have expressed disappointment in the seeming inability of Black people to follow Garveyism.

In the *Jamaican Observer* in 2014, Dixon writes about how the 'Black race needs Garveyism now more than maybe ever before'.

'It appears that, for the most part, the majority of Africans are not conscious of their own dignity and the dignity of their fellow Black brothers and sisters,' she opines. 'If the current generation of Black leaders and parents were properly steeped in Garveyism, then every person, regardless of age, would live in a state of being conscious that they are worthy of respect.

'It is my belief that one of the best and worst things that ever happened to the Black race in the diaspora was the granting of affirmative action, a policy born out of the Civil Rights Act of 1964. It was the best policy to attempt to eradicate discrimination, particularly against members of the Black race and women in general.

'However, on the negative side, it lulled Black people into a drunken, drugged-out delirium that caused many to think that they were "free at last, free at last".' As Dixon reflects, Garveyism extols group pride, self-help principles and solidarity.

[Dixon, 2014]

Audre Lorde (1934–1992)

Lorde's most famous words, 'Revolution is not a one-time event', are often quoted to define her as one of the 20th century's most important Black thinkers and feminists. Yet her six words ring out with as much clarity in the 21st century as when she struck them in 1982.

Her influence on many Black antiracism analysts of today is to deepen and corroborate their experiences.

Her address, *Learning From the '60s*, delivered at the Malcolm X weekend at Harvard University, allowed Lorde to explain: 'One of the most basic Black survival skills is the ability to change, to metabolise experience, good or ill, into something that is useful, lasting, effective. Four hundred years of survival as an endangered species has taught most of us that if we intend to live, we had better become fast learners.'

She advocated 'alliances and coalitions' among Black people as a counter to supremacy, emphasising that the focus of Black 'rage for change' should not be upon other Black people, but rather upon the enemy.

The African nationalists

Kwame Nkrumah (1909–1972)

A scientific socialist and Marxist, Nkrumah was the leader of Britain's 'model' West African colony, the Gold Coast. Then he led the newly named Ghana to independence from Britain in 1957 and served as its first prime minister and president until he was deposed, his reputation harmed, in 1966.

A staunch believer in Pan-Africanism, Nkrumah was a founding member of the OAU, having been an advocate of, at best, a Union of African Socialist Republics, but otherwise of a decolonised, federal United States of Africa. The vision was that this would have complementary regional structures, each separately governed, but each with a limited sovereignty.

From the time he was a student in the US and England, Nkrumah studied and caucused with other Black intellectuals on how to overthrow colonialism with African socialism – a revolutionary act. He got his moment when the grievances of thousands of former Second World War soldiers were taken to the streets in the 1948 Accra Riots. These spread throughout the country.

Ghana gained independence on 6 March 1957 – the first of Britain's African colonies to get majority rule. To this day, the country remains heroic to other Africans and within BC. Nkrumah was determined to seize his country back from the British with an African outlook that imperialist powers had not seen on the continent. Demonstrating decolonisation at every cue, he adopted a dedicatedly African image by wearing the traditional Kente cloth of the south of his country, and the fugu robes of the north.

But there were problematic tendencies in him, and an ambitious economic and social policy would spell doom for Ghana's path forward. Massive development spending was designed to lift the country out of its colonial dependency, but plummeting prices for its primary commodity, cocoa, ate into shrinking reserves, leading to unemployment, food insecurity and unmanageable prices.

Nkrumah demanded austerity, but his Marxism may have been too conservative for a burgeoning young African democracy. To match that, he began to lose sight of his popular role, absurdly declaring himself President for Life, banning opposition, censoring the media and conjuring up a cult, which he dubbed the Nkrumahist Gospel, by 1964. Perhaps most dangerous, however, was his crackdown on traditional leaders, whose position in Ghanaian society had until that point been unchallenged.

In 1966, Nkrumah was visiting President Ho Chi Minh in the Democratic Republic of North Vietnam to discuss a strategy towards the Resistance War Against America when his government was overthrown in a military coup. Operation Cold Chop saw Ghana's army and police assume control, dismiss Nkrumah and ban his ruling Convention People's Party. That moment, for all that it was a painful reflection on Nkrumah, entirely changed Ghana's path to African socialism. Instead of looking east, and focusing on forging closer ties within the African continent to build power blocs, it looked west.

Soon, the International Monetary Fund (IMF) and the World Bank were directing the swing of the economy.

Nkrumah went into political exile in Guinea, where President Ahmed Sékou Touré made him honorary co-president. He died of prostate cancer in April 1972 at the age of 62. Nkrumah was awarded honorary doctorates by his US *alma mater*, Lincoln University, as well as Moscow State University, Cairo University, the Jagiellonian University in Kraków, Poland, the Humboldt University in East Berlin and others.

But it took 43 years for Nkrumah to be recognised in Ghana, when President John Atta Mills declared 21 September – Nkrumah's 100th anniversary – as Founder's Day.

Julius Kambarage Nyerere (1922–1999)

Africa's ultimate 'mwalimu' or teacher retained a mutual respect with his beloved continent until the day he died. An early adherent of Fabian thinking, honed when he was studying in Scotland, Nyerere's dream was to see socialism segue with traditional African communal life.[30]

In 1954, Nyerere formed the legendary Tanganyika African National Union (TANU), seeing Tanganyika gain internal self-government under his administration in 1955, and then full independence as Tanzania in December 1961. Nyerere was elected president of a poor country with a foreign debt crisis, facing struggling commodities prices, in 1962. But he worked on a different method to accepting Western economic models, through ujamaa (traditionally, 'the state of being a family', in Swahili), collectivised or co-operative work and nationalisation.

This was not an untold success. Times were hard. The economy battled. Peasants were not united as to the benefits of ujamaa. But admiration for Nyerere was generally solid, and he achieved in other areas of social development, if not in building a radiantly socialist African economy.

---

30 The Fabian Society, which founded the London School of Economics and Political Science in 1895 'for the betterment of society', was a British socialist organisation that believed not in revolution but reformist democracies.

Nyerere's love for Africa was undisputed. Tanzania hosted soldiers from the ANC, PAC, Frelimo and the Zimbabwe African National Liberation Army, and Nyerere famously oversaw the invasion of Idi Amin's Uganda after Amin flouted Tanzania's borders in 1978. Tanzania helped restore Ugandan leader Milton Obote to power.

Nyerere remained president until 1985 when he stepped down, although he stayed chair of his party, the Chama Cha Mapinduzi, until 1990. He died of leukaemia in a London hospital on 14 October 1999.

Ahmed Sékou Touré (1922–1984)

The *New York Times* writer Eric Pace wrote a compelling obituary of Sékou Touré, the President of Guinea, when he died at 62 in a hospital in Cleveland after an apparent heart attack: 'A towering, charismatic and radical figure in Africa's post-colonial history', Pace penned, 'Mr Touré proved so strong a figure since becoming President in 1958 that he was called the Elephant and was repeatedly re-elected.'

Pace described Sékou Touré as a self-proclaimed descendant of the African hero Samory Touré, who fought against French rule until his capture in 1898.

As if by destiny, the handsome and brilliant orator Sékou Touré then led Guinea – a desperately poor nation – to independence from France in 1958. In control for 26 years, he was at the time of his death the longest-serving head of state. Sékou Touré's words 'Guinea prefers poverty in freedom to riches in slavery' are immortal, particularly as decolonisation became increasingly urgent. He rejected ties with France, the colonial power, but his creation of a Soviet-leaning enclave and declaration that his own Democratic Party of Guinea be its only political organisation somewhat defied the BC so closely aligned to his name.

Oppression – and, in Sékou Touré's case, gross human rights violations and assassinations of 'fifth columnists' – is not an aspect of Consciousness, and the flight of more than a million of his compatriots into exile under his rule belied his original intention.

[Pace, 1984]

Patrice Lumumba (1925–1961)

A memorable piece published in *The Guardian* in 2011 called the murder of Lumumba 'the most important assassination of the 20th century' as it reflected upon his death on its 50th anniversary.

Written by Georges Nzongola-Ntalaja, professor of African and African-American studies at the University of North Carolina at Chapel Hill and author of *The Congo from Leopold to Kabila: A People's History*, the analysis recorded how the 'heinous crime was a culmination of two inter-related assassination plots by American and Belgian governments'.

The headline quoted Ludo de Witte, Belgian author of *The Assassination of Lumumba*. Relating how 'Congolese accomplices and a Belgian execution squad [were used] to carry out the deed', Nzongola-Ntalaja says its 'historical importance lies in a multitude of factors, the most pertinent being the global context in which it took place, its impact on Congolese politics since then and Lumumba's overall legacy as a nationalist leader'.

He takes his readers back 126 years, to when 'the US and Belgium... played key roles in shaping Congo's destiny'. 'In April 1884, seven months before the Berlin Congress, the US became the first country in the world to recognise the claims of King Leopold II of the Belgians to the territories of the Congo Basin.' But as Nzongola-Ntalaja records, 'there were millions of fatalities' as brutal economic exploitation took place. The Congo's unparalleled natural resources saw the US seize uranium to manufacture the Hiroshima and Nagasaki bombs. But Lumumba, as Nzongola-Ntalaja writes, was determined to achieve genuine independence partly in order to 'have full control over Congo's resources... to utilise them to improve the living conditions of our people'.

As the US connived at devastating human cost to combat Soviet interests in Congo, Lumumba became a threat to Western interests. 'To fight him,' writes Nzongola-Ntalaja, 'the US and Belgium used all the tools and resources at their disposal, including the UN secretariat under Dag Hammarskjöld and Ralph Bunche, to buy the support of... Congolese rivals, and hired killers.'

To illustrate the urgency with which those colonialist powers needed to be rid of Lumumba, he was killed less than seven months after independence. Using the nefarious services of a firing squad commandeered by Belgian mercenary Julien Gat, Joseph-Désiré Mobutu (1930–1977) – chief of staff of the Congolese National Army imperialism – had Lumumba executed in Mobutu's own interests and those of Western imperialism. The kleptocrat Mobutu, who was to become a homicidal dictator, would change his name to Mobutu Sese Seko Kuku Ngbendu Wa Za Banga, and that of the DRC to 'Zaire'.

The 'second independence' regrouping by a 'mass movement of peasants, workers, the urban unemployed, students and lower civil servants would later found an eager leadership among Lumumba's lieutenants in Brazzaville, across the Congo river from Kinshasa'.

Nzongola-Ntalaja describes Pierre Mulele, a leader of that movement, as having 'selfless devotion to radical change for [the] purposes of meeting the deepest aspirations of the Congolese people for democracy and social progress'. But trade unionist and insurrectionist Christophe Gbenye and future leader Laurent-Désiré Kabila, who helped develop a National Liberation Council after Lumumba's assassination and then overthrew Mobutu, were 'more interested in power and its attendant privileges than in the people's welfare'.

[Nzongola-Ntalaja, 2011]

Aimé Césaire (1913–2008)

In its obituary in April 2008, *The Independent* in London described the poet and founding father of Négritude as 'the most influential Francophone Caribbean writer of his generation'.

Born into a peasant family in Martinique in 1913, Césaire's education saw him mix 'with the assimilated middle classes and emerge as the complex product of a double socialisation'. *The Independent* writes about how, together with the French Guyanese Léon-Gontran Damas and the Senegalese Léopold Sédar Senghor, Césaire launched the magazine *L'Etudiant Noir* (*The Black Student*) in 1934: 'The three young men drew inspiration from the Harlem Renaissance's efforts to promote the richness of African cultural identity and particularly opposed French assimilationist policies.' But it is Césaire's own book, *Discourse on Colonialism*

(1950), which has remained a classic of Black political literature.

Césaire – who taught Fanon – coined the term 'Négritude' in his most famous poem, 'Cahier d'un retour au pays natal' (*Notebook of a Return to My Native Land*) in 1956. 'The poem took its inspiration from the Martinican landscape and Toussaint Louverture, the leader of the first phase of the Haitian Revolution, whose biography Césaire would later write,' wrote *The Independent*. He brilliantly combined 'high' French with Martinican colloquialisms, says Bloodaxe Books, which published a French-English version of *Notebook* in 1995 (translated by Mireille Rosello and Annie Pritchard). The publisher describes how Césaire opposed the ideology of colonialism 'by inventing a language that refuses assimilation to a dominant cultural norm; a language that teaches resistance and liberation'.

'The poem,' said *The Independent*, 'explores the distinctiveness of Black cultural identity in a historically grounded manner that prefigures the BC movements of the 1960s.'

A communist in the earlier days of his political life, he later allied himself, at the age of 93, with the Socialist Party in France, supporting Ségolène Royal[31] in the 2007 French elections.
[Thieme, 2008; Bloodaxe Books, 2020: https://www.bloodaxebooks.com/ecs/product/notebook-of-a-return-to-my-native-land-392]

Thomas Sankara (1949–1987)

The African Che Guevara – whose iconic red beret was adopted by his acolytes, Julius Malema and the Economic Freedom Fighters (EFF), in South Africa – was a military man whose revolutionary posture did not waver through his four short years of rule in Burkina Faso.

An unwavering crusader for the power of young people to sustain revolutionary beliefs, Sankara's legacy is still so strong in his country that in 2014, when leader Blaise Compaoré – once Sankara's deputy – tried to illegally hold onto power, a movement called Le Balai Citoyen ('the citizens' broom') campaigned against him. Among other acts of discipline, pride and Black citizen control, Sankara – a Pan-Africanist Marxist – had insisted that people clean their own streets.

---

31 Ségolène Royal is a French politician and former Socialist Party candidate for President of the French Republic.

Compaoré ascended to power after his radical compatriot was assassinated against the backdrop of threats of a coup in October 1987.

Writer Leo Zeilig described Sankara's murder this way on *Africa is a Country* – the online intellectual commentary source about the African continent, found at www.africasacountry.com – in 2015: '[A] meeting was under way when shooting erupted in the small courtyard outside... Sankara's driver and two of his bodyguards were the first to be killed.

'Upon hearing the gunfire, everyone in the meeting room quickly took cover. Sankara then got up and told his aides to stay inside for their own safety: "It's me they want."

'He left the room, hands raised, to face the assailants. He was shot several times, and died without saying anything more.

'If his exit from the room was intended to save his comrades inside, it failed. The gunmen, all in military uniform, entered the meeting room and sprayed it with automatic weapons fire. Everyone inside was killed, except for [one].'[32]

The BBC (www.bbc.com) reported in 2015 how an ex-Liberian warlord, allied to former Liberian president Charles Taylor, had testified before that country's TRC that Taylor – who is serving the remainder of a 50-year prison sentence in England for war crimes, including terrorism, rape, murder and the use of child soldiers – engineered the assassination. But it was widely believed that Compaoré organised for Sankara to be killed.

Sankara's body was dismembered after his murder and buried in an unmarked grave. Thereafter, Compaoré reversed nationalisation and gave over some control of Burkina Faso's economy to the World Bank and the IMF.

Compaoré was the dictator of his country for 27 years.

[Zeilig, 2015]

---

32   Zeilig is a writer and researcher who authored *Patrice Lumumba: Africa's Lost Leader* and *Frantz Fanon: Philosopher of Third World Liberation*.

The philosophies
Black (Africana) existentialism
This theory affirms the liberation from oppression of Black people in Africa and the diaspora.

Widely ascribed to Vanderbilt University professor of philosophy and African-American and diaspora studies Lucius T Outlaw (1944–), who has specialised in the BC intellectual tradition, it examines efforts to articulate new identities in the context of racial oppression and supremacy.

This critical theory looks both at the massive limits placed upon Black people through racism, and new social orders not determined by white liberalism.

Outlaw – author of *On Race and Philosophy* (Routledge 1996) and *Critical Social Theory in the Interest of Black Folks* (Roman and Littlefield, 2005) – is highly influential in a field of existentialism otherwise dominated by writers and thinkers like Du Bois, Richard Wright (1908–1960), James Baldwin (1947–1985) and Ralph Ellison (1913–1994).

Ellison's *Invisible Man* is regarded as the archetype of Black existentialist literature as it examines Black men's alienation in the last century in the US. The 'invisibility' points to the way in which Blacks were given names by whites during slavery.

Wright, whose most acclaimed work was *Native Son*, was greatly influenced by French philosophers Sartre (1905–1980) and Simone de Beauvoir (1908–1986). *Native Son* exposed a system in which young Black men could be arrested for crimes they did not commit and then be imprisoned through the complicity of white prosecutors.

Baldwin introduced interracial and bisexual relationships into his profound writing on Black life, particularly in *Another Country*. But it was the pain of the unchanging political odds which cast Baldwin back into the global spotlight in 2020, after the death of George Floyd.

The *New York Times* bestselling author Eddie Glaude Jr reveals *this* Baldwin in his 2020 book, *Begin Again: James Baldwin's America and Its Urgent Lessons for Our Own*.

Brenton Blanchet of *The Daily Gazette* – an independent newspaper in Schenectady, New York – writes: 'The distinguished Princeton professor of African-American studies and MSNBC contributor... uses Baldwin's words as a scope for the modern day, looking at what he calls "the lie": "the broad and powerful architecture of false assumptions by which white lives are valued more than others".'

Glaude tells Blanchet: 'I knew that Jimmy [Baldwin] had gone through his own depression, his own despair, his own moment of acknowledging the country's betrayal, and tried to figure out how to pick up the pieces and how to bear witness in the face of that betrayal.'

A great modern proponent of Black existentialism is Lewis R Gordon (1962–), a Biko biographer and recipient of the Nelson Mandela visiting professorship in the department of political and international studies at Rhodes University. Gordon is a professor of philosophy and African-American studies at the University of Connecticut at Storrs, where he also researches phenomenology, postcolonial thought and philosophies of liberation.

His *Existence in Black: An Anthology of Black Existential Philosophy* (Routledge, 1997) is a leading text, written as a series of short chapters divided into four parts. Yet his first book, *Bad Faith and Antiblack Racism* (1995), is an even more robust examination of the effective denial of Black humanity.

Employing Sartrean analysis – which shows how human beings seek to run away from their innate selves, and also develop numbers of identities as a form of self-deception, moving from 'subject' to 'object' depending on the scenario – it exposes an array of inauthenticities. These include 'expectations of sincerity' in white engagement.

Gordon is chairperson of the Caribbean Philosophy Association's award committee.

Black Feminism

This can be traced back to the 19th and early 20th century in the writing of distinguished scholar and Black liberation activist Anna J Cooper (1858–1964), who argued that a person's worth should be based on their contribution. To this end, Black worth, particularly the worth of Black women, said Cooper, exceeds that of many whites.

Other prominent feminists working in this field include the cultural critic, artist and writer bell hooks (1952–) and Professor

Hortense Spillers (1942–), who writes most prominently in the field of gender.

hooks has concentrated on the intersectionality of race, capitalism and gender, and how these perpetuate oppression. To this extent, in 2016, hooks drew attention for expressing the view that 'a part' of superstar Beyoncé (1981–) was 'a terrorist, especially in terms of the impact on young girls', explaining that 'the major assault on feminism in our society has come from visual media'. hooks's concern followed a lightly clothed Beyoncé appearing on the cover of *Time* magazine's 2016 'The Top 100 Most Influential People' issue. Her view was that Beyoncé was 'ascribing to the dominant standard' and that she was part of the problem of women being encouraged to uphold impossible beauty standards.

Black feminist scholar and literary critic Spillers has had a momentous impact in studies of Black gender construction. Professor at Vanderbilt University, her *Comparative American Identities: Race, Sex, and Nationality in the Modern Text* (Routledge, 1991) and *Black, White, and In Color: Essays on American Literature and Culture* (University of Chicago Press, 2003) are seminal to Black feminist existentialism.

Yet it is Spillers's 1987 essay, 'Mama's Baby, Papa's Maybe: An American Grammar Book', which remains her most important piece and one of the most cited scholarly articles in African-American literary studies.

Central to it is a devastating critique of the 1965 Moynihan Report (also known as 'The Negro Family: The Case For National Action'), written by American sociologist Daniel Patrick Moynihan (1927–2003), who was assistant secretary of labour in the Johnson administration.

In focusing on 'Black poverty' in the US, Moynihan's position was that the high rate of Black families headed by mothers would 'hinder progress of Blacks, especially Black men, toward economic and political equality'.

Moynihan, through his white liberal racism, identified a 'tangle of pathology' which would 'perpetuate itself' unless there was 'assistance from the white world'. At the core was a notion that 'the state' should 'provide Black men with masculinity'.[33]

This approach, male-centric and layered in deep racism and cultural stereotypes, continues to be widely condemned, especially in the Black world. But it is Spillers's letting loose, particularly on the trope of 'the absent Black father', that draws blood.

She argues that 'the absent Black father' is in fact the white slave master who rendered a state of *partus sequitur ventrem* upon enslaved Black mothers, giving them the status of 'a father'. Since neither Black men or women were awarded 'a gender' under slavery – with all in the same legal state, which was 'property' – when Moynihan or any other racist refers to a 'male', they are manufacturing some legal description that their ancestors never used.

In Spillers's view, this means that Black women, since enslavement, effectively exist without 'a Black patriarchy' and operate as they have done since slavery, in law, from an 'androgynous boundary' or what she calls 'massification' – 'ungendered'.

That whites regard Black family structures as 'deficient' is only in comparison with 'white family structures' which refuse to grasp even a 'role reversal' within Black families where a mother is, as she always has been, the family authority.

This particular form of sexism and racism is as much an indictment of whiteness and white culture as any. That 'Black matriarchy' is undermined by whiteness does not make it any less powerful in reality.

Arguably the most celebrated Black feminist is the 1993 Nobel Prize for Literature winner Toni Morrison (1931–2019), who, like hooks, developed her existentialism around the rejection of the supremacist prism and the cult of white womanhood.[34]

Black women remained enslaved if they adored the appearance of white women for their whiteness, and could find themselves exploited

---

33   Scholar Roderick Ferguson, Professor of Women's, Gender and Sexuality Studies and American Studies at Yale University, described this in his book, *Aberrations in Black*. A scholar of Marx, Ferguson noted that historical materialism was an appropriate response to capital's 'gendered, racialised sexual ideals'. Those who failed capitalism's test in this regard – mostly Black women – were seen as 'pathological'.

34   Morrison was the first Black woman of any nationality to win the Nobel Literature prize.

for their labour, with their own sexuality debased. Black women were, after all, 'breeders' for white slave-owners as Black children became 'property' too.

That social control was the bedrock of white male capitalism, which today rejects Black mothers who seek the assistance of the state. Black women, for the most part, no longer fit the 'corporate' control which the slave owner once exerted over their labour in the plantations.

It is still astonishing that even the women's movement of the mid-20th century in the US failed to acknowledge the power of Black women's labour, with most Black women working while most white women did not. Work for women was considered something 'aggressive', rather than a means of supporting a family or of showing personal ambition. The stay-at-home white mother was appealingly 'passive'.

Without being given credit for their labour, and with their labour not being considered 'good enough' unless it occupied a status equal to that of white women, Black women workers were devalued in terms of class, race and gender.

Morrison's novel *Beloved* (1987) – which set in motion a trilogy of sorts, followed by *Jazz* and *Paradise* – is one of the most profound studies of this mental 'slavery' of Black women drawn into horrific, transgenerational despair. Yet her books *Song of Solomon*, *The Bluest Eye*, *Sula* and *Tar Baby* were each created out of Morrison's Black feminism whose existentialism inspires BC at its core.

[Crosley Coker, 2014]

Négritude vs Black nihilism

A sense of pointlessness about Black existence and a lack of self-worth is not only a theory but a lived experience for many Black people in Africa and the diaspora.

Nihilism was a central aspect of Fanon's *Black Skin, White Masks* (1952), in which he argued that there is no model in the modern world of 'a normal Black adult'. Fanon's view was that a Black person was instead a 'white construction' and that Black people have been placed in a position where they must seek white recognition and affirmation, which are self-deceiving acts.

Négritude, the BC movement coined by Césaire, would enable Blacks to love themselves by rejecting white reason. Anti-imperialist and anti-colonial, its intention was to assert pride in African cultural values.

Sartre's 1948 text, *Black Orpheus (Orphée Noir)*, had an important impact on Fanon, as it essentially opposed the 'integration' that white liberals proposed between Blacks and whites, and advanced Black existentialism as being at the core of a revolutionary working class. Biko was influenced by these ideas in *I Write What I Like*, saying that whites who were antiracist could be 'Black'.

[Fanon, 1952]

The Brazilians: Paulo Freire, Abdias do Nascimento and Hamilton Borges dos Santos

SASO and the UCM introduced innovative methods of training young South Africans at gatherings they referred to as 'formation schools'. The organisations used the ideas of Brazilian scholar Freire (1921–1997) to conscientise, imparting techniques of literacy to interpret experiences in Black people's own terms and extrapolate these to the wider world.

Freire was banned in South Africa during apartheid, but that did not prevent his 1968 classic, *Pedagogy of the Oppressed*, from significantly influencing BC.

The apartheid regime wished, and fully intended, to shut down Black minds. Those who refused had to organise underground – and read, learn and teach underground. It made sense to use Freire. As Dan Magaziner, the Yale historian who specialises on South Africa, says, Freire taught that 'all oppressed people needed to develop their own critical faculties rather than have some vanguard force an ideology upon them'.

The South African Paulo Freire Institute (PFI-SA) was established within the Centre for Adult Education (CAE) at the University of KwaZulu-Natal in 2004, joining 50 other institutions around the world 'which work to stimulate, promote and strengthen Freirean thought and pedagogy'.

Pedagogy was enough to get many intellectuals banned under the regime, especially those who recognised the Black experience in South Africa with their own. And so it sought to isolate Brazilian academics like Abdias do Nascimento, whose lives were devoted to BC.

Nascimento (1914–2011) was a Pan-African activist who created the Black Experimental Theater in 1944, and the Black Arts Museum in 1950. He was a primary organiser of the diaspora in Brazil and was determined to celebrate Brazilian Blacks and Black culture in the Americas.

Nascimento was Professor Emeritus at the State University of New York at Buffalo and served as Rio de Janeiro state secretary for the Defense and Promotion of Afro-Brazilian People and Secretary of Human Rights and Citizenship. He won honours for his work, including UNESCO's special Toussaint Louverture Award for his fight against racism. He received that prize in 2004, the same year as Césaire.

Brazilian intellectual and activist Hamilton Borges dos Santos would have been *persona non grata* during apartheid had he been of their generation. A protagonist of the Black Movement in Brazil in 2001, he went on to develop it as the grassroots React or Die! (also, React Or Be Killed!) campaign.

Do Santos grew up in Liberdade, Salvador (Bahia), which is regarded by many as the capital of the African diaspora. It attracted many African-Americans to its shores over decades as an 'Afro-paradise', but also, from the early 2000s, was the site of transnational politicisation as Black people in Brazil and the United States faced many of the same issues.

With a Bachelor of Laws degree, Dos Santos's work centres on anti-Black police violence in Brazil, unjust incarceration there, reparations for Black victims of abuses and their families, extrajudicial executions, militia and death squads whose attacks are racially motivated or happen in majority Black communities in the former Portuguese colony.

Among Dos Santos's important works are *General Theory of Failure* (2017) and *Salvador, Cidade-Titerio* (2018).

Cornel West (1953–)

In May 2017, activist, writer and public intellectual Cornel West was trending for a shouting match he had on live TV with American channel HBO's political talk show host Bill Maher over the 2016 Democratic presidential nominee Hillary Clinton (1947–).

Among others, left-wing online news organisation *RawStory* wrote how Maher had confronted West for calling Clinton and President Donald Trump (1946–) 'equally awful'.

'A prominent backer of Senator Bernie Sanders (1941–), [West] insisted that the Vermont independent could have won the election, and took a shot at Clinton after Maher pointed out that one of the former Secretary of State's first speeches as a candidate was about mass incarceration that disproportionately affects young Black men.

'"Hillary gave speeches about a whole lot of stuff," West shot back, "but it didn't have a whole lot of integrity in it, brother."

'Maher's response was immediate: "That is such bullshit."'

In 2020, West – a radical democrat and socialist – was more critical than ever, calling the US 'imperial' and reminding people of their responsibility in assuring Black freedom. Interviewed by Azad Essa of *Middle East Eye* in June after the death of George Floyd, he said: 'What we have to do is recognise that the funeral of George Floyd, where tears are flowing... they have [similar] funerals in the West Bank because of US policy [and] US bombs mediated through [the] Israel Defense Forces...

'They have funerals like that in Yemen... they got funerals like that in Pakistan, in Afghanistan. They've got funerals like that in Mali.

'... So in the tradition of Martin Luther King Jr, we have to be morally consistent in our critique of US racism, militarism, poverty, as well as materialism.

'I think that the fundamental impulse behind the rage is the indictment of elites who are unaccountable. So it has to do with police power and police murder in the Black community. It has to do with Wall Street power and Wall Street crimes in terms of the legalised looting that's been taking place for so long on Wall Street, with high levels of wealth inequality flowing from there. It has to do with Pentagon power.'

Dr Brad Elliott Stone, professor and graduate director of Philosophy at Loyola Marymount University in Los Angeles, observes how West 'formulates the need to move past the traditional Marxist approaches to the question of race, namely, by reducing race to one more type of economic struggle'. This was articulated in West's essay 'Toward a Socialist Theory of Racism' published in his classic 1993 collection, *Prophetic Fragments: Illuminations of the Crisis in American Religion and Culture.*

Stone records: 'Although economics is indeed a major part of the story of race in America, Marxism is inadequate because it fails to probe other spheres of American society where racism plays an integral role – especially the psychological and cultural spheres.'

West, says Stone, employs a similar approach to that of French philosopher and historian of ideas Michel Foucault (1926–1984). This would be 'a genealogical inquiry into the ideology of racism, focusing on the kinds of metaphors and concepts employed by... supremacists' and '... an analysis of the mechanisms that sustain white supremacist discourse in the everyday life of [Black] people'.

This might include the 'assistance' of other neoliberals with whom the world possibly more easily identifies. MEE wrote that West, for example, 'reserved some of his choicest criticism for President Barack Obama [1961–] who spoke in favour of the Black Lives Matter protests in 2020'.

'It's amazing to see brother Barack Obama out there acting like he's part of the vanguard and struggling against police power when Black Lives Matter emerged under his administration, with his Black attorney general, with his Black [secretary of] homeland security,' West said.

'But he helped militarise those police departments. He helped generate the levels of poverty when he had bailed out the Wall Street criminals...

'My experience on the ground is that when people now see the politicians and people now see the neoliberal spokespersons come forward and act as if they are so militant, act as if they are so radical, they say: hey, we were born at night, but not last night.'

MEE writes: 'West, once a supporter of Obama, has been an ardent critic following Obama's handling of the financial crisis, which saw his policies bail out banks and ensure major bank executives were let off the hook for their roles in the crisis.'

West called Obama 'a black face of the American empire' and said that 'talking about the connections between Black Lives Matter and US militarism should not be treated as a "luxury".'

'In the end, if you really want Black people to be free, and I do, Black people will never be free under a system of predatory capitalism... I get pretty fired up when people want to try... downplay the systematic character of the oppression...'

West is also a spoken word artist who confronts the 'radical conditionedness' of societies.

[Raw Story, 2017: This website carries a report and a video of the 'shouting match' between Maher and West; Essa, 2020: Middle East Eye]

The South African intellectuals
Pumla Dineo Gqola

Gqola is one of the most important scholars of contemporary BC and is especially linked with the movement's relationship to gender issues.

Formerly a professor of African literature at Wits in Johannesburg, she joined the University of Fort Hare in Alice in the Eastern Cape as dean of research in 2018.[35]

Gqola – who holds MA degrees from the universities of Cape Town and Warwick, UK and a PhD from the Ludwig Maximillian University of Munich, Germany – has interests in feminism, African, Caribbean and Black British literature, slavery and memory, and the media and its relationship to post-colonial sexualities.

Her notable works include: the acclaimed *Rape: A South African Nightmare* (MFBooks Joburg, 2015), an award-winning book which examined the relationship power, wealth, status and race have to the rape pandemic in South Africa; *A Renegade called Simphiwe* (MFBooks Joburg, 2013), which sought to present BC vocalist Simphiwe Dana's work as it analysed and challenged the social positioning of Black people; and *Reflecting Rogue: Inside the Mind of A Feminist* (MFBooks Joburg, 2017), a series of autobiographical essays on power, sexuality,

---

35   Fort Hare has a special place in BC for being the *alma mater* of, among other Africanists, Robert Sobukwe, Seretse Khama, Julius Nyerere and Robert Mugabe.

relationships, feminist rage and other topics.

Among Gqola's other important writings are *What is Slavery to Me? Postcolonial/Slave Memory in Post-apartheid South Africa* (Wits Press, 2010), 'Black women's bodies as battleground in Black Consciousness literature: Wayward sex and (interracial) rape as tropes in *Staffrider* 1978–1982' in *Imagining, Writing, (Re)reading the Black Body* (Unisa Press, 2009) and *Regarding Winnie: Feminism, race and nation in global representations of Winnie Madikizela Mandela* (editor).

Gqola's writing for the Steve Biko Foundation's *Frank Talk* fifth edition, published in January 2013, was a vital addition to the redevelopment of BC. In the essay, 'Contradictory locations: Black women and the discourse of the Black Consciousness Movement in South Africa', she discussed the space afforded women in the BCM and how the movement related to issues of race and gender, exploring how the language of BC was often found lacking in the way it addressed issues specific to women.

Gqola highlighted that one of the movement's flaws was an inability to recognise the 'material differences' between the oppressions of Black people at the hand of the apartheid system, leading 'to a situation where, in spite of its power as an ideology, the tendency to shy away from differences between Black people proved to be one of the biggest areas of weaknesses for BC .

'The quest for Black solidarity took precedence over the need to criticise other Black people and organisations opposed to apartheid.'

Gqola's popular role as a public intellectual has made her one of the most recognisable protagonists of Black feminism. She writes 'Black woman' as 'Blackwoman' – a single word that describes how feminism, to her, is an intersectional study and way of life. – *Masego Panyane*

[Gqola, 2009, 2010, 2013]

Nigel C Gibson

Gibson was a militant during the strike of 1984–85 under British trade unionist, the National Union of Mineworkers (NUM) leader, Arthur Scargill. When coal pit closures were announced by Margaret Thatcher's Conservative Party government with the loss of around 20 000 jobs, NUM started industrial action in Yorkshire and

Scotland, with which Gibson was involved.

Gibson had been exposed to the BCM in the 1970s when he lived in London and met South African exiles. This led to a raft of academic work about the BCM before he moved to the US where, among others, he studied with Edward Said and became a central theorist on Fanon.[36]

After basing himself in South Africa, Gibson became a foremost protagonist of social justice programmes, which operate outside a traditional NGO paradigm. Chief among these was radical Durban-based Black shack-dwellers' organisation Abahlali baseMjondolo. Gibson was outspoken about the state-sanctioned violence enacted against its members.

Gibson co-edited *Biko Lives! Contesting the Legacies of Steve Biko* with Andile Mngxitama and Amanda Alexander. The book forms part of Palgrave Macmillan's Contemporary Black History series edited by Manning Marable and Peniel Joseph.

Gibson's essay in *Biko Lives!*, 'BC after Biko: The dialectics of liberation in South Africa (1977 to 1987)' is an explosive examination of politics in the pre-democracy period. It begins with Gibson recounting his journey as a 'young anti-Stalinist, anti-apartheid activist', goes on to critique the way in which BC tried to graft 'class' onto 'race', the possibility for Marxist humanism as a method for the late struggle period, and Black Theology .

Gibson was previously the assistant director of African studies at Columbia University and a research associate in African-American Studies at Harvard University.

He went on to become associate professor at the Institute of Interdisciplinary Studies, an honorary research professor at the Humanities Unit of Rhodes, and a member of the Committee for Academic Freedom in Africa.

He is a recipient of the Fanon Prize of the Caribbean Philosophical Association.

(Mngxitama, Alexander & Gibson, 2008)

---

[36] Edward Wadie Said was a professor of literature at Columbia University, a public intellectual, and a founder of the academic field of postcolonial studies. He was a Palestinian-American born in Mandatory Palestine, and a citizen of the US by way of his father, who was a US Army veteran.

Patrick Bond (1961–)

Professor of political economy at the Wits School of Governance and previously with the University of KwaZulu-Natal, where he directed the Centre for Civil Society from 2004 to 2016, Bond spent a brief part of his childhood in Alabama in the US during the civil rights era after his family moved there from Northern Ireland.

Educated at the University of Pennsylvania, he did his PhD on the topic of 'Finance and Uneven Development in Zimbabwe' at the Johns Hopkins University department of geography and environmental engineering in 1993 after working for social justice agencies in Washington and Philadelphia in the 1980s.

Bond arrived in South Africa in 1990, where he put his skills to use in the NGO sector before authoring and editing policy papers including the Reconstruction and Development Programme (RDP) and the RDP White Paper.

His exemplary research on the political economy of Africa, the fraught effects of international finance on Black communities and, broadly, environmental and development issues in South Africa has seen him contribute to a growth in knowledge about BC.

Bond's arguments about the ANC's neo-liberal governance and the failure of capitalism to serve Black South Africans are among the most influential in the world.

His major publications include *Zuma's Own Goal: Losing South Africa's 'War on Poverty'*, edited with Brij Maharaj and Ashwin Desai; and *Talk Left, Walk Right: South Africa's Frustrated Global Reforms*; *Looting Africa: The Economics of Exploitation*; and *Against Global Apartheid: South Africa Meets the World Bank, IMF and International Finance*.

Bond has been published by, among others, Aakar Press and Jacana Media, Africa World Press, Capitalism Nature Socialism, Haymarket Books, HSRC Press, *Journal of Contemporary African Studies*, *Law, Social Justice & Global Development*, Merlin Press, Monthly Review Press, New Internationalist, *openDemocracy*, www.pambazuka.org, Pluto Press, *Review of African Political Economy*, *Third World Quarterly*, Unisa Press, the University of Arizona Library, the University of Cape Town Press, the University of KwaZulu-Natal Press, Urban Forum, Weaver Press, Zed Press and a range of media sources.

Mabogo Percy More

A philosopher working in the area of Black existentialism, including examinations of the intellectual foundations of the BCM, and of the life and work of Steve Biko, More was awarded the Frantz Fanon Lifetime Achievement Award by the Caribbean Philosophical Association in 2015.

More is a Turfloop alumnus who was in class with [Abram Onkgopotse] Tiro. A former professor of philosophy at the University of KwaZulu-Natal and the University of Durban-Westville, he taught political philosophy in the department of political science at the same university, and in the departments of philosophy at the University of Limpopo and the University of the North.

More's fascination with BC philosophies began when he was a student. He related a story to Kwanele Sosibo in the *Mail & Guardian* in 2015 about how S'bu Ndebele, then an assistant librarian at Turfloop, smuggled radical literature like *The Wretched of the Earth* out to young acolytes like More.[37] That had a marked influence on his mind and thoughts.

But More faced many of the racist obstacles which other Black philosophers are limited by in many other countries in the world.

His belief, as he told Sosibo, is that there are two 'obvious reasons': 'First, the European construction of the African as the absolute Other, and second, the constructed... self-conception of the philosophy itself. Africa and the Africans supposedly lack what both the European and philosophy share: rationality.'

More – who is, among other texts, the author of *Biko: Philosophy, Identity and Liberation* (https://www.hsrcpress.ac.za/books/biko) – completed his master's at Unisa with a thesis 'about pacifism as a way of exploring the Fanonian notion of therapeutic violence'.

More tells Sosibo: 'You couldn't say violence was right or you would go straight to jail. But the point is Steve Biko [who was heavily influenced by Fanon] was not a pacifist. He only claimed non-violence to try setting his comrades free [as a witness in the 1976 BPC/SASO trial].

'Biko at a personal level didn't take any nonsense. He beat up security policemen twice. He even took one policeman's tooth out...

---

37   Ndebele later became a government minister.

Maybe that explains why he was killed with his hands tied behind him because he wouldn't let them touch him.'

More earned a scholarship to Indiana University in 1981 and was exposed to African-American and Afro-Caribbean philosophy, including works like Leonard Harris's *Philosophy Born of Struggle: Afro-American Philosophy from 1917*. Frustrated by the narrowness of South Africa's philosophy arena for Black minds, he then attended Birmingham University, the University of Illinois and Harvard University, until he finally returned home to teach at the University of Durban-Westville.

[Sosibo, 2015: mg.co.za/article/2015-01-15-no-country-for-brilliant-thinkers/]

Christopher Mouy Rutledge

Rutledge is executive director of the Mining Affected Communities United in Action, and Women Affected by Mining United in Action Advice Office. He was previously the South Africa mining and extractives co-ordinator at ActionAid, an international organisation which works in 45 countries on poverty and injustice. The methods of these organisations are steeped in the same philosophy as BC: people using their own power for the benefit of community and society.

Rutledge's confrontational and well-crafted analyses of issues ranging from the ANC's kleptocratic tendencies to the devastation wrought by international mining companies on the potential in Black life became essential reading in print and on social media.

Salim Vally

An associate professor and the director of the Centre for Education Rights and Transformation (CERT) at the University of Johannesburg (UJ), Vally was previously a senior researcher at the Education Policy Unit at Wits and is a visiting professor at the Nelson Mandela Metropolitan University in Port Elizabeth. He studied at the University of KwaZulu-Natal's Howard College campus, York University and Wits, where he did his MEd in 1995, and has been a visiting lecturer at Columbia, Virginia, York and Fort Hare universities.

Among his significant contributions is exposing the potential in marginalised Black communities through class analysis, a deep understanding of human rights, antiracism and critical pedagogy. Vally uses the broader arena of grassroots scholarship and research to bring this potential and the barriers against it to the fore and, through that, to plot a way forward with communities.

His primary areas of interest are education rights, curriculum issues and social justice.

He serves on the editorial boards of several global organisations and academic journals, including UJ's *Education as Change*, the *McGill Journal of Education* and the *Journal for Critical Education Policy Studies* while remaining active in social movements and solidarity organisations.

Vally, who has been an activist all his life, is a foremost proponent of Palestinian freedom, and in 2017 wrote the introduction to a special issue of the University of Edinburgh's *Journal of Holy Land and Palestinian Studies* in memory of Edward Said, whose writings Vally describes in that introduction as 'an effective antidote to the undisguised venom and crassness of imperial hegemony today'.

Vally's recent books are *Reflections on Knowledge, Learning and Social Movements: History's Schools* (co-edited with Aziz Choudry; Routledge, 2017) and *Education, Economy and Society* (co-edited with Enver Motala; Unisa Press, 2014). He was awarded the Hiddingh-Currie prize in 2015 and voted runner-up in the 2016 inaugural National Institute for the Humanities and Social Sciences (NIHSS) awards in the edited non-fiction category.

[Vally, 2017]

Nurina Ally and Shireen Ally

The two South African academics contributed the important essay 'Critical intellectualism: The role of BC in reconfiguring the class problematic in South Africa' to *Biko Lives!*.

In focusing on the impetus for academics' allegiance with BC in the 1970s, especially the rise of the left-wing white academia,' they '[rescript] BC into the intellectual history of South Africa by examining the dramatic role played by the movement in inspiring... debate' about its influence. That 'debate' vitally centred on 'the relationship between race and class in ... the socio-political structure of South Africa', as it still does more than a half-century after the first democratic elections.

At the heart of it, they believe, the BC 'critique on liberalism, and the alienating politics of race engendered by it, proved a pivotal determinant in the shift toward critical Marxist thought among white, English-speaking intellectuals in the 1970s'.

Nurina Ally is a specialist in constitutional and administrative law whose research includes movement lawyering. Now at UCT's department of public law, she served as the executive director of the Equal Education Law Centre in Cape Town.

She obtained her BA and LLB degrees from Wits, where she graduated as the most distinguished scholar in law. She also holds a Master's in African Studies from the University of Edinburgh and a Masters in International Human Rights Law from Oxford.

Shireen Ally has an MSc and PhD in sociology from the University of Wisconsin-Madison and taught in the department of sociology at Wits after 2004, where she is Chair in Local Histories and Present Realities. She has done memorable work in the colonial histories of domestic service, published, among others, by Cornell University Press. Hers is a meticulous investigation into an immense area of Black life, and the impact of colonial cruelty on Black women.

[Ally & Ally, 2008: Biko Lives!]

Vuyolwethu Seti-Sonamzi

Dr Seti-Sonamzi's 2019 thesis, 'On Blackness: The role and positionality of Black public intellectuals in post-94 South Africa' has a fierce energy in its immediate and direct call to the BC generations after apartheid.

She 'explores the role and positionality of ... Simphiwe Dana, Ntsiki Mazwai[38] and Sisonke Msimang[39]' using what is a rather unusual study choice for bodies of work: their Twitter postings 'on various social matters

---

38   *Ntsiki Mazwai* (1980–) is a poet, author, social activist, producer and blogger.

39   Sisonke Msimang is the author of *Always Another Country: A Memoir of Exile and Home* (2017) and *The Resurrection of Winnie Mandela* (2018). Her work focuses on race, gender and democracy, and she has written for, among others, the *New York Times*, the *Washington Post*, *Newsweek* and *Al Jazeera*. Msimang held a fellowship at Yale University, and is a fellow at the WiSER Institute at Wits.

that concern the condition of the Black in post-1994 South Africa'.

Seti-Sonamzi used Fanon's 'native intellectual consciousness as a lens... to capture and evaluate an emergent form of "cyber" activism in the country'. Against the backdrop of a regular backlash against Mazwai's tweets, in particular – as she persists in taking on all notions and perpetuation of anti-Blackness – the Unisa academic posits that intellectualism 'must undergo a complete overhaul...'

The daughter of a PAC family who was exposed to Black intellectuals from a young age, Seti-Sonamzi says 'Black Twitter is the communicative plane on which Blackness performs and articulates itself, for itself'. Her aim is to make Blackness public 'by allowing it to think, and speak through its pain as opposed to the usual pathologising white gaze'.

Her methodology of decolonialism is that of an indigenous 'imbadu (a gathering of a group of people who sit and discuss issues in isiXhosa culture, or African culture in general) in the face of (a) debilitating colonial hangover'.

She advances that 'the chosen intellectuals who are feminists by choice, think and speak from Blackness albeit being silenced by oppression' and, as such, she was driven to produce 'a pedagogical contradiction to the orthodox axiology of a detached scholar and (write) in the autobiographical form'.

[Seti-Sonamzi, 2019: https://www.nihss.ac.za/content/blackness-role-and-positionality-black-public-intellectuals-post-94-south-africa]

Mbuyiseni Quintin Ndlozi (1985–)

Economic Freedom Fighters (EFF) MP and formerly its national spokesperson, Ndlozi was introduced to South Africans as an intellectual whose path into mainstream politics had come through the South African Students Congress (SASCO), the ANCYL and the Young Communist League (YCL). But Ndlozi has adopted a more left-wing, revolutionary position than many of his fellow EFF MPs, having served in the Palestinian and Cuban international solidarity movements. He has also studied widely in the field of African politics.

A member of the parliamentary portfolio committees of telecommunications and communications, Ndlozi is a notable firebrand whose popularity has extended beyond his party.

He did not abandon his intellectual path upon entering democratic South Africa's fifth parliament in 2013. Ndlozi earned his PhD in August 2017 from Wits. His doctoral thesis covered the psychological implications of apartheid's military push into the so-called Vaal Triangle townships in the 1970s and 1980s. The 'Vaal Triangle' incorporated greater Johannesburg.

Ndlozi is himself a child of that area, having been born in Evaton township, some 50 kilometres outside Johannesburg.

Khanya College, Johannesburg

A great number of intellectuals, culture activists, workers for liberation and aspirant politicians helped develop this independent and now-legendary Johannesburg NGO from its roots in 1986. It celebrated 30 years of continued existence in 2016.

Khanya College's focus was on working-class and poor Black communities, its motto being 'Education for Liberation'.

Among those who worked at Khanya College was American James Kilgore (1947–), better known during his time in southern Africa as John Pape, who was later arrested in Cape Town as a fugitive member of the Symbionese Liberation Army, a left-wing American revolutionary organisation and petitioner vanguard army. He spent more than six years in prison in the US.

Some SLA members, not including Kilgore, were involved in murders and acts of violence. Kilgore was underground for 27 years, and during that time built a reputation as an activist and educator.

The lie that is promised when we say #AllLivesMatter
Patrisse Cullors, Alicia Garza and Opal Tometi

Black feminist activists started Black Lives Matter, the social movement for policy changes to bring about Black liberation for all Black people in July 2013. Cullors, Garza and Tometi started #BlackLivesMatter as an online network in response to the death of Trayvon Martin[40] and

---

40   Trayvon Martin, a 17-year-old African-American high school student, was killed in Sanford, Florida, in February 2012 by George Zimmerman, a mixed-

the acquittal of his killer, George Zimmerman.

Cullors (1984–) is an artist, organiser, educator and public speaker, and faculty director of social and environmental arts practice at Arizona's Prescott College. She was also the founder of Dignity and Power Now, a grassroots organisation, in her hometown of Los Angeles. Cullors was recognised as one of *Time* magazine's '2020 100 Women of the Year' and is a *New York Times* best-selling author, together with journalist and writer Asha Bandele, of *When They Call You a Terrorist: A Black Lives Matter Memoir* (2018).

Garza (1981–) is an Oakland-based organiser, public speaker and writer who has featured in *Time*, *The Guardian*, *Essence*, *Democracy Now!* and the *New York Times*, and is special projects director for the National Domestic Workers Alliance.

She was named on *The Root* list of 100 African-American achievers and influencers in 2016; she was also a recipient of the *Glamour* Women of the Year award and the *Marie Claire* New Guard award.

As a queer Black woman, Garza 'challenge the misconception that only cisgender Black men encounter police and state violence'. Her view is that 'in order to truly understand how devastating and widespread this type of violence is in Black America, we must view this epidemic through a lens of race, gender, sexual orientation, and gender identity'.

Tometi (1984–) is a New York-based Nigerian-American student of liberation theology, writer, strategist and community organiser credited with creating the social media strategy at the beginning of Black Lives Matter. She has been honoured among 'The world's 50 greatest leaders' in by *Fortune* and *Politico* magazines, and leads the Black Alliance for Just Immigration, the Pan-African Network in Defense of Migrants' Rights, and the Black Immigration Network. She has presented at the United Nations and the US Congress, and is featured in the Smithsonian's National Museum for African-American History and Culture.

[Black Lives Matter, 2020: https://Blacklivesmatter.com/our-co-founders/]

---

race neighbourhood watch co-ordinator for his gated community. Martin, who was unarmed, was visiting relatives at the time of the shooting. There was an altercation between the two and Zimmerman claimed self-defence.

Black Lives Matter

This global network began as a chapter-based, member-led organisation whose mission was to 'build local power and intervene when violence was inflicted on Black communities'. Its commitment was to 'struggling together and to imagining and creating a world free of anti-Blackness, where every Black person has the social, economic, and political power to thrive'.

Its first major event was the Black Lives Matter Freedom Ride to Ferguson[41] after the death of 18-year-old Michael Brown in Missouri in 2014. Always true to its non-violence policy, Black Lives Matter protests took hold in 2015 and 2016 after more Black deaths through police brutality, toxic masculine violence and transphobia.

The power of the movement drew heightened attention to injustice in the Philando Castile[42] case when the policeman who killed him was acquitted in 2017. Black Lives Matter was also prominent that year when its supporters joined counter-protestors at the supremacist Unite The Right rally in Charlottesville, Virginia.[43]

Black Lives Matter prominently faced off against the Los Angeles Police Department in the matters of Grechario Mack[44] and Kenneth

---

41   Michael Brown Jr, an 18-year-old Black man, was fatally shot by white police officer Darren Wilson in Ferguson, St Louis, Missouri, in August 2014. His death led to days of significant protest in Ferguson with police enforcing a nightly curfew despite criticism over militarised tactics. The US department of justice ultimately concluded that Wilson shot Brown in self-defence.

42   Philando Castile, a 32-year-old African-American man, was fatally shot during a traffic stop in St Paul, Minnesota. Jeronimo Yanez, a 28-year-old Hispanic police officer, shot Castile in front of his partner, Diamond Reynolds, and her four-year-old daughter.

43   Unite the Right saw Klansmen and other white nationalists openly display anti-Black, anti-Muslim and antisemitic symbols and slogans. Initiated after the removal of Confederate monuments that began after the Charleston church shooting in 2015, in which a supremacist murdered nine Black people, the Unite the Fight rally resulted in numerous injuries and the murder of counter-protestor Heather Heyer.

44   Grechario Mack, a 30-year-old African-American man, was shot and killed by two Los Angeles Police Department (LAPD) officers while going through a mental health crisis. The LAPD ruled that officers Ryan Lee and Martin Robles followed policy when they fired initial shots at Mack, but that shots fired once he was on the ground violated protocol.

Ross Jr[45] in 2018. In supporting the men's families, said *The Guardian*, it took 'on one of the deadliest police systems in the US, where law enforcement killings of black mentally ill residents are so normalised, families struggle to be heard'.

The newspaper said the organisation and the families '(faced) an uphill battle in the most secretive state in the US for police misconduct, in a region where officers who shoot are never prosecuted'.

In defending the rapper 21 Savage[46] in 2019, Black Lives Matter also protested the detention and deportation of Black and Brown immigrants.

Syreeta McFadden, writer and professor of English at the Borough of Manhattan Community College, City University of New York, explained in *The Atlantic* in September 2020 that the objective of Black Lives Matter today is not 'direct action... (that is) never the primary component of a movement's longevity'.

She quotes Allen Kwabena Frimpong, resource mobiliser and co-founder of the AdAstra Collective which supports and studies social movements in the US: 'It... works in concert with a multitude of efforts. Movements frequently face setbacks and fierce resistance, and some even wait decades to capture the national imagination.

'When the cameras turn off, when there's not as much attention to the issues in mass media or social media, we think that the movement activity has somehow ended. But it hasn't.

'It's that what is required of us has shifted... in this phase of the cycle. It's a time to build strategy.'

Black Lives Matter has, rather, become 'an energising and connecting force for Black people around the world... a political home for many', winning 'critical legislation to benefit Black lives', and changing 'the terms of the debate on Blackness around the world',

---

45   Kenneth J Ross Jr, a 25-year-old African-American man, was shot multiple times, including in the back by LAPD officers in a Los Angeles park. Ross had bipolar disorder and schizophrenia.

46   Atlanta rapper 21 Savage (She'yaa Bin Abraham-Joseph, 1992–) was arrested and detained by the US Immigration and Customs Enforcement (ICE), which said he was British and had illegally overstayed a visa. Black Lives Matter responded that the detention of Black immigrants was endemic in the US and an aspect of violence criminalising Blackness.

as it describes itself on its website. Vitally, as a BC movement, it has 'catalysed other movements and shifted culture with an eye toward the dangerous impacts of anti-Blackness'.

[McFadden, 2020: *www.theatlantic.com*; Black Lives Matter, 2020]

George Floyd (1973–2020)

Many parts of the world were under lockdown or under pressure to survive due to the COVID-19 pandemic in May 2020 when a video showing a white police officer killing a Black man by kneeling on his neck in Minneapolis went viral.

The death of George Floyd – an African-American man under arrest after a store clerk alleged he had passed a fake $20 bill in Minneapolis – through the actions of Derek Chauvin, changed the spectrum of protest about and commitment to ending violence against Black people. The focus was predominantly on police brutality in the US, with Black Lives Matter, activists from other organisations and ordinary antiracism protestors leading campaigns for months.

The response to these actions, and condemnation of the violence shown in the video – Chauvin knelt on Floyd's neck for more than eight minutes – was global. The name 'George Floyd' would become a phrase for justice for Black people.

Chauvin was charged with second-degree murder, raised from an initial charge of third-degree murder and second-degree manslaughter, and three other officers who were present were charged with aiding and abetting second-degree murder and aiding and abetting second-degree manslaughter.

Black sports stars: 'Enough. Enough is enough.'

Basketball players including LeBron James (1984-), Dwayne Wade (1982-), Carmelo Anthony (1984-) and Chris Paul (1985-) were among the first American sports stars to publicly endorse campaigns for Black equality in the Black Lives Matter era.

The four National Basketball Association (NBA) superstars used the opening of the 2016 ESPYs (sports awards presented by US TV network ABC) to reach millions on the subjects of race hate and violence against Black people. Wade demanded the end of the shoot-to-kill mentality, famously saying: 'Enough. Enough is enough.'

James, who urged the 'renouncing' of 'all violence', had previously spoken out when Black people were killed through police action, and in the verdict in the Brown case.

In August 2020, James joined worldwide cries for justice in the Breonna Taylor[47] case, wearing a modified MAGA ('Make America Great Again', a Trump campaign slogan) hat calling for the arrest of the police officers who shot and killed her.

In the same month, James was among Los Angeles Lakers and Milwaukee Bucks players who boycotted NBA playoffs to protest the shooting of Jacob Blake.[48] Many other professional sports teams also refused to play scheduled games, leading to some games being postponed. Leagues that took part in the protests included the Women's National Basketball Association, Major League Baseball, the National Hockey League and Major League Soccer.

James came out in support of National Football League (NFL) star Colin Kaepernick (1987-) who was transformed from player to civil rights activist in 2016 when he declined to sing the national anthem as a protest against the systemic oppression of Black people.

This led to a deeper and broader reaction from some other players, coaches and team owners, and the political establishment. Kaepernick remained unsigned after that season.

African-American sports agent C Lamont Smith, who founded and was president of the Denver, Colorado-based All Pro Sports and Entertainment Inc and Above the Rim Management, representing many top American athletes, pointed to the core issue – Black Consciousness. Campaigns in favour of Black equality are significant

---

47   Breonna Taylor, a 26-year-old African-American woman from Louisville, Kentucky, was killed by police who used a battering ram to enter her apartment on 13 March 2020. Her name was at the centre of protests against police brutality and racism. Since her death, police in Louisville are no longer able to forcibly enter homes without warning. Sports teams and athletes were prominent in campaigns aimed at justice for Breonna. In particular, the Women's National Basketball Association (WNBA) dedicated their season to Taylor.

48   Jacob Blake, a 29-year-old African-American man, was seriously injured by a police officer in Kenosha, Wisconsin when the cop shot at Blake seven times. Marches, rallies and protests followed.

and consequential, but if there is no lasting shift to BC, that support is not enough.

In Smith's view, as quoted in the *Marquette Sports Law Review*, 'The sports and entertainment industry is to (Black people) what technology is to the Japanese and oil is the Arabs. It is incumbent upon us to work to control our natural resources.'

[Athreya 2020: www.essentiallysports.com; Shropshire, 1996: *Marquette Sports Law Review*]

Stans and pro-Black TikTokkers

The 2020 protests around the world after the death of George Floyd brought about an extraordinary unity among especially young people driven by antiracism.

Even American capitalist enterprises, which had previously kept a distance from Black Lives Matter, showed open support for the movement. Associate Professor Eugene Y Chan of Purdue University, a public research institute in West Lafayette, Indiana, noted in August 2020 that 'it seems as if most major companies including Apple, Amazon and Facebook have endorsed the movement – or at a minimum pledged millions of dollars to fight racism and vowed to do more to end discrimination in their workplaces'.

Chan, who studies the psychology of consumer behaviour, believes a primary reason was 'the pressure of young people', with a *Business Insider* poll – using social networking app Yubo and online learning platform StuDocu – showing 'nearly 90% of members of Generation Z (Gen Z) – those born from 1997 to 2005 – believe African-Americans are treated differently and support Black Lives Matter'.

'That compares with just 60% of respondents under 30 who said they supported the movement back in 2016.'

Chan noted that 'as of 2020, there were 82 million millennials – born from 1981 to 1996 – and 86 million members of Gen Z in the US, compared with 69 million baby boomers. The spending power of millennials was estimated at $2.5-trillion', an amount which 'could grow significantly in the coming years as they inherit $68tn in wealth from their baby boomer parents, which will constitute one of the greatest wealth transfers in modern times'.

That 'millennials say it's important companies they buy from share their values, which is also true for Gen Z', would enhance (and repudiate) the way in which Black lives were viewed – vitally, not as commodities, as slavery had intended, but as human beings.

The potency of video-sharing social networking service TikTok in spreading messages against injustice and brutality on Black bodies was also shown in 2020. *USnews.com* reported how the hashtag #blacklivesmatter 'shot up TikTok's trending list with 3 billion views', giving the example of 'TikTok superstar Charli D'Amelio, whose 60-million followers is nearly twice the number of HBO's US subscribers, hit pause on showing off dance moves to discuss George Floyd'.

'I will continue to spread these messages and be an ally,' said D'Amelio, who is white, in a post which garnered more than 47.7m views and 12m likes.

'TikTok's emergence as a platform for political discourse for teens follows a tradition of media platforms evolving beyond their founders' initial designs – such as Twitter's role in the Arab Spring protests in 2011[49] and the MTV cable TV network's role in galvanising young voters [around social and political issues, particularly voting] in the early 1990s.'

Even zealous fans of K-Pop (South Korean) supergroups like BTS (the name drawn from 'Bangtan Sonyeondan', or 'bullet-proof Boy Scouts') momentarily overcame their online divides – where 'tone-deafness', cultural appropriation and outright racism are expressed even as numbers of Black stans – fans and antiracism allies – grow.

When BTS donated US$1 million to the Black Lives Matter movement in June 2020, 'the ARMY', as fans are called, used the Twitter hashtag #MatchAMillion to donate the same amount. The BBC reported: 'One In An Army – the fan collective that spearheaded the donation drive – said in a press release, "We stand in solidarity with Black ARMY. They're an important part of our family. And we

---

49   The Arab Spring was a series of anti-government protests and armed rebellions that spread through North Africa and the Arab world from the early 2010s. This began in Tunisia and led to a number of insurgencies including in Morocco, Algeria, parts of Iran, Lebanon, Sudan and other countries. There were large demonstrations in countries as far apart as Djibouti and Mauritania.

stand with Black people everywhere. Your voices deserve to be heard".'

'BTS's social media following is known for its devotion and activism and had already organised online protests in support of Black Lives Matter. K-Pop fans took over the hashtag #whitelivesmatter, posting *en masse* to drown out white-supremacist or racist posts using the hashtag.' It was, however, also the case that some K-Pop fans used #whitelivesmatter for its literal meaning, facing a backlash from 'stans'..

Asian support of Black liberation is historically most powerful in China, dating back to Mao Tse-tung's overt support during his rule, and the Black Panthers' tendency towards Maoist politics. Aspects of that were revived during the 2020 protests, although not without criticism of Chinese allies failing to understand that this was not their moment to be spotlighted or even to try and share the 'attention'.

Journalist Taylor Weik reported for NBC News on how 'signs and artwork bearing the slogan "Yellow Peril Supports Black Power" started appearing at protests and on social media following the death of George Floyd'. He tells of how the slogan – 'repurposed by Asian Americans as a show of solidarity with the Black Lives Matter movement' – traced its roots to the 1960s.

'The term "yellow peril" originated in the 1800s, when Chinese labourers were brought to the US to replace emancipated Black communities as a cheap source of labour. Chinese labourers... became victims of racist backlash from white workers who saw them as a threat... This fear led to... the Chinese Exclusion Act of 1882, the first law to restrict immigration based on race.

'... In the 1960s, Asian Americans tried to reclaim the racist term and their histories... (and) students of colour at San Francisco State University and the University of California, Berkeley, formed a coalition called the Third World Liberation Front, calling for campus reform... and protesting the Vietnam War.'

Asian-American activist Connie Wun PhD – co-founder and executive director of AAPI (Asian American Pacific Islander) Women Lead – told NBC Asian America: 'We need to interrogate how our privileges as Asian Americans are made possible by anti-Blackness.'

Wun 'challenged individuals to think about whether their actions work to combat police brutality against Black people, or if they're centred around their own feelings'.

'"People have to centre Black liberation and freedom in their politics and in their practice. That's what it means to be in solidarity. It's not going to be easy, but that's part of the work. Racial solidarity is a goal that requires struggle".'

[Chan, 2020: *www.theconversation.com*; Black Lives Matter, 2020: *Blacklivesmatter.com/about/*; BBC.com, 2020: https://www.bbc.com/news/world-asia-52960617; USnews.com, 2020; Chaudhry, 2020: theverge.com; Weik, 2020: *www.nbcnews.com*]

'To love our Blackness is to resist'

Janet Smith interviews American Black Lives Matter activists Mervyn Marcano of movementforBlacklives.org and Thenjiwe McHarris of the US Human Rights Network on anti-Black racism, the war on capitalism and love. They met at a retreat in Johannesburg's northern suburbs in March 2017 while Marcano and McHarris were in South Africa to discuss solidarity networks with local #FeesMustFall activists.

Mervyn Marcano: Anti-Black racism is an important question for any political movement. Blackness is founded as the ultimate Other, and certainly whiteness, in its own sort of flattening way, doesn't exist without Blackness. Whiteness as a dominating, all-seeing, all-knowing force doesn't exist without a flat notion of Blackness.

Where I think the short-cut has been made in many societies around acknowledging racism is to acknowledge that whiteness as a concept is a bad thing, and that Blackness as a concept is a bad thing.

This leads us to say, let's not acknowledge race. We are all one people. We are all one human race. [But] this is another flattening; it erases lived experience and political realities. It creates conditions that allow for the continued perpetuation of oppressive dynamics, while promoting a social falseness. This can rely on the co-option of concepts such as *ubuntu*, 'be nice to me, I'll be nice to you', but don't allow for the realities of a country like South Africa, a 90% Black country with incredible levels of poverty and denigration of Black people. So anti-Blackness, anti-Black racism, is pervasive and it is insidious and it can survive and re-adapt if it is not dealt with directly.

The reason that anti-Blackness as a notion is important is because it has been so long-lasting and gives whiteness an identity. It informs everyone's identity. The notion of Blackness as the ultimate bottom in any society gives other folks meaning in terms of where they sit in the culture. And so in order for us to find our own dignity as people, we have to attack anti-Black racism, because it is the concept on which capitalism is built. Critics of capitalism specifically call it out, [but] in the US, anti-Black racism has a very codified structure – from Jim Crow laws during slavery up to today.

It is important to talk about the ways in which anti-Black racism exists politically and inter-personally, because you can essentially end up with a presidential candidate like Donald Trump who trades on anti-Blackness, while not specifically denigrating Black people.

This is a very dangerous concept because he can be called anything from an everyday fascist to the anti-Christ, yet he is not calling me a n---er.

He is not saying that I don't deserve to live, but he is saying our 'inner cities' are 'falling apart' and he has to send in the National Guard to restore order. This is essentially coded anti-Blackness. He is specifically talking about 'inner cities' like Detroit, like Chicago and Black political centres, and he is specifically talking about the failure of Black leadership. And saying that in order for law and order to come back we have to restore order and send in the National Guard ... essentially it's easy to see that as not being anti-Black.

After all, there are National Guards who are Black. There are Black people who will participate in such an effort.

What it does, though, is essentially target Black communities, strip Black communities of their self-sufficiency to whatever extent they have been able to build them up, and will trade on 'Black political failure' and the super-predator of Blackness as being the core social ills that bring us all down. If white folks don't actually call that out for what it is, we will continue to see insidious notions of anti-Blackness.

In South Africa, I (kept) hearing what a failure (former President) Jacob Zuma was. While there may be concerns, I wonder sometimes about the political opportunity it gives the white ruling class to continue to focus on the failure of Black political leadership without discussing the very entrenched economic privilege that it has.

In the US, if we rest on the laurels of the civil rights movement that was essentially about access to political power, we lose the opportunity to transform our political system and social fabric. Because now we have the opportunity to see the failure of certain efforts of the civil rights movement – access to the ballot box, to the franchise, to political representation.

But what does that mean? The process shifting to accommodate the realities of Black folks? We had a Black president, but at the time we had stagnant Black employment. Have Black folks impacted on every economic and social level, to a greater degree than most other folks in our country?

If we're not willing to have those conversations, instead trading on the notions of 'let's be nice to each another', we won't progress.

Globally, people are valued based on how light they are, on how dark they are, and so to deal with racism means you have to unearth Black radical thought, essentially the radical Black imagination.

To confront [anti-Black racism] forces us to deal with the relationship Black suffering has to the suffering of [anyone whose life is] seen as less valuable wherever they are in the world. It's also about the relationship to capitalism. It's not just the battle of who is more oppressed; it's also an ideological framework we have to confront to move towards liberation.

We can't confront white supremacy, capitalism, without recognising that people are valued based on how much they have, where they live, how masculine they perform in the world, what family means to them. I imagine a world in which we have rid ourselves of this deep desire for domination. When Black people get through, we all get through and that's the notion that makes us say Black Lives Matter.

Black folks must get free, and by free I don't just mean politically free. I mean human dignity free. If we can do that, then it frees white folks of this falsehood of supremacy and they can become full human beings instead of the monsters Black folks have come to know.

It would allow folks to acknowledge that when we say Black Lives

Matter, whether you are a Black American or an Indian migrant coming on a foreign visa, you are aligning yourself with a political and moral compass that says: I actually don't stand in a system that will denigrate those that white people see as less. And I am chaining my human dignity and my political value with those who are being oppressed in this system.

The promise for Black folks, whether you are African-American or a migrant, Puerto Rican, is essentially what whiteness is promising you. That is a notion of 'respectability', that, somehow, if you work really hard, you will ascend over all the muck. That's the lie, and it's the lie that is being promised when we say #AllLivesMatter.

Thenjiwe McHarris: A couple of things are surfacing for me. We need to talk about caste systems. We need to talk about why the darker you are, the less value you have. White supremacy and capitalism are integrally involved with one another the ways in which capitalism is racialised, and only sustained off the exploitation and suffering of a population who looks a particular way.

We need to talk about the adaptive nature of capitalism and the adaptive nature of white supremacy. The racist nature of capitalism continues to reinvent itself; it wants to avoid emerging norms and still be able to profit off Black bodies.

We've moved from a place where there was enslavement, such as our ancestors [had to endure]. We are currently in a place where more of our people are 'in cages' and enslaved. I keep thinking about that question of needing to disrupt the pattern of history. We have to be courageous enough to think about an alternative to free our people.

So, if we frame our movement around just the abolition of prisons or police brutality, there will be another reason why our people are being caged, held and tortured, brutalised, taken from us. How do we disrupt that? It's about training ourselves on the adaptive nature of white supremacy and capitalism, which doesn't just affect Black folks in the US, but around the world.

MM: We have to ask ourselves what kind of victory is it when you have conservatives in the US Congress who would never utter the word 'n--

-er', who celebrate Black History Month, who would never say that we should go back to slavery, who would say full-heartedly that that's terrible [to name someone like that], and if you believe it is not, you are a terrible person.

At the same time they will legislate for the complete elimination of healthcare and the privatisation of school systems, even though [being American] is essentially our commons, no matter what we think of the way our state currently functions. They would legislate [that] away for private interests.

What kind of antiracism is that? It's not something that gets us anywhere closer to freedom. It's essentially a negotiation with capitalism, and when I say a negotiation with capitalism, I don't want to sound like I'm at a '70s Beatbox poetry thing saying words that people don't understand. A politic that allows powerful white people to not utter a negative word about Black people but takes the rug out from Black people, that denies Black people access to water, equal education, employment and human dignity and essentially incarcerates them at rates of 10 times anyone else, a politic that says that's okay, is racist.

It's not about whether someone can call me a name, which they can't. We can overcome this kind of inter-personal ugliness, even some of this structural ugliness, but instead we have a politics that tolerates a level of torture and brutality that should be unacceptable.

TMcH: That this can happen even under a Black president ... So what does it mean to have a Black president and yet the material conditions for Black people do not change? What is it like to have a Black president and see tanks in Missouri?

We can't be so desperate that we are willing to sacrifice our imagination. We can't be so desperate that the face of a Black man in the White House means more than our children eating or our ability to access quality healthcare or housing.

We always speak about the next generation of organisers. We need to [concentrate on that] rather than focus on how victorious it was to put a Black man in the White House. It's a question that is more difficult.

It's more challenging. It's more painful, but it's readied them for a struggle, especially against the administration we have in 2017, and also for what we see happening globally. They're strategic enough on the Right that they are starting to create a global agenda.

We need to be courageous enough to prepare our children for what's coming their way. The Right is threatened by us acknowledging that winning is possible and that it is only possible together.

MM: When we think about what 'duty' [within BC] means, I don't hear conscription; I don't hear that every Black person at the age of 15 must perform their two hours of being in the movement. I do hear a critique of the *laissez-faire* attitudes to this kind of work. And so when I hear that it is 'our duty' to fight for our freedom and it is our duty to win, I see it as a call to make sure our work is authentic, that it is worth doing and is actually calling out a problem and attacking it.

I hear in that a critique of charity work. I hear in that a critique of the be-all, end-all NGO. I hear in that a critique of technology being the thing that solves all our problems. I hear in that a framework that we should apply.

I think we have a duty to attack anti-Blackness everywhere. In some cases that might mean running for office, making sure people have access to the ballot particularly in a local context.

There are offices we constantly cede to the opposition or the power structure, for example district attorneys who decide what kind of sentences people will get, and which kind [of] cases should [be] prosecuted.

There is no *one* way to participate in the movement.

Not everybody is going to wield a spear. Some people are going to file lawsuits, some are going to write, some are going to do door-to-door organising, some are going to teach. If there is anything we have learned from past movements, it's that it is best to incorporate as many people as possible, and that we have a duty to see each other as we are.

We need an extensive notion of Blackness so that as many people as possible can participate. This means we have a duty to let go of this myth of the singular Black male leader.

[For instance] we cannot talk about Black lives mattering if we cannot talk about transgender women being killed in Black communities. Some people would say that's not a state violation. That's not police killing a Black man.

[But] you know what *is* a violation? It's that Black man who does not value her life, who doesn't see her as a human being – and neither does the DA [district attorney].

Black queer women have led the Black Lives Matter movement; they are in the frontlines physically and in our meanings and our spaces as we build up our infrastructure, leading the charge invisibly and emotionally. If we continue to rely on the trope of the singular Black male leader, which we know not to be true, we cannot have a real movement.

We have this myopic focus on Black men and ignore what Black women have had to shoulder. We also ignore how Black women have been brutalised, yet our families are way multi-dimensional. We grew up in families with grandmothers caring for children, cross-bloodlines, where multiple adults care for the children.

If we fail to see the many ways that Black folks make families, we are failing to see how Black folks can contribute to the transformation of our culture in a meaningful way.

TMcH: We cannot over-simplify Blackness, because when we do, we make Black suffering invisible. When we cannot imagine leadership outside the Black 'head-men', we're not allowing [ourselves] to build the kind of Black liberation resistance we can build.

I'm hoping we can get to a place where we can disrupt the compulsion towards individualism. People need to see both themselves and people around them as valuable, in spite of how much or how little they have.

I think the duty for those who want to challenge the *status quo* takes on a different form for me. What's the intervention you wish to make? There's caring and loving yourself and those around you, but what's the intervention you'll make, like our elders and ancestors did for us.

In reading some of Biko's writings, something struck me: the letter to his family, about having to sacrifice being the kind of father he should have been, [that] he did not do it out of negligence or arrogance, but [because] he wanted to see a South Africa in which Black people and white people had equity.

There are sacrifices to be made, but I think you can be part of Black resistance or a liberation struggle while also loving the hell out of your family. I think you can be part of a movement at home. My grandmother was my first teacher. She taught me how beautiful it was to be a Black girl in the Bronx, and it did not matter how much she was mistreated, that she cleaned homes for white people ... it hurt her, but it never robbed her of her dignity, her understanding of her Blackness and how beautiful it was.

MM: Black Lives Matter is a network. There is a Black Lives Matter organisation that does a specific set of work, and then there is also the broader movement for Black lives – hundreds of organisations that have been active over the last few years and certainly even before that, working on racial justice issues.

TMcH: It's important for us to acknowledge the current generation of our movement is carrying on the legacy of our elders and ancestors who not only acknowledged racism and white supremacy, but taught us the beauty of Blackness. Our movement is not about exclusion. It's about forcing our country to deal with white supremacy, with the history and legacy. To love our Blackness is to resist. White supremacy doesn't affect just Black people, it affects all people.

MM: The movement for Black lives has, for instance, opened up lots of conversations in Latino communities around their anti-Blackness. There is a conversation, a political Blackness, at a certain point within every community we are dealing with. The movement for Black lives has opened up ways in which Blackness is way more expansive than we could ever have imagined and way more beautiful than we could have ever imagined – and politically challenged in every corner.

TMcH: I have been politically active for 11 or 12 years. In my political homes, it was okay to use the term 'white supremacy', but in more public spaces I could not use that term, and if I did, I was making a particular strategic choice. I think we have entered into [a different space now]. I think a lot of this is due to decades of organising, of movement and resistance work that happened before me and by those who taught me and helped build us.

I think it's also a product of not just where we are in the States but what's happening globally. Young people, in particular, resist in ways that are inspiring around the world, and I think we saw some of that with the #FeesMustFall uprising [in South Africa].

We can let the media name what is happening in our streets, or *we* can name what's happening within our communities. I think there was a concerted effort [among us] now to name what *we* saw happening.

MM: The constant question we are struggling with is patriarchy. And if that's our movement's contribution, to fight that, at the moment, then that is our movement's contribution.

TMcH: That's the most important thing for me. Are we giving the next generation of organisers a fighting chance? It's also about what we leave behind. We search for history so that we can find answers because we are tired of sitting with the questions.

The point of the use of terms ... I had an elder once tell me, because we kept saying 'police brutality, police brutality', that you can say 'police torture', which makes me ask why am I uncomfortable to use the term 'torture' when that is what it is.

We are so [sentient] to white anxiety, so while you can pose some challenging things, you must not trigger white anxiety to the point where you will be alienated. I think that is an important thing: how we talk about Black suffering from the perspective of a white gaze. To love my people is to say that when you resisted in the streets, it wasn't a 'riot', it was an 'uprising'. Saying it like that is to love my people. I say it because I love my people enough to say what is happening to us is so terrible, it amounts to a term that I am not supposed to use.

MM: What is the definition of a struggle for liberation? We seem to only have the narratives around what liberation looked like 50 years ago, 100 years ago, and with our limited knowledge of them, we often

Raised fists seen during a youth month commemoration held at Regina Mundi Church in Soweto on 16 June 2006 (Photo: Paballo Thekiso)

Steve Biko speaking at the second General Students Council of SASO at the University of Natal in July 1971 (Photo: SAHA)

Vuyelwa Mashalaba is considered the mother of Black Consciousness and many believe the movement might have died without her inspiration and grace. (Photo: courtesy of the Mashalaba family)

Crowds attend Biko's funeral held in King William's Town on 25 September 1977 (Photo: SAHA)

Grave of Steve Biko (Photo: SAHA)

A guard of honour protects a coffin carrying the remains of Khotso Seatlholo, a young leader of the June 16 uprising. He was reburied next to his comrade Tsietsi Mashinini at Avalon cemetery, Soweto, in 2006. (Photo: Paballo Thekiso)

Photo Shows Ntsiki Biko (31), widow of dead South African political detainee Steve Biko, who died while in police custody, defiantly gives the Black power salute with their children Samora (2) (left) and Nkosinathi (6) in front of their home at King William's Town, South Africa, shortly after hearing of his death. "Steve may be dead but his struggle will continue,'" said Mrs Biko. (Photo: Keystone Press/Alamy Stock Photo)

Barney Pityana was a founding member of SASO with Steve Biko. (Photo: Media24)

Professor Harry Nengwekhulu speaks from his office at UNISA, where he works as a lecturer, about his early days with Steve Biko and the start of the Black Consciousness Movement (Photo: Paballo Thekiso)

Former press photographer Bokwe Mafuna, seen here at his house in Roodepoort, played an important and unique role in the Black Consciousness Movement before he was forced into exile. (Photo: Paballo Thekiso)

University Christian Movement (UCM) delegates from Natal campaigned together for BC. Steve Biko is in the middle of the front row. (Photo: Paddy Tiber archive files/Blogpost)

BC supporters Malusi Mpumlwana, Nohle Mohapi and Dr Mamphela Ramphele are seen here with Mohapi's attorney Griffiths Mxenge during an October 1979 hearing at the Grahamstown Supreme Court. Mohapi was suing the apartheid minister of police for claiming her husband, Mapetla Mohapi, had written a suicide note. (Photo: *Sunday Times*)

Shamima Shaikh was one of South Africa's best-loved human rights activists, a notable Islamic feminist and a journalist who defied conservatism. (Photo courtesy of the Shaikh family)

Ishmael Mkhabela, now chairman of the Steve Biko Foundation with its offices in Johannesburg and in Biko's village of Ginsberg, has remained true to his calling as a community change activist. (Photo: Paballo Thekiso)

Family members of Khotso Seatlholo walk past a poster bearing a picture of him and his June 16 comrade, Tsietsi Mashinini, after a church service at Regina Mundi Church held to mark Seatlholo's reburial in 2006. (Photo: Paballo Thekiso)

Priests walk solemnly past an RIP memorial during Khotso Seatlholo's reburial at Avalon cemetery, Soweto. A number of activists were interred on its grounds, including 1976 heroes Hector Pieterson and Hastings Ndlovu. (Photo: Paballo Thekiso)

Reverend Moss Ntlha is the chairman of the South African Christian Leadership Initiative, and has a long history of faith-based activism for social justice at local, national and international levels. His activism straddles both church and society and he is an active participant in civil society struggles, including the Save South Africa campaign. He is a pastor and general secretary of the Evangelical Alliance of South Africa. (Photo: Paballo Thekiso)

Poet and political activist Don Mattera holds on to the tombstone of 1976 student leader Tsietsi Mashinini at Avalon cemetery in Soweto. (Photo: Paballo Thekiso)

Political activist, writer, member of the BPC, vice-president of AZAPO and president of SOPA Lybon Mabasa speaks at a youth day commemoration held in Regina Mundi Church, Soweto, in 2006 (Photo: Paballo Thekiso)

Dikgang Moseneke being congratulated by his wife, Khabonina, after being admitted as an attorney in 1978. (Photo: Gallo Images/Avusa)

Activist Omar Badsha's photography, resistance art, activism and writing made an incalculable contribution to the meaning of being 'South African'. (Photo: Media24)

end up with these really masculinist notions of freedom: using your body, putting your body on the line, fighting somebody with your fists, with a gun. That is people's ultimate vision of liberation.

Even at the protests, the protest is not legitimate unless you are punching a cop in the face. These very particular modes of being in a Black body in terms of resisting power are very limited tellings of history. There's even a very limited understanding of who Malcolm X was.

There's this picture of Malcolm X standing with a rifle that every young Black male organiser has as a profile picture on Facebook. It is a very limited sort of notion in which we erase and eclipse these incredible ruptures that we have generated as a people over the last few years, the cultural shifts that have happened as a result of this movement.

I think the success of a movie like *Moonlight* is just as valuable as five people sitting in a corner talking about how we are going to take over a building or some very ill-thought-out strategy about how power operates.

We are in a different moment, we are in a different time.

Capital operates differently, the role of the state is different. We have to give ourselves credit for adapting to the moment that it is.

TMcH: I think there are many tactics people employ around the world, but a difficult question is: What is winning? We have to deal with this obsession with domination.

MM: There is also a question around whether Black Lives Matter is an anti-capitalist movement. Is capitalism dying? Is it morphing?

The question I know I have personally struggled with, and I think other folks struggle with, is when we talk about how the bread gets buttered, how the cookie gets baked, the means of production, who owns the production, whose labour is used and valued.

We are in a moment in our global history that requires some new thinking around what is labour, what is production and what are the means, and I think every movement around the world is struggling with this question.

We are using models of understanding production that are hundreds of years old, even as our world is moving towards automation, away from human labour, toward a liberal notion of the commons.

When you have captains of industry talking about a universal basic income in our country, we are on very different territory in terms of understanding capitalism.

Mervyn Marcano and Thenjiwe McHarris worked with student activists in South Africa to create a broader global identity for young Black activists.

Ibram X Kendi (1982–)

How to Be an Antiracist became much sought-after in the weeks and months after George Floyd was killed as protests for Black Lives Matter marched around the world. Its themes of structural justice and accountability revealed BC in its true nature: as an act of humanity. Kendi's book reached No 1 on the *New York Times* bestseller list, seeing trading in excess of 1 million copies.

This was not the author and intellectual historian's breakout publishing event. Kendi's 2016 book *Stamped from the Beginning: The Definitive History of Racist Ideas in America* won a National Book Award (among many other prizes and accolades), although it entered the *NY* bestseller list only in 2020 as a result of the accelerating interest in Kendi's work.

Writing in *GQ*, ZZ Packer described the professor as having 'a Jedi-like prowess for recognising and neutralising the racism pervading our society'.

'His method: to apply a laser focus on racist ideas – not mere surface-level epithets, but deeply entrenched prejudices with their own intellectual lineage.

'Kendi's dismantling of those ideas starts with his very definition of the term "racist", which he unyokes from the intent or the relative moral goodness or badness of the person expressing it [in *How to Be an Antiracist*], and instead ties [it] solely to actions that perpetuate racial inequity.'

Packer explains how 'Kendi breaks down [the] continuum into three modes: segregationist, assimilationist, and antiracist. He likens being antiracist to loving someone and accepting them no matter how different from you they may be. The assimilationist says he likes you only to the degree that you resemble him and incorporate his manners and ways. The segregationist cannot accept you at all because your differences from him are grounds for expulsion from the circle of brotherhood.'

The author – who was born Henry Rogers – and his wife Sadiqa jointly adopted the surname Kendi ('loved one': Meru, Kenya) during a naming ceremony when they got married in 2013. Ibram Kendi also chose Xolani ('peace': isiZulu, South Africa) as his middle name at that time.

The professor leads Boston University's new Center for Antiracist Research, having previously created the Antiracist Research and Policy Center at American University in Washington DC.

[Packer, 2020: https://www.gq.com/story/ibram-x-kendi-antiracism-scholar-profile]

Layla Saad (1983–)

The author's best-selling *Me and White Supremacy: Combat Racism, Change the World and Become a Good Ancestor* grew out of her 2018 Instagram challenge under the hashtag #MeAndWhiteSupremacy, which led to a digital workbook and then her book, which is a guide to a life of antiracism.

Saad advances the principles of Black humanity to oppose the 'densensitisation' of white people. This is reiterated in her June 2020 *The Guardian* review of *When They Call You a Terrorist: A Black Lives Matter Memoir*, written by BLM co-founder Cullors and award-winning journalist Asha Bandele.

There, Saad reflects on how whites are so used to 'seeing Black lives snuffed out on their mobile phones that they are often unable to connect the dots to see that each person had loved ones, desires, relationships, quirks and dreams'.

She pointed to the need to focus 'not only to the atrocities committed against Black Americans, but also to the humanity of those whose lives were taken, and those who, still living, continue to fight for justice...'.

Saad – who grew up in Wales with Zanzibari and Kenyan parents – hosted the *Good Ancestor* podcast in which she spoke to people about their ancestry or how individuals in society impacted them. She lives in Qatar with her family.

[Saad, 2020; www.theguardian.com]

From The Little Red Book to Guerrilla: Conscious Black solidarity

The theory of the Black Panthers

The practices of the late Malcolm X, assassinated in 1965, were deeply rooted in the theoretical foundations of the Black Panther Party. The Party also adopted Malcolm X's words 'Freedom by any means necessary' as its slogan.

Malcolm X was a militant revolutionary for oppressed minorities, who – among other fights – sought positive social services as a primary aspect of his Consciousness work. This was a mutual quest for the Black Panthers who also followed Malcolm's belief of international working-class unity across race and gender in unity with other revolutionary groups.

With Maoism as an ideology, the Party was envisaged as being in the vanguard of the revolution, while from Marxism, it addressed the capitalist economic system, embraced dialectical materialism and encouraged workers to assume the means of production.

The history of the Black Panther Party

At the same time as the UCM was being founded at a divided NUSAS congress at Rhodes University in South Africa, and Biko and other Black students were plotting their rebellion against NUSAS after being excluded from white accommodation and dining facilities, the first issue of *The Black Panther* was making waves across California.

It was April 1967, and the Black Panther Party's official news organ had gone into distribution. In May, the Party marched on the California state Capitol in Sacramento fully armed in protest at the state's attempt to outlaw carrying loaded weapons in public. It thereby put itself on the world's radar – and effectively committed itself to armed struggle.

Co-founder Bobby Seale read a statement of protest, and the police responded by arresting him and 30 other armed Panthers. This act of political repression kindled the fire to a burning resistance movement in the US. Soon it led to some Black workers also taking up arms and new Panther chapters being formed outside California.

In October 1967, the police arrested the defence minister of the Panthers, Huey P Newton, for killing an Oakland police officer. Ex-convict Eldridge Cleaver then began the movement to 'Free Huey' – a prominent Panthers struggle – and would quickly become the party spokesman while editing *The Black Panther*.

The Party meanwhile spread its roots further into the American political spectrum, forming coalitions with a range of revolutionary entities.

Stokely Carmichael, the former chairman of the Student Non-Violent Coordinating Committee (SNCC) and a proponent of Black Power, was recruited, becoming the Party's prime minister in 1968. Carmichael was adamantly against allowing whites into the Black liberation movement, believing whites could not relate to the Black experience and had an intimidating effect on Blacks. This position stirred some division in the Panthers.

Carmichael explained in 'The basis of Black power', a Panthers document, at the time: 'Whites who come into the Black community with ideas of change seem to want to absolve the power structure of its responsibility for what it is doing, and say that change can only come through Black unity, which is the worst kind of paternalism. If we are to proceed toward true liberation, we must cut ourselves off from white people [otherwise] we will find ourselves entwined in the tentacles of the white power complex that controls this country.'

The lengthy student strike at San Francisco State University in 1968 helped pull away those tentacles.

Led by the Black Student Union and the Third World Liberation Front, it demanded the university fund an Ethnic Studies programme, and support an end to the Vietnam War.

In 1968, the Party made Chinese Communist Party chairman Mao Tse-tung's *The Little Red Book* compulsory reading for student adherents. This also assisted the funding of the purchase of shotguns.

Meanwhile, the FBI under J Edgar Hoover initiated the COINTELPRO (counterintelligence programme) to break up growing unity among revolutionary groups. These included the Peace and Freedom Party of Cleaver, Carmichael's SNCC, and union leader and labour organiser Cesar Chavez and others in the farm movement. Then, to destroy the Panthers, the FBI began a programme of 'surgical assassinations': targeting leading members of the Party who could not otherwise be subverted.

Arrests and a programme of psychological warfare were designed to split the Party politically and morally, using espionage and *agents provocateurs*.

To this end, a 17-year-old Panther, Bobby Hutton, lost his life in April 1968 in West Oakland, killed by the police. An unarmed Hutton was shot more than 10 times after he was caught in a gun battle with police.

In the interests of hype to see Newton freed, Cleaver had led an ambush of the cops during which two were wounded. Cleaver was also wounded, but Hutton – who had stripped down to his underwear to show he was not armed – wouldn't make it out alive. Martin Luther King, whose champions included top American entertainer Harry Belafonte, had been assassinated just days earlier. King had started rethinking his own doctrine of non-violence and started to explore other unions. Two months later, Robert F Kennedy, widely recognised in the minority community as one of the only politicians in the US 'sympathetic' to the civil rights movement, was also assassinated.

But there was positivity, too. In January 1969, the first Panthers Free Breakfast for School Children Program was initiated at St Augustine's Church in Oakland. By the end of the year, the Panthers had set up kitchens in cities around the US, feeding more than 10 000 children every day. Nonetheless, Hoover publicly stated that the Panthers were the 'greatest threat to the internal security of the country'.

Twenty-one-year-old Panthers leader Fred Hampton was a victim of this. He had been involved in activist programmes on the west side of Chicago, in particular a door-to-door programme of sickle cell anaemia tests. (Sickle cell anaemia, a group of blood disorders inherited from one's parents, occurs more frequently among people of African origin.) The Party's Chicago branch had also reached out to local gangs to bring them into the class war.

Hampton was killed by police during a raid on an apartment,

along with another Panther, 17-year-old Mark Clark, while four were wounded. According to the findings of an investigation, 90 bullets were fired inside the apartment, with only one coming from Clark's shotgun, which he kept in his hands while he slept. Surviving Panthers were, however, arrested for 'attempted murder of the police and aggravated assault'. No police officers were held.

In the summer of 1969, the alliance between the Panthers and SNCC began pulling apart. One of the main points of contention was the role of whites in the struggle – a dispute that would lead to an open gunfight at the University of California at Los Angeles (UCLA) against the group US, led by Maulana Karenga. This left two Panthers dead.

US, for 'Us Black people' – a Black nationalism and social change organisation – was co-founded by Hakim Jamal and Karenga (Swahili for 'keeper of tradition'). Karenga studied Swahili, Arabic and Africana at UCLA, mentored by Jamaican anthropologist and Négritudist, Councill Taylor.

By the end of 1968, the Party had maintained its original 400 or so members and reached more than 5000 people in 45 chapters and branches.

Newton was convicted of voluntary manslaughter in 1969, although the conviction was overturned in 1970 on procedural errors.

Seale was indicted the same year for protesting during the Democratic National Convention, convicted on 16 counts of contempt and sentenced to four years. He would later be charged for killing a cop, but met a hung jury. On Newton's release from prison, he developed the Panthers' 'socialist survival' programmes in Black communities, which continued free breakfasts for children, established free medical clinics, helped the homeless find housing and gave away free clothing and food.

But in March 1970, the FBI began to sow seeds of factionalism in the Black Panthers, in part by forging letters from groups outside the Panthers to Panthers themselves, from rank-and-file members to leaders. The split came when Newton went onto a TV talk show with Cleaver – who had been particularly targeted with forged letters encouraging dissent – on the phone in Algiers. That was where Cleaver and wife Kathleen had settled after jumping bail following charges of murder in the Oaklands ambush, which had resulted in the death of Hutton.

The Cleavers had fled the US in 1968 – first to Cuba and, after Algeria, to France. Cleaver had occupied the position of head of the international section of the Panthers, later claiming that his stipend while in Africa had been funded by the North Vietnamese – who were, at that time, at war with the US. Cleaver also travelled to North Korea where he explored *juche* or 'self-reliance' – the state ideology under which the masses are to act as the 'masters of the revolution and construction'. Kim Il-sung (1912–1994), around whom a cult of personality was created, developed the ideology out of Marxism-Leninism.

Cleaver expressed his disdain for the Panthers during the TV show, and even attacked its children's breakfast programme as 'reformist'. As a result of his anti-Party statements, Cleaver – accused of having murdered a man suspected of having an affair with his wife – was expelled from the Panthers' Central Committee.

He started up his own Black Liberation Army, which promoted his belief in armed resistance and urban guerrilla warfare.

In 1973, Seale ran for mayor of Oakland. Although he received 40 per cent of the vote, he was defeated.

Seeing the Party ripped apart by factions, Newton, like many, became disillusioned. In 1982 he was accused of embezzling state aid to a Panther-founded community school, and it was in the wake of the embezzlement charges that he disbanded the Black Panther Party. The embezzlement charges were dropped six years later after Newton pleaded no contest to a single allegation of cashing a state cheque for personal use. He was sentenced to six months in jail and 18 months' probation. But he no longer wanted to lead the Party, although people demanded otherwise of him. He threw himself into self-doubt instead and, having advocated putting down the gun and working on social programmes to directly benefit Black communities, he became dependent on cocaine, heroin and other narcotics.

Newton remarked in one of his public speeches in the 1980s – where he showed sparks of his earlier, brilliant clarity, but then became incoherent and rambled – that he was 'killing himself' by 'reactionary suicide' through the vice of addiction. On 22 August 1989, Newton was shot dead on the streets of Oakland during a drug dispute.

Seale resigned from the Party, while Elaine Brown (1943–) took the lead in continuing the Panther community programmes. A writer and activist, she created the Panthers' music albums, *Seize the Time* and *Until We're Free*, and was editor of the Black Panther publication in the Southern California branch before becoming a member of the party's central committee as Minister of Information, replacing the expelled Eldridge Cleaver. (Brown later ran for the Green Party presidential nomination in 2008 and worked for radical newspaper *Harambee*).

In 1975, the Cleavers returned from exile as born-again Christians, and became involved with right-leaning religious groups including North Korea-born messiah claimant Sun Myung Moon's Unification Church. (Moon also formed an association with Nation of Islam leader Louis Farrakhan, among others.)

In 1979, all charges against Eldridge Cleaver – whose 1968 prison book of philosophical and political essays *Soul on Fire* made a major impression even in the *New York Times* – were dropped after he struck a bargain with the state and pleaded guilty to 'assault' in that fatal 1968 shootout.

Cleaver is accused by some of using the book to attempt to 'justify' his rape of Black women as 'practice' for the 'delighted' serial rape of white 'prey', which he called 'politically inspired ... revenge an insurrectionary act. He did, however, renounce his position on rape – which had helped convict and put him behind bars – and instead promoted Black Theology, at first. After that bargain was struck with the state in 1979, Cleaver got five years' probation. In his twilight years, he entered dubious business ventures, and became a crack addict and conservative, very public, GOP Republican.

By the beginning of the 1980s, attacks on the Panthers and internal divisions saw it fall apart. Many remaining Panthers were either killed or forced to flee the US.

[Material drawn predominantly from the USA History Archive at www.marxists.org, especially the sections from Stokely Carmichael; Seale & Newton, 1995; Epstein, 1969; Democracy Now!, 2015]

Rules of the Black Panther Party
Speak politely.
Pay fairly for what you buy.
Return everything you borrow.
Pay for anything you damage.
Do not hit or swear at people.
Do not damage property or crops of the poor, oppressed masses.
Do not take liberties with women.
If we ever have to take captives, do not ill-treat them.
Obey orders in all your actions.
Do not take a single needle or piece of thread from the poor and oppressed masses.
Turn in everything captured from the attacking enemy.

[edited from the list of rules on www.marxists.org]

Huey P Newton (1942–1989)

A student in San Francisco when he joined the Afro-American Association (AAA) which sought Black separatism, Newton was a follower of Karl Marx, Vladimir Lenin, Fanon, Malcolm X, Mao Tse-tung, 'father' of modern sociology and French academic Emile Durkheim, and Che Guevara.

He and fellow student Bobby Seale founded the Black Panther Party for Self Defence in October 1966, with Seale becoming the chairman and Newton the minister of defence. At first, the Panthers concentrated on compelling government to recognise the right of self-defence for Black Americans, firmly rooted in the broader Black Power movement, which sought justice in housing, jobs and education.

Newton believed fervently in Black people's personal development, and his revolutionary recruitment was centred on improving people's knowledge of institutions and their rights.

But there was much political and personal conflict ahead.

Newton spent six months in prison after being convicted of assault with a deadly weapon for repeatedly stabbing another man in 1964. And in 1967, when he was out of his probationary period, a fracas with Oakland police led to the death of one officer and the wounding of another. Newton took a bullet to the abdomen and was arrested. He was later convicted of voluntary manslaughter for the killing of the policeman, although the charges were dismissed.

Newton and a small group of Panthers visited China in 1971, legendarily greeted by thousands waving copies of Mao's *The Little Red Book* and displaying Black Power placards when they arrived. Newton met representatives from North Korea, Tanzania, North Vietnam and South Vietnam while they were in China, a country he described as 'free and liberated'.

But he would again be associated with violence in 1974 when he shot an 18-year-old woman who later died, and assaulted his tailor. He then fled to Cuba where he remained until 1977, after which he returned to the US to stand trial for those crimes.

Chaotic testimony saw him acquitted of the assault – although he was convicted on illegal arms possession – and eventually not tried for the murder after a key witness suffered an assassination attempt at the hands of the Panthers, and declined to testify.

Newton got a PhD in social philosophy at the University of California, Santa Cruz, in 1980 for his dissertation 'War Against the Panthers: A Study of Repression in America'.

He was murdered in 1989 in West Oakland, California.

[Hevesi, 1989; www.lib.berkeley.edu]

Bobby Seale (1936–)

Seale grew up mostly in poverty in Texas and California, joining the US Air Force after leaving school early. He was dishonourably discharged after a battle with a commanding officer in South Dakota, and then decided to study engineering. He soon signed up for the AAA as a student, whereupon he and Newton formed a close bond.

Seale was intent on social programmes that would give Black teenagers insight into Black American history and teach them community responsibility.

Before they founded the Panthers, Seale and Newton created the Soul Students Advisory Council whose aim was to develop young Black leadership 'and serve the Black community in a revolutionary fashion'. Seale saw the Panthers' fight as being against a 'racist decadent, capitalistic system', and believed white radicals could be incorporated into that fight.

Seale's 1970 book *Seize the Time: The Story of the Black Panther Party and Huey P Newton* is a rarity in publishing as its material was derived mainly from tape recordings he made to give an understanding of the Party and the oppression of African-Americans.

Seale was jailed after an uprising following protests over the Vietnam War at the Democratic National Convention in Chicago in 1968, and his revolutionary outbursts in court saw musician Graham Nash[50] devote some of the lyrics of the song 'Chicago' to him. Poet Gil Scott-Heron[51] also referred to 'the chaining and gagging of Bobby Seale' in his 'H2Ogate Blues'.

Seale served four years and was released in 1972 but was again in the sights of law enforcers when he was implicated in a murder after the mutilated remains of his wife Artie's lover, fellow Panther Fred Bennett, were found. No charges were pressed.

Newton and Seale were later said to have had a harrowing and violent physical encounter, which apparently left Seale needing bouts of treatment for his injuries. Newton was alleged to have been assisted in that terror by armed bodyguards. Although Seale then seemingly went into hiding and ended his association with the Panthers, he denied the fight with Newton.

His autobiography, *A Lonely Rage*, came out in 1978.

Seale generally devoted himself after that to youth leadership,

---

50   Graham Nash (1942–) wrote 'Chicago/We Can Change the World' for *Songs for Beginners* with title and lyrics referring to the trial of those arrested at the Democratic National Convention in Chicago. Dubbed the Chicago 8, they were charged by the US government with conspiracy to incite a riot. Bobby Seale, the only Black defendant, was shackled for outbursts in court, hence the first line of Nash's song: 'So your brother's bound and gagged, and they've chained him to a chair.' Defendants included Abbie Hoffman and Tom Hayden. All were acquitted.

51   Gil Scott-Heron (1949–2011) was an American poet and musician whose 'The Revolution Will Not Be Televised' has held power since 1970. In its obituary, the *Guardian* described Scott-Heron's debut LP, *Small Talk at 125th and Lenox*, as 'proselytizing spoken-word... set to a sparse, funky tableau of percussion... [which] served as a militant manifesto urging Black pride (Power, 2011: https://www.theguardian.com/music/2011/may/28/gil-scott-heron-obituary).

education and upliftment, although he also taught Black Studies at Temple University in Philadelphia and continued to speak at many campuses about his experiences as a Panther and on how to organise and raise people up within Black communities.

[www.marxists.org; Epstein, 2001]

Assata Shakur (1947–)

Born JoAnne Deborah Bryon in 1947, the Black liberation activist renamed herself Assata ('she who struggles') Olugbala ('for the people') Shakur ('the thankful one'), describing herself as 'a 20th-century escaped slave'. (She is also cited as JoAnne Chesimard, which is her married surname.)

Shakur was radicalised by opposition to the Vietnam War, saying of the anti-Communist ideologies rife through her childhood: 'Only a fool lets somebody else tell him who his enemy is.'

She joined the Harlem branch of the Black Panthers in 1970 but became disillusioned and joined the more radical Black Liberation Army (BLA), which tilted at armed resistance. Shakur was accused of kidnapping, armed robbery, attempted murder and murder between April 1971 and January 1973, but it was only in May 1973, when she and two other BLA members were stopped for a traffic violation, that the authorities were able to get her behind bars on an actual charge.

Shakur, who was shot twice during an ensuing gunfight with the New Jersey State Police, was put on trial for the killing of police officer Werner Foerster. Convicted of first-degree murder, and despite a debilitating wound she received during the shoot-out, she was sentenced to life plus 30 years in 1977.

Shakur spent more than six years in prison, during which time a cassette was smuggled out in which she was recorded as saying: 'I have declared war on the rich who prosper on our poverty, the politicians who lie to us with smiling faces, and all the mindless, heartless robots who protect them and their property.

'I am a Black revolutionary and, as such, I am a victim of all the wrath, hatred and slander that amerika is capable of. Like all Black revolutionaries, amerika is trying to lynch me.'

But Shakur was able to escape the maximum-security wing of the

Clinton Correctional Facility for Women in New Jersey in 1979, and she then lived as a fugitive before being given asylum in Cuba by Fidel Castro.

'Because of government persecution, I was left with no other choice than to flee from the political repression, racism and violence that dominate the US government's policy towards people of colour,' Shakur writes on her website, www.assatashakur.org.

'I am an ex-political prisoner and I have been living in exile in Cuba since 1984. I have been a political activist most of my life, and although the US government has done everything in its power to criminalise me, I am not a criminal, nor have I ever been one.'

The FBI placed Shakur on its Most Wanted list.

Shakur was slain rapper Tupac Shakur's godmother. Tupac was himself immersed in the Black Panthers and Black revolutionary politics from an early age. Renamed before he was two after Túpac Amaru II – the 18th-century Peruvian revolutionary executed after leading an indigenous uprising against colonial rule – his mother Afeni and his father Billy Garland were active Panthers.

Tupac was born just weeks after his mother was acquitted of more than 150 charges of 'conspiracy against the US government and New York landmarks'. Tupac's godfather, Elmer 'Geronimo' Pratt, was also a Panther, as was his stepfather, Mutulu, who spent four years at large also on the FBI's Most Wanted list for having helped Assata Shakur, his sister, escape from prison.

In July 2017, American left-wing activists came under fire in some reactionary media in the US after a tweetstorm ensued in defence of Shakur on her 70th birthday. The activists call her a 'civil rights leader', while her detractors and political enemies were quick to describe her only as 'a convicted cop killer'. In June 2017, Trump called on Cuba to send Shakur back to the US. He was widely reported in the international media as saying: 'Return the fugitives from American justice, including the return of the cop killer Joanne Chesimard.'

[www.assatashakur.org; Socialist Worker, 2020]

Angela Davis (1944–)

In her biography on www.blackpast.org, Davis's middle-class birthplace, Dynamite Hill in Birmingham, Alabama, is described as having been named that way as so many Black homes had been bombed over the years by the Ku Klux Klan.

Davis's mother Sallye, a teacher, was active in the Southern Negro Youth Congress, and it was when Angela moved to New York City and attended the Elizabeth Irwin High School that the teenager became more deeply politicised. (The school was considered 'leftist' because a number of its teachers were blacklisted during the McCarthy era for their earlier alleged communist activities.)

Davis was so moved by the horrifying deaths of four girls in the racist bombing of the Sixteenth Street Baptist Church in her home town in 1963 that she first joined the civil rights movement, then the Black Power movement and, finally, was associated with the Black Panthers.

She got her MA at the University of California at San Diego in 1968, the same year she joined the American Communist Party – a decision that got her dismissed from her post as an assistant professor of philosophy at UCLA.

Davis's earlier work concentrated on improving prison conditions for African-American inmates and a campaign to release the 'Soledad Brothers', George Jackson, Fleeta Drumgo and John Clutchette, who were charged with the murder of a white prison guard and jailed in the notorious O wing of Soledad State Prison in California.

She was placed on the FBI's Most Wanted list after Jonathan Jackson, George's younger brother, attempted to free the men while they appeared in court. The judge, Harold Haley, and three others, including Jonathan Jackson, were killed, and although Davis did not take part, she was a suspect when it was found that the guns Jackson used were registered in her name.

Davis fled and, although she spent 16 months behind bars and was later put on trial, she was acquitted. Among her many supporters were John Lennon and Yoko Ono, Castro, Erich Honeker of East Germany, and Russian dissident and Nobel Laureate Aleksandr Solzhenitsyn. This didn't help her secure a job as a teacher, as then

California Governor Ronald Reagan campaigned to prevent her from being employed in the state university system.

She did get hired, though – as a lecturer in women's and ethnic studies at San Francisco State University in 1977. Since then, Davis has authored several books, and is a pre-eminent figure in the prison abolitionist movement in the US.

She has also run for office as vice-president of the US on the Communist Party ticket and continues to be an activist in her role as Distinguished Professor Emeritus of History of Consciousness and Feminist Studies at the University of California at Santa Cruz.

Davis was prominent and active throughout the 2020 protests and uprisings, accentuating the ideologies of Black Power as she always has. In a virtual American University (AU) event on 23 September 2020, the first in a Black Lives Matter speaker series, Davis 'discussed the inherently racist structures of society today in the US and other countries'.

The Eagle, which carries the views of and news about the AU, wrote: '[Davis] said the resistance... has collectivised on an international level against these structures, such as during a protest that occurred in Palestine over the killing of George Floyd in support of the BLM movement.

'"Despite BLM being a largely American-based movement, supporters have made themselves known around the world," Davis said. '"We can't understand racism, and we certainly can't develop strategies to eliminate it unless we look at it in a global context."'

[www.blackpast.org; Manhattan, 2020: https://www.theeagleonline.com/article/2020/09/angela-davis-calls-for-justice-not-just-diversity-and-inclusion-at-virtual-au-event]

The Nation of Islam (NOI)

Although the NOI leadership has in recent times shifted towards L Ron Hubbard's Scientology, it started as a Black political and religious movement in Detroit, Michigan, in 1930. It was founded by Wallace Fard Muhammad with the goal to 'improve the spiritual, mental, social, and economic condition of African-Americans in the US and all of humanity'.

In spite of the fact that it is an independent Muslim movement distinct from the mainstream Islamic community, it has been described as 'Black supremacist', 'anti-Semitic' and a 'hate group', and its membership runs to the tens of thousands.

Elijah Muhammad succeeded Fard in 1934, and established NOI temples and mosques, and the Muhammad University of Islam. The NOI also owns farms and other property and land in the US and abroad.

The suspension of former NOI senior leader Malcolm X had a profound effect on it. Malcolm X was later assassinated by a member of the NOI while speaking at a rally for his Organisation of Afro-American Unity in Washington Heights, Manhattan, in 1965.

After Elijah Muhammed died in 1975, his son Warith Deen Mohammed tried to convert NOI to a Sunni Muslim-focused ideology, but leader Farrakhan rejected Mohammed's leadership and re-established the NOI on the original model.

The Caribbean and Britain's Black Power movement

In 2013, *The Guardian* published arts correspondent Mark Brown's review of a new biography of the Trinidad-born radical journalist, writer and civil liberties campaigner, Darcus Howe. *Darcus Howe: A Political Biography* (Bloomsbury) was written by Robin Bunce and Paul Field, and caused a stir for its searing critique of Britain's relationship to Black liberation politics.

A pro-independence activist born in Trinidad, Howe (1943–2017) joined the British Black Panthers in the 1960s after he arrived in England to study law. He gained widespread attention when he was named one of the Mangrove Nine who marched to the Notting Hill, London police station in 1970 to protest raids of the legendary The Mangrove restaurant.

He then gave up his studies to pursue Black politics and journalism in an act which would surely have made his uncle, the admired Trinidadian intellectual and Marxist historian CLR James, proud. James fundamentally believed in the Black working class.

The Mangrove, a 'decolonised' venue, 'served as a wider Black culture community centre', writes Brown, who reflects on how

'Britain's Black power movement is [now] being written out of recent cultural history because it does not fit into the "utopian" narrative of the UK being a nation of civilised fair play'.

He quotes Cambridge academic Bunce as saying, 'There is a fundamental danger of erasing the very notion of a struggle at all. There have been so many occasions when people have said to me: "There was no Black struggle in Britain. You're thinking of South Africa or America."'

Bunce's view is: 'The narrative that feeds it is the one that Britain is the utopia of fair play. We have such a commitment to individual rights, we have such a commitment to common sense and decency that there is no systematic racism in Britain.'

Bunce and Field argue that 'there has been a resurgence of outright denial, linked to the romantic, dumbed-down ... view of history that suggests racism was always someone else's problem'.

They examine how former British prime ministers and Labour Party leaders Tony Blair and Gordon Brown gave speeches in which they spoke about how Britain had abolished slavery, 'not how the nation was complicit in it'.

Their summary is that this effectively meant 'there was no need for a Black rights movement [and] any Black person who says they are being discriminated against is clearly just making it up, because the British are just so fair'.

Black Power really took off in Britain after Black resistance leader Stokely Carmichael gave a speech in London in 1967 that led to the establishment of the United Coloured People's Association and the British Black Panthers.

Bunce writes in the Howe biography about how The Mangrove was suspected as being a place for 'terrorists' to gather in a system which 'fundamentally believed Black radicalism was criminal'. Although the Mangrove Nine were acquitted when an all-Black jury was demanded, and Howe was later a co-organiser of the 1981 Black People's Day of Action to protest police mishandling of a fire in which 13 young Black people died, there was very little known about the Black Power movement until this biography was published in 2013. This, says Bunce, is despite the movement helping to create 'real social change' and a 'cultural shift' that led to greater equality.

Four years later, in April 2017, Bunce and Field were writing Howe's obituary for *The Guardian*, describing how 'his aims were radical, and he brought them into the mainstream by articulating fundamental principles in a strikingly outspoken way'.

Yet they fear Howe, like so many other Black Power activists of his era in Britain, could still be largely forgotten if the British Black struggle is not brought into schools in the UK, and is not debated and discussed enough to simply become part of more mainstream British thought.

Howe and the Race Today Collective recorded significant BC-driven grassroots campaigns in Britain and abroad from 1973. Led and organised mostly by women, the collective included his wife, Leila Hassan Howe (1948–), a prominent British editor, writer and activist.

Involved in Black Power activism since the late 1960s, she was a member of the Black Unity and Freedom Party and the British Black Panthers.

Among her own BC political actions, Hassan campaigned for Arts Council England to recognise the Notting Hill Carnival as an art form and was also co-organiser of the 20 000-strong Black People's Day of Action march through London.

Others involved in the Race Today Collective were the great dub poet Linton Kwesi Johnson,[52] celebrated writer and broadcaster Farrukh Dhondy and human rights activist and *Bandit Queen* writer Mala Sen (who was once married to Dhondy).

Tension grew around the 1981 Black People's Day of Action, leading to the three days of the Brixton Riots.[53] Not much seemed to

---

52   Linton Kwesi Johnson (1952–), also known as LKJ, is a Jamaican dub poet and activist who has lived in the UK since 1963. A prize-winning writer and performer, LKJ is a Trustee of the George Padmore Institute, earned Jamaica's Order of Distinction and was given an Honorary Doctorate of Literature by Rhodes University in South Africa. LKJ's albums include *Dread Beat an' Blood* (1978) and *Bass Culture* (1980), and one of his most well-loved poems is 'Di Great Insohreckshan', a response to the 1981 Brixton Riots.

53   The Brixton Riots were a confrontation between the London Metropolitan Police and thousands of mostly Afro-Caribbean protestors in the depressed area of Brixton, South London between 10 and 12 April 1981. 'Bloody Saturday', April 11, saw multiple injuries. A public inquiry was commissioned and a new

have shifted between 1970 and 1981. Thereafter numbers of uprisings broke out in Black and Afro-Caribbean communities around England.

Howe – who had worked with Guyanese scholar, Pan-Africanist and political activist Walter Rodney on political programmes in Brooklyn, New York – was publicly associated with his friend Dhondy after Dhondy commissioned Howe's prime-time TV series, *The Bandung File* (which ran from 1985 to 1991), for Britain's Channel 4.

Rodney, who was assassinated in Guyana in 1980, was a dazzling mind – and such a threat to colonial 'peace' that he was effectively banned from Jamaica in 1968 because of his activism among the working poor.

The decision to refuse Rodney entry led to deadly uprisings in Jamaica still known as the Rodney Riots, but the uprisings also heightened Black political consciousness throughout the Caribbean.

Rodney then founded the Working People's Alliance in opposition to the government. He was killed by a bomb in his car in 1980 at just 38, having returned to his home country after attending independence celebrations in Zimbabwe.

Howe would, however, be given a safer, if still challenging, space to put race and class front and centre in *The Bandung File*, where he steered traditional white British authority into the general gaze – confronting it, making it uncomfortable and compelling it to account.

Howe continued in that vein with the documentaries *White Tribe* (2000) and the three-part *Slave Nation* (2001) in which, say Bunce and Field in their obituary in *The Guardian*, he examined 'Britishness and whiteness ... with considerable foresight'.

Even in 2011, Britain had clearly not yet come to terms with its flawed relationship to Blackness. There were uprisings across England after police shot dead a 29-year-old Black man, Mark Duggan, in Tottenham, north London, while he was being arrested on suspicion of planning to use a handgun in an attack. Duggan's death and those uprisings are still the subject of considerable controversy.

---

code for police emerged in 1985. After Black British teenager Stephen Lawrence was murdered in a racially motivated attack in April 1993, another investigation concluded the police force was 'institutionally racist'.

Not long before he died of prostate cancer, wrote Bunce and Field, Howe was working with the production team of Black British director John Ridley's political TV drama *Guerrilla*. He and his wife, Leila, advised them on the politics of the 1970s and the British Black Power movement.

The Guardian's Ellen E Jones told how *Guerrilla*, which first aired in 2017 on the Sky Atlantic channel in Britain, tells 'an imagined story of a couple as they form an underground cell to fight oppression'.

Co-starring Frieda Pinto and Idris Elba and 'set within the real-life context of London's 1970s Black Power movement', *Guerrilla* was designed to reveal a history which few Britons know anything about.

Jones writes that 'most people know more about the US history of slavery and civil rights than they do about Britain's own involvement in the slave trade, the Brixton uprisings or the Mangrove Nine'. But Ridley – who won an Oscar in 2013 for Best Adapted Screenplay for fellow Oscar-winner Steve McQueen's film *12 Years a Slave* – may have achieved something even the activists have not yet been allowed to do.

His six-part mini-series on Black Power was well received, writes Jones, and because Britons are keener on TV than almost anything else, they may indeed have absorbed a truth to which they had not been introduced before. Racism is real. Anti-Blackness is real.

Hassan Howe co-edited *Here to Stay, Here to Fight* (2019), a collection of radical Black writing from the *Race Today* journal.

[Brown, 2013; BBC, 2017]

Steve McQueen (1969–)

Ridley's *Guerrilla* opened the way to more such television and filmmaking, with the epic Black British and Black Indian anthology, *Small Axe*, predominant among these. It started shooting in 2016 under director McQueen, who also co-wrote it, with the BBC the original commissioning channel.

Top film industry and review website, *Indie Wire*, captured its context which is rooted in BC as it concerns the arrival of the ship Empire Windrush in June 1948 – 'a landmark of post-war mass migration of Caribbean people to Britain'.

'That multi-decade history – which lasted through the 1970s – has been largely ignored by popular culture. McQueen [aims] to rectify that oversight with [this] ambitious ... anthology series [comprising] five original films, set from the 1960s to the 1980s, which collectively tell the story of Britain's West Indian community.

McQueen – who had been trying to make *Small Axe* for 11 years – describes the anthology to *Indie Wire* as that of 'people ... shaped by their own force of will despite rampant racism and discrimination'.

'Raised by a Grenadan father and Trinidadian mother in London' McQueen said he was 'one of only a few storytellers given the opportunity to explore the culture in question'.

'We're missing two generations or so of Black artists in the UK because that industry was not welcoming to Black people. There's a hole in our narrative. These stories shaped the history of the UK.'

'The title, *Small Axe*,' explains *Indie Wire*, 'comes from a proverb that has resonance throughout the Caribbean ... popularised by Bob Marley in The Wailers song 'Small Axe' from the album *Burnin'* (1973): "If you are the big tree, we are the small axe." This speaks to the little-known stories of Black pride and resilience demonstrated during what has come to be known as the Mangrove March.

'And while that story is unique to British history, it resonates globally today against the backdrop of Black Lives Matter, and especially following the tragic deaths of George Floyd, Breonna Taylor, and Ahmaud Arbery.'

Three of its films – *Lovers Rock*, *Mangrove* and *Red, White and Blue* – premiered at the New York Film Festival in September 2020 and were included in the official Cannes 2020 selection. 'When McQueen's films were selected for Cannes, he said in a statement that he was dedicating the projects to Floyd's memory.'

'The two-hour *Mangrove* ... – which begins after Enoch Powell's "Rivers of Blood" speech in 1968.'[54] – celebrates the courage of the women and men known as the Mangrove Nine – Darcus Howe, Frank

---

54   *Indie Wire* explains: 'Enoch Powell was an English far-rightist who gave a now infamous speech attacking the British government's immigration policy, calling it "a dangerous delusion". He said Britain had to be crazy to allow more immigrants into the country. "In this country in 15 or 20 years' time, the Black man will have the whip hand over the white.. Like the Roman, I seem to see the river Tiber foaming with much blood."'

Crichlow, Altheia Jones-LeCointe, Barbara Beese, Rupert Boyce, Rhodan Gordon, Anthony Innis, Rothwell Kentish and Godfrey Millett – who took on systemic racism…'

McQueen was appointed Officer of the Order of the British Empire (OBE) in 2002, Commander of the Order of the British Empire (CBE) in 2011 and was knighted in 2020 for services to film. He is thus Sir Steven Rodney McQueen (CBE).

[Obenson, T, 2020: https://www.indiewire.com/2020/09/small-axe-steve-mcqueen-interview-1234586832/]

Farrukh Dhondy (1944–)

Born in Pune, India, Dhondy is a writer, playwright, screenwriter and left-wing and race activist, who has lived in England since he won a scholarship to study in Cambridge to read natural sciences. He then switched to English and, after lecturing in Leicester, got involved with the Indian Workers' Association and then the British Black Panther movement.

Dhondy, whose BC extends across academic theory to Bollywood, has a significant literary output. So diverse is his body of work that it includes a biography of the Trinidadian Marxist CLR James and the children's book *KBW (Keep Britain White)*, about a boy's response to anti-Bengali racism.

Three

Black Consciousness and Christianity

Compiled by Janet Smith and Paballo Thekiso

Christianity was a natural springboard for BC. Priests, nuns, theologians, clerics and worshippers across denominations played an unassailable role in raising consciousness, often more fearlessly than politicians, academics and artists. Faith, as can be interpreted from the Bible, offered activist Christians an invisible cloak, which atheists and non-believers experienced in its unflinching human flutter.

Christianity played an enormous role in the birth of BC in South Africa. And while it is indeed true that our consciousness would have emerged with or without particular individuals, the overarching community that Black churches and their leaders offered to the oppressed helped guide the country to certain freedom.

From 'guerrilla priest' Anglican Rubin Phillip to the Lutheran Manas Buthelezi, from the Pentecostal razzmatazz of Allan Boesak to Afrikaner renegade Beyers Naudé and Europeans funding liberation using god as their cover, Christianity and BC are entwined like incense smoke in the apse.

'God's not dead': Fighter priests, the University Christian Movement (UCM) and the hot pew

In the early 1960s, white Catholics, Anglicans, Methodists, Presbyterians, Congregationalists and Baptists lived in segregated neighbourhoods, worshipped separately from their 'non-white' brothers and sisters, and revered their 'mother' churches abroad as they shared the provision of Sunday's meat and two veg for their mostly foreign clergymen.

Apartheid had been declared just over a decade earlier, in 1948. Its tenets entrenched a national Christian ethos which, said the ruling National Party, meant God had ordained distinct 'development' for whites and Blacks. Still some distance away from the 'African culture' con of the bantustans and a decade from sanctions, South African whites were hardened to their Black compatriots' lives. Ruled by supremacist Christian nationalists, Black people freshly agonised by the massacre in Sharpeville were subjected to increasingly savage repression. But white people still filed into church in their suburban and rural masses.

God was, after all, on their side. For them, there was no struggle.

South Africa became a Christian Republic in 1961 with apartheid the law. Church benches, like all benches, were not allowed to be shared. It would take a white Christian Afrikaner nationalist to rattle that perspective because such a person was the only type other whites listened to. They didn't know that Beyers Naudé – with his French Huguenot refugee roots and a father who served in the Anglo-Boer War – would not only support the liberation of Black people, but BC.

The ability, not to say the potential, for Black people to even think for themselves was not in the heads of most white people. They pledged themselves to a racist god, with a Bible – used as a racist instrument of propaganda – that agreed with them.

A Stellenbosch University graduate whose sociology lecturer was the chief architect of apartheid, HF Verwoerd, Naudé was ordained in the white- and Afrikaner-controlled Nederduitse Gereformeerde Kerk (NGK, Dutch Reformed Church), just as the Second World War started in 1939.

As was the tradition of those favoured within the white patriarchy, he joined the Broederbond and then also became a moderator at his church synod. These were very specific powers within the white Afrikaner community. With the backing of the Christian faith, they represented considerable access.

Naudé was settled among other well-off Afrikaners in the Aasvoëlkop NGK community in Northcliff, Johannesburg, when Sharpeville happened in March 1960. Shocked and requiring a response, the World Council of Churches (WCC) – to which the NGK belonged – approached eight South African church denominations, including the NGK, for a consultation in the wake of the state-sanctioned killings. That gathering happened nine months later in Cottesloe, Johannesburg, and many of the 80 church delegates there agreed on its unexpected conclusion.

Naudé – who had spent his career as a preacher abiding by a Christian morality that sought to justify apartheid – was ultimately among those who then refused to continue to condone a scriptural or theological basis for apartheid. This was even as Verwoerd instructed the NGK delegation at Cottesloe to repudiate the consultation.

The NGK would quit the WCC in disgust while Naudé would in turn abandon the church of his calling and resign from the Broederbond. There was no going back for him from there.

The consultation looked at ways to resist apartheid, discussing the rejection of a theological rationale for white supreme rule.

Its resolutions included that the prohibition of mixed marriages was not supported in the Bible; migrant labour had a destructive effect on Black families; no Christian 'believer' should be excluded from any church on the grounds of race; and, importantly in terms of a theme which dominated within the BCM years later, owning land was an inherent right.

The Cottesloe Consultation has, however, been somewhat diminished in liberation history for being a largely white event at which Black people were not much more than token delegates. But such was the rage from the white Christian Afrikaner community after Cottesloe that Naudé became its favoured pariah. And so, by 1963 – 36 months after liberation movements had been banned by the regime – he was instead dedicating himself to the development of the Christian Institute (CI), 'an ecumenical interest group', and its monthly anti-apartheid journal, *Pro Veritate*.

His ideal, if not his dream, was that a 'confessing community' – modelled on the Confessing Church in Germany in which thousands of clergy embarked on collective action to oppose genocidal Führer Adolf Hitler and his Third Reich – could be established among Blacks and whites in South Africa. But even the CI, with its philosophical basis in the franchise for all, could not entirely shake off a dominant white value system inculcated in many of its members from birth.

More than a decade later, for instance, CI seemed prepared to give its backing to support for the bantustans. The Bantu Homelands Citizenship Act, passed in 1970, said Blacks could be 'legal citizens' in areas designated for different ethnic groups, but in no way did this Act give them citizenship, or civil and political rights. Transkei then 'gained' what the apartheid regime dubbed 'independence' in 1976, followed by Bophuthatswana in 1977, Venda in 1979 and Ciskei in 1981. The rest – Gazankulu, KaNgwane, KwaNdebele, KwaZulu, Lebowa and QwaQwa – would remain 'self-governing territories'.

On the face of it, and especially four decades later, it seems a blight on his history that Naudé issued a joint statement in 1976 with Buthelezi in support a year before. (Later, the IFP and supporters of the ANC would be involved in what amounted to a merciless civil war that would come to include two massacres – Trust Feed, which left 11 people dead in a rural village in the Natal Midlands in December 1988, and Boipatong, which left 45 people murdered in 1992 after 300 armed men from a hostel in the nearby township of Sebokeng attacked them.)

In retrospect, that joint statement is a source of confusion, perhaps clearly reflective of CI's internal struggles.

With his Black Power posturing and initial support from the ANC in exile, Buthelezi had long gained the trust of the established English liberal camp led by Harry Schwarz of the United Party. But as early as 1967, Buthelezi was ignored if not ostracised by the nearly 90 South African clerics and students who attended the inaugural congress of the UCM in Grahamstown.

There had been pressure from Christian organisations abroad since Sharpeville and, in particular, the World Student Christian Federation (WSCF) had kept vocal and public its objections to apartheid. Its relationship with its South African affiliate, the Students Christian Association (SCA) – which operated in racially divided schools and on campuses across South Africa – was affected by this, although the SCA had both Black and white leadership in its national council.

The WSCF had already in 1964 'deplored' the failure of the SCA 'to disassociate itself in word and act' from apartheid, and the federation had been among those organisations that had urged sanctions against the Republic. And so the SCA withdrew from the WSCF, disbanded in 1965 and replaced itself with four bodies ostensibly distinguished by way of language: English and Afrikaans whites; Black people, and coloured and Indian Christians.

Liberal white Christian students and young Black Christians then began to caucus outside these organisations in 1966 as an ecumenical movement, finally gathering in Rosettenville, Johannesburg, to plan their next stage that December.

Ideas were developed for what would become the UCM and it was decided a conference would be held in Grahamstown the following July. SASO would be born out of the UCM's second 1968 conference in Stutterheim, and so that juncture – Rosettenville – is vital to a timeline of the movement.

Father Colin Collins, a priest working for the South African Catholic Bishops Conference, was one of the first leaders of the UCM. He explained that most of the white students who came to the UCM in its first couple of years were interested in finding a meaning for their Christianity in an apartheid society and wanted to become actively involved.

'On a theological level, the "God is dead" controversy was predominant.

'Most of the Black people who came into the UCM were, from an ecclesiastical viewpoint, far more conservative and traditional than the whites. They were mainly in the UCM because it was an organisation in which they could get together to discuss the South African situation and their position in it.

'At that point in time, the UCM was the only suitable organisation in existence where this could take place.'

Collins, however, importantly observed that even had the UCM not been formed, BC would still have 'taken place'.

'What animated those of us who initiated the UCM was a deep sense of social justice. The polarisation strategy was a direct result of the Black people themselves discarding their own sense of inferiority; the encouragement that they received from within the UCM was to "go it" on their own. The BCM was created by young Black leaders and by them alone.'

Collins's fellow theologian Basil Moore was elected president of the UCM and, together with teacher Winnie Kgware, was on the first UCM executive.

In the citation for Moore as a doctor of laws *honoris causa* at Rhodes in April 2011, Professor Paul Maylam, head of the department of history and distinguished professor, described how 'a general mood of acquiescence' towards apartheid from the SCA had helped bring the UCM to life. It quickly attracted 3 000 members who established 30 branches across South African campuses within two years. Black students made up a significant majority of those members.

Maylam tells how the UCM 'organised interracial "work" camps and group discussions, promoted Black Theology, prioritised the pursuit of social justice and practised a free, unconventional style of worship'.

Within a year, that second, even more critical UCM congress was held in Stutterheim, a small town in the border region of the Eastern Cape. This was the one that Biko attended with Pityana and others who would steer BC. Young Anglican priest Desmond Tutu was there along with other theologians who would provide moral support, such as the Reverend Simon Gqubule, who much later became president of the Rhodes Convocation. (Attached to the Federal Theological Seminary, based close to Fort Hare in Alice, Gqubule, Tutu and Aelred Stubbs would later informally teach UCM members.)

In the citation for Moore, Maylam noted that 'it was Gqubule who ordained Moore almost 50 years ago – the first time a white Methodist minister had been ordained by a Black minister in South Africa'.

He also related the history as it unfolded: 'At this Stutterheim conference, it was decided to establish a Black caucus, out of which would emerge SASO, the first major BC organisation to be established – the body that brought Biko to the forefront'.

In the background, the *Message to the People of South Africa*, a 'directive' from a collective of mostly white church leaders, was issued, stating that apartheid was 'authoritarian and racially repressive'.

But there was no such *mea culpa* from Rhodes, which is why Maylam said in the citation: 'It might be thought that the award of this honorary doctorate is just an act of repentance on the part of Rhodes University ... There is much more to it than this ... [Moore] was a brilliant teacher with an exciting, radical vision of the Christian faith ... and a deep antipathy to racism which rubbed off on renowned figures like Steve Biko and Beyers Naudé.

Then, in 1969, Naudé's CI and the SACC launched what was to become a pre-eminent inquiry: the Study Project on Christianity in Apartheid Society (SPRO-CAS). A strategy that came out of the partnership established at the Cottesloe Consultation, the study happened against a backdrop of growing international church and other funding and support being garnered for the liberation movements including the PAC, Swapo and the ANC in exile.

SPRO-CAS co-ordinator Peter Randall – then assistant director of the SAIRR – oversaw the project's publication of anti-apartheid writing, including poetry by BC champions James Matthews and Gladys Thomas. Randall later became director of Ravan Press, which was started at the height of repression against the BMC in 1972 by Naudé, the rebel Afrikaner cleric Danie van Zyl and Randall (Ravan is an anagram of their names).

SPRO-CAS 2 followed, with Biko and Khoapa agreeing with Randall to divide the Study into a BCP and a 'white consciousness' programme, to allow the BCM to properly develop its own projects for Black communities. (The white programme was led by Kleinschmidt.) SPRO-CAS 2 ran until the bannings of 1977, operating a number of commissions and issuing reports on social justice from a Christian perspective that remain part of the significant record of the BCP.

Particularly important among these were the writings of Rick Turner. Like Biko, Turner contributed to SPRO-CAS 2, although he was perhaps more radical than Randall. That said, Randall, who provided intellectual support to BC, put forward important challenges such as what the WCC, which was helping to fund the liberation movements, imagined the politics of southern African countries would look like should those movements enter power.

Randall also defended socialism even on public platforms as late as 1977.

There was ideological push and pull. While bolstered by foreign agencies and some white congregants and clergy in South Africa, BC continued to openly reject white liberalism. Meanwhile SPRO-CAS 2, which had worked to exceed the Christian liberal roots of its predecessor programme, would face opposition from some reactionary members of the SACC.

It was conflict like this that presented challenges for the SACC, especially around BC. It was having to define itself in the early to mid-1970s amid widespread state crackdowns. Its UDF-era secretary-general Frank Chikane would as late as 1987 admit it had engaged in internal battles.

What was it? A theological body? A political body? Was it possible to say it represented Black people and rejected apartheid without being considered so 'political' by some of its white membership that it became irrevocably divided? That said, when the UCM was declared an 'affected' organisation, unable to receive foreign funding and effectively shut down by the apartheid state in the early 1970s, the SACC was forced to react. It was, after all, indirectly a supporter of SASO.

Certainly, the UCM founding congress in Grahamstown, which took place directly after a divisive NUSAS congress, had presented an alternative picture of a unitary future as Black students, many of them Catholics and Anglicans, dominated. And they came from all over the country, among the most prominent being Pityana from the Eastern Cape, Nengwekhulu and Machaka from what is now Limpopo, and Goolam Abram from Durban.

The UCM flouted all apartheid's expectations of the Black student. It brazenly introduced Black Theology and Latin American and African-American-style liberation theology and it was also at the first congress that Freire's thought took hold, in part by way of Moore and

Collins. The two men then started publishing a journal, *One for the Road*, which propagated those liberation and Black theological concepts.

A certain internationalism would also influence the UCM as especially American donors put money into the movement, encouraging other overseas Christian organisations to do the same. But there was no such support from the university administrations. In much the same way Rhodes had sought to intimidate and alienate Moore and others, Fort Hare's rector Professor JM de Wet refused a request by law students and BC student leaders Barney Pityana and Justice Moloto for recognition for the movement.[55]

As had happened at Rhodes around Moore, the students at Fort Hare protested and the police were brought onto campus. But De Wet struck back further. A decision was taken to cancel the registration of all students in 1968. They would have to reapply for admission and this of course meant that those Black students deemed too radical for the white leadership could simply be excluded.

SASO members Moloto, fellow law student Madibeng Chris Mokoditoa and [Stanley] Ntwasa – who would go on to become an Anglican priest and a close friend of Biko – were the only full-time UCM staffers. Ntwasa, who was from Kimberley, had been a student at St Peter's Seminary in Rosettenville and was an exponent of Black Theology.

But the axis between the two organisations was such that UCM, which had the donor funding and global solidarity because of its Christian ethos, could successfully partner SASO in its recruitment and work on the ground. *Samizdat*, or underground political publications, could also be distributed using the channels afforded by the UCM.

In the end, though, it was the dissemination of that 'prohibited' literature that got the UCM barred from 'bush' campuses Turfloop, Fort Hare, the University of Zululand-Ngoye and UWC.

Undeterred, Naudé lobbied a printing press out of the Dutch

---

55   Moloto became a judge at the International Criminal Tribunal for the former Yugoslavia in The Hague, having been a judge at South Africa's Land Claims Court. Pityana, who also studied theology, became director of the Programme to Combat Racism at the WCC in Geneva, chairperson of the South African Human Rights Commission, vice-chancellor of Unisa, president of Convocation at UCT and served on the African Commission.

and German church sponsors of SPRO-CAS: a key intervention as most commercial printers were not prepared to print underground material due to the heavy-handed response from agents of the apartheid state. Even more vicious was the state's approach to Christian renegades and the BCM.

Collins, who came under a banning order and house arrest, was forced into exile in 1971, followed by Moore. Moloto and Ntwasa were also banned.

Ntwasa was training at St Peter's when he was placed under house arrest in Kimberley. Anglican monk Stubbs, who was a mentor of Ntwasa's, described him as 'a passionate advocate of BC', and explained that Ntwasa had been 'permitted to interrupt his ministerial training for a year in 1971 to act as travelling secretary of the UCM with special responsibility for promoting the growth of Black Theology ... on campuses all over the Republic'.

It was that 'subversive' activity which got Ntwasa banished.

The great Durban cleric, Bishop Rubin Phillip – who was dubbed 'the guerrilla priest' – described Ntwasa as 'a legend'. He told journalist Carlos Amato that Ntwasa was 'a tall, awkward guy who drank too much and smoked too much and everything else. But he had the best political brain I'd ever known, and he taught me so much about connecting theology and poverty, theology and the struggle.

'At first we asked the question: "Surely this is a white thing? What are we doing here in the first place? It's a white god who has brought the Afrikaners to this country, and certainly they saw it as a divine mandate to come here."'

In 1972 and 1973, the apartheid regime began its most insidious fight-back yet when it appointed the Commission of Inquiry into Certain Organisations, better known as the Schlebusch/Le Grange Commission, whose mandate was to limit or cut foreign donor funding and seize the assets of the CI and other organisations.

Alwyn Schlebusch (1917–2008), a National Party MP for Kroonstad, was the only vice-state president of South Africa. Louis le Grange (1928–1991) was a lawyer and later deputy minister and minister under racist prime ministers BJ Vorster and PW Botha.

Although it was called a 'commission', it was not judicially mandated, and the typically secretive nature of its intent was revealed in that the panel sat *in camera*. Names of those who appeared before it were withheld. There was no cross-examination permitted and, in the end, evidence wasn't published.

Its thrust was unashamedly at shutting down Christian and church funding support for BC and other anti-apartheid structures. It centred on an apparent 'duty' to resist 'un-Christian' activities. As expected, the Commission's final report announced that a number of CI's activities indeed 'posed a danger' to the apartheid state.

It also investigated the UCM, NUSAS and the SAIRR, and all bar the SAIRR were declared 'affected', with their foreign donors cut off by 1975. The SAIRR's output was deemed to be 'propaganda'. Despite this destructive outcome, the CI and other Christian bodies defied the state in 1974 by taking the Hammanskraal Resolution, which prominently urged members of the SACC to 'look seriously at the possibilities of conscientious objection to [white] military service'. This, wrote David Thomas in *Pro Veritate*, 'put the [SACC] through its own trial of fire', calling it 'Christ's call' to object to conscription.

Although there has been criticism that the CI's activity was too focused on the white community, it was a partner to BC. This was expressed in projects, training and programmes developed for Black communities in the interests of self-sufficiency and in how the CI was able to get international publicity through its connections to white-owned media. That introduced it to funding that the BCM may otherwise not have been able to access.

Yet Black theological organisations like the African Independent Churches Association (AICA) and the Interdenominational African Ministers' Association (Idamasa) had a closer political alliance with BC.

That threw down the gauntlet to the English-speaking churches and in 1970 the Catholic Church in particular was challenged when the Black Priests' Manifesto was issued. Headlined 'Our Church Has Let Us Down', it was published by five priests including Mkhatshwa, and expressed their view that there was some pretence around the condemnation of apartheid from within the Catholic Church, while it seemed clear that the church could still accept many of its practices. The manifesto said that 'Catholics pretend to condemn apartheid.

And yet, in practice, they cherish it'.

Attempts to escape white control of the Christian churches also came from bodies like the Broederkring ('circle of brothers'), drawn out of Black NGKs in the Western Cape. These organisations provided more of an inter-Black contact than the CI could do, although the CI was among 18 organisations banned by the apartheid regime on 19 October 1977.

That repression forced it to close. Naudé – also known as Oom Bey (Uncle Bey) – was banned, along with other CI leaders.

Four years later, the government appointed a judicial Commission of Inquiry under the chairmanship of Justice CF Eloff to 'investigate the inception, development, objects, history and activities of the SACC, as well as organisations and people giving money or assets to the Council'. Academic Dr Ben Khumalo-Seegelken, based at the Carl von Ossietzky University in Oldenburg, Germany, records how the 1982 testimony of Afrikaner theologian and academic David Bosch – 'a profiled co-operative contemporary of the CI of international standing' – provided an extraordinary record of the CI's (and the SACC's) relationship to Black communities.

The Eloff Commission failed to slow a steady path out of anti-Blackness for many Christian churches, with the Belhar Confession happening in 1982 and the Kairos Document being issued in 1985. The Belhar Confession, a Christian statement of belief written in Afrikaans in 1982 and adopted by the Dutch Reformed Mission Church in 1986, stated that unity is 'both a gift and an obligation for the church' and that 'individual, racial and social segregation is sin'.

The NGK originally rejected the Confession as a statement of liberation theology, although it is now compulsory to adopt it within the NGK. It has also since been adopted by some Christian church movements in Namibia, Belgium, the US and the Dominican Republic. The Kairos Document is a theological statement issued in 1985 by a group of mainly Black ecumenical pastors and is regarded as an example of liberation theology in action. Although the names of those who initiated the process were not released at the time, it is believed that the Pentecostal churchman Frank Chikane was its protagonist. A mere 11 000 words long, the document, which criticised 'State and Church theology' and advocated a more grassroots approach, at first included more than 150 signatures, but was later signed by many more. '*Kairos*' is a Greek word meaning 'special moment'. State theology is defined in the document as 'the theological justification of the status quo with its racism, capitalism and totalitarianism'.

[Maylam 2011: www.ru.ac.za/media includes the full Citation for Moore; Stubbs in Biko, 1975; Thomas, 1975; Kalley, Schoeman & Andor, 1999; Hewson, 1961; Collins, 1979; De Gruchy, 2005; Walshe, 1983; Fatton, 1986; Naudé, 1995; Magaziner, 2010; Khumalo-Seegelken, 2014; Amato, 2020]

The Kairos document preface
25 September 1985, Johannesburg

[This] is a Christian, biblical and theological comment on the political crisis in South Africa today. It is an attempt by concerned Christians in South Africa to reflect on the situation of death in our country.

It is a critique of the current theological models that determine the type of activities the church engages in to try to resolve the problems of the country. It is an attempt to develop, out of this perplexing situation, an alternative biblical and theological model that will in turn lead to forms of activity that will make a real difference to the future of our country.

Of particular interest is the way the theological material was produced. In June 1985 as the crisis was intensifying in the country, as more and more people were killed, maimed and imprisoned, as one Black township after another revolted against the apartheid regime, as the people refused to be oppressed or to cooperate with oppressors, facing death by the day, and as the apartheid army moved into the townships to rule by the barrel of the gun, a number of theologians who were concerned about the situation expressed the need to reflect on this situation to determine what response by the church and by all Christians in South Africa would be most appropriate.

A first discussion group met at the beginning of July in the heart of

Soweto. Participants spoke freely about the situation and the various responses of the church, church leaders and Christians. A critique of these responses was made and the theology from which these responses flowed was also subjected to a critical analysis. Individual members of the group were assigned to put together material on specific themes which were raised during the discussion and to present the material to the next session of the group.

At the second meeting the material itself was subjected to a critique and various people were commissioned to do more investigations on specific problematic areas. The latest findings with the rest of the material were collated and presented to the third meeting where more than 30 people, consisting of theologians, ordinary Christians (lay theologians) and some church leaders.

After a very extensive discussion, some adjustments and additions were made especially in regard to [a] section entitled 'Challenge to Action'. The group then appointed a committee to subject the document to further critique by various other Christian groupings throughout the country.

Everybody was told, 'this was a people's document which you can also own even by demolishing it if your position can stand the test of biblical faith and Christian experience in South Africa'. They were told that this was an open-ended document which will never be said to be final.

The 'working committee', as it was called, was inundated with comments, suggestions and enthusiastic appreciation from various groups and individuals in the country. By the 13th of September 1985 when the document was submitted for publication there were still comments and recommendations flowing in.

The first publication therefore must be taken as a beginning, a basis for further discussion by all Christians in the country. Further editions will be published later.

[https://kairossouthernafrica.wordpress.com/2011/05/08/the-south-africa-kairos-document-1985/]

SPRO-CAS 2 publications

'The Eye of the Needle': Rick Turner (1972, banned in 1973)

A significant introduction to a new kind of egalitarian politics for South Africa, this publication was distributed to nearly 4 000 people, especially trade union members and activists.

Importantly in terms of the class analytic, Turner looked at the links between capital and Christianity and discussed how those who control the means of production exploit Black labour. Turner, who took socialism as his ideological theme, critiqued white liberalism while urging readers to re-examine the New Testament to see that Christians should take issue with capitalism. He quotes from Matthew 19: 24–25: 'It is easier for a camel to go through the eye of the needle, than it is for a rich man to enter into the Kingdom of God.'

Turner was in Paris studying at the Sorbonne in the period before the 1968 student uprisings. Young activists like him were inspired by Marx as they turned away from capital and staged massive uprisings with workers numbered in the hundreds of thousands.

'Black Viewpoint': edited by Steve Biko (1972)

A publication of the BCP, based in Durban, it has continued to carry weight predominantly for Biko's editorials.

As was the position of the BCM, Biko encouraged Black people to express themselves in print to counteract and indeed circumvent the white viewpoint. Biko edited the work of, among others, Njabulo S Ndebele, a student at Roma University in Lesotho at the time. Ndebele went on to become a professor and writer, and the vice-chancellor and principal of UCT and chancellor of UJ.

His topic for *Black Viewpoint* was on tradition versus modernity – a major subject within BC formation schools and discussion groups.

Strike! A Dossier on the Durban strikes (1973)

Dubbed 'The Great Zulu Strike', the event which lay behind this dossier concerned the brick and tile workers' victory of a wage hike of R2 per week.

That was a driver, but this document rather sought to expose the liberal English as being just as conservative as Afrikaners when it came to paying workers.

'Cry Rage': James Matthews and Gladys Thomas (1972, banned in 1973)
This volume of poetry spoke of the fury, pain and rage of those subjected to the oppression of apartheid.

'White Liberation': edited by Horst Kleinschmidt (1972)
The BC idea that white people need to liberate themselves from their embedded acceptance of a system that prefers them and return to their own communities to raise a consciousness there has become prevalent. Yet Kleinschmidt was already of that mind back in 1975 when he was expressing support for a 'confessing' church in South Africa.

Turning God into a racist

Paballo Thekiso, photographer and videographer for this book, has a strong spirituality, which led him to become a pastor in a Johannesburg church. Believing 'we are all on our own journey', Thekiso found a mentor in Moss Ntlha, also a pastor in Johannesburg and the general-secretary of the Evangelical Alliance of South Africa (TEASA). Moss is a former anti-apartheid activist. The two met in Johannesburg in 2020 to discuss how BC's new role in South Africa is to restore Black Theology.

A theory in the US in 2010 was that Christianity wasn't keeping pace with other institutions in terms of 'diversity' not because of 'racial animosity', but because of parishioners preferring to worship with others 'who look like them'.

Such was the contention in the study, 'Race, Diversity, and Membership Duration in Religious Congregations', written by Christopher P Scheitle of the Pennsylvania State University and Kevin D Dougherty of Baylor Institute for Studies of Religion.

'People choose churches where they feel comfortable,' Dougherty, a sociology professor, told CNN. 'Maybe they get challenges there, but they're going for the comfort.'

Nine out of 10 congregations in the US were segregated 'with a single racial group' accounting for 'more than 80 percent of their membership'.

This was, as noted in Scheitle and Dougherty's paper, more than 50 years after Reverend Martin Luther King Jr, 'speaking from the pulpit of Dexter Avenue Baptist Church' to Americans as a 'nation', said: 'You must face the tragic fact that when you stand at 11:00 on Sunday morning to sing *All Hail the Power of Jesus Name* and *Dear Lord and Father of all Mankind*, you stand in the most segregated hour of Christian America.' As we have seen in recent years, and especially in 2020 after the brutal murder of George Floyd, the silence of the white evangelical church has revealed which side it is on. The words of psychotherapist Steve de Shazer represent this behaviour: 'Where you stand determines what you see and what you do not see. It also determines the angle you see it from. A change in where you stand, changes everything.'

Many, if not most, Black people living in South Africa are Christians if they are spiritual. Fewer are Pentecostalists than they are evangelicals, much like numbers of Black Americans, and the British missionary-driven tradition of Christianity in South Africa has similarities to the US.

Emanating as it did out of the Church of England breakaway movement of the 1700s, it became embedded in white settler colonisation. Indeed, many Christian churches that have high numbers of Black worshippers and Black elders in both countries today bear the distinguishing marks of empire in their services.

Yet, even as the white missionary influence recedes to almost negligible levels as Black evangelism grows, Western-dominant culture church practices still reflect those racist origins.

As spiritual people and believers, Black South African Christians must challenge themselves to develop BC in their churches. We should take inspiration from Christian migrants from West and North Africa who have arrived in our country over the past two decades after apartheid.

Just as it was in the US when North Africans began to move there in greater numbers over the last century – mostly from Egypt, Tunisia and Morocco – South Africa is seeing a more varied influence in Black faith practices.

Do we need white Christians to progress?

Inasmuch as Black Americans and Black Africans share the story of bigotry and white supremacy theology, we also share the story of using our churches during segregation to organise campaigns against state violence and anti-Black legislation.

That so many of our churches failed to make systemic changes that mirrored Black power gains in society could be a reflection of us not prioritising BC.

We know where we come from. We know the depravity of white Christians who didn't believe Black people were really 'human' and so did not possess souls. We know that even liberal white Christians promote a 'white Jesus' narrative – in the songs they sing, the authors they quote and the whole 'Sunday experience'.

Blacks attending those churches are left with a choice to assimilate and never complain, or go to a Black church. This widens the gap of 'the 11:00 segregation', and leaves the church more divided than united.

Whether intentionally or not, white theology is the elevation of whiteness over other cultures, and in the church, this comes in the form of predominantly white, capitalist values such as individualism but also hierarchy, a defensiveness towards 'the other', the 'right' to comfort, and maintaining control over all things. To most Black Christians, these values are opposite to what the Bible teaches, and opposite to our culture.

The question of whether a BC ideology can help churches overcome this whiteness can be answered with Genesis 1:27: 'So God created human beings in his own image; in the image of God created he … them.'

This scripture has always been the message of BC. To remind Blacks of their beauty and worth is to take them back to their original design and connect them with their creator. As Biko taught us, denying Blackness is an insult to the creator.

This is found at the beginning of the Bible, and how it is that white racist Christians chose to misunderstand it, baffles me. What confuses me further is how such an antiracist scripture could be twisted by white Christians such that they found a way to turn God into a racist. One understands why many Black people, especially young people, drift away from Christianity, arguing that it is an irrelevant white man's religion that is out of touch with their daily realities.

We are seeing that decay of spirituality that used to be a wall of consciousness in the hearts and minds of many. Young Black people are looking for a religion that relates to their everyday experience. They are looking for practical answers to deal with the racist world they face in which the white church fails them.

They see the effects. Raising justice issues in white churches leaves many Black church leaders out in the cold and labelled as 'troublemakers'. White theology calls issues of justice 'politics' and wishes to keep social injustice at a distance, leaving Black church leaders facing the battle of deliberately not being heard, or gaslighted or publicly undermined by the white leadership.

And it is not just whites who equate 'Black' with 'politics'. Blacks who have been brainwashed by white theology are also inclined to see us as 'instigators', and their behaviour is not new. At the height of BC in the 1970s, there were Blacks in the church who refused to be called Blacks and wanted to be referred to as 'non-whites'.

That is a form of slavery. Biko, a believer, said: 'We are oppressed because we are Black. We must use that very concept to unite ourselves and to respond as a cohesive group. We must cling to each other with a tenacity that will shock the perpetrators of evil.' [Biko: *I Write What I Like*, page 97]

Being Black in white spaces remains a battle of the mind. We have heard what whiteness has to teach, and it has not helped us progress. White Christianity sought in recent times to 'diversify' congregations by bringing in a few Black faces. Yet, while 'diversity' as a value is a public good, it is only one of many steps. White churches that have failed to deeply recognise, acknowledge and reject the sin in white theology have not yet repented from it, dismantled it or joined the quest to bring about Black liberation.

Supremacy is not only dangerous and oppressive for Black people, but also for white people. As American Black Liberation theologian James H Cone put it: 'Any theology that is indifferent to the theme of liberation is not Christianity theology.'

Ntlha was one of three UCM members to travel to Cleveland, Ohio in 1967 when a fledgling UCM was being established there. He says one of the others who went on the trip turned out to be an undercover security branch policeman. The third, Bob Kgware, was murdered when a bicycle spoke was driven through his heart by 'unknown assailants' – presumably the security police – shortly after the trio returned to South Africa.

The tragedy hit hard. They had come back with rejuvenated BC through their direct introduction to the Black Power movement and its political strategies, and their access to books and writing that were banned in South Africa, including that of Cone, who they also met.

Like BC, Christianity is a way of life. It is impossible to separate yourself and your actions from it. The counter-hegemonic approach of Black Theology identifies with a Jesus who was born poor, who struggled and who was dehumanised for believing in liberation. BC was, perhaps, never more important in the Christian church than at this moment with the dominant culture of whiteness in its terminal phase, doomed to extinction.

As Ntlha says, 'We can never kill the truth because after three days it will rise again'.

He explains that 'as a trained theologian now under the influence of James Cone, I wrote an exploratory study paper, "Towards a Black Theology", in 1970, which was distributed to members, affiliates and the sponsoring churches.

'The immediate and tangible effect was that the UCM established a Black Theology Project and appointed [Sabelo, or Stan] Ntwasa as its full-time organiser. Out of this came a sequence of conferences on Black Theology across the country during 1971, with the publication at the end of the year of a selection of conference papers. It was immediately banned by the South African government ... but was then published by Christopher Hurst in London, under the title "Black Theology: The South African Voice".'

Black Theology, says Ntlha, took its understanding of 'Black' from the BC movement, which used it as a positive identifier, but it also 'referred specifically to those victims of racism who were engaged personally and directly in the liberation struggle'.

'"Black", if you like, referred exclusively to Black freedom fighters... Black Theology had to grow out of and be part of the liberation struggle.'

Ntlha deepens the argument for Black Theology here, saying 'What was most distinctive about it was its theological method. In essence this was grounded in the conviction that in a racist society, racism not only structures the experiences of the oppressors and their victims differently, it also makes them "see" and interpret things differently.

'As such, the nature and meaning of the Gospel is understood differently when it is approached within the experiential context of white oppressors from what it is when Black experiences and aspirations inform the interpretation.

'Thus, whites are likely to see the heart of the Gospel as being about salvation of the soul. Whereas for Blacks, the primary message is that Jesus came to set the oppressed free. It is about liberation.'

Eminent Black Theology protagonist Mokgethi Motlhabi, who was a leader in the Black Theology Project, believed that 'to allow others to rule over us and make decisions for us compromises our dignity and authenticity as human beings'.

'This argument was carried over into an attack on the authoritarian images of God – omnipotent, king, ruler, Lord and so on – under which we were supposed to obey "His" will.'

'This was seen as locking human beings into a permanent childhood and legitimating the social manifestations of authoritarianism in both church and state. Throughout the UCM and thus also in early Black Theology there was a relentless quest to find ways, especially theological ways, of affirming human beings as adults.

'It was argued by Ntwasa that we need to explore "relational" images of God rather than remain locked in the "traditional person" images. He said in the scriptures there are two sets of images of God – one … like King, Lord, Father, etc., and the other … [those which] assert that God is love, peace, justice, etc..

'If we persist in giving priority to the "person" … we also [ended] up … subjecting God to the Race Classification Act, according to which God [was] undisputedly "white".'

Ntlha raises a meaningful historical record that showed how Blackness in South African church life was encouraged through the UCM developing "occasion-specific liturgies" to shift that 'white God, white church' framing.

'They were modelled on relational images of God and human beings. They used dance and drama extensively. They drew for their music and songs on the protest song traditions of Europe, the US and South African Black workers, Black townships and Black universities. There was, thus, an unmistakeably political thrust…

'There was [also] experimentation with liturgies which set worship in the context of the Black liberation struggle to promote [it] … [to fire] the will to resistance by supporting people in the struggle and by exploring resistance strategies. Specifically they used traditional African "praise songs" to celebrate leaders of the liberation struggle.'

During the 1971 Black Theology conferences it was these acts of struggle-based worship that were 'most consistently broken up by the security police'.

Ntlha says he knows 'of no copies of those liturgies which survived the police raids'.

It's BC which survives, and 'if the church is going to survive … the church must stop calling the Black Lives Matter "a debate" [versus "All Lives Matter"], because it is not.'

'Calling it a "debate" gives it life and gives it legitimacy. It is not a debate, it is a fact that Black Lives Matter. Any church that refuses to agree with this fact, are disagreeing with God.'

Conscious cassocks

Aelred Stubbs (1923–2004)

Perhaps best known for his personal memoir, 'Martyr of Hope', published in Biko's *I Write What I Like*, Stubbs was an Anglican priest and monk who became close to the Biko family after he moved from the St Peter's Theological College in Rosettenville – forced to close by the apartheid regime because it was in a white group area but taught Black students – to form the Anglican constituent college in the ecumenical Federal Theological Seminary in Alice.

Khaya, Biko's older brother, had been expelled from Lovedale College in Alice with more than 40 of his comrades in 1963. Arrested and charged with membership of Poqo, the military wing of the PAC, they were being held in Fort Beaufort Prison when Stubbs was asked to secure a defence and bail for them.

LL Mtshizana, the attorney representing most of those being held, was detained under the 90-day law by the Security Branch on the eve of their trial, which was compromised in every way by the state to prejudice the accused.

Stubbs gave evidence in mitigation for Khaya Biko, who received a two-year sentence, 15 months of which were conditionally suspended. During and after the trial, however, Stubbs spent a significant amount of time getting to know the Biko family, in particular Steve, who had many questions around Christianity, being schooled as he was by Catholics in Mariannhill.

At first, Stubbs and Biko corresponded by way of letters and Stubbs said Biko 'showed an unusual facility of expression as well as a sharp and enquiring mind'. Stubbs also came to know Biko's compatriot Pityana, whom he described as 'a deeply committed Christian'. Writing that Biko regarded him as 'a father in Christ', Stubbs reflected on how the seminary in Alice was once a bastion for NUSAS, but once Biko became the president of SASO, 'it began to make progress even on [their] campus'. Describing Biko's 'extraordinary magnetism', Stubbs said 'his hold on his all-Black audiences was almost frightening; it was as if they were listening to a new "messiah".'

Stubbs got to know Biko better after he was banned in February 1973 along with SASO leaders Pityana, Jerry Modisane, Nengwekhulu, Strini Moodley and others.

In 1974, Biko wrote Stubbs a letter in which he said he had learned 'to develop a strong faith in God'.

Stubbs was known as 'Father A' to most of the BC leaders, but Biko insisted on calling him 'Father Stubbs'. It was Stubbs who collected Biko's writings to compile these into *I Write What I Like*.

Biko biographer Xolela Mangcu wrote that Stubbs died in 2006 after living quietly in the grounds of a convent in Lesotho for some years.

[Stubbs in Biko, 1975; Mangcu, 2013]

Right Reverend Rubin Phillip (1948–)

Bishop of the Anglican Diocese of Natal, Phillip – who grew up in poverty in Clairwood, Durban – gained impetus for a new generation of BC activists as a strong supporter of shack-dwellers movement Abahlali baseMjondolo (AbM) in the 2000s. Yet the struggles of the poor in South Africa have always been a focus for the bishop, who South African journalist Carlos Amato revealed afresh in 'The guerrilla priest' for *New Frame* in 2020.

Phillip had recently been awarded the Bremen International Peace Award[56] on the grounds of his work in the struggle against apartheid and his ongoing work to offer solidarity to the displaced people, victims of persecutions and detainees'.

The following year, Phillip received the Diakonia Award[57] in recognition of his involvement with the anti-apartheid movement, his advocacy and involvement in the Zimbabwe crisis,[58] and his solidarity with AbM.

There's a far-reaching history to his activism from a BC mind-set, as Phillip was a close comrade of Biko. Today, writes Amato, Phillips see Biko as 'increasingly significant to South Africa's political moment – first, because of the resurgence of [his] intellectual legacy, and second, because that resurgence has been marred by what [Phillips] sees as a crudely essentialist mutation of BC, most obviously in the rhetoric of Julius Malema and the Economic Freedom Fighters (EFF).'

'My sense is that some BC principles are there [in the EFF], about

---

56   The Schwelle Foundation – a German NGO – selects nominees for the International Bremen Peace Award presented every two years to honour setting 'a good example in … work for peace, justice and the integrity of creation'.

57   Diakonia is an international development organisation with Christian values. It is funded by Brot für die Welt [aid organisation of Protestant churches and free churches in Germany], Church of Sweden [former state church, now an evangelical Lutheran church], the DT Hudson Trust [named for British Special Operations executive Colonel Duane Hudson, who set up a charitable trust in part to unite churches in South Africa] and Misereor [German Catholic Bishops' Organisation for Development Cooperation].

58   This particularly refers to events in 2008, as Amato explains, when 'a shipload of Chinese-made arms bound for Zimbabwe docked at Durban harbour… [Workers] wanted to refuse to offload the arms.. Phillip and a number of comrades were able to persuade a judge to issue an order blocking the offloading in what was seen as a triumph of defiance by workers of.. Thabo Mbeki's "quiet diplomacy" – a policy stance that closely resembled craven enablement of the [Robert] Mugabe regime'.

pride and achievement. But there is a kind of rotten materialism that runs like a thread through it all. I'm appalled at Malema buying outrageously expensive clothes and so on.'

Biko's vision of liberation was broad, argues Phillip: It held that white oppressors also needed mental liberation...'

Phillip says 'fundamentally, it is about pride. The level of killing and destruction in our communities are just a sign of lack of self-worth and self-love. And unless and until we as a people affirm who we are, not only in material terms, we cannot win this struggle for genuine independence.'

'We need to reach the point where a man is so proud of himself, so accepting of himself and of the other, that he won't rape a young woman. She is a sister. The fact you have R10 000 in your pocket is not going to stop you from abusing a 12-year-old. There is an intangible thing in the soul that is lacking.'

Casting a warm light on Biko as a person and a leader, Phillip tells Amato, 'that ideological breadth was underpinned by a radically open political style, a willingness to debate, if not to compromise, with one's enemy'.

The men worked side-by-side when Phillip was elected deputy president of SASO and Biko president.

'Biko asked Phillip to join him on a drive from Durban to Pretoria, where he would meet some activists in Mamelodi. [He relates how], "It gave us time to talk, and we shared the driving in his Toyota. At one point on the N2, I was driving at the time, and ... [we saw some defence force hitchhikers, who Steve decided we would lift] ... I think they were very sorry that they did. Steve really grilled them. Eventually, about two hours later, they asked to get out..."'

'"Steve was at heart an extremely kind person, who was genuinely interested in other people and wanted to know what they thought [about the SADF killing us Black people. Killing our mothers and our children]. So they felt a bit uncomfortable... He wasn't nasty to them, but they were in an awkward position. They responded in very short sentences. They were out of their depth, and I bet it got them thinking, but we'll never know. And that wasn't unusual [for Steve]."'

Phillip and Biko both played at No 8 in the University of Natal Medical

School (Black section) rugby league on opposing sides, 'much to Phillip's dismay'.

Phillip tells Amato: 'Steve took a fancy to really bashing me on the field. And I said to him one day, "Is this personal?" And he said, "No! I just love it!". Bastard!'

Phillip says he was fortunate to be raised in a conscious family, 'which wasn't always the case among most Indian people, who tended to close ranks against Black, as in African, folk – and to some degree that still happens, I think. Part of that has to do with Indians being such a minority group, being protective of their culture and ideas and race.'

He became involved in the Anglican church social action programmes at high school, meeting Ntwasa, Drake Tshenkeng and others who, like Biko, 'saw the church as a Western invention to dull our minds, but ... [also] where Black people drew their inspiration and strength'.

Phillip did his master's in New York in the early 1980s where his research deepened his interest in Peruvian Dominican priest Gustavo Gutiérrez[59] and Freire, whose 'Marxian lens' positioned 'Jesus Christ as liberator' in his mind. Phillips completed his degree at the Union Theological Seminary, affiliated to Columbia University, where his teachers included Cone – who was sympathetic to liberation theology – and [Cornel] West.

It's fascinating to note, as Amato shows, that Phillip had issues with Black Theology [versus liberation theology] as 'it ... focused on race alone].

'Of course that had relevance here in South Africa, because the problem was essentially a race one... But the Latin American liberation theologians, like Gutiérrez, were saying, "What about class?"'

Phillip was banned during apartheid and sentenced to house arrest. He, however, remained at the forefront of the SACC's support of families of political prisoners.

---

59   Gustavo Gutiérrez (1928–) is a Peruvian philosopher, Dominican priest and a founder of liberation theology. He was a visiting professor at a number of universities. At the time Phillip was studying abroad, Gutiérrez would come under fire from Pope John Paul II who disagreed with the Marxism inherent in liberation theology. A Vatican report was produced under his successor, Cardinal Joseph Ratzinger, which agreed that Marxism was incompatible with Catholic teaching.

Amato describes Phillip as 'a street-level priest – a guerrilla of pacifist struggle, [whose] work terrain is shacks and hospitals and cemeteries, giving direct support to those tormented and bereaved by apartheid tyranny or its post-democracy mutations'.

[Amato, 2020: https://www.newframe.com/the-guerrilla-priest/]

David Russell (1938–2014)

A young Anglican priest in 1973 when Biko was banished to King William's Town, he worked among the poor of the area and shared friendship and intellectual stimulation with Biko during the first months of Biko's banning.

Biko later wrote in a letter to Stubbs after Russell – who spoke fluent Xhosa – had been moved from 'King': 'David's going away left a gap which cannot be closed. The evenings we spent together were very good palliatives to the mental decay which so easily sets in.

'Besides this, he was a person full of life and always with something new to pursue. He was strong and reliable and made life purposeful. I am aware that I must have served a purpose in the many consultations we had, and this was good to know.'

Biko described Russell to Stubbs as 'a political person, a friend, an equal, a schlenterer,[60] a comrade I could easily ask him about his family ... and adopt freely any attitude I like towards this'.

[Biko, 1975]

Enos Zwelabantu Sikhakhane (1917–1993)

The history of the Methodist Church in Africa would be incomplete without a chapter on Reverend Sikhakhane, says the church's website.

The founder of the influential Edendale Lay Ecumenical Centre in 1965, this visionary 'Christian gentleman' – as he was described by the executive secretary of the Methodist Church in South Africa, Reverend Vivian Harris – became one of the most revered and loved ministers in the church. 'He was gifted with the talent of organising people around him and the ability to motivate community self-reliance. This was in keeping with the BC philosophy,' said Harris.

Having combined his church work with community work during

---

60   Popularly – here, affectionately – 'a person who manipulates behind the scenes'.

the 1950s, Sikhakhane personally collected funds, even going abroad to appeal for support, to build the Edendale centre.

> [Material drawn largely from an obituary by the Natal Society Foundation, 1993]

The Interdenominational African Ministers' Association (Idamasa)

Originally known as Tiama (the Transvaal Interdenominational African Ministers' Association), Idamasa was founded in 1915 at a time when the newly established ANC was picking up momentum. Tiama spread its work into other provinces, founding similar regional organisations in Natal, Free State and the Cape Province. Among its early projects was the establishment of the Mendi Memorial Scholarship that helped students through Fort Hare.

The Interdenominational African Ministers' Federation (IDAMF) was founded in Bloemfontein in 1945. The Federation existed until 1965 when it was transformed into Idamasa through the adoption of a constitution that made it possible to employ permanent staff.

Idamasa's activities involved Black education, research into African traditions, the advancement of Black youth and women, representations to local and national government and the creation of rapport among churches and religious organisations. Idamasa would grow to 117 branches and a membership of more than 1 000, operating independently of individual churches.

In 1972, an Idamasa conference was held in Umtata at which a report made it clear that 'Africans [should] dedicate themselves to the crystallisation and propagation of Black Theology'.

Idamasa was affiliated to the SACC and the All Africa Council of Churches.

African independent churches

In the 1970s, at the height of BC, it was believed that at least 4 million Blacks belonged to independent churches represented by the African Independent Churches Association (AICA), the Reformed Independent Churches Association (RICA) and the Assembly of the Zionist and Apostolic Association (AZASA). Of these, the most important was AICA.

In 1964, a group of independent African church leaders approached Naudé's CI for guidance in the field of theological training for ministers. This was occasioned by a restriction by the apartheid government in 1960 on ministers' recognition where they had not been formally trained. The leadership believed that a strong association to look after the interests of the independent churches would be to their advantage. And so, at a conference in Queenstown in 1965, AICA was established. Primarily providing mentorship to Black theologians, with a theological seminary in Alice, it received funding from churches in Germany, Holland and Switzerland.

But AICA was later riven by complaints about how its finances were being handled, and by 1969 a small group had split from it and formed an allegiance instead with the Dutch Reformed Church, which was working with the Department of Bantu Education.

Blame for the splits was, however, imputed to the CI, until 1972 when a special conference was convened in White City, Jabavu, with 216 member churches represented. Sadly, the strife continued.

The Lay Ecumenical Centre

Situated south of Pietermaritzburg, it was administered entirely by Blacks and became a symbol of African initiative. The site where it was built was bought by Blacks and supported by Nzondelelo, an African organisation within the Methodist Church in Natal.

Through the centre, nearly 40 Black organisations and 'educated African representatives' aimed to create an 'informed Christian leadership prepared to take community responsibility and leadership seriously'.

'The present situation of a professional elite who have become alienated from their fellows causes anxiety in African communities where "belonging to each other" is an important component of African personality,' opined a view of the centre in its early days.

The centre aimed to 'serve the emerging African industrial workers and urban dwellers. The African is a community man who has to regain his awareness of himself as a human'.

The centre's programmes consisted of youth action training, skills training, leadership courses, women's programmes and consultation.

Teachers' organisations, religious groups, women's groups,

cultural organisations, youth groups and students' organisations all used its space, as did SASO for its leadership training courses. The BCP used the centre – which was affiliated to the SACC – for major conferences, and the BPC also used it as its conference site during its formative stages.

> [From the archives of the Digital Institute of South Africa (DISA), by way of the Interdenominational African Ministers' Wives Association of South Africa, www.disa.ukzn.ac za/sites/default/files/pdf_files/ Br1972.0376.4354.000.000.1972.pdf]

Khoza Elliot Mgojo (1932–2018)

A presiding bishop of the Anglican Church in the 1980s and president of the SACC from 1990 to 1996, he also served on the TRC under chairperson Desmond Tutu.

Known to his peers by his clan name, Mbuyisa, Mgojo was born into a Methodist family in 1932 in uMzimkhulu, Natal.

Mgojo studied theology at Fort Hare, and completed his MA in theology *cum laude* at the University of Chicago. He read for his PhD at Harvard.

The Natal Society Foundation records how Mgojo's 'relations with some of the key liberation struggle leaders in exile enabled him to play a significant role in helping to pave the way into exile for some of the young students who were leading the resistance struggle against Bantu Education in the Seventies.

'Together with his colleagues, he fought an intense battle not only to keep the seminary alive in the face of the onslaught of the apartheid forces, but also to keep the church in the frontline of the struggle.'

In 1976, after the Soweto massacre, together with the Reverends Ernest Baartman, Andrew Losaba, F de Waal Mahlasela and others, he formed the Black Methodist Consultation 'with the intention of helping locate the Methodist Church of Southern Africa at the heart of the liberation struggle'. Serving as its first general secretary, he was 'yoked with Tutu, Chikane, Reverend Dr Allan Boesak, Dr Brigalia Bam and others to pilot the responsibility of holding Black people together through the church…'.

> [Natal Society Foundation, 1993]

Allan Boesak (1946–)

Giving a lecture about Biko at the University of KwaZulu-Natal in Durban in 2011, the veteran theologian said that 'the philosophy of BC is resurfacing and the values it espouses are essential for public life'. *The Witness* newspaper reported on how Boesak's lecture was divided into a series of four: BC as a liberating consciousness; as an empowering consciousness; as an engaging consciousness; and as a critical consciousness.

Boesak, said *The Witness*, was critical of what he called the ANC's 'deliberate fading' of the historic role of BC 'in its own almost total claim on the history of South Africa's liberation struggle'.

'Biko knew exactly who and what the apartheid regime was, but he also understood clearly that the white [Afrikaner] regime could as easily be used as a scapegoat for all whites, especially the liberal white who claimed to criticise the apartheid regime, but had no qualms soaking up the benefits the white racist structure provided.'

Boesak said lessons that can be drawn from BC are 'crucial for a search for a meaningful life' in South Africa, and 'our struggle for justice, equality and human dignity, and in our effort to give meaning to the term "reconciled nationhood".

'All South Africans should simply be convinced that in embracing the humanity of others they are embracing their own, and in that greater scheme of being, pigmentation and what is called "race" are entirely irrelevant.'

Boesak was born in Kakamas, Northern Cape and worked as a child labourer to help support his family. At 14, he became a sexton in a coloured NG Mission Church and would later graduate from the Bellville Theological Seminary before working as a pastor from 1967. From 1970 to 1976, he studied at theological institutions in Holland and in New York, gaining a PhD in Ethics titled *Farewell to Innocence*, which remains a vital liberation theology text.

On his return to South Africa in 1976 to Bellville, Boesak increased his political activities through the church.

In 1981, various Black Reformed churches founded the Alliance of Black Reformed Christians in Southern Africa and elected Boesak as chairperson. The website *www.sahistory.org* writes that the alliance's statement reflected many of Boesak's beliefs. It rejected the use of religion as a cultural or racist ideology ... [and] divorcing religion from political activism.

'Boesak and the alliance believed that the struggle against apartheid represented a struggle for Christianity's integrity.'

It was when Boesak introduced a motion at a World Alliance of Reformed Churches (WARC) gathering in 1982 in Canada, asking it to declare apartheid 'a heresy', that he drew international attention. WARC adopted the *Declaration on Racism*, suspended the South African Dutch Reformed Church from membership, and unanimously elected Boesak president, making him 'spiritual leader to over 50 million Christians'.

In the background however were serious political effects for the BC movement.

As Boesak, who had once championed the BCM, gained an international political profile, he called for 'a united front' in South Africa, and his repositioning as a political figure assisted in creating a leadership that would ultimately set up the United Democratic Front (UDF) in 1983. This umbrella organisation came to life at a time when a racist new South African constitution had introduced the Tricameral Parliament, which provided separate chambers of Parliament with limited powers for coloured and Indian minorities. The Black majority was still excluded.

The UDF and Boesak – elected its patron – would gain significant political mileage out of protest at that event, but the effect on the BCM was significant.

Boesak would later be beset by scandal, including of extra-marital affairs and, most damaging, in 1999, fraud charges after the 'diversion' of Danish funding from his social justice programme into a private bank account. He had a short spell in prison thereafter, although he was pardoned by Thabo Mbeki in 2005 and returned to the church, as much an advocate of Black Theology as before.

In 2009, he articulated it thus: 'On the one hand, there has been the theology we inherited from western Christianity: the theology of accommodation and acquiescence. It engendered an individualistic, other-worldly spirituality that has no interest in the realities of this world except to proclaim the existing order as the God-ordained order.

'On the other hand, there was a theology of refusal; a theology that refuses to accept that God was just another word for the *status quo*; a theology that understood that the God of the Bible is a God who takes sides with the oppressed and who calls persons to participate in the struggle for liberation and justice in the world.'

Boesak's 1982 collection of sermons, *The Finger of God*, covered Black ministry and the death of Biko.

His 18th book, *Pharaohs on Both Sides of the Blood-red Waters*, was published in August 2017.

Manas Buthelezi (1935–2016)

Buthelezi served as the director of the Natal region of the CI in Pietermaritzburg from June 1973. He was banned for five years under the Suppression of Communism Act in the same year. Buthelezi became a BC spokesperson and theologian after his banning order was lifted unexpectedly before its expiry date.

The Lutheran World Federation (LWF) – of which he was a former vice-president – described him as 'a prophetic voice with a passion for justice, peace and reconciliation'. A bishop (emeritus) when he died in April 2016 aged 81, Buthelezi was considered 'a great African theologian of the 20th century'. He served as bishop of the Central Diocese of the Evangelical Lutheran Church in southern Africa for 20 years.

LWF general secretary Reverend Dr Martin Junge said: 'His deep and visionary theological analysis, his prophetic voice, his charismatic leadership and commitment to ecumenism and global Lutheranism have marked the lives of many people around the globe.' Buthelezi 'helped open ways for Lutherans to continue reading biblical texts through the eyes of the oppressed'. Buthelezi's position was that 'apartheid had distorted true Christian unity by instituting segregation based on race'.

Educated at Umphumulo Theological College, and then Yale, Buthelezi taught for a time at the University of Heidelberg in Germany. A leading exponent of Black Theology, he played a major role in the SACC, the All Africa Conference of Churches and the WCC. In 2000 he retired to his birthplace, Mahlabathini.

[www.lutheranworld.org: The Geneva-based Lutheran World Federation publishes this website, which featured this obituary of South African Lutheran bishop Manas Buthelezi]

Oshadi Jane Mangena (1931–2015)

Born in a toilet on 12 June 1931 when her father's employer refused to allow her mother to wait for an ambulance inside her home, as she was Black, Mangena exceeded all the hateful expectations for her of supremacists.

Mangena was a full-time nurse when she became actively involved in BC politics from the late 1960s, reaching the heights of executive director of the Association for the Education and Cultural Advancement of South Africa and national president of the Young Women's Christian Association (YMCA) from 1974 until it was banned in 1977.

Mangena left her career as a nurse in 1973 to join the CI, to which she was elected regional director in 1976. She worked closely with Naudé, attending the All Africa Conference of Churches in Lusaka as an observer in May 1974 and being part of the movement within the member churches of the SACC, which in August 1974 tabled the Hammanskraal Resolution.

Mangena initiated and co-ordinated an array of grassroots projects involving people in rural areas and spoke on issues ranging from attempts to sensitise and motivate pastors and teachers, to how to participate in community initiatives for human rights.

Mangena was detained after the June 1976 uprising, and after spending months at The Old Fort prison in Johannesburg, she was banned and restricted to Mamelodi township in Pretoria. In April 1977 she went into exile, working closely with the BCM as the European representative for the CI until 1980 when the institute closed down.

She earned a BA in political science and public administration at Unisa while in exile, a master's in development studies from the Institute of Social Studies in The Hague and her PhD in social sciences from the University of Amsterdam. She lectured in development studies at the University of Amsterdam from 1984 to 1996.

Mangena returned home in 1998 to work as a consultant in development studies. She was also one of the founding members of

Pitseng Trust Women's Fund and a member of the National Working Committee of the World Affiliated YWCA of South Africa.

[SAHO, 2019: https://www.sahistory.org.za/people/dr-oshadi-maphefo-jane-mangena]

Colin Collins (1918–)

Colin Collins, a Catholic priest, completed his philosophy studies with the Dominicans in Stellenbosch, then did four years of theology with the Oblates of Mary Immaculate in Pietermaritzburg.

Ordained in 1940 at the age of 22, he said he learned about 'racial and religious prejudice' when he was at Pretoria University: 'The Catholic Church to the Afrikaner was the *Roomse gevaar* ('Roman' danger) – as evil as Communism.'

Collins worked unhappily for the Vatican representative for southern Africa and then for the South African Bishops Conference, during which time he was the chaplain to the National Catholic Federation of Students. That was where he became 'increasingly angry with the lack of action on the part of the bishops in the struggle against apartheid [turning to] young pastors in the Protestant churches'.

Collins recalled Biko, his political comrade, as a 'highly charismatic student ... one of the most impressive individuals that I have met'.

In 1971, Collins went to Canada to study Freire. Unable to return to South Africa, he accepted a job in Adelaide, Australia, where his friend, Basil Moore, was already teaching. He then worked in Brisbane in palliative care.

[Collins, 2012]

Basil Moore

Politicised in the early 1960s when he was a divinity student at Rhodes, where he served as SRC president, Moore became involved in the UCM when he was registered for a PhD. He was then serving as the Methodist chaplain.

But Moore's UCM involvement 'attracted ... an unseemly response from the university authorities', said Professor Paul Maylam upon giving Moore his Honrarary Doctorate of Laws at Rhodes in 2011. 'Although the university Senate endorsed a recommendation for

[Moore] to be given a lectureship, the conservative university council (twice) overturned it, clearly on political grounds.'

When the council refused to give reasons for not hiring Moore in 1969, campus protests and a student sit-in at the council chamber ensued. Moore's passport had already been seized by the apartheid government in 1968; preventing him from travelling for research purposes.

In what became known as 'the Basil Moore affair', the sit-in resulted in the eight-week suspension of 13 students and the dismissal of temporary politics lecturer, David Tucker.

Moore nonetheless completed the research for his PhD, and spent two years stationed in Carltonville, a strongly white nationalist mining town in Johannesburg of which he said: 'I survived two years there. [It] was not exactly the kind of place for someone with my history and ideas to try to minister.'

Thereafter he became full-time theology director of the UCM and director of the leadership training programme of the AICA until he was banned and placed under partial house arrest in December 1971. In August 1972, Moore was finally given permission to leave the country but at the same time declared a 'prohibited immigrant' – a ruling which took him and his family into exile in Australia from which he was unable to return until bannings were lifted on all liberation movements and most activists from the late 1980s.

When Maylam conferred the Honorary Doctorate on Moore, Moore also received an apology from Rhodes for the events which took place during the apartheid regime.

[Maylam, 2011: full citation at www.ru.ac.za]

Reverend Al Sharpton (1954–)

A child prodigy, Sharpton was licensed and ordained a Pentecostal minister of the Washington Temple Church of God in Christ (COGIC) in Brooklyn, New York, by Bishop FD Washington when he was 9 years old. Sharpton famously preached his first sermon at the age of four.

The church became one of the largest congregations in the US.

COGIC is a Pentecostal-Holiness Christian denomination with a predominantly African-American membership, although it has some international and 'multi-ethnic' elements.

Sharpton didn't remain in the church, though, deciding to become a Baptist after Washington's death in the late 1980s. Rebaptised as a member of the Bethany Baptist Church in 1994, Sharpton then became a Baptist minister, famously defending his beliefs in a public debate, 'Is God Great?, with writer Christopher Hitchens, who was an overt atheist, in 2007. The event, held at the New York Public Library, attracted widespread attention.

thegrio.com reported on how the argument was driven by the title of Hitchens's book, *God is Not Great*, with the acerbic British writer insisting religion 'poisons everything' from individual relationships to international ones. *The Grio*'s Joyanne Reid wrote, 'Sharpton and Hitchens went several rounds, and in the end, gained a mutual respect'.

Sharpton has been an activist for more than 40 years, defending individuals, neighbourhoods, communities and organisations which he supported, no matter the personal odds.

Journalist Jacqueline Cutler writes that his 'fiery anger gives off more light than heat' in her piece about Sharpton's 2020 book, *Rise Up: Confronting a Country at the Crossroads*', remarking that 'if your opinion of Sharpton remains mired in images of the tracksuit agitator from 40 years ago, consider the president and founder of National Action Network's explanation of his look back then.

'"The medallion I often sported in the 1980s – the one Rudy Giuliani[61] told James Comey[62] to bring to him as a trophy for protesting police brutality – was given to me as an award for my work in civil rights",' Cutler quotes Sharpton. '"So, let's be clear: I may have adopted the swagger of a showman – all the better to get eyeballs on the causes I was bringing into the light – but I also put in the work".'

Sharpton tells Cutler he likes to remind people that 'he is a

---

61   Rudi Giuliani (1944–) is an American attorney and politician who was New York mayor from 1994 to 2001. He was former US President Donald Trump's cybersecurity advisor in 2017 and joined Trump's private legal team in 2018.

62   James Comey (1960–) is an American lawyer who was director of the Federal Bureau of Investigation from 2013 until his dismissal under the Trump administration in May 2017.

Sharpton because that was the name of the white family which owned his relatives' under slavery: 'So, I'm shocked when people tell me all I see is race because I'm shocked that they *don't* see it.'

Sharpton had a sustained and profound influence on the development of BC through the 2020 uprisings. He gave the 20th annual Steve Biko Lecture from New York in September 2020. Broadcast live on TV news channels in South Africa, Sharpton reflected on the very close connections between Black people in the US and in South Africa.

'Us as a minority in the United States and you as a majority in South Africa, parallel movements, different methods and tactics, different ways of dealing with issues but the same goal of empowerment and freedom of our people and protecting our existence.'

[Reid, 2011: https://thegrio.com/2011/12/17/when-christopher-hitchens-debated-al-sharpton/; Cutler, 2020: https://www.nydailynews.com/entertainment/ny-sharpton-crossroads-country-book-20200918-wn5gfhtgozbptpnuwmi7cqwnc4-story.html; https://www.sabcnews.com/sabcnews/live-20th-steve-biko-memorial-lecture-by-rev-al-sharpton/]

Four

The Soweto Massacre and the Growth of a New Black Consciousness

Written and compiled by Baldwin Ndaba and Janet Smith

There were many events during apartheid that deserved an unqualified, final push for *uhuru*,[63] yet the brutal control of Black South Africans by white oppressors was unlike any other experienced on the African continent. With the exception of some acts of war from the PAC's military wing, Poqo, and AZAPO's APLA, whites were, however, not tortured in retaliation.

There was no revenge even for the massacre of schoolchildren in Soweto in June 1976 – events expressly agonising among the atrocities

---

63 *Uhuru* means 'freedom' in Swahili. The word gained wider use after Kenya's first post-independence vice-president Jaramogi Ajuma Oginga Odinga (1911–1994) wrote his autobiography, *Not Yet Uhuru*, in 1967. Odinga's view that Kenya was not yet free when he wrote his book related to his conflict with Kenya's first president Jomo Kenyatta and Kenyatta's successor Daniel arap Moi, leading to Odinga being placed under house arrest once he assumed the position of opposition leader.

of the security forces unleashed by the National Party to secure supremacy. The uprising that followed changed the way activists and revolutionaries saw their path.

Led by the bravery of teenagers who had, in turn, been inspired and encouraged by their BC elders, 1976 delivered a generation so consciously powerful that it is only now beginning to be replicated.

Heroes like Ishmael Mkhabela, Neville Alexander, the teachers of the '70s townships and Dulcie September – who had to be killed to stop her from telling the truth – are being re-examined and honoured for their many contributions.

We revisit some of those here, exploring influences and futures for BC.

'I went through the torture myself, but I did not succumb': The story of Mike Matsobane

Baldwin Ndaba talks to the PAC and Bethal Trial veteran at his home in Krugersdorp about how the June 16 uprising was planned from within BC structures

June 16, 1976 did not only mark the outbreak of a widespread Black uprising. It also marked the day when the apartheid regime was caught unawares by the secret plans of BC and PAC township cells.

For more than a year, the police and BOSS were oblivious to former political prisoners and other community leaders, including the PAC's second president Zephania Mothopeng, plotting the greatest rebellion yet in the country's history.

One of those leaders was Mike Matsobane, a former Robben Islander who served his time for PAC-related military activities, and is now in his mid-70s. He reveals how the group of Black radicals successfully conspired to launch a revolution through the courageous acts of Soweto's schoolchildren from 1975.

Mothopeng had just returned to his home in Soweto after being banished to the Free State following his release from Robben Island for his participation in the 1960 anti-pass campaign, which led to the Sharpeville massacre.

Matsobane was released from Robben Island in 1967 after serving four years for attempting to overthrow the apartheid government. But imprisonment failed to deter either of them. Matsobane's greatest worry had, rather, been what he perceived as a 'political lull'. It concerned him that even some of his own PAC comrades, who had spent time on the Island too, were no longer showing interest in activism.

After lying low for about eight years, Matsobane started to organise underground to find a new strategy to fight the apartheid regime, and it was agreed that a Christian youth club – the Youth African Christian Movement (YACM) – would be formed as a front. This was immediately well received in churches and schools, especially around the Kagiso area east of Johannesburg, and in Soweto.

'We projected it to the people as a non-political movement whose primary objective was to fight alcohol and drugs,' Matsobane explains. The name was later changed to the Young African Religious Movement (YARM) to accommodate the Muslim community, which was fervently opposed to the scourge of abuse, but also had very strong activist tendencies. Matsobane said the clandestine preparations included meetings at his own house, and, finally, a major conference in December 1975 in Kagiso.

'The keynote speaker at the event was Desmond Tutu. At the time, Bishop Tutu was the Dean of Joburg.'

That conference got the attention of BOSS agents who arrived at Matsobane's house to question him about speeches made there. 'They wanted to find out why we were using militant words such as "fight against drugs and alcohol" and they also wanted to know why I addressed the conference and called people "African students". I told them that we are serious about our fight against drugs. But in my mind, I knew that they suspected the movement was a front for the PAC.' The agents left, saying they did not have the power to arrest him as 'they were only the intelligence arm of the police'. And that, chuckles Matsobane, was his last such meeting with henchmen of the apartheid government.

Meanwhile, plans continued to be made during further secret meetings, and, says Matsobane, it was Mothopeng who announced 16 June as the date for the resistance action.

The first signs of the onslaught came a little earlier, however – on 14 June in Kagiso, when residents torched beerhalls in the area. Two days later Soweto was on fire, and the 1976 uprising rapidly spread across the country as apartheid police resorted to state-sanctioned violence and killed hundreds of Black people.

Not long after the uprising, Matsobane, his brother Dan, Mothopeng and 15 others were behind bars again, charged with treason under the notorious Suppression of Communism Act in December 1977.

Theirs would be known as the Bethal Trial – the first ever secret political trial in the history of South Africa. Not even family members of the accused were allowed in court. Proceedings went on for more than 18 months.

Newspapers at the time were also reluctant to cover the trial. Editors allegedly said it was costly to send reporters 200km from the offices and give them allowances for food and accommodation. The court would hear that the reason proceedings were secret was for the safety of state witnesses, who included co-conspirators.

Matsobane has a different view. He says the *in camera* nature of the trial was to allow Judge DJ Curlewis to sentence all 18 of the accused to death.

'Judge Curlewis had the highest number of cases where he sentenced a lot of African people to death.'

When asked whether he harbours hate towards those PAC members and co-conspirators who ultimately testified against the Bethal trialists, Matsobane says: 'I do not. They were tortured to testify against us and some of their testimony was exaggerated to satisfy the prosecution. You must understand our threshold of resistance cannot be the same. I went through the torture myself, but I did not succumb.'

After his release in 1987, Matsobane's wife, a retired teacher, bought a house and, by uncanny coincidence, one of their new neighbours was the state's main witness in the trial, a former primary school principal named James Sejanamane.

But Matsobane is resolute: 'I did not have a problem with him. I get along well with all the family members of those who testified against us.'

The PAC has steadfastly maintained that the June 16 uprising was its revolutionary work. And indeed for Matsobane and many others, this is true. It is also true, however, that many in South Africa still believe the June 16 resistance was planned by members of the ANC, and it is recorded like that in many histories of the time. The most harmful of all the fractures within the liberation movements during the apartheid era – that between the PAC and the ANC – is, perhaps, made most painfully real in this memory. But what remains is that the young leaders of the uprising were followers of the BCM, and that cannot be erased.

[This piece, edited for this book, was first published in *The Star* on 16 June 2016, on the 40th anniversary of the massacre. It is reproduced here with kind permission from Independent Media.]

The teenage activists
Tsietsi Mashinini (1957–1990)

Mashinini was an active member of the Methodist Church and chair of the Methodist Wesley Youth Guild when he was at Morris Isaacson High in Soweto. He was regarded as an outstanding pupil, his acumen most marked in his debating skills. The legendary BC intellectual, Tiro, who was hired after he was expelled from Turfloop, taught Mashinini. Tiro was a primary influence, developing the teenager's BC tendencies and introducing him to the world's great Black writers, theorists and philosophers.

Once Mashinini had joined SASM and become its president at his school – as well as, after June 16, the president of the SSRC – he was committed to revolutionary struggle. He was among hundreds of Soweto schoolchildren who gathered at the Donaldson Orlando Community Hall to discuss strategies against Bantu Education two days before the uprising, but the planning had happened over a considerable period.

The children were dominantly against the introduction of the colonial settler language, Afrikaans, as a medium of instruction, with Mashinini offering a substantial understanding of the situation to a London-based interviewer in October 1976 and March 1977 in interviews published by Intercontinental Press. These are now housed in the ANC-SMFC Collection archives at Fort Hare University, according to the South African History Archive. (Mashinini was regarded as a fugitive at the time; hence, the interviews are not readily available.)

Mashinini said that 'with the type of education we have and where you do not have much material to research on, students find difficulty understanding concepts involved in physics, biology and geography. And now, if you do all these things in a language you are not conversant in, and the teacher has never been taught to teach in Afrikaans ... and all the time for almost 11 years, you have been taught through the medium of English, it is difficult to switch over.'

But he emphasised that the language issue was only an aspect of the systemic oppression to which Black children were being exposed.

'I realised that people were fed up with this sort of thing, but nobody had the guts to start anything. I decided that if we were to demonstrate, it would have an effect because there had never been a demonstration before in Soweto. There were demonstrations some time before we were born or when we were little kids, like Sharpeville ... of which we know very little because any written material about Sharpeville [was] banned.'

What wasn't banned, yet, was a placard Mashinini and his fellow scholars put up on the Morris Isaacson gate, reading: 'Notice – no security branch allowed. Enter at risk of your skin.'

That was four days before the massacre.

In the interviews, Mashinini directly addressed the question around student support for the ANC and PAC, and their position vis-à-vis BC. Today, the child heroes of 16 June are sometimes portrayed as having been a proxy for the liberation movements in exile at a time when political activity was at its most dormant due to the aggression of the apartheid state.

The interviewer asked him: 'Do you think there is a different political outlook between the old movements, the ANC and PAC, and the Black Consciousness Movement?'

Mashinini answered: 'Yes there is. There were a number of clashes between ANC and BCM leaders, because the ANC leaders did not want to recognise the BCM as a liberation movement.'

'Why didn't they want to recognise the BCM?' asked the interviewer.

'They did not want to understand why BCM was formed when ANC was the liberation movement. But ANC was banned inside the country, so a new liberation front had to come,' said Mashinini. He then went on to carefully elaborate on the history of the BCM, including describing the roles of SASO, SASM, the BPC, the Black Allied Workers Union and the affiliated Black women's federations.

'Their ideology is the same,' Mashinini told the interviewer, 'to make the Black man more conscious of the evil of the white man, elements of oppression and so on. The ideology is to peacefully bring about a change in the South African social aspect and to bring about total liberation of the Black man... As long as there is a Black person oppressed in South Africa, there will be Black movements, which will result in the concept of Black Power – the eruption of the Black masses.

'Black Power is every Black person in South Africa, Namibia and Zimbabwe. The ideology of the BCM defines "Blackness" as an attitude of the mind, and not of the colour of the skin.'

Before the uprising, Mashinini had been elected to lead an 'action committee', which later became the SSRC. He is particularly remembered for how he took to the podium during assembly on 16 June and began to sing, whereupon his fellow pupils did the same, and soon the children were walking peacefully together out of their schoolyard towards an assembly point.

Gradually, children from other schools moved in, and estimates say that up to 20 000 in their school uniforms had joined the mass march by the time it was ready to go.

Mashinini provided leadership, emphasising to the others that this was a peaceful event. Meanwhile, armed apartheid police were closing in around the children.

The bloodshed which ensued, with the first casualties being Hector Pieterson and Hastings Ndlovu, did not deter Mashinini.

Although he quickly became the Most Wanted child in South Africa, he continued the rallying cry against the regime as the uprising radiated into other provinces. He would not give up. He told his fellow pupils that the regime had embarked on an act of war.

Finally fearing imprisonment, torture and even assassination, he fled to Botswana a month after the massacre. Once over the border, Mashinini was feted at the highest levels especially in Guinea and Nigeria, eventually living and getting married in Liberia.

Such was his power that the UN invited him to address its General Assembly about apartheid. Still, Mashinini remained non-partisan in terms of the liberation movements in exile.

Much like his comrade Khotso Seatlholo, Mashinini did not die under the most salubrious of circumstances for a freedom fighter of his distinction. More moving was that he died in 1990, just as exiles were returning home. The cause of his death in Guinea – after he was hospitalised for multiple injuries and left maimed – remains a mystery.

Nonetheless, the BCM did not deny him his stature. AZAPO hosted a funeral service for him at Jabulani Stadium in Soweto. Mashinini was also honoured posthumously with the national Order of Luthuli in Gold.

[SAHO, 2010: This website carries a biography of Tsietsi Mashinini, from information contributed by Mashinini's brother Dichaba Mashinini; *Daily Sun*, 2017]

Khotso Seatlholo (1958–2004)

Seatlholo was a pupil at Naledi High in Soweto when, together with Mashinini, he became a leader of the SSRC. He took over the presidency of the SSRC when Mashinini was forced into exile, later joining Mashinini in Botswana.

He was captured in South Africa and charged under the Terrorism Act when he re-entered to recruit young people for the South African Youth Revolutionary Council (SAYCRO), the military wing of the SSRC.

Seatlholo spent 15 years in prison, and his death was a particular tragedy for the BCM as he died largely alone and somewhat forgotten.

Seth Mazibuko (1957–)

Mazibuko gained a particular power for being the youngest member of the action committee that gathered at the Donaldson Orlando Community Hall to strategise for the uprising. Aged just 16, Mazibuko was later arrested and held in solitary confinement at the notorious Number Four Prison at The Fort in Braamfontein, Johannesburg, before he spent seven years on Robben Island.

Mazibuko – who earned his education degree in prison – has, however, seldom been a background figure.

As recently as 2016, he was again being carried upon supporters' shoulders to the sound of protest songs, laced in the shadows of clenched fists, when he was released after being arrested following a violent protest against the installation of pre-paid electricity meters in Orlando East, Soweto. He was charged with common assault, public violence and malicious damage to property after the state claimed he had helped vandalise Eskom electric meter boxes as part of a long-running conflict between the parastatal and his community.

Mazibuko – who had declared his intention to run as an independent candidate in the 2016 local government elections – was reported in *Sowetan* newspaper as saying: 'It is the community that has been charged, not me. I still believe that the people shall govern. I pray to God that he gives us ethical leaders. This struggle is not new.' He had requested police protection after alleging that ANC councillors in Soweto had 'threatened' him after he held a meeting with members of the Orlando East community who had formed an Orlando Task Team (OTT) in 2014 focused on local government issues, including water and electricity problems and evictions.

[Xaba, 2016; Malefane, 2016]

The teachers

It was not only the children who were activists in June 1976. Many teachers were also BC supporters, well aware of how educators had laid the groundwork and protested when the apartheid government announced Bantu Education in 1953.

The regime expected teachers who had been trained in English to use Afrikaans as a medium of instruction for half the subjects in Standard 5 (current Grade 7) and in the first form (current Grade 1), even when many were unable to speak the language in its proper grammatical form themselves.

Although Afrikaans, as it is today, was a *lingua franca* in Soweto and other townships as it had been integrated into *iscamtho* or *tsotsi-taal* – a pidgin language across especially urban South Africa – there was little widespread knowledge of it in the formal, structured sense. For most teachers, it was, at best, a third language.

Once the apartheid minister of bantu affairs and development, MC Botha, introduced it as a determinant in Bantu Education from Standard 5, Afrikaans became a far more heightened political issue. It came against the backdrop of the development of the bantustans and accelerated marginalisation of actual South African citizenship to Black South Africans, but also against the inspiring backdrop of decolonisation across southern Africa. Maths, geography and history were to be taught in Afrikaans, while science, biology and practical subjects such as housecraft and woodwork – menial pursuits which were, however, also taught in white schools of the time – would be taught in English.

Forced upon Black teachers and children, Afrikaans – which was used almost exclusively by the regime's bureaucracy – was then no longer a language of the streets, but a lever for deeper control. It was a mark of enslavement.

The South African Democratic Teachers Union (SADTU), among other organisations and researchers, has narrated the response of many Black teachers to the crisis, during which the African Teachers Association of South Africa (ATASA) argued that 'the Black child would be seriously threatened'. It recognised that the apartheid government was using Afrikaans to deny Black children a role in the wider South African and world economy and access to 'an international future'.

Teachers were often powerful and courageous supporters of their students during protests over the months prior to the uprising in June 1976. Many teachers had already been fired for joining their pupils in these demonstrations, out of anger; others had been given no choice but to resign. Those who remained in class were largely behind the children whose increasing BC – rather than support for a particular liberation movement – ignited a complementary fire in themselves.

Teachers, particularly coloured teachers, were an especially driven community within the BC frame, inspired from as far back as 1913 when the Teachers League of South Africa was established in reaction to the announcement of a white Union of South Africa in 1910. Although more contemporary analysis has argued that there was a peculiar pattern within some coloured communities, which aspired towards a more elite education, and therefore a reactionary submission to the white value system, by the 1950s organisations like the Cape African Teachers' Union, the Natal African Teachers' Union, the Orange Free State African Teachers' Association and the Transvaal African Teachers' Association were becoming more unified and more activist. Any elitism appeared to have vanished by 1976.

Instead, teachers were by then increasingly critical of a colonial-centred history, which had touted especially church mission-style schooling as beneficial to Black South Africans. They berated the educational conservatism, and indeed the racism that was embedded in that system – aided and abetted by traditional leaders.

By 1976, they would help their pupils take on the apartheid state.

Many sources, including *www.joburg.co.za*, have quoted Wits academics Phil Bonner and Lauren Segal from their book *Soweto: A History* where they opine that one of the reasons the regime cracked down on the use of Afrikaans in schools at that precise moment was that television was finally to be introduced to South Africa in 1976, and 'Afrikaans-speaking conservatives feared that it would strengthen the position and status of English in the country'.

'It was also felt that Black school children were becoming too assertive and forcing them to learn in Afrikaans would be a useful form of discipline,' wrote Bonner and Segal.

White children, they recorded, had free schooling, 'but Black parents had to pay R51 – about half a month's salary – a year for each child, in addition to buying textbooks and stationery and contributing to the costs of building schools. 'The disparity in the government subsidy was telling: R644 was spent on each white child, but only R42 on each Black child.'

Meanwhile, not all Black teachers had the requisite qualifications to lead a classroom either, yet many of their former pupils remember them with a profound fondness: for how they politicised them; for how they developed a sense of Black community in them.

Former deputy chief justice Dikgang Moseneke – who sat on the Constitutional Court from 2002 to 2016, and whose memories are detailed in his book, *All Rise: A Judicial Memoir* (2020) – is one of those. Moseneke holds a significant place within the history of the BCM for being the youngest prisoner on Robben Island after being arrested, detained and convicted under the Terrorism Act at the age of 15 in 1962.

A member of the PAC by the age of 14, he spent a decade on the Island where he earned a BA in English and political science and then a B Iuris degree.

Moseneke writes in his 2016 autobiography, *My Own Liberator*, about how his teachers were his 'liberators', too: 'They spat at inferior Bantu education and ensured that they produced confident and well-rounded individuals.'

[Bonner & Segal, 1998; www.joburg.co.za, 2007; Matlhaku, 2017; SADTU, various: they can be found on www.sadtu.org.za]

Popular education

Since the 1970s, the BCM has tried to introduce pedagogy to strengthen popular education in South Africa. But it's not a smooth progression as public education in the country is so poor, and might, according to some analysts, even be the opiate of the people.

We must question why there is no improvement in the way our children are taught, despite no apparent national budgetary constraints. Could it be that if the Black masses were properly educated and able to righteously enter society, access all its resources and contribute, the neo-liberal political agenda would no longer be viable?

These are issues that the Johannesburg-based National Institute for the Humanities and Social Sciences (NIHSS), started in March 2013, tackles as it places its focus on BC-style pedagogy to strengthen popular education. Led by Professor Shirley Walters of UWC and honorary professor Astrid von Kotze of the University of KwaZulu-Natal, its projects are steered by an illustrious reference group that includes teachers, community leaders and trade unionists.

Among them are Omar Badsha of www.sahistory.org; Grischelda Hartman of the Development Institute for Training, Support and Education for Labour (Ditsela), which was established in 1996 by the main trade union federations; Derrick Naidoo of the Popular Education Programme (PEP); and Thami Nkosi of Ndifuna Ukwazi (NU).

Naidoo has particular importance as a role model among young conscious people. He was among a group of BC activists who went on a 41-day hunger strike in 1981 when they were being held under the infamous Section 6 of the Terrorism Act.

Also a leading internationalist – another important feature of BC – Naidoo is an activist for Palestinian freedom. A former teacher, he has, for example, been a vocal supporter of Palestinian hunger strikers against Israeli settler-colonialism, warning in *The Daily Vox* in 2016: 'In my own experience, assurances given by the regime to stop eventually were betrayed and never honoured.'[64]

Popular education activists like Naidoo use their background 'in South Africa in the 1970s and 1980s, [when] there was a proliferation of community organisations that identified strongly with anti-apartheid struggles, alternative development paradigms and social justice agendas'.

The Institute reminds us that 'most had a recognisable educational component: seeking to conscientise people who often had had limited access to formal education and, at the same time, impart practical skills and literacy.

'They operated outside of and often in direct opposition to the formal education system ... a reflection of authoritarian and racist relations in which [white] masters were deemed to be the experts inducting [Black] ignorant people into Western/European knowledge.'

As the BCM 'became the political home of many young people who refused to bow to the hegemonic forces of dehumanising schooling',

---

64 Naidoo's daughter, Leigh-Ann, a former Olympic athlete, #FeesMustFall activist and PhD scholar in education, was the South African delegate on the Women's Boat to Gaza. The Women's Boat to Gaza campaign is part of the international Freedom Flotilla Coalition, a grassroots solidarity movement working around the world to end the illegal Israeli siege of Gaza.

People's Education became a movement. Its struggles might seem contrary, as it ascribes some of the difficulties of expanding across Black communities to the fact that not everyone 'associates the values of liberation and humanity with education'.

'Similarly, few have heard of or read African and other philosophers and writers such as … Césaire, Fanon, Freire … Nkrumah, Nyerere … some of the people who inspired the BCM, community organisations, trade unions and people's education.'

Among other activist acts, the Institute is now bringing 'forgotten traditions' to the fore to 'ignite optimism and hope' – as has been the case with the BCM throughout its existence.

[Naidoo, 2016; www.populareducation.co.za]

The weave of language, policy, class and power: Neville Alexander's revolutionary legacy

Jean-Michel Jarre's song 'September' was composed for a friend and fellow revolutionary of Neville Alexander. And while few would dispute that Dulcie September (1935–1988), the activist assassinated outside 28, rue des Petites-Ecuries, the ANC's Paris office, was not deserving of the conceptual artist's attention, it seems unjust that Alexander (1936–2012) – an activist to the end – does not have his own composition. After all, Peter Gabriel took 'Biko' onto vinyl and the Dave Matthews Band picked out '#36' in honour of the murdered SACP leader, Chris Hani.

Yet perhaps it's fair to say that Alexander is not the ideal subject for a musical work. Neither iconic in his look – as were September, Biko and Hani – nor an especially romantic figure within the literatures of liberation, he instead ended up challenging the intellectual space in the interests of seeing Black communities build a new society.

If one imagined Alexander recalled in a piece of music, though, it might be infused with Beethoven, a favourite of Karl Marx – as long as the orchestra was not too dogmatic. There would almost certainly be a remix to include the clatters and clangs of the communal cells on 'the University of Robben Island' where Alexander spent 10 surprisingly human and fruitful years for conspiracy to commit sabotage. And there would surely be the happy voices of a children's choir from Cradock, the rural town of his birth, to remark upon his insights as a devout educator.

Certainly, Alexander must have been moved to see how September was remembered – and not only by Jarre. The New York-based German artist Hans Haacke modified a defunct fountain in front of the Grande Halle de la Villette in Paris to create *One Day, the Lions of Dulcie September Will Spout Water in Jubilation*. And a square in the 10th arrondissement in Paris was inaugurated in her name in March 1998 to mark the 10 years after her death.

Alexander and September spent many hours, days, months in each other's company together with fellow activists, first in the Teachers League of South Africa, an affiliate of the Non-European Unity Movement (NEUM), then in the named Yu Chin Chan Club (YCCC) – the independent organisation, among others, for whose activities Alexander was jailed in 1964. The YCCC would later form the basis for the National Liberation Front (NLF).

September, aged 52, had just collected the mail and was unlocking the door of the ANC's office in Paris when she was shot five times from behind with a .22-calibre rifle. A silencer meant she fell to the ground as quietly as her killer had stepped up. Her murder has lost none of its relevance as September was investigating weapons trafficking – allegedly also nuclear materials – between South Africa and France. The arms trade has dogged a free South Africa and its principles for more than two decades of liberation.

Alexander had been out of prison for more than a decade when September was killed. He might have contemplated their plots as activists, and what could have become of the YCCC had the members of that small 'study group' achieved their more militant aims.

The YCCC surely deserved a longer life just for the allure of its name, which incorporated the words for guerrilla warfare favoured by Mao Tse-tung. Others in the 'club', like Fikile Bam (1937–2011) – who went on to become judge president of the Land Claims Court and a member of the Goldstone Commission, among other achievements – might have agreed.

But the NLF had the potential to be a more serious platform for its co-founder Alexander, who was archly anti-colonialist, strongly anti-Stalinist (unlike many compatriots in the SACP) and a believer that the bourgeois should also be prodded into revolution.

His was a different path of resistance after prison, however. The NEUM – with which Alexander was associated through the Teachers League towards the end of the movement's rather fragile existence – may have started out in the earlier part of the century with the tacit support of Black minds CLR James and George Padmore. But it had very little activity that could be measured beyond newsletters, journals, pamphlets and books.

Alexander didn't seem content with constant theorising. Instead, while his compatriots in the NEUM were drawing up plans they would never enact to combat restrictive measures against Black peasant farmers' traditional cattle-herding grounds, he was meeting Cubans and Algerians while on the Alexander Humboldt Foundation scholarship in West Germany. It was the late 1950s. Why wouldn't such a mind be meeting people who could help him hone his ideological direction?

The NEUM was a grouping of Trotskyists who admirably determined to unite African, coloured and Indian South Africans under one banner – much like the BCM – but seemed incapable of gathering forces on the ground. It's furthermore debatable whether the NEUM had any radical policies that could come alive in the real world. Alexander, on the other hand, was a prescient soul who recognised intersectionality before it went vogue in the 2000s.

Unlike the NEUM, the socialist Alexander had a sustainable theory and, as academics Salim Vally, Brian Ramadiro and Jane Duncan wrote in 'The revolutionary who changed many lives', a tribute to him in the *Mail & Guardian* upon his death in 2012: '[He] remained committed to using the analytical tools of Marxism to develop this.

'His Marxism was not vulgar; it was enriched by his deep understanding of the South African situation.

'Ultimately that is the calling of a political movement: to garner empathy for its ideology and build mass support.'

Unlike many within the NEUM, Alexander knew he couldn't only live loftily in his head and imagine that, because he thought something should happen, it had already happened.

He also demanded a moral responsibility be placed on intellectuals – for instance, at the very least, to acknowledge they could already be in the morass into which the elite had waded in South Africa post-1994.

Saying the intelligentsia was in fact part of those 'power elites', Alexander continued rather sadly: 'Those of us who fought consciously and often at great personal cost for the liberation of South Africa from the shackles of apartheid and colonialism, are left asking ourselves whether this is the kind of society we had in mind' (from *South Africa Today*, a lecture Alexander gave at the 10th anniversary celebration of the Foundation for Human Rights in Pretoria in 2006).

His concerns about the intelligentsia had not softened by 2011, when he said it was 'high time' they accepted 'that language, policy, class and power are tightly interwoven and that, unless we devise our own agendas in the interest of our people as a whole, we are willy-nilly carrying out others' possibly nefarious agendas' (from 'The centrality of the language question in post-apartheid South Africa: Revisiting a perennial issue', published in www.scielo.org.za in 2012).

Although Alexander's time with left-wing organisations like the YCCC and the NLF should predominate in any revolutionary analysis of him, it is surely rather his later fight to see South Africans educated, and their languages and culture treated equally and admired, which matters more. That was his 'permanent revolution'.

That was a positive aspect of his years on Robben Island. Not only did he and others, including prominent members of the ANC, dream up 'the Society for the Rewriting of South African History' – which saw them debating everything from Shakespeare to Hegel – but the prisoners came to respect each other's personal histories. This gave Alexander the confidence to learn how to speak Xhosa again, and for illiteracy to be all but eradicated on the Island through their efforts by the end of their time there.

Once he was released, among other roles he became the Cape Town director of SACHED, the secretary of the Health, Education and Welfare Society of South Africa, a leader of the Workers Organisation for Socialist and Action and, finally, director of the Project for the Study of Alternative Education, a unit attached to the University of Cape Town. Alexander showed he was in fact a most effective post-democratic revolutionary.

His book *One Azania, One Nation: The National Question in South Africa* (first published under the *nom de guerre* of No Sizwe, and then banned) was about trying to wrestle national unity out of the disparate movements within the liberation fold. It remains a vital text.

Of course, Alexander was right: Unless we know each other – and that would come naturally by studying and learning to love each other's culture and languages – we cannot realise consciousness. It's likely he, however, did.

[Vally, Ramadiro & Duncan, 2012; Alexander, 2006]

'Three weeks later, Biko was dead'

There's a part of Alexander's story which disturbs some who consider him an exemplary revolutionary. They feel it detracts from what he stood for. They believe it isn't properly contextualised by those who have allowed an impression that he 'betrayed' Biko to go mostly unchallenged for 40 years. Meanwhile, a further impression, that Alexander spent the rest of his life in sorrow for what happened, also suggested that this was, in the end, the only event that mattered in his rather large life.

This part of the story starts in 1974 when Alexander had been released from prison, banned and placed under house arrest for five years. That would take him up to 1979, a time during which he deepened and widened his connections with those who shared his vision of a socialist future. Alexander intended to continue the fight for that in South Africa.

He hosted 'study groups' between members of the then Unity Movement (UM) and the BCM while, in the background, plans continued for nationwide mass action against the apartheid government's declaration of the Transkei's 'independence' the previous October. This had been held back when the bloodshed of June 1976 happened.

Alexander was, however, also wary about being exposed to the extent that he could be jailed again. Biko had himself been banished to King William's Town in 1973 and was actively pursuing the BCP. During that time, he was consulted on an almost continuous basis by people representing all sorts of forces with different agendas.

Both Alexander and Biko were thus using their time under 'house arrest' productively for political ends. Neither was attached to either the ANC or the PAC. Yet it was a problematic political moment. For Biko, there must have been some ideological confusion around the BCP, and where next to take the BCM.

In some ways the BCP and the BCM were distinct as the BCM wished to remain 'pure', and not rely in any way on white liberals or white capital for its survival or growth. The BCP was instead drawing closer to the ANC's policy of using whatever resources were at its disposal in accepting funding, even from business corporates. Truth was, though, that the BCP had little choice. If it rejected such funding on the basis of an ideological conflict – the intrinsic link between race and class – the programmes would likely collapse. There was no money to sustain it in the Black community and so the stealth of white monopolistic capital might have to be overlooked.

(That would also be the case for the UDF, the ANC's proxy in the 1980s. It too had little choice but to take that kind of funding, although the difference was that the ANC had a leaning towards neo-liberalism, and an indisputably non-racial position. Yet accepting that funding would naturally make it increasingly difficult to extricate itself from the power that white capital would ultimately hold over it.)

No doubt the BCP's relationship with its funders clashed with the BCM's stated protocol of building Black communalism and self-reliance, rejecting both white capital and white liberalism. The funders, on the other hand, probably preferred it if the BCP toned down open discussion about actual revolutionary intent.

Another great concern was that members of the BCM in Cape Town, led by dedicated soldier of the movement Johnny Issel, seemed to be fomenting their own rebellion, apparently frustrated with the BCM's ambivalence around assuming a more radical posture. There was for instance a significant divide over Biko having met US Senator Dick Clark – who chaired the influential Senate Subcommittee on

African Affairs – in Ginsberg, in the area to which he had been banished, the previous December. There was also ongoing criticism of a plan by a cohort in exile to get Biko to Gaborone, Botswana, to meet Tambo, although papers had been written inside the movement on how to forge closer ties with the ANC and the PAC. Of course, the ANC would not have been able to look the other way if the BCM rose on the ground at home while it struggled with political dormancy.

Not only had the BCM delivered some of its finest cadres into the ANC's surrogacy in exile after the Soweto massacre the previous year, it had not fallen into the PAC's 'Africa First' camp.

The political simplicity of the BCM was that it was largely non-partisan. But had it had the capacity to properly organise across the grassroots, and develop its ideology to the extent that it could reach into the unionised working class and the broader poor, the BCM could have grown into a serious and independent political contender. That wouldn't have worked for the ANC. By 1977, the BCM, like the ANC and the PAC, was still grappling not only with its leadership being mostly banned, in prison or in exile, and the savage might of the apartheid regime's security forces, but also with how to secure the ordinary Black person's support in every house, street and community across the country.

The ANC felt it could offer the BCM a mutually beneficial relationship. In 1977, Biko drove out of his area of banishment with his colleague Peter Jones, hoping to meet Alexander in Cape Town to have a discussion about common ground. Despite being under alarming threat if he was caught, Biko was determined. But either Alexander could not take that risk or the political circumstances in terms of more important allegiances on the ground were too great.

Fikile Bam was one of many mediators between the two parties. Biko's superlative biographer Xolela Mangcu writes that 'Bra Fiks' even travelled to Ginsberg, where Biko stayed under his banning, to discuss unity talks. Bam was himself banned at the time and restricted to the Transkei.

There are differing versions of what happened, and who was on whose side, but it seems clear that when news got to Alexander that Biko was in Cape Town, he indicated he wouldn't see him. Bam – who was also in Cape Town – then apparently acted as a mediator again, and drove Biko to Alexander's house in Grassy Park on the Cape Flats under cover of night on 17 August; but while to-ing and fro-ing between the car and the house went on for quite some time, Alexander himself never came out. Biko was not able to leave the car.

Alexander told Mangcu that 'it was a clash of cultures': 'We were a disciplined underground movement. On their side, they were carried away by their own spontaneity. They thought if they just showed up, I would see them. But my house was literally besieged by the cops for weeks on end. We were sent to prison for such little mistakes.'

Finally, Biko and Jones had no choice. They had to head back to King William's Town, which was a journey of more than 10 hours. They were within an hour of their destination when they were pulled over at a roadblock. Mangcu writes how Jones was taken to Algoa police station, and Biko to Walmer. Both police stations were in Port Elizabeth.

While Jones was detained and repeatedly tortured for nearly 18 months, Biko was tortured while kept naked and manacled for 20 days before being transferred to the Sanlam Building in Port Elizabeth. Like John Vorster Square in Johannesburg, that building's name was a byword for the violence of the security police.

Between 6 and 7 September, Biko sustained 'at least three brain lesions occasioned by the application of force to his head'. The district surgeon Dr Ivor Lang could 'find nothing wrong' with Biko and recommended he be driven to the Pretoria prison hospital. On 11 September, Biko was loaded into a Land Rover without support, in that horrific condition, and taken 700km away – a journey of more than 12 hours.

He died on 12 September, the 46th person to die in prison since detention without trial was legalised in South Africa in 1963, and would become the most important name among those.

Alexander told Mangcu that this 'was one of the most tragic moments of my life': 'There was a contradiction between commitment to organisational discipline and my own wish to meet a person I really should have spoken to that evening.'

In June 1997, the Truth and Reconciliation Commission's health hearings witnessed UCT pharmacology head Professor Peter Folb apologising directly to Biko's widow Ntsiki and his brother Khaya, saying 'the medical profession continued to address the ethical issues which the Biko case had raised'. The SAPA report on the hearings documented that 'although an inquest magistrate had found there was a prima facie case of professional misconduct and/or negligence against the district surgeons treating Biko, Folb said the South African Medical and Dental Council (SAMDC) took no action against them'.

The Medical Association of South Africa then declared that the SAMDC 'had been correct in its findings', and it was only after a group of doctors brought a Supreme Court action that the Council finally launched an inquiry into the conduct of district surgeons Lang and Benjamin Tucker.

It found Tucker guilty of disgraceful conduct and Lang guilty of improper conduct, but the punitive measures were slight. Tucker was suspended from the medical register for three months, with the sentence itself suspended for two years, while Lang was cautioned and reprimanded.

There was a collective 'sound of anguish' at the TRC hearings, wrote the great South African human rights lawyer George Bizos, when it was described how Biko 'was chained to the interrogation room door in mock crucifixion, his legs attached by shackles to the grillwork'.[65]

Bizos further wrote how the deplorable Minister of Justice Jimmy Kruger 'joked with the foreign press', saying: 'A man can damage his brain many ways. I have also felt like banging my head against a brick wall many times, but realising now, with the Biko autopsy that may be fatal, I haven't done it.'

Thirty-seven days after the atrocities against Biko happened, the apartheid regime banned 18 BC organisations and Black newspapers on what is still known as Black Wednesday.

The BCM's next layer of leaders were in prison. Many of the most talented and fearless young Black leaders of the June 1976 generation

---

65   Bizos is quoted from his book *No One to Blame? In Pursuit of Justice in South Africa* in the paper 'Stephen Biko and the torture aesthetic' written by Marian Eide in 2014 for *Ufahamu: A Journal of African Studies* at the University of California in Los Angeles.

were either behind bars, banned or had fled into exile. It was a tormented and agonising time.

As to whether his decision not to see Biko that night defines Alexander in any way: surely this is not so much moot as unjust.

[Mangcu, 2012: 255; www.justice.gov.za/trc/media; Bizos, 1998 in Eide, 2014]

The fight against the Black comprador bourgeoisie: The story of AZAPO

AZAPO declared 2017 to be the Year of the Rescue of the Revolution, as 2016 was 'downright more painful for the majority of us than we deserved'. Its New Year's message said history would 'never forgive us for handing back our own freedom and liberation on a platter to the colonialists, racists and the white settler-minority regime'. Dubbing the ANC a 'Black comprador bourgeoisie', and attacking the 'national tragedy' of corruption, AZAPO's lively, revivalist language urged its supporters to 'take collective blame' for 'colluding'.

For many in its movement, this would indeed have been a painful moment. Ten years before AZAPO struck its founding document in 1978, Black students were on the rise. Attending a UCM conference to strategise on how to protest against the apartheid clause that forbade them to remain in a designated white area for more than 72 hours, they began to formulate setting up the Blacks-only student movement that later became SASO.

Then came the BPC, designed as the flagship of the burgeoning BCM. Its primary influences were the global student protests; the thought leadership of Anton Muziwakhe Lembede of the ANCYL of the 1940s; the Unity Movement (UM); and Sobukwe. Although there were a number of tenets of the BPC, its belief in Black 'communalism' was primary, and this gave it a closer allegiance to Nyerere's *ujamaa* and other 'Black first' convention-style movements on the continent.

Even when the first major wave of bannings against the BCM had taken place after the Schlebusch Commission, activities continued under the aegis of the Black Consciousness Movement of Azania

(BCMA). It brewed underground and then actively in exile after 1974. By 1980, its members were popular even in London's left-wing circles. There were BCMA chapters in southern Africa as well as in the US and Canada, and in England, France, Belgium and Germany. And it wasn't only a political and intellectual exercise.

The BCMA had witnessed the burgeoning conquest in the ANC's method out of its Kabwe Conference in 1975. The ANC had agreed there to a broader version of armed struggle, one that would have a greater appeal to young Black people; it gave them a sense of purpose and direction, which organisations like the UM and even the BCM were unable to do with their concentration on theory. BCMA's formation of the Azanian National Liberation Army (AZANLA) reinvigorated the militants within BC, and with support and funding from Black Power and solidarity circles around the world, it could send them for training in China as well as in Libya and Eritrea. Those were not the ANC's conventional partners. It had been much closer to the Soviet Union than to China, and Libya and Eritrea had not hosted its military camps, unlike Angola and Tanzania. The BCMA, which dreamed of creating a 'democratic socialist Azanian state', was thus a bit of a bulwark for AZAPO.

Although there were a number of heroes in its fold, it found a leader in Mosibudi Mangena, who had helped establish the BPC back in 1972. He was a popular candidate. He'd spent five years on Robben Island after being sentenced under Section 6 of the Terrorism Act in 1973 for BPC activities and was then banned for five years after his release, as was the customary practice of the apartheid government.

The Mangena family had little choice but to go into exile in Botswana. Although some BCM activists joined the ANC at that point, Mangena instead developed the BCMA first out of Gaborone and then in Zimbabwe. Based largely in Harare from then on, he only returned to South Africa in 1994, when he was elected president of AZAPO.

The organisation did not contest the first democratic elections, having vociferously objected to concessions, particularly on land and minority rights, required to seal the Declaration of Intent of the Convention for a Democratic South Africa (CODESA) in 1991.

(CODESA was a series of negotiations between 1990 and 1993 held between the apartheid-era National Party (NP) and the ANC and other political organisations. Its 'Sunset Clauses', which effectively guaranteed the NP a 'peaceful transition' from white minority rule while retaining substantial benefits for many of those white beneficiaries, is still a source of anger and bewilderment.)

In the background, AZAPO had been trying to tie together a Patriotic Front with the PAC in Zimbabwe, calling for a constituent assembly elected on a One Person, One Vote basis to draft a new constitution. Meanwhile, CODESA – which saw representation by more than 90 organisations – seemed, at its essence, to be a negotiation only between the National Party and the ANC. A second round, dubbed CODESA 2, was an abysmal failure largely because those two parties were by then unendingly at odds over a minority veto in an interim government.

Although AZAPO's decision not to take part in 1994 is still debated today, its primary reason for not participating was its abiding concern that Black people would never be fully emancipated by CODESA's clauses.

Those who think it should have gone ahead anyway and then tackled the problems once in government asked whether it was judicious for a BC party to step into the cold on principle while the ANC was sharing a Government of National Unity (GNU) with De Klerk's National Party and Buthelezi's IFP. (The PAC remained small, bitterly divided and marginalised.) The GNU lasted from 27 April 1994 to 3 February 1997 under the leadership of the ANC.

AZAPO had not been inactive in terms of consolidation, though, as AZAPO and the BCMA merged organically in 1994 in what is known as the Shaft 17 Congress. The BCMA then melted away and AZAPO represented the whole. It did take part in the next national elections in 1999, when Mangena was chosen to represent it as its only MP. He was later made the deputy minister of education and, then, minister of science and technology, and given the Order of Luthuli in Silver in 2013 in recognition of his role in the struggle for freedom.

It might be fair to say, however, that AZAPO was isolated from the *zeitgeist* during Mandela's years of 'reconciliation'. (Later the BCM veteran and former Robben Islander, Pandelani Nefolovhodwe, also became an AZAPO MP. He had been a student leader at Turfloop with Tiro before being expelled by the racist administration. After teaching for a while, he returned to university and was elected president of the SRC and national president of SASO in 1974. Nefolovhodwe helped organise the Frelimo rally in October 1974, after which he was arrested and charged with terrorism. He was a defendant with Moodley, Lekota and six others in the SASO 9 trial.)

Although the BCMA provided solidarity after AZAPO was founded in 1978, it had been a complicated 15 years for the BCM. The ANC had assumed the psychological advantage after 1977 when the BCM was no longer able to operate in the open after the bannings of Black Wednesday a month after the talismanic Biko was murdered. Then in the early 1980s, the ANC seized its chance at popular politics again and birthed the UDF.

A number of BC people were involved, including Issel, the vociferous Western Cape activist who had urged more radical politics from the BCM, even discussing this with Alexander in the days before Biko's arrest.

Issel (1946–2011) then joined forces with Cape-based activist Trevor Manuel in the early 1980s and is credited with organising the UDF's massive launch in Athlone on the Cape Flats in 1983. (Manuel would later become minister of finance, and has now joined capital. There have been allegations about a role he might have had in protecting the white Afrikaner elite in the early years of democracy, and he was hamstrung by an apparent lack of insight, and insufficient moral investigation or intervention into the so-called 'arms deal' – the Strategic Defence Procurement Packages – finalised by the ANC in 1999.) That was such a different moment to the early 1970s when the BCM was starting to reverberate across the country, steadily reinventing Black politics against the backdrop of a cowed ANC and PAC.

Were it not for the BCM, the children of the 1976 resistance might not have been mobilised. Were it not for BC, the ANC might not have been bolstered by conscientised young bravehearts who fled the bullets of apartheid and joined its ranks in exile.

AZAPO emerged out of a time of political chaos. Of the struggle years until then, 1976 and 1977 were the most desperate and the bloodiest as the regime shamelessly turned its guns on children in school uniform. The government was sanctioning the assassinations of its enemies with gunshots in the back and by parcel bomb. It was pushing them out of high windows. But the activists who vowed they would never submit, even under horrifying torture, knew it was unlikely their most valiant actions would yet shut down the violent racists who ruled.

That would only come when the regime finally had no money left; when it had been cornered enough by international solidarity to no longer be able to afford to keep the oppression going under the radar. Such is the way of capitalism, and in the South Africa of the 1970s, the axis between race and capital had at last been recognised by the liberation movements and the BCM, although the BCM never quite managed to pull a workers' alliance together.

This was despite Koka's recruitment under Biko to set up BAWU in 1972. The regime quickly banned Koka, first detaining him for months in solitary confinement.

Out of sorrow and fury, AZAPO determined to destroy that very axis in 1978. It wanted to find a new way forward to allow Black people to lead, but without an allegiance to the ANC.

It was a tough environment. The media might technically have been free in that the state did not own or directly control it, but Black Wednesday had blocked the few avenues that still existed for BC's public resistance.

A reminder of the organisations that were banned on that day: the BPC; SASO; SASM; NAYO (National Association of Youth Organisations) and all its affiliates; the BCP; the Medupe Writers' Association; the Zimele Trust Fund; the Black Women's Federation; the UBJ; and the Association for the Educational and Cultural Advancement of the African People of South Africa. *The World* and the *Weekend World* newspapers and heroic editor Percy Tshidiso Qoboza were also banned.

The regime had toughened up its laws by then, replacing the Suppression of Communism Act with the more onerous Section 10 of the Internal Security Act. There was almost no escaping.

Qoboza was among dozens detained without trial. He effectively disappeared for six months and, when he was released, had little choice but to leave. He and his family moved to the US where he worked in part for the *Washington Star*. Qoboza, who was also a prestigious Nieman Fellow at Harvard, went on to edit *City Press* newspaper in Johannesburg from 1984 upon his return home, but died in 1988 on his 50th birthday after a heart attack earlier had left him in a coma.

BC was, however, far from dead, even if the ANC was seizing its moment. Some of the most influential names in South African journalism would continue to serve its philosophy in courageous endeavours of the pen. These included Joseph (Joe) Nong Thloloe, Joyce Sikhakhane-Rankin, Thami Mazwai and Sandile Memela.

Thloloe and Mazwai were closely identified with the PAC, with Thloloe going on to become the president of the UBJ and later the Media Workers Association of South Africa. He served as the executive director of the Press Council.

Mazwai became a media entrepreneur and publisher, and honorary professor of entrepreneurship at UWC and Fort Hare. He was also on the National Planning Commission instigated by the ANC-led government and, somewhat controversially, a special adviser to the small business development ministry.

Sikhakhane-Rankin, who has a BSc Honours degree from the Open University in the United Kingdom, is a legend in South African media, having been an activist, writer, TV producer and consulting editor.

Memela is a journalist and columnist of long-standing repute and has been a strategic media adviser and spokesperson within government.

The Congress of South African Students (COSAS) grew out of the banned SASM in 1979, gaining mileage for its aggressive campaign to support MK operative Solomon Kalushi Mahlangu (1956–1979), who would be executed by hanging after being found guilty on two counts of murder and three charges under the Terrorism Act. Mahlangu, who had been trained by MK in Angola and Mozambique, re-entered South African in June 1977 through Swaziland with ammunition, explosives and pamphlets. Two fellow guerrillas – Mondy Johannes

Motloung and George 'Lucky' Mahlangu – accompanied him.

It was only two days later that they were detected by police in Goch Street, central Johannesburg, and a gun battle ensued. Two ordinary citizens were killed and two wounded, and Mahlangu and Motloung were arrested. 'Lucky' Mahlangu escaped. But as Motloung had suffered debilitating brain damage during the arrest, he couldn't stand trial and, as common purpose had been formed, Mahlangu was able to be convicted on all counts.

Mahlangu's name was proudly brandished during the 2015 #FeesMustFall campaigns at Wits when Senate House was renamed by the students, many of whom were BC *redux*. Their passionate cry for the name of a students' hero to be given an honour such as that was ultimately heard by the Wits management, and Senate House is today officially known as Solomon Mahlangu House.

Although COSAS is most closely associated with the ANC, and supported the establishment of the UDF, its BC roots are undeniable. That was also the case with the Azanian Students Organisation (AZASO) of the late 1980s. Its leader then, Tiego Moseneke, is the brother of former deputy chief justice, Dikgang Moseneke. Tiego, on the other hand, was a Wits Black Student Society (BSS) president in the 1980s, but has had a cloud over him on and off over the past 10 years on discomfiting allegations of nepotism and fraud. He was struck off the roll of attorneys in 2006.

But such was Tiego's reputation as a student activist that, when #FeesMustFall was unfolding, he became the spokesperson for the South African Student Solidarity Foundation for Education. This was a fund to help facilitate access into higher education institutions and to raise fees for students who cannot afford them.

It gave Tiego Moseneke an unexpected entry into current BC politics, offering him a platform to say in the Wits student newspaper, *Vuvuzela*, in 2016, that 'There are too many able young people denied a good education because they are poor', and to advocate for the first time in 30 years for 'a mass movement that will reverberate across the country'. But Tiego Moseneke, like all too many others from that era, has not yet told the whole story of his experience of the often-deadly turf wars between the ANC-aligned student organisations and those from BC formations.

Although AZASO was defiantly formed in 1979 as a means of substituting for the BCM's banned crown jewel, SASO, it would by the 1980s be effectively co-opted into the ANC camp. AZASO would then morph into the South African National Students Congress (SANSCO) and finally come full circle when SANSCO and NUSAS – SASO's old nemesis – merged to form the South African Students Congress (SASCO) in 1991 at Rhodes.

AZAPO, meanwhile, had to replace the renegade AZASO with the Azanian Students Movement (AZASM) in 1983 when BC students found themselves at a loss for a political home. The Western Cape-based Students of Young Azania (SOYA) was also created as a barrier against AZASO's reinvention, SANSCO. AZASM had to quickly build credibility, and its first move was to invite BC stalwarts Nefolovhodwe and Moodley to address its inaugural conference. SANSCO had instead asked Diliza Mji and Lekota – both former BCM leaders, but by then supporters of the UDF – to do the same.

Mji is now a surgeon in Cape Town and the founder of Black-owned private healthcare group Busamed, but he received adverse press over his alleged links to a Corvette gearbox deal attached to arms trading. When those links were claimed, Mji was the ex-chairman of the Independent Development Corporation. He has also been a non-executive director of Telkom SOC Limited.

Lekota is the leader of the ANC breakaway party, the Congress of the People (COPE), which now has three seats in the National Assembly.

But AZASM could never reach the numbers which SANSCO and then SASCO could attract, although it had a foothold in some secondary schools. This was a painful dilemma, as attacks against some of AZASM's members chipped away at its political self-confidence. That pattern was repeated for AZAPO itself. Although Mangena was a particularly good leader working hard to see the ANC and the PAC in a unified front with AZAPO, its revolutionary impetus may quite simply still have to bide its time. Even the NF which eventuated at AZAPO's 800-delegate-strong congress in 1983, the year the UDF came about, and intended to be a unifier for the liberation movements, was unable to soar to the heights of the UDF.

While the BCMA and AZAPO were meeting with the PAC in

Zimbabwe for the Kadoma Consultation, which hoped to bring about a Patriotic Front, the Harare Declaration was bringing the ANC into the frame of the OAU ahead of the final drive towards the unbanning of the liberation movements in 1990.

The BC Azania People's Manifesto was never as powerful as the now-mainstream Freedom Charter, with AZAPO being walled up against the 'Charterists' until today.

AZAPO and the BCMA were surely a tremendous force in helping to end apartheid, even if neither has been justly recognised as such. Especially in terms of the cultural boycott, which played a most influential role in global solidarity to bring about freedom, the BC cohort made a relentless push for Black self-determination, while the ANC was straightening its lapels, checking its cigar boxes and polishing its high-end shoes to meet Afrikaner intellectuals in Dakar, Senegal.

[Boso, 2016; www.pmg,org.za; www.azapo.org; Seekings, 2000; Mangcu, 2012]

Ishmael Mkhabela

A man of immediate gentleness, despite the impact of a violent apartheid regime on his struggle history, former schoolteacher 'Ish' Mkhabela has spent his life within BC.

He was undeterred after the BCM was banned in October 1977, turning his attention within a month to the Soweto Action Committee. The roots of that organisation lay with the Committee of 10, formed by prominent BC-aligned Soweto residents who wanted complete autonomy for the township. The apartheid regime was having none of that and continued advancing the control of its Bantu Administration Board.

It then detained most of the members of the Committee of 10, led by its most outspoken 'ambassador', businessman and physician Nthato Motlana. His wife, Sally – an ardent activist for Black consumer rights and a leading member of the Black Women's Federation – was detained. (Motlana was a founding member of the BCP, but such was his leaning towards business that he is today better known as the father of Black Economic Empowerment.)

Mkhabela defied the expectations society may have of a person of his stature. He was the founder chairperson of AZAPO – which was formed with Mabasa, AZAPO's current leader Itumeleng Mosala, Cooper, Strini Moodley, Mangena, Myeza, Nefolovhodwe, Nchaupe Mokoape and others on 28 April 1978 in Roodepoort outside Johannesburg – but remained focused on the day-to-day problems of Black communities.

In any event, not a month after AZAPO was formed, Mkhabela and Mabasa were arrested in Soweto. Held under the General Law Amendment Act of 1963, they were charged with terrorism and banned.

Perhaps Mkhabela would have been more comfortable with being charged for standing up to the power charge of the UDF five years later. His concern then was what lay beneath overtures from the UDF to BC formations. There had been murder victims on the AZAPO side, and violent clashes had characterised some encounters between the UDF and AZAPO on the ground.

Mkhabela, now chairman of the Steve Biko Foundation with its offices in Johannesburg and in Biko's village of Ginsberg, has remained true to his calling as a community organiser and change activist. He became particularly well known as a negotiator in challenging face-to-face situations. Mkhabela serves as the chairperson of the Johannesburg Innercity Partnership and is the deputy president of the SAIRR. He was the CEO of the Interfaith Community Development Association which he founded, together with the Witwatersrand Network for the Homeless.

Mkhabela – who is married to Bongi Mkhabela, a vital proponent of BC throughout her life and now the CEO of the Nelson Mandela Children's Fund – is a member of the board of the Nelson Mandela Children's Hospital Trust in Johannesburg. He is also a member of the board of the Centre for Development and Enterprise and the Donaldson Trust, the oldest fund for Black social development in South Africa.

The Steve Biko Foundation

Its stated purpose is to 'create an inclusive platform' to promote the legacy of Steve Biko, who believed in Black self-reliance. Biko's inspiration has led the Foundation to establish that platform through education and training, but always with the intention of helping people find their identity.

Just as Biko was himself an intellectual resource for many people in his time, the Foundation endeavours to be that too, with its most ambitious project the Steve Biko Centre in Ginsberg. It wants to focus on community-based organisations there 'to provide essential services' and develop cultural industries. At the same time, it looks to build mass participation in national dialogues.

The Foundation has hosted the annual Steve Biko Memorial Lecture since 2000. Its alumni include Professor Njabulo S Ndebele, Professor Zakes Mda, Professor Chinua Achebe, Ngũgĩ wa Thiong'o, Nelson Mandela, Archbishop Emeritus Desmond Tutu and the Reverend Al Sharpton.

It also hosts the Robert Sobukwe Memorial Lecture, which honours the legacy of the late Pan-Africanist, and its alumni include Professor Es'kia Mphahlele, Archbishop Emeritus Njongonkulu Ndungane and Justive Dumisa Ntsebeza.

Among the Foundation's other projects is the Matthew Goniwe Youth Leadership Conference, an annual gathering which brings together delegates from 70 community-based organisations to interact with society leaders.

Its *Frank Talk* forum, which recalls Biko's column in the SASO newsletters of the early 1970s, brings together young professionals to discuss issues.

Tiyani Lybon Mabasa and the Socialist Party of Azania

Formed in March 1998, nearly two decades after AZAPO, the Socialist Party of Azania (SOPA) emerged out of that very organisation. Its luminaries in its ranks have included Mabasa, Rose Ngwenya, Dr Gomolemo Mokae,[66] Lekgantshi Console Tleane,[67] Ashraf Jooma[68]

---

66   Gomolemo Mokae (1964–) is an author, medical doctor, screenwriter, film maker and political commentator who writes in English and Setswana.

67   Lekgantshi Console Tleane was City of Tshwane spokesman from 2007 until 2011 when he moved on to work for the metro police. He is a contributor to the *Monthly Review*, an independent Socialist magazine.

68   Ashraf Jooma was general-secretary of the Azanian Section of the Fourth International (AS-FI), the South African chapter of the international

and Strini Moodley and his wife, Asha (see *The Art of Black Consciousness*).

SOPA blends into its ideological mix humanist Marxist-Leninism, the political thought of Biko, BC and pedagogy.

Its view, similar to that of the EFF, is that Blacks in South Africa are not yet liberated and that the 'neo-colonial' ANC is akin to a proxy white party whose success is contingent upon it adhering to the demands of white capital. SOPA stated its positions as land expropriation without compensation; nationalisation 'of the commanding heights of the economy', starting with the mines; the building of a socialist project, and the struggle for the name Azania 'as the first symbol of a break with colonialism and imperialism that imposes restrictions on our country, including the repayment of the apartheid debt and the subordination of the country into the clutches of the Bretton Woods financial institutions that have imploded many economies throughout the world'.

SOPA regards the World Bank, the World Trade Organization and the IMF as 'imperialist' organisations.

It urges instead a Black united front 'to advance the struggles of the Black working class and the Black majority', finding an affiliation with the EFF, the Association of Mineworkers and Construction Union (AMCU, which was formed in Marikana) and the National Council of Trade Unions (Nactu) 'for a revolution of the proletariat and an abolishment of private ownership of the means of production'.

Although it is not in a formal political bond with AZAPO, the two bodies have attempted to find a common purpose.

BC veteran Mabasa, SOPA's president and a SOPA candidate on the EFF's list of 830 names for the 2014 national election, delivered SOPA's membership of the International Liaison Committee for the Workers International. But to Marxists such as themselves, it's also important they remain Trotskyists and therefore remain welcome within the Fourth International, which works at bringing about socialism and international communism. SOPA forms the Azanian Section within the Fourth International.

---

organisation of the working class, and editor of *Black Republic*, the Azanian newsletter published by supporters of the Organising Committee for the Reconstitution of the Fourth International.

Mabasa was conscientised through SASO. He enrolled for a BA in English and linguistics at Turfloop, but was quickly more involved in the student Christian movement on campus. Refused readmission in his final years because of his politics, Mabasa then started teaching at Meadowlands High School and joined the BCP. After being held for four months by security police after the 1976 massacre, Mabasa helped plot AZAPO before being arrested under Section 6 of the Terrorism Act in that year.

Mabasa was AZAPO's vice-president and later its president. His Facebook page is a strong source of BC material and ideas.

[www.pa.org.za; Ndaba, 2013; www.economicfreedomfighters.org; Sosibo, 2014]

Rose Ngwenya

When the EFF under commander-in-chief Julius Malema contested the 2014 national elections, it announced it had established 'working relations' and reached agreements with several organisations on candidates. Primary among these were SOPA and the BC Party, which did not intend to stand independently for election, but would share their capacity with the EFF. Their candidates were to be listed as EFF members.

For many BC supporters, SOPA representative Ngwenya was an advantage for the EFF. She had been as important to the progress of BC in the late 1960s and early 1970s as were the men, working alongside women like Deborah Matshoba and Nomsisi Kraai. Ngwenya says she is a feminist, and takes that ideology to the AZAPO women's wing, Imbeleko, of which she is president.

Khehla Shubane

A Wits graduate who served time on Robben Island for his BC activities, Shubane has swept his influence way above the prison buckets and bunches of keys. Having returned to community and Black politics upon his release, Shubane participated in the life of the Soweto Civic Association until he was drawn into more corporate and academic work.

Known for his research work at the Centre for Policy Studies, where he was also a director, he is a prolific writer, an independent policy analyst and works in business. He has also served the Nelson Mandela Foundation as its CEO.

Philip Kgosana (1936–2017)

A revered leader of the PAC and a hero for our times, Kgosana was beloved for his powerful spearheading of the 30 000-strong march from the township of Langa to Cape Town on 30 March 1960. It was a mere nine days after the apartheid police had cold-bloodedly slain dozens of Black people at Sharpeville.

Kgosana was only 23 years old, and yet was able to stand his ground and negotiate with police to try and arrest the bloodshed.

The immense courage saw him immortalised when Cape Town's De Waal Drive was renamed Philip Kgosana Drive in 2017.

Workers' College, Durban

The educational philosophy of this unusual and vibrant institution is Recognition of Prior Learning (RPL), which poet and cultural worker Mphutlane wa Bofelo (Workers' College), information worker Anitha Shah (Workers' College), former teacher trade unionist Kessie Moodley (director, Workers' College), academic Linda Cooper (associate professor, School of Education, UCT) and consultant researcher Barbara Jones (UCT) discuss in an article for the *McGill Journal of Education*.

They describe RPL as 'a form of radical pedagogy' – 'an educational philosophy which aims to build the competencies of activists in labour and community organisations, facilitate their self-affirmation and dignity, and provide an access route to post-school education'.

The vibrancy of South Africa's predominantly Black working-class trade unionism is rooted in left-wing politics and BC, and the Workers' College continues to conscientise in the classroom in Marxism, colonialism, liberalism and capitalism.

'The educational philosophy of the College is to begin with learners' struggle knowledge, to reflect on it, validate it through peer engagement, and link experiential knowledge to radical political theories of social change, as well as to the codified knowledge base of academia.'

[Wa Bofelo, *et al*, 2014: *McGill Journal of Education*]

'Dude, what the hell. Check the guns out!': The story of #FeesMustFall

Arguably the most powerful act of defiance by the country's youth since the 1970s, #FeesMustFall and its protagonists, the 'Fallists', was a seismic event in South Africa in 2015.

By the time that student movement took hold, it was built upon other uprisings – such as #RhodesMustFall and #OpenStellenbosch – at individual universities where decolonisation was at the centre of struggles for access to university.

That had long been impeded by unaffordability, but #FeesMustFall threatened something far greater than young, mostly Black, South Africans taking to the streets in their numbers. Its catalyst was an increase in fees for tertiary education, yet it threatened a *coup* not only within the education system but at state level from those who felt abandoned by the system.

The anger and disappointment with South Africa's democracy from its Born Frees found its voice by implementing a complete shutdown of institutions of higher learning using poverty as a lever.

Universities were of course easy targets as post-colonial relics. This was a conscious age in an African state where the rise of Black people had been denied through neo-liberal economic policies and 'Sunset Clauses' that protected a white minority.

Fees were believed to have increased by at least 40 to 50% over a period of five years in what was a *de facto* bar for poor students. Within radical thought, that 'bar' maintained a *status quo* that supported the white upper 10% and a Black elite, and continued to deliver a desperate Black majority as voting fodder for the ANC.

Young people had had enough, and #FeesMustFall put their questions to the world.

Was the denial of access to higher education for the Black masses an actual plot? How should it affect a 'woke' Black middle class? And, in terms of BC and its historic ideological clash with the ANC, was collaboration with the management of liberal academic institutions essential if the party was to keep up the ruse of having been the only viable force in liberating the country?

Irrespective of multifarious political allegiances on campuses, these were BC questions.

Building upon the popular discourse of Freire, who influenced the Biko generation, #FeesMustFall confidently demanded to know why Black South African history had been disseminated in the way it had, post-1994. They queried the assumption that their generation should – like that of their parents – acquiesce to government's gradualist policies because its ruling party was a former liberation movement and its leaders were Black.

Most Fallists were Born Frees. They had not experienced apartheid as a reality, but they certainly experienced it in effect. They were feeling the consequences of the ANC's determined 'non-racialism' which sought to blur the lines between Blacks and whites under the Mandela administration and thereafter, meaning capitalism of the kind which had always dominated South Africa, was still deciding their fate.

This Black pushback was wholly discomforting for the ruling party whose 30 years of cosying up to money had already taken a distinctly dark turn under the Jacob Zuma.

The shift began at Wits on the morning of 8 October 2015, when a handful of predominantly Black students who had successfully organised a protest two days before against the outsourcing of workers.

Their activities brought the university to a standstill, and by lunch time that day, a march organised by the SRC saw students gathering in large numbers outside the august Great Hall. Protest intensified as exits were closed.

By the second day, word was out that Wits students were in control, and so began mass demonstrations. Most university campuses in the country would be shut down by the end of that week in solidarity, students' demands at other sites also rallying around the insourcing of workers and free education.

At the beginning, the catalyst of #FeesMustFall was then no different from the impetus of Biko, the UCM and SASO 40 years before: equality and access for Black students in universities. Institutionalised racism conspired as it always had to keep them out. And in a 2000s environment, universities in South Africa could also be comfortably accused in other struggles affecting young Black people: sexism, homophobia, transphobia, ableism, xenophobia and granular class issues.

So far, a predictable set of modern battles. But as the students geared up their fight and got the attention of the country and the international community, they were quickly having to sharpen their ideological weapons behind the scenes. #FeesMustFall was the heir of the BCM. Their uprising was at its core Blackness versus the white-dominant economy perpetuated by the ruling ANC for 20 years. And that meant #FeesMustFall would be treated in similar ways to the BCM. It could not be tolerated.

By the time the movement was quelled by the ANC-led government in cahoots with capital, hundreds of young Black people were traumatised, peripheralised and having to pick up the pieces of their lives and their politics. There were clear signs of future forms of Black South African protest among children abandoned to inferior public education, but the road had been left bloodied. The revolution was still coming of age.

Wits, for example, reacted with violence in the same way as the universities of the 1970s had done, bringing heavily armed police onto campus and into surrounding streets, including on the world-famous Mandela Bridge in Johannesburg's university town of Braamfontein.

That meant that the tactics and confidence which had propelled Fallists in 2015 were dimmed through fear and intimidation in 2016, at the same time as deep political conflicts broke down their internal leadership.

At Wits, the leadership was steered by two Black women – both ANC-aligned SRC presidents: Nompendulo Mkhatshwa and Shaeera Kalla – whose relationship with the 'unity' grouping, the Progressive Youth Alliance (PYA),[69] was key.

When Wits and other universities presented a much-touted 0%

---

69   The Progressive Youth Alliance (PYA) is made up of the South African Students' Congress Organisation (SASCO), the ANCYL, the Young Communist League and high school representative body, Congress of South African Students (COSAS). The PYA was cast into the spotlight in 2008 when its leaders included Julius Malema (now leader of the EFF). Representing youth organisations affiliated to the ANC, it had enough clout to be designated by the ANC to alert the media to the 'recall' of president Thabo Mbeki in favour of Jacob Zuma.

fee increase for 2016 after negotiations at the end of 2015 with the students and other interested parties, there was no plan in place for 2017 and beyond. Many Black students believed their leaders had 'sold out', leaving the EFF's student supporters especially aggrieved and determined to right the wrongs.

The realisation that political parties had cynically and violently used a Black youth movement to service their own ends – an escalation of the war for power between the EFF, then a new party led by former ANCYL president Julius Malema, who was expelled from the ANC, and the ruling party itself – broke the students' morale.

That damage would quickly assist the EFF's intentions of dramatically growing its support base. It certainly benefited from the emergence of young Black revolutionaries like Simamkele Dlakavu,[70] Naledi Chirwa,[71] Vuyani Pambo[72] and Anele Nzimande.[73] But there were also casualties of the 'war'. An example might be Mcebo Dlamini, a former Wits SRC president expelled in 2015 for misconduct, who will not be forgotten – or forgiven – for pro-Hitler comments, but whose arrest in 2016 for serious crimes including violating a court order, theft, public violence, assault and malicious damage to property during #FeesMustFall also put him in the history books. In March 2020, the Johannesburg Magistrate's Court sentenced Dlamini, who represented the ANC at Wits, to two years, wholly suspended for five years, for public violence.

Numbers of students were arrested and jailed at the height of

---

[70] Simamkele Dlakavu has a master's in African literature from Wits, where she was a Fallist and a decolonialism activist. A former television producer, she is now a lecturer in gender studies at UCT whose writing has been widely published in the media.

[71] Naledi Nokukhanya Chirwa (1993-) is a feminist and former student activist based at the University of Pretoria during the #FeesMustFall uprisings of 2015 and 2016. Chirwa is now an EFF MP.

[72] Vuyani Pambo (1990-) was the head of the EFF's student command at Wits. An award-winning filmmaker, he is now an EFF MP, a member of the party's central command team and its spokesperson.

[73] Anele Nzimande (1993-) has a law degree from Wits and worked as a legal researcher at the Centre for Applied Legal Studies. A leader during #FeesMustFall, she was also active in the Wits Law Students' Council. Nzimande is the founder of a fashion and content marketing brand and has contributed analysis to a range of publications.

#FeesMustFall. Ultimately, the most prominent was Kanya Cekeshe, a media student at a college in Braamfontein, who was imprisoned for setting a police vehicle alight during the 2016 protests.

Cekeshe was among thousands of convicts given a remission of sentence for certain categories of prisoners by President Cyril Ramaphosa in December 2019. He had spent two years behind bars after being sentenced to eight years, three of which were suspended, for public violence and malicious damage to property.

Nzimande recalled #FeesMustFall in a powerful opinion piece in the *Saturday Star* newspaper in 2017, where she said 'there was a point where some of us were accused of treason [for diverting from ANC positions]…'

'It was the most terrifying time of my life … I thought people were going to die. If not that, I thought some of us would disappear after the protests without a trace.'

There were serious triggers for the 1976 generation, many of whom were family members of the 2015 Fallists. Pain reverberated.

Nzimande said she had 'had no confidence in the state at all because the level of intimidation was beyond anything I ever could have imagined'. The 'fault lines' that appeared in the movement and 'tensions in the PYA camp' were understood as part of an 'identity' struggle. '[They were] embroiled in the ruling party and … standing up for student issues meant they had to denounce the ANC to some degree.'

The 2015–2016 period crucially marked the chaotic meltdown of the corrupt Jacob Zuma administration when it was all bad hands on deck as the former president sought to cling on to patronage. Thus, the students who aligned themselves with the ANC were psychologically bound to the party led by Zuma, if not by his own dirty faction within it.

The devastating abuse of state resources on Zuma's watch destroyed the country's economy, the real cost calculated during the pandemic of 2020. The victims of that were Black, most of them the grandchildren and great-grandchildren of the BC generation of the 1970s.

By September 2020, the Gauteng provincial government estimated that at least 18% of children had not returned to school as the virus response reached 'Level 1', which allowed classrooms to reopen. So fractured was South African society, and so mortally damaged by the economic crash, that it was difficult not to believe this was another lost Black generation. The Fallists were shattered by then.

'The possibility of death didn't frighten us,' Nzimande wrote in 2017, 'but it did make things very fraught ... #FeesMustFall was reverberating across the country. It was riveting. Everyone was watching.'

She recalled the police presence and its effect on students: '"Dude, what the hell, check those guns out", someone said, pointing [at the phalanx of police] ... There was a slight commotion, people unsure of whether we should charge on or turn back. We couldn't cross Mandela Bridge to make it to Luthuli House[74] because there were guns in our way.'

Nzimande believes she was 'protesting from a place of anger not only at the establishment, but also my former self'.

'I had been co-opted by the oppressive anti-Black systems without my knowing and this was a chance for me to redeem myself, to absolutely, and unequivocally declare that I would no longer participate in systematic racism and oppression – in this instance, the exclusion of (Black) students from an opportunity to potential radically transform their socio-economic conditions through obtaining an education. This was an experiment.'

In retrospect, she placed significance on 'Mandela Bridge [which] shook under the weight of Hector Pieterson ... [one of the 1976] children, tired of seeing their parents humiliated by the violence of the state and knowing that if they did nothing about it, that too would be their fate'. And she noted the agonising links between that generation of 'children who had to reintegrate into a society that remained violent and unchanged, just days after they had buried their peers' and her own, who also had to 'continue going to class, writing exams, sleeping in the same home and community, after that moment of rupture that had caused unspeakable devastation in the lives of everyone around you'.

[Nzimande, 2017: https://www.iol.co.za/saturday-star/opinion/sacrifices-of-a-different-kind-9831630]

---

74 The ANC headquarters in Johannesburg, named after former party president and Nobel Peace Prize-winner Albert Luthuli. 'Luthuli House' is a metonym for the party's leadership.

Five

The Art of Black Consciousness

Compiled by Rabbie Serumula, Therese Owen and Janet Smith

There is no politics without art and no art without politics. Revolutionary movements all over the world would have been far the poorer, if they tried to exist, without writers, poets, painters, musicians, photographers and filmmakers empathetic to their cause.

The words of extraordinary writers Njabulo S Ndebele and Bessie Head and poets Wally Serote and Don Mattera have an intergenerational Blackness. So too the boisterous art of Lefifi Tladi and Shugasmakx. None could be together without the militancy of Strini Moodley and Saths Cooper's theatre or Keorapetse Kgotsitsile's influential Harlem years now reborn in his son, the prodigy, Earl Sweatshirt. Art messes with the mind as it must.

Hip hop and Black Consciousness
It is not by coincidence that hip hop culture is marred by patriarchy, sexism, ageism, who is better than whom, who owns what wealth, the texture of hair, body stature, shades of Black. None of this is by any

means a blunder. It is all by design.

There is a multitude of negative from wherever you may find yourself. Yet hip hop culture is synonymous with Black culture. Heads and tails of the same coin.

The 'design' was not birthed on the banks of the James River in the colony of Virginia in 1712 by one Willie Lynch, 'owner of a modest plantation in the West Indies, invited to address slaveowners in early America'. But the letter, 'The Making of a Slave' – which appeared on a nascent Internet in 1993 attributed to Lynch, the fiction, and spun out into urban legend after that – is all about the 'design'.

'Lynch' said the best way of spreading hate, or indeed killing Black people, was to set them against each other by all means. That idea was not a hoax. That reality is at the core of hip hop.

'Lynch' would have it that the colonisers' best intent would be to tear down the pillars that define Blackness, from the seams; to disassemble a Black man's mental strength 'while grooming the Black woman to train her offspring in early years' to submit to the dehumanising ill omen of white masters. 'Lynch' has been explored in many ways in hip hop, with musicians and poets knowing that what was presented in 'A Letter' to stir Black mayhem within Black communities, had some truth to it. But as the decades pass, it is clear that BC will not allow that disintegration.

BC-rich content has grown in hip hop since the early 1990s, interpreting and re-interpreting the divisive methods which slaveowners and the systemic racism that they engendered, used and still employ. Now in its fourth decade, the genre persistently reminds us that the Black mind has a strong drive to correct and re-correct itself over time.

Knowledge of Black history is the teacher.

We cannot ignore the risqué, demeaning, vulgar, criminal, delinquent and obscene tones in this art form, but we also cannot deny that it places its fingerprints on the base of that history. The Black man may have been asphyxiated by the stranglehold of oppression, but hip hop breaks the Black mind free.

South African rapper and poet Stogie T (Tumi Molekane, 1981–) released an EP in November 2019 as a prequel to his 2020 full-length album, which is a musical manifestation of this. *The Empire of Sheep* vividly situates the anti-Black mindset in the second track, as it shows that hip hop is a pillar that maintains the consciousness of Black youth.

They're too enchanted by the rhythm and poetry to accept they are 'Nobodies':

> *Not human beings, but human resources, work force/*
> *No faces but arms, no names but just numbers/*
> *No pages in the annals of history/ Just papers with gossip/*
> *The open veins of nations discarded, Galeano depicted/*
> *Nobodies ain't worth the bullet that kills them/*

Stogie T was born in exile in Tanzania to parents fighting in the struggle against apartheid. He was first the lead vocalist of Tumi and the Volume, an African hip hop music ensemble officially disbanded in 2012 that conscientised many young Black South Africans out of ever-narrowing circles of fear, mistrust and envy – circles used for control.

Hip hop is that phenomenon slaveowners warned each other about. But we are not unfortunate young Black men and women, if some of us were the sons and daughters of those unfortunate fathers. We are sons and daughters of pharaohs, the Queen of Sheba, Mansa Kankan Musa, of Shaka Zulu, King Moshoeshoe of the Basotho, Sekhukhune, Modjadji. We accept that we are 'Nobodies' to them, but we are sons and daughters of Steve Biko, and the children of Black Lives Matter.

The transcripts of the minutes leading up to George Floyd's death revealed that he told officers more than 20 times that he couldn't breathe as white cop Derek Chauvin rubbished that and wedged his knee deeper into Floyd's neck, saying: 'It takes a heck of a lot of oxygen to talk.'

Lil' Baby (Dominique Armani Jones, 1994–), an American rapper, singer and songwriter from Atlanta, Georgia, threw his hat in the ring about police brutality on the track, 'The Bigger Picture', in June 2020.

The song opens with clips from news broadcasts reporting on the protests after Floyd's death, mixed with protestors' 'I can't breathe' chants, and Lil' Baby detailing his own distaste for the police as a result of a few brutal experiences.

This kind of work in hip hop is part of the Black history of racial violence and injustice, stemming from the first prominent hip hop song to provide a social commentary like this – 1982's 'The Message' by Grandmaster Flash and the Furious Five.

Lil' Baby reminds us that the system continues: institutional racism, the fear of being Black in America, corrupt law enforcers and the fight for freedom are as alive in 2020 as they were in 1982, as they were in 1712.

Oppressors of the Black mind, there isn't much new about Black people scattering – like an intrusion of cockroaches when the light goes on – from tear gas and rubber bullets whooshing through the air, locked on to Black bodies. Yet there is another clear message – a flock follows. Hence, the allegory of sheep from Stogie T, as he shows how a gregarious instinct dictates a desire to stay close for protection.

This theme was also well-drafted by South African author, musician and activist Sizwe Mpofu-Walsh (1989–) on 'Imbi Lendawo', a track from his 2017 *Democracy and Delusion* album:

> *Our people still waiting for service/*
> *They need water, electricity, leaders of authenticity/*
> *They've struggled so long they deserve it/*
> *Three hours on a taxi to work/*
> *Just to arrive and be treated like dirt?/*
> *This whole township's a prison/*
> *We're down, we're stuck in the system/*

Oppressors of the Black mind, there isn't much new about Black people suffering. Plenty, however, is new to Black people in how we are evolving. Hip hop, along with many other art forms, is continually interrupting the system.

Without Black ideas, creativity would scarcely have been inflamed over the last centuries as Black minds have shaped and shifted American culture and economics.

J Cole (Jermaine Lamarr Cole, 1985–), an American rapper, singer, songwriter, record producer and record executive used these words in his 2016 album title track, '4 Your Eyez Only':

> At a glance, I'm a failure/
> Addicted to pushing paraphernalia/
> But Daddy had dreams once, my eyes had a gleam once/
> Innocence disappeared by the age of eight years/
> My Pops shot up, drug-related, mama addicted/
> So Granny raised me in projects where thugs was hanging/
> Blood was staining the concrete/

The song served as a message to both J Cole's then-new-born son and Nina, the daughter of a deceased childhood friend of his who got caught up in the streets and was killed at age 22.

The first three verses on the track are from his friend's perspective to Nina, recounting his life so she can always have an image of her father.

Cole hereby also expresses how Black passes down love through pain, with love of self the backbone of consciousness. He uses the form of an Hadith – a collection of sayings of the prophet Muhammad and a major source of guidance for Muslims – which reads: 'None of you [truly] believes until he loves for his brother what he loves for himself'.

This revolt against hate of Blackness, this re-education and enlightenment through hip hop is not by any means a blunder. It is a reaction to the 'design'. One of the Greatest of All Time (G.O.A.T.), Tupac Amaru Shakur, advised that fear is stronger than love.

Oppressors of the Black mind, there isn't much new about Black humanity.

In 2018, the music world and fans were somewhat shaken by Childish Gambino's 'This Is America' music video. The artist (born Donald Glover, 1983–) opened minds to Black possibilities, reflected *insider.com*, as it touched 'on gun violence, the precarious state of Black bodies in the US, and how we've historically used entertainment to distract us from pervasive cultural and political problems'.

There was significant commentary, as Jacob Shamsian wrote,

'including from *Dear White People*[75] creator Justin Simien, (who interpreted that a key) pose (adopted by Childish Gambino in the video) resembles a classic illustration of Jim Crow, the racist character that characterised African-Americans as lazy, stupid and inherently less human.[76] 'Glover's exposed torso [was] there to remind us that he is Black and vulnerable, according to Yahoo's Ken Tucker. 'Glover wants to remind us that violence is committed against Black bodies like his with some regularity and with no heed to whether the body in question is that of a celebrity or an ordinary citizen,' Tucker writes.'

Shamsian commented on other reminders in Childish Gambino's video of the 'historical violence inflicted upon African-Americans, and … the ways we're continually distracted from that history'.

None of this is by any means a blunder. It is all by design.

[University of Missouri-St. Louis, Thomas Jefferson Library reference department, 1993: *https://web.archive.org/web/20070808080232/http://www.umsl.edu/services/library/blackstudies/narrate.htm*; Shamsien, 2018: *https://www.insider.com/this-is-america-music-video-meaning-references-childish-gambino-donald-glover-2018-5*]

'The full injustice': Art, media and being 'woke' to BC

Advertising firm McCann and a client whose work was with technology company Microsoft came under fire in June 2020 when London-born, New York-based visual artist Shantell Martin (1980–) was approached to paint it a Black Lives Matter mural 'while the protests were still relevant'.[77]

The artist then published the email request the company had sent her 'that insinuated the … movement was a passing trend' – on her social media accounts. In an extended comment, Martin posted:

---

75 *Dear White People* emerged on the big screen in 2014 as an American comedy-drama, written, directed and co-produced by Justin Simien and focusing on escalating racial tensions at an Ivy League institution. It was developed into a TV series in 2017.

76 White American performer and playwright Thomas D Rice created the character in blackface, using African-American forms of speech in song and dance in the early 1800s at the original minstrel shows.

77 Grindell, 2020: https://www.businessinsider.com/artist-slammed-microsoft-for-asking-make-mural-while-still-relevant-2020-6?IR=T

'Here's an example of what it's like to A) be reminded of my Blackness, B) how Black pain and oppression is commodified with performative allyship, C) what systematic racism looks like within corporations.' Although management apologised for 'insensitive language' in the original approach made to Martin, the artist was clear: 'We can see the trend. We are aware. We are conscious.'

'The mural was intended to be put up on the Microsoft store located at 5th Avenue in New York City. The store (was) boarded up – as (was) much of Manhattan – because of the protests in New York over George Floyd's death.'[78] We saw events in 2020 that challenged BC philosophy at its core. Related to George Floyd, viscerally connected with Black Lives Matter, these challenges were commonly in the US, often directed at art and played out in different micro-aggressions and efforts at change. To understand which was which within a defined context of BC required remaining resolutely true to its principles, and that outlawed the momentary, capitalist opportunism that drove many 'black square' endorsements.

One aspect of the movement in the pandemic year was the ubiquity – for a short time, at the height of media attention on the protests – of the 'black square'. It became an artwork of its own. An image. A picture of history. The 'black square' was the social media avatar of millions of individuals, corporations, organisations and institutions as the world looked to the widespread fury at Floyd's murder playing out in the US, at times as an alternative to the catastrophe of a global shutdown in the wake of a devastating virus.

Ultimately, *Vox* put it best: the 'black square' was not about consciousness of Blackness for many. Instead, it was 'a virtue signal of solidarity by brands, corporations, and influencers'. Was it even ever a symbol of BC, at a time in history where there were only two events at play: COVID-19 and Black Lives Matter?

'To many activists and even consumers, the square is seen as a cop-out and counter-productive to spreading resources related to the nationwide protests. For institutions like the Guggenheim Museum, which did not invite the first Black guest curator in its decades of history to a panel about her work, a post appears meaningless if there

---

78   Ibid.

is no commitment to change.'

Chaédria LaBouvier lead the show *Basquiat's 'Defacement': The Untold Story in 2019*, exploring Jean-Michel Basquiat's work in New York in the 1980s. *Essence* magazine reported that 'LaBouvier showed up to the panel (which had excluded her) to say ... the museum had used her. "What has gone down is so violent. It's so violent," she said, "and it's meant to be that way. And of course it's an institution that condones and looks the other way but there's also a very traceable step of how that happens".'[79]

And herein lies the challenge that was also put to Martin, and countless other Black artists at the turning point of June 2020.

There was suddenly an inconceivable amount of attention upon Black artistry in much of the content on the internet. Some came from citizens of a social media utopia. Others were racers who chased euphoria through trends. Within those quests was the same holy grail: Clout. But the tool was 'BC' – in quotes.

Clout is having fame, influence and types of power for 'performative wokeness'. The byword would be widely used by Black American artists like Lil Uzi, Lil Yachty, Vert, Wiz Khalifa, Offset, Ty Dolla $ign, Cardi B, Denzel Curry and numerous rappers.

By definition, however, 'chasing clout' moved away from awareness, and the further the audiences in fact were from being truly aware, the closer they leaned towards self-destruction. That was a challenge. At times, it felt like a red herring, or abuse from within. If a tilt at BC could make money, could its roots be denied?

'Consciousness' and 'woke' are not synonymous.

Certainly, 'woke' was coined by a Black American – the gratuitously forgotten writer, William Melvin Kelley.[80] The word first appeared in an Op-Ed he wrote in 1962, published in the *New York Times* under the

---

79   https://www.essence.com/entertainment/chaedria-labouvier-guggenheim/
80   *The New Yorker* calls Kelley (1937–2017) 'the lost giant of American literature', who 'turned his considerable intellect and imagination to ... what it is like, for all Americans, to live under the conditions of white supremacy – not just the dramatic cross-burning, neo-Nazi manifestations ... but also the everyday forms endemic to our national culture'. Journalist Kathryn Schulz described how 'Kelley first addressed these issues at length in his début novel, *A Different Drummer*.

headline: 'If You're Woke, You Dig It.'

Kelley pointed out that much of the beatnik slang created by those who participated in social movements of the 1950s and early 1960s stressed artistic self-expression and the rejection of the mores of conventional society. The beatniks were 'the people who know what's up and are aware of current events'. Hence, 'woke'.

But there were more cynical, mocking undertones to the term in 2020.

An internet troll, on the premise of a quick Google search, posting maddening statements or comments to elicit emotional responses in people, was not 'woke'. Neither was being aware, but not part of a Black solution.

There would be other righteously BC messages, which had paramount potential to conscientise, but these were not prominent in 2020 even as they continued in the background as consciousness through art.

An example would be the work of Mozambican anti-war activist Gonçalo Mabunda (1985–), who creates masks, figures, sculptures and thrones from AK47s, rocket launchers, rockets, pistols, parts of tanks, soldiers' boots and bullets, and other military equipment. These were the instruments of death, the objects of the destruction, that laid waste his homeland through relentless civil war.

Mabunda uses these deactivated weapons to represent human beings in diverse ways, with his work shown at the Center Pompidou in Paris, the Venice Biennale, the Museum of Art and Design in New York, the Museum Kunst Palast in Düsseldorf, the Mori Art Museum in Tokyo, the Johannesburg Art Gallery, the Sweden Army Museum and at multiple other exhibitions. His work began in 1995, inspired by the Christian Council of Mozambique, which collected weapons around the country when the war ended. Artists were given the opportunity to use these for sculpture and other artforms, with more than 800 000 weapons used against Black lives assembled through the humbly named 'Transforming Guns into Hopes' campaign.

There would be other art forms that focused on BC in 2020. A fine example would be a warmer spotlight on the 2019 Oscar-winning animated short film, *Hair Love*, by Matthew A Cherry, that tells the story of an African-American father learning to do his daughter's hair for the first time. This was a vivid, impactful expression of Blackness.

Wokeness manifests growth. Growth is change – in perspective, ideology or view of self. To be woke is to understand the full injustice. [Nguyen, 2020: https://www.vox.com/the-goods/2020/6/3/21279292/blackouttuesday-brands-solidarity-donations]

Keorapetse Kgositsile and Earl Sweatshirt: Two generations of revolutionaries

Affectionately known as 'Bra Willie' (brother Willie) in South Africa, Kgositsile (1938–2018) used poetry as politics with a BC beat that reverberates strongly in the DNA of his son, American hip-hop artist Earl Sweatshirt (1994–).

A writing force so powerful that he was named South Africa's second National Poet Laureate in 2006, 12 years after the first democratic elections, Kgotsitsile's legend is drawn most deeply from his years in exile in the US.

Along with numbers of other South African artists, he was supported on that complicated journey by a newly banned ANC. At the time he was banished in 1961, Kgotsitsile was a 21-year-old journalist on Johannesburg-based left-wing newspaper *New Age*, where he attracted the adverse attentions of the apartheid regime.

Kgositsile first travelled as a journalist to Tanzania where the ANC had a base. His arrival in the US was dislocating and severe, but it gave him a chance to dedicatedly study literature and culture to the point where he would become a celebrated activist and artist himself, especially in New York's Black music scene.

There, Kgotsitsile delved into oral history as performance art and earned the reputation of a revolutionary. He illuminated a nascent spoken-word circuit and his spirit there remains strong.

In an obituary in 2018, the *New York Times* wrote that '[Kgotsitsile's] poetry addressed themes of Black solidarity, displacement and anti-colonialism with an uncompromising directness'.

'In their declaratory rhythms as well as their content, his poems often echoed the music of Black America and of Africa. "I believe my work is contemporaneous with me," he told *Callaloo*, a journal of Black literature, in 1972. After moving to the US, he said, "my acceptance of my environment did not erase my memories of Africa on the continent".'

Poet Sterling D Plumpp (1940–) – who is today also an educator, editor, critic and the author of numerous books – introduced Kgotsitsile to Cheryl Harris,[81] an African-American academic active in politics in Chicago, with whom Kgotsitsile found a shared love of radical jazz.

They moved to Los Angeles where both were teaching – Harris, law, and Kgotsitsile, English, at UCLA – and where their only child, Thebe Neruda Kgositsile ('Thebe' is Setswana for 'shield'; 'Neruda' is a tribute to Chilean poet Pablo Neruda) was born in 1994.

In his time in the US, Kgotsitsile earned, among many other accolades, the Harlem Cultural Council Poetry Award and a National Endowment for the Arts Poetry Award. He graduated from Columbia University in 1971, whereupon he became integral to the uptown Black Arts Movement[82] and was involved in the fabled Black Arts Theatre in Harlem.

Kgotsitsile looked on this arts community as militant in its own way, 'destroying the symbols which have facilitated our captivity. We will be creating and establishing symbols to facilitate our necessary and constant beginning.'

His keynote anthology, *My Name Is Afrika*, carried a distinguished introduction by Pulitzer Prize-winning poet Gwendolyn Brooks.

Kgotsitsile – who was at times known as K William Kgotsitsile in

---

[81] Cheryl I Harris is the Rosalinde and Arthur Gilbert Foundation Chair in Civil Rights and Civil Liberties at UCLA School of Law. A graduate of Wellesley College and Northwestern School of Law, Professor Harris was a key organiser of major conferences that helped establish a dialogue between US and South African legal scholars during the development of South Africa's first democratic constitution. Harris has produced ground-breaking scholarship in Critical Race Theory and lectured widely on issues of race and equality.

[82] The Black Arts Movement (BAM) was active from 1965 into the 1970s, using culture to develop institutions honouring Black pride and Black Power. Poet and playwright Amiri Baraka (known as Leroi Jones at the beginning of the movement) was a prominent founder of BAM, and among those who established the Black Arts Repertory Theatre School in Harlem which inspired similar centres in other American cities. Among celebrated members of the BAM were Audre Lorde, Gwendolyn Brooks and Maya Angelou.

America – left the US in 1975 to take up a teaching position at the University of Dar es Salaam in Tanzania where he met and later married the ANC exile, Baleka Mbete, who was living there. He renewed his activities with the ANC, founding its department of education in 1977 and its department of arts and culture in 1983. He became a deputy secretary of the party in 1987 while he taught at schools in Kenya, Botswana and Zambia. Throughout this period he was still banned in South Africa, and was only able to return from 1990, after nearly 30 years away.

In 2008, Kgotsitsile was awarded the National Order of Ikhamanga in Silver 'for excellent achievements in the field of literature and using these exceptional talents to expose the evils of the system of apartheid to the world'.

He died on 3 January 2018 in Johannesburg after a short illness.

Kgotsitsile's son, Earl Sweatshirt, is regarded as a hip-hop prodigy, described by Kelefa Sanneh in *The New Yorker* a year after his sensational arrival on the Los Angeles skateboarders and scenesters arena in 2010 at the age of 16, as 'the most exciting rapper to emerge in years, a virtuoso who was just starting to figure out what he could do with words'.

Earl's brilliance as a lyricist and musician was not over-praised by his father. Kgotsitsile was based in Johannesburg during Earl's childhood and teenage years. He told *The New Yorker* in 2011 that he had 'heard about his son's growing reputation among hip-hop fans', but that he hadn't listened to the successful young music collective which included Tyler the Creator, Frank Ocean and Syd tha Kyd, in which Earl Sweatshirt played a key role..

'"When he feels that he's got something to share with me, he'll do that," Kgositsile said. "And until then I will not impose myself on him just because the world talks of him."' Sanneh wrote that Kgositsile '[resisted] the suggestion that, through hip hop, his son [was] carrying on the family business, and [suggested] that Thebe's emergence as a second-generation lyricist might be "coincidence".'

Kgotsitsile remarked that he was 'not a fan of "commercially promoted" hip-hop: "I really don't think it's about anything of relevance, socially, other than young people saying they're hurt"

– and his verdict on his son's career [was] that "Frantz Fanon said that each generation must find its own mission. If he's part of those that have found their mission, then I'm very happy."' Interviewed on National Public Radio (NPR) in the US in December 2018, Earl told host Ari Shapiro about his new work, the studio album, *Some Rap Songs*, and his feelings about his identities as both Earl and Thebe.

'I'm trying to get … back to what it is. Black expression is directly related to pain. At least this Black expression is. And then if you want to compare it to jazz when it started getting *avant garde*, niggas was wailing, niggas using these instruments to express very crazy emotions that come as a result of these sometimes cursed existences.'

Shapiro spoke of how Earl had planned to reunite with his father, who he had not seen for years before 'he died very suddenly'. 'Playing Possum', a track on *Some Rap Songs*, samples Kgotsitsile's voice and Harris's voice.

Earl became a major star as a teenager together with, Odd Future, at the helm of which was Tyler Okonma, better known as Tyler the Creator. Among Earl Sweatshirt's most iconic lyrics were these, as discussed by *The New Yorker*, from 'Blade', which featured on Odd Future's 2010 album, *Radical*:

I'm half-privileged, think white and have nigger lips/
A tad different: mad smart, act ignorant—/
shit, I'll pass the class when my dad starts giving shits,/
but as long as our relationship is turdless, I'm-a/
keep burning rubber and fucking these beats with burnt dick…/

Yet, Earl's words were somewhat prefigured, albeit more violently, in 'Towards a Walk in the Sun'. Sanneh writes in *The New Yorker* that Keorapetse Kgotsitsile, as the poet, 'imagines his own demise – or, at any rate, his obsolescence. There is a gruesome, hallucinatory catalogue of racially charged horrors and insults, most of them phrased as accusations':

You who bleached the womb of your daughter's/

*mind to bear pale-brained freaks. You who bleached/
your son's genitals to slobber in the slime of missionary-\
/eyed faggotry..*

Their shared BC – against the curiosity of an over-abundance of white fans, in Odd Future's and Earl's case, and the fightback against historical supremacy, in Keorapetse Kgotsitsile's case – would make for a fascinating debate.
[Sanneh, 2011: https://www.newyorker.com/magazine/2011/05/23/wheres-earl; NPR, 2018: https://www.npr.org/transcripts/673227162]

The Last Poets

A pounding echo came out of Harlem in 1968 when a group of Black poets stepped up to the stage in a park, absorbed the anger and spat it back at the crowds on the grass. Soon, everyone was chanting, louder and louder.

It was an *ad hoc* beginning that still today has incredible resonance and bears a history of supreme significance.

The Last Poets' name, also decided on the spur of the moment, recalled South African activist Kgotsitsile's poetry. An exile, he'd had an impact in the area, and now also on how these future legends would work words and sound. Black nationalist pioneers of hip hop, they bolstered his name and the themes of his most well-known poem, 'Towards a Walk in the Sun'.

Critic Jason Ankeny – who was on the editorial team of the *All Music Guide* and has been published by *Rolling Stone*, among others – is often referenced on the Last Poets through a piece where he said: 'With their politically-charged raps, taut rhythms, and dedication to raising African-American consciousness, the Last Poets almost single-handedly laid the groundwork for the emergence of hip-hop.'

The artists went through painful, even violent, turf wars among themselves as they rifted into different incarnations. Founding members David Nelson, Gylan Kain and Abiodun Oyewole broke into versions of the group featuring other Black Power protagonists including percussionist Nilaja Obabi, Jalaluddin Mansur Nuriddin, Baba Donn Babatunde, Umar Bin Hassan, Suliaman el-Hadi and the leader of the Young Lords [the Puerto Rican version of the Black

Panthers in New York], Felipe Luciano.

For all their fights and hurts, brilliance and evanescence, all those involved are considered as having had a critically important influence on music and culture.

British music magazine *NME* include the Last Poets among those artists who 'paved the way for the many socially-committed Black [emcees] a decade later'.

Their biographer, Christine Otten, wrote in *The Guardian* in 2016 about their 'self-critical, militant poems ("Niggers are scared of revolution. Niggers love anything but themselves") which not only influenced generations of hip-hop and soul artists – such as Public Enemy, Ice Cube, Ice-T, 2Pac, Common, Mos Def and Erykah Badu – but also the likes of David Bowie and Mick Jagger'.[83] Each has a story of exceptional and insurgent intent. Nuruddin, for example, learned to 'spiel' (from the Yiddish 'schpil') – meaning to talk at length persuasively, and an early form of rap – when he was incarcerated in the late 1960s. He dubbed these 'spoagraphics', meaning 'spoken pictures' – a rhythmical spoken word performance style also known as 'toasting', which was accompanied by impromptu percussion by fellow inmates.

Although Nuruddin, who died in 2018 at the age of 74, is specifically known as 'the Grandfather of Rap', the other members of the original collectives are hailed too as forerunners of the huge global movement that the genre became.

The Last Poets first appeared on 19 May 1968 – born in what is now Marcus Garvey Park in Harlem on Malcolm X's birthday, 'in the years, months and days after Martin Luther King, Robert F Kennedy and X had been murdered' – as three political spoken word poets and a conga drummer. In 2020, their memory, and some of the members, were there still.

[Otten, 2016: https://www.theguardian.com/books/2016/nov/21/the-last-poets-america-in-poetry-from-black-power-to-black-lives-matter; Mills, 1993: https://www.washingtonpost.com/archive/lifestyle/style/1993/12/12/the-last-poets/e31c20d9-a35e-430a-b887-9ae095f65716/]

---

83 *The Last Poets* by Christine Otten, translated from the Dutch by Jonathan Reeder, is published by World Editions.

The publishers
Skotaville

Poet Jaki Seroke, journalist Muthobi Mutloatse and writer Miriam Tlali were among the founding members of Skotaville Publishers, a project of the African Writers Association.

Skotaville resonates for some with the name of the Kimberley-born Black intellectual, Mweli TD Skota (1893–1976), who was described as a 'human encyclopaedia'. He worked at the *Abantu-Batho* newspaper and in the South African Native National Congress, the forerunner to the ANC, later becoming secretary-general of the ANC.

Skotaville, the publishing house, was a leading progressive publisher during the Cultural Struggle when artists, writers, musicians, performers and creatives of all types rallied under the banner of liberation. Most of Skotaville's titles were politically inclined works supportive of that liberation, all true to its motto: 'Publishing by the people, for the people.'

Skotaville published dozens of books, many of them international classics, including *The Trial of Andrew Zondo* and *Higher than Hope* by Fatima Meer; the play *Have You Seen Zandile?* by Gcina Mhlope, Maralin Vanrenen and Thembi Mtshali; the autobiography of fine art giant Durant Sihlali; *Mihloti* by Tlali and cult BC anthology, *Azanian Love Song* by Don Mattera.

Skotaville's topics covered politics and government, Black life, theology, Christianity, the Chimurenga War in Zimbabwe, economic policy and education with its authors – in addition to the above – including Desmond Tutu, Lindiwe Mabuza, Sipho Sepamla, James Mata Dwane, Nathaniel Ndazana 'Nat' Nakasa, Nelson Mandela, Philip Kgosana, Boyd Makhoba, Jonathan Jansen, Charles Villa-Vicencio, Es'kia Mphahlele, Lewis Nkosi, Fatima Dike and Noni Jabavu.

There can be no doubt of the importance of Skotaville to the library of apartheid South Africa and, most valuably, to the BCM.

[www.openlibrary.org; www.oxfordreference.com]

Black Viewpoint

Biko's seminal statement when *Black Viewpoint* was launched in 1972 reverberates: 'It is significant that in a country peopled to the extent of 75% by Blacks and whose entire economic structure is supported and maintained, willingly or unwillingly, mainly by Blacks, we find very few publications that are directed at, manned by and produced by Black people. *Black Viewpoint* is a happy addition by the BCP to all those publications that are of great relevance to the Black people.

'Our relevance is meant to be in the sense that we communicate to Blacks things said by Blacks in the various situations in which they find themselves in this country of ours.

'We have felt and observed in the past, the existence of a great vacuum in our literary and newspaper world. So many things are said so often to us, about us and for us but very seldom by us.'

Black Viewpoint was designed, said Biko, to negate a 'dependency mood amongst us which has given rise to the present tendency to look at ourselves in terms of how we are interpreted by the white press.

'We Blacks must on our own develop those agencies that we need, and not look up to unsympathetic and often hostile quarters to offer these to us'.

The Classic

The quarterly literary magazine of predominantly BC thought was a journal of township and Pan-African literature. Edited by Barney Simon from 1964 to 1971, it was founded by Nakasa.

The *New York Times* had presented Nakasa, a *Drum* writer, with an unparalleled opportunity in 1961 when it asked him to write on the 'human meaning of apartheid' after the Sharpeville massacre. This gave him a platform to apply for international funding, bringing forth the first edition of *The Classic* in June 1963.

It was magnificent for its writing, featuring greats like Mphahlele, Can Themba, Dollar Brand (later Abdullah Ibrahim), Casey Motsisi, Doris Lessing and even Senegalese poet Leopold Senghor, who would later become president of his country. But it battled to stay alive, especially as the apartheid state ratified the onerous Publications and Entertainment Act in 1963, allowing it to ban and censor as it saw fit.

After Nakasa went to the US on a Nieman Fellowship in 1962, he was banned for five years under the Suppression of Communism Act. Sadness, loneliness, frustration and lapses in his mental health contributed to Nakasa committing suicide in 1965. This left Simon to continue *The Classic* without his substantial contribution, except by literary osmosis.

Poet and Skotaville publisher Seroke – who was jailed by the apartheid regime in 1987 – would also edit *The Classic* (and *Staffrider*).

The writerly renaissance brought on by BC was promoted in many other publications, including *Spearhead* (in Dar es Salaam), *Ophir*, *New Coin*, *Donga*, *Wietie*, *Purple Renoster* and *Bolt*; these journals and magazines encouraging contributors to express their Black identity.

[www.saha.org.za; www.sahistory.org.za]

New Age

A leftist newspaper produced in Cape Town, founded in 1954 by trade unionists and intellectuals with links to the ANC leadership. Among its founding editors were ANC and SACP leader Govan Mbeki – who was imprisoned from 1963 to 1987 on charges of terrorism and treason with Mandela, Walter Sisulu, Raymond Mhlaba, Ahmed Kathrada and others for their roles in creating the ANC's armed wing, MK – and Ruth First, an anti-apartheid activist and scholar, assassinated in 1982 in Mozambique where she was working in exile.

New Age provided a detailed, monthly chronicle of the apartheid state and the struggle between 1954 and 1962.

The Congress of South African Writers (COSAW)

An organisation that was 'partly formed in response to the notion that culture and art be regarded as a weapon of struggle against apartheid, [and] brought together experienced and new writers across all genres'.

Its former president Njabulo Ndebele explains on his website (www.njabulondebele.co.za) that 'as more experienced, older writers shared their experience, they were in turn energised by the perspectives of younger, relatively inexperienced writers. It made for a dynamic mix of energies.'

'A mobile, disreputable bearer of tidings': The story of *Staffrider*

Nick Visser interviewed Mike Kirkwood — an English literature academic appointed by the Christian Institute to be the founding publisher of Ravan Press — in the magazine's office in Johannesburg in September 1980. Designed to be a multidisciplinary journal which was not only anti-apartheid but championed BC, Staffrider *— a product of Ravan — was to host many community-based Black arts groups, and white activist artists. It was banned at first, but later found its way around onerous apartheid legislation to keep distributing as best as it could. This interview was published in* English in Africa, *and is now hosted by South African History Online on its website www.sahistory.org. This is an edited version.*

How did Staffrider *start? Whose idea was it?*

In 1977, the year before I went to Ravan Press, I was talking to what is now called the Mpumalanga Arts Group in Mpumalanga, which is part of Hammarsdale township, halfway between Durban and Pietermaritzburg.

There was a group of about 10 writers – Mafika Gwala, Nkathazo Mnyayiza among them – and the discussion came to the matter of regionalism. Natal writers, both Black and white, felt themselves ignored by the big metropolitan centres.

The Mpumalanga writers felt that there should be a magazine that would not only carry work from all around the country but would also give a certain amount of autonomy to the various groups of writers.

Nobody wanted the kind of editorial policy that comes from the top.

I wanted Ravan to have a literary magazine that would respond to the new creative forces inside South Africa. Not knowing where to begin with such a project, I got in touch with Mothobi Mutloatse. I knew, of course, about the Medupe Writers' Group, which had been banned in October the previous year.

From what Mothobi said, it was clear that there were a lot of individuals around who were beginning to coalesce in writers' groups. He began to talk to people about the magazine, and from early on the discussions centred on the idea of groups that were based in particular townships and grew out of particular communities.

My first insight into how powerful and well supported an arts group could be came, in fact, when Matsemela Manaka walked into the office, coming not as an individual but carrying with him, as it were, a whole group of writers ...

The [Ravan] director, Peter Randall, had just been banned and it had become known as a publishing house that would not only listen to Black writers but would do at least some of the things that Black writers wanted it to do ...

When Mothobi and I were talking over various possibilities that had been suggested as a suitable name for the magazine, he mentioned that somebody ... had suggested the word 'staffrider'. I said, 'Well, what does that mean?' He explained that a 'staffrider' is somebody who rides 'staff on the fast, dangerous and overcrowded trains that come in from the townships to the city, hanging on to the sides of the coaches, climbing on the roof, harassing the passengers: A mobile, disreputable bearer of tidings.'

The idea had a certain flavour that made it right for the magazine. It was definitely outside the bounds of institutional life in South Africa; it focused on an area of experience – travelling to work and back – that is central to most Black lives in this country. It incorporated the notion of a daredevil, somebody who would go a little bit further than most. I suppose we drew a comparison between the liberties the staffrider took with the law and the liberties we wanted the magazine to take with the censorship system.

You don't use commercial distributors. How do you recruit distributors?
The whole Black readership in this country operates largely outside the normal channels of bookshops. And, from the beginning, *Staffrider* has been trying to express the cultural force that rests outside the institutional framework. So we use non-commercial outlets, outlets that derive from the writers' groups that we publish. This is part of an attitude to writing.

Mothobi says in his introduction to *Forced Landing* that the writer's job isn't done when he's written his piece; he has to be part of getting that piece to the people and part, even, of the people's response to the piece that he's written.

In other words, we see the connection between the writer and his audience not as an abstract thing, but as a matter of concrete connections.

Would you say that there are a number of writers **Staffrider** *has encouraged to such an extent that one can think of them as created by* **Staffrider***?*

Perhaps one can distinguish between three kinds of writers that *Staffrider* has had to do with. First, let's take the case of the writer who is in the first place an oral poet, someone like Ingoapele Madingoane. He was very well known before *Staffrider* came on the scene, and has become even better known since, not through *Staffrider*'s efforts but through his oral performances.

Then there's somebody like Miriam Tlali, whose career was already established before the *Staffrider* period by her novel *Muriel at Metropolitan*. During the *Staffrider* period her range of writing has expanded; the magazine has also brought her to more readers.

Of the writers who've become known mainly through publication in *Staffrider*, the best example is probably Mtutuzeli Matshoba, who published in the magazine before going on to do his first book.

What position do Ravan Press and **Staffrider** *hold regarding the censorship apparatus in this country? What effect does censorship have on the editorial policy in general?*

Strange as it may seem, I can't think of one instance in which we have turned down a piece of writing that we really wanted to use simply because it would get the magazine banned. We have perhaps elided a word here or there in case it would alert the censors, as long as the absence of the word wouldn't actually weaken the force of the story.

[SAHO, 2016]

Essential reading for the Conscious
Bessie Head (1937–1986)

The writer's personal story bears repeating, not only for its powerful content, which was reflective of so many apartheid lives, especially Coloured lives, but also because it goes some way to explaining the profundity of her writing.

Born in Pietermaritzburg, KwaZulu-Natal, Head never knew her biological parents, described with customary apartheid dismissiveness as 'an unstable white woman and an unknown Black man'. Her mother, 'Toby', was indeed troubled: She was a patient at the Fort Napier Mental Hospital in Pietermaritzburg who gave up her daughter for adoption to a white family, and died when Head was only six. As happened all too many times in a racist country, when the white adopters realised that Head was not white, they refused to raise her and she was then put into the care of Nellie and George Heathcote, a Coloured couple. Head's biological grandmother, the mother of 'Toby', sent the Heathcotes money to help take care of the little girl, but when 'Toby' died, the cheques also stopped.

Head, who had believed Nellie Heathcote was her mother, was then sent to the Anglican boarding school St Monica's, a care home for Coloured girls near Durban, at 12. She had only standard 4 at that time but found a certain peace, especially in the library.

Head found out that Nellie was not her mother when she was refused an invitation to visit the Heathcotes at Christmas when she was 14. Instead, she was brusquely told in a magistrate's court not only that Nellie was not her mother, but that 'your mother was a white woman and your father was a Native'. Head struggled with that shock and the cruel 'announcement' throughout her life, finding reading books and writing her salvation.

Although she went on to unhappily become a teacher and then, somewhat more successfully, a journalist, working for the Black newspaper *Golden City Post* and living in District Six, the anti-Blackness she said she found in that otherwise 'non-racial' Cape Town community only entrenched her own instability. She believed her dark complexion was an additional source of discrimination against her.

It was only when she moved to Johannesburg to work for the weekend magazine *Home Post* in 1959 and met Black journalists who mentored her, that her life shifted. Introduced to the PAC, Head joined the party where she became an activist and was arrested in the aftermath of the

Sharpeville massacre. A prolific letter-writer who corresponded with dozens of people all over the world for many years, Head had a long friendship with Sobukwe – one of her greatest heroes – by mail.

Not long after Sharpeville, Head self-published a newspaper she called *The Citizen*, which expressed her pro-Africanist views.

Marrying journalist Harold Head – a member of the Liberal Party who helped publish *Contact*, a liberal newspaper – meant moving back to District Six where the couple had a son, Howard, in 1962. But their marriage was all but over two years later, and with her exceptional short novel *The Cardinals* in hand, Head applied for a teaching post in the thriving town of Serowe in the Bechuanaland Protectorate, when Botswana was two years away from independence. The apartheid regime refused to give her a passport and her writer-friend Patrick Cullinan helped her to get a one-way exit permit, which meant she could never come home.

An array of personal issues dogged Head throughout her life in Botswana, although, financially strapped and tormented as she was, she still produced the magnificent *When Rain Clouds Gather*, a lynchpin of African and world literature, *Maru*, her acclaimed autobiographical novel, *A Question of Power*, the bewitching *The Collector of Treasures and Other Botswana Village Tales* and the long historical novel *A Bewitched Crossroad: An African Saga*.

Head died in the mid-1980s after liver failure, having found some solace in alcohol. She is buried in the old Serowe cemetery 'amid trees and flowers'.

Although she was made aware many times through the adulation she received around the world for her writing that she was an explosive talent, Head refused to be called 'an African writer, a Black writer, a feminist writer, or a revolutionary writer'. She said she wrote for all people, everywhere, but she knew that she had an unstable mind, which she called 'my curse'.

Thousands of her documents were given to the Khama III Memorial Museum in Serowe where these are catalogued in a dedicated reading room. Her photographs, desk and typewriter are on display in a special Bessie Head Room.

The Order of Ikhamanga, South Africa's highest presidential

award, was bestowed on Head in 2003, 17 years after her death.

Her house, Rain Clouds, is still standing in Serowe where her son Howard lives.

[Bessie Head Heritage Trust, 2006]

[Thanks to www.thuto.org[84] and writer Tom Holzinger for this edited biography.]

Gladys Thomas (1934–)

A clothing factory worker at 15, Thomas was always a writer. But because her work was so critical of apartheid, it was inevitable that much of it would be banned – in particular when her playwriting was noticed and praised by *The World* newspaper.

Three of her plays were prohibited in 1979 and Thomas was detained. That year, however, she received Kwanzaa honours for 'writing under oppressive conditions'.

Kwanzaa, meaning 'first fruits of the harvest', derived from the Swahili phrase 'matunda ya kwanza', is an African diaspora celebration. First celebrated in 1966, it takes place from 26 December to 1 January in some Black diaspora communities. Its aims are: *umoja* (unity); *kujichagulia* (self-determination); *ujamaa* (co-operative economics); *nia* (purpose, which intends to restore Black people to their 'traditional greatness'); *kuumba* (creativity), and *imani*, which is faith.

Thomas's poems, stories and plays were sparked by the way apartheid laws affected ordinary people. She gave survivors of torture and torment a face. When a Cape Town ghetto community was bulldozed in 1986 to make room for a white suburb, for example, Thomas interviewed the youngest among the dispossessed and told their stories in *Children of Crossroads*.

She based her work *The Wynberg Seven* (1987) on her interviews with parents who watched their teenagers being taken into Pollsmoor Prison. Being selected to attend the International Writing Program in

---

[84] The website www.thuto.org, an academic website which was administered by the history department at the University of Botswana, states that the facts are drawn from the biography, *Bessie Head: Thunder Behind Her Ears* (Eilersen, 1995). Further, that the initial research and structure of the piece were borrowed from the authors of the Bessie Head travelling exhibit of 1987 to 1989. Writer Holzinger added his own commentary.

Iowa City in 1983 assisted in giving her a more international profile. Her work, including pieces published in the collections *Cry Rage* (1972) and *Exile Within* (1986), was published in newspapers, journals and anthologies. Her best-known play is *Avalon Court* (*Vignettes of Life of the Coloured People on the Cape Flats of Cape Town*) (1992).

[www.thepresidency.gov.za; King, 2011; www.sahistory.org.za]

Nokugcina Elsie Mhlope (1958–)

For years, 'Gcina' Mhlope has made a living out of writing, telling, reading and performing stories to children. And not just any stories.

This bringer of vespers and verses, lightning, suns, waxing moons and a sweeping sky – who in public seemed to suppress a BC doctrine in favour of lyrical visions – has delivered a love of worlds within Africa to thousands over generations.

But away from the suburban libraries, halls and bookshops, Mhlope had been writing other stories that straightened the spine of BC. Perhaps her most famous piece, *My Dear Madam*, is an antidote to the comfortable mythology that grew up around her – telling, as it does, how it feels to be 'the worker for the white'.

'You must forget that you are Black,' said the 'madam'[85] to 'the domestic servant' in Mhlope's short story, 'and life will not be so difficult'.

'She said this, smiling, and went on before I could even say anything. Maybe the way out is to call them "baas".'[86]

Mhlope earned honorary doctorates from the Open University in London and the University of KwaZulu-Natal.

Miriam Tlali (1933–2017)

Muriel at Metropolitan has not had the resurgence it deserves in this era. It's a lively, boundary-pushing and political read by BC writer Tlali as she tip-taps into life the semi-autobiographical story of her experiences as a Black clerk in an apartheid office.

When Tlali wrote it in 1969, it was novel within South African

---

85 The naming convention under apartheid designed to diminish Black people in how they addressed white women.

86 The naming convention under apartheid for Black people to address white men; from 'boss'.

literature and so it took six years for any publishing house to pay it attention until Ravan Press picked it up in 1975. The editors at Ravan were careful. There was a lot in the book that could be censored, so they did some trimming beforehand. But that didn't help. *Muriel at Metropolitan* was banned almost immediately.

It took another four years before Longman was willing to give it another go, changing the title to *Between Two Worlds*, and seeing it translated rather into Japanese, Polish, German and Dutch.

Speaking in Amsterdam upon the invitation of the Committee Against Censorship many years later, Tlali said: 'We Black South Africans, we are not going to write in order to qualify into your definition of what you describe as "true art". Our duty is to write for our people and about them.'

Tlali's second novel, *Amandla*, was based on the 1976 Soweto uprising. That too was banned in 1980. *Mihloti* was then released by Black publishing house Skotaville, which Tlali co-founded.

Her work was finally unbanned in 1986.

Mafika Gwala (1946–2014)

Born in Verulam near Durban, Gwala's beginnings were in manual labour and in the classroom, but this writer of sublime intent found a position much closer to his true calling when he joined Biko's *Black Review* as a publications researcher in 1973.

His BC anthologies *Jol'iinkomo* (1977) and *No More Lullabies* (1982) should as a matter of course be introduced to young South Africans, filled as they are with superlative poetic technique and an astonishing breadth of literary influence, from African proverbs to San Francisco and New York's Beat Poet scene of the 1950s .

Duma ka Ndlovu and the Medupe Writers' Association

Poet, journalist, director, producer and playwright Ndlovu (1954–) started writing for *The World* newspaper during the 1970s, but it was the Medupe Writers' Association, a nationwide cultural group that encouraged young Black writers, which gave him a spotlight to more prominently espouse BC.

[Njabulo] Ndebele wrote a paper in 1987 in which he examined six major waves of writing during and after the BC generation, one of which was Medupe.

'The Writers' and Artists' Guild of South Africa was established in 1974. Then there was the phenomenal mushrooming of writers' and cultural groups in the townships throughout the country in the mid-1970s, when at least 25 were recorded. PEN (Johannesburg) followed in 1978. When it disbanded in 1982, it was immediately replaced by the African Writers Association. In 1985 the Writers' Forum was created, and in July 1987 it became COSAW.

'The emergence of numerous cultural groups in the townships in the mid-1970s was, without doubt, a singular event in the contemporary cultural history of South Africa. They came in various names and from different parts of the country: Creative Youth Association of Diepkloof, Soweto; Moakeng League of Painters and Authors (MALEPA) of Bloemfontein and Kroonstad; GaRankuwa Art Association; the Guyo Book Club of Sibasa; Mpumalanga Arts of Hammersdale; Community Arts Project of Cape Town; Peyarta (Port Elizabeth Young Artists Association), and several others.

'This phenomenon was a product of the climate of resistance that owed much of its character and thrust to the BCM... Its distinguishing characteristic was advocacy of the performing arts. A group such as ... Medupe was an outstanding example: Poetry was recited to the beat of drums; there was much drama and music.'

Ndlovu was Medupe's president until October 1977 when the regime banned the association along with 17 others in the wake of Biko's murder. This was intolerable for Ndlovu, who then went into exile in the US.

He wouldn't remain dormant on the writing front, however, and nearly a decade later, in 1985, he founded the Woza Afrika Foundation as a funding mechanism to support South African arts.

[Ndebele, 1987: https://www.sahistory.org.za/sites/default/files/archive-files/the_writers_movement_in_south_africa_by_njabule_s_ndebele.pdf]

Mandlenkosi Langa (1950-)

Better known as Mandla Langa, the writer is well remembered for what many say is his most important poem, 'Banned for Blackness'.

The reason is that Langa used it to call for Black resistance and his call was uncompromising.

A writer of such a breadth of quality that he would win the prestigious Commonwealth Writers' Prize (Africa region) in 2009 for his novel, *The Lost Colours of the Chameleon*, Langa grew up in KwaMashu township outside Durban. His brother, Pius, would later serve as chief justice. Langa went on to study English and philosophy at Fort Hare, and then returned to KwaMashu as a teacher while he was a leader of SASO. Effectively an activist of the 1976 generation, he, like thousands of others, was quickly driven into exile – although he first had to spend 101 days in jail for trying to leave the country without a passport. But he used his time behind bars wisely.

Langa wrote and wrote in order to improve his skills and, upon release, fled to Botswana, was trained by MK in Lesotho and lived in Mozambique, Zambia, Hungary and England.

Although closely associated with the ANC, Langa invested his writing with a robust BC. This can be seen in powerful works like *Tenderness of Blood* (1987) and *The Naked Song and Other Stories* (1997).

This would appear to have a great deal to do with the personal circumstances that troubled Langa when he was in exile.

His brother, Ben – an activist from Natal – was killed in 1984 by MK operatives who accused Ben of being an informer. It's been documented that Langa heard about the murder in a 'cruel and casual' fashion from a representative of the ANC in Lusaka, where Langa was based at the time. Two of the MK killers would be sentenced to death and hanged, although such was his forgiveness and conviction that Pius Langa, a lawyer, would publicly rail against capital punishment. The ANC would later admit in front of the TRC that it had made a mistake in killing Ben Langa.

Mandla Langa's *The Naked Song*, however, documents that haunting time, and the love he had for his brother.

In 2007, Langa received the National Order of Ikhamanga (Silver) for literary, journalistic and cultural achievements.

He has been the chairperson of the Independent Communications Authority, and chairman of the board at MultiChoice South Africa and served on the boards of the Institute for the Advancement of Journalism, the Independent Broadcasting Authority and the SABC.

In 2017, Langa completed the second part of Mandela's memoir *Long Walk to Freedom*, titled *Dare Not Linger: The Presidential Years*.

Maishe Maponya (1951–)

Playwright, poet, lecturer, actor and director, he founded the Bahumutsi Drama Group of Soweto, later becoming a lecturer at Wits. Maponya has described his as a 'theatre of the dispossessed', and he made it a politically spiritual mission to reflect BC in works like *The Cry* (1975), *The Hungry Earth* (1979), *Dirty Work* (1984) and *Gangsters* (1984), which were performed at the Market Theatre and, in the case of *The Hungry Earth* in 1983, at the National Theatre in London, after which it toured Britain and Germany.

Maponya was dogged by security police during apartheid, and refused a passport in 1984 to go overseas with his plays.

The recipient of the Standard Bank Young Artist Award for Drama at the National Arts Festival in Grahamstown in 1995, he would later work as a director in the department of arts, culture, science and technology.

Mtutuzeli Matshoba (1950–)

A founding member of Ravan Press and contributor to *Staffrider*, his accomplished collection of short stories, *Call Me Not a Man*, was published by Ravan Press. Tackling the experiences of the Black and migrant worker after the 1976 uprisings, it won the English Academy Pringle Award in the Creative Writing category.

Matshoba's short stories eventually attracted the attention of filmmakers, which resulted in him moving into scriptwriting himself. In a long and diverse career since, Matshoba was involved with the TV series *Soweto, The History*, *Yizo Yizo*, *Stokvel*, *Scoop Schoombie* and *Zero Tolerance*, among others.

He raised his game to making feature films, starting with Ntshaveni wa Luruli's *Chikin Biznis*, a hit comedy which won Best Film in 1999 at the Pan-African Film and Television Festival of Ouagadougou (Fespaco), a biennial attraction in the Burkina Faso capital.

Don Mattera (1935–)

Without Mattera, the word, the concept, the dream of 'Azania' might not have been as widely heard, accepted or envisioned. His pointed, irreverent and pained anthology, *Azanian Love Song*, is probably the only must-have book from the 1980s for BC people and the white Left alike. In it, Mattera – who later became a source for healing and memory, especially in Sophiatown – depicted the haunting power of literature to make a case for politics.

'People who love lyrical poetry which cries out from the depths of the heart and soul, complaining of man's inhumanity to man; of the pain of the orphan ... of the phantom dreams of chained people of Africa and its sons and daughters will find a spiritually rich mixture in this book of poetry,' records a note on www.apartheidmuseum.org, Mattera's work being such an essential collection for any visitor to South Africa to take home.

This is despite its circulating for more than 30 years.

'He writes of the destruction of Sophiatown, the children gunned down in Soweto and Sharpeville; what it is like to live in a slum; what it is like to be oppressed, banned, exiled.' Yet, as the website continues, a truth not only all of those familiar with his work will honour, but also all of those familiar with the man himself, is that Mattera's message is one of hope.

This is not a trite hallelujah: 'It is strong poetry because it is autobiographical'.

Mattera's autobiography *Memory is the Weapon* is indeed 'a brutal story', as independent South African bookstore Xarra Books describes, 'as it traces his rise to political consciousness. In his journey from notorious gangster to activist and poet, Mattera introduces the reader to such major figures as writer and dissident Robert Resha, and to forces of resistance that originated in that period and have remained active in the struggle for liberation.

'Powerful, honest, and full of insight, Sophiatown is an extraordinary testimony to the triumph of the spirit over the devastating effects of apartheid.'

Ezekiel Mphahlele (1919–2008)

When 'Es'kia' Mphahlele died aged 88 in 2008 in Limpopo, he was widely mourned – especially at Wits, where he'd founded a phenomenon in accomplishing the setting up of the African literature department where he was also professor.

Born in 1919 in Marabastad on the outskirts of Pretoria, Mphahlele studied to be a teacher but was banned from the chalkboard in the early 1950s because he vocally opposed the Bantu Education Act of 1953. With his trenchant writing skills, where else would he land up but at *Drum* magazine as an editor. But editing was not satisfying enough, and by 1959 Mphahlele had written one of the most affectionate and wry observational novels in South African literary history: *Down Second Avenue*.

This gave him the impetus to further pursue his studies, which he did by getting an MA at Unisa. Then he went into exile in Kenya, Zambia and Nigeria, became an editor of the *Black Orpheus* literary journal and earned his PhD in Denver before teaching at the University of Pennsylvania.

Mphahlele, a beloved figure, was back in South Africa by 1977. AZAPO was bereaved when he died in 2008, saying: 'Among some of the concerns raised by Ntate[87] Mphahlele was the deterioration of African cultural norms in our society. You [Mphahlele's family] are not the only ones who have lost, but the entire nation of South Africa. Azania will miss this gifted son of the soil.'

[Adenekan, 2008; SAPA 2014a, 2014b]

Mothobi Mutloatse (1952–)

A co-director at Ravan Press and a creative force behind Skotaville Publishers, Mutloatse was also a journalist and feature writer on the independent apartheid-era publication, *The Voice*.

Author of the short stories collection, *Mama Ndiyalila* (1982), he was editor of others' stories, essays and social commentary, too, most notably in *Forced Landing: Africa South: Contemporary Writing* (1980), *Reconstruction: 90 Years of Black Historical Literature* (1981) and *Umhlaba Wethu* (1984).

Mutloatse's devotion to the outstanding *Drum* writer, Casey 'The Kid' Motsisi saw him eulogise Motsisi's literary output, which, like Mutloatse's own in *Mama Ndiyalila*, was about contemporary Black life.

---

87   From Sesotho, meaning 'an older man'; a title of respect.

Mbulelo Vizikhungo Mzamane (1948–2014)

The first sentence anyone researching Mzamane is likely to read is that he was described by Mandela as a 'visionary leader and one of South Africa's greatest intellectuals'. The ubiquitous Mandela link may well be an attempt on the part of those who wish to sanitise history by situating Mzamane in the political mainstream. But this would not be accurate. He was the epitome of BC.

A twist of fortune saw him taught by the legendary Can Themba at high school at St Christopher's in Swaziland, before achieving his MA in English from the University of Botswana, Lesotho and Swaziland (Roma Campus) and PhD in English literature from the University of Sheffield .

Mzamane held academic positions in Nigeria and the US, where he was in exile, as well as Lesotho, Botswana, England, Germany and Australia, and won awards for creative writing, scholarship and human rights advocacy.

He returned to South Africa in 1993 and 1994 and became the first post-apartheid vice-chancellor and rector of Fort Hare, where he was a professor in the department of English studies and comparative literature.

Committed to BC, Mzamane was a board member of the movement's Umtapo Centre in Durban. The centre's Arun Naicker described him as 'a giant who remained humble, nurturing and who was a great mentor'. She told *The Witness* after Mzamane's death in 2014 that he 'believed that history would one day judge the BC movement as being a major force on the South African political landscape'.

Naicker noted that at the inaugural Strini Moodley Commemoration Lecture, Mzamane said: 'What history should record, therefore, is that BC was not just an intellectual movement: it was the premier Black intellectual movement of 20th-century South Africa. It took the country by storm, and transformed the thinking of Blacks and whites in less than a decade.

'There is nothing in South African history in any period to compare with its mass impact and radical reorientation.'

Any new reader of Mzamane is advised to start with *Mzala*, his radiant collection of short stories published by Ravan Press in 1980.

[Naidoo, 2014]

Njabulo S Ndebele (1948–)

Professor Ndebele relates his life story in an irrepressible manner on his website, www.njabulondebele.co.za, beginning with his birth in 1948 at Coronation Hospital (now the Rahima Moosa Mother and Child Hospital) in Johannesburg where his mother, Regina Makhosazana Ndebele, uMaTshabangu, was a nurse. His father, Nimrod Njabulo Ndebele, was a maths and Zulu language teacher at 'the prestigious' Madibane High School in the Western Native township, also in Johannesburg.

Ndebele was proud of his parents, and recalls how Archbishop Emeritus Desmond Tutu, a former pupil of Ndebele senior, said his father was 'an outstanding teacher who got the best out of us without a beating!'

Like the great writer Mzamane, Ndebele went to St Christopher's in Swaziland, finding a number of other Black South African boys there whose parents wished them to escape Bantu Education, in addition to boys from all over Africa. Their teachers came from different parts of the African continent, as well as Britain, the US, the Netherlands, Canada and France. Ndebele enjoyed this school experience, calling it 'internationalist and cosmopolitan', as well as intellectually rigorous, as the boys didn't only do the regular syllabus but also debated decolonisation, Cold War economics, Cuba and more.

Just like Mzamane, he studied English (and philosophy) at Roma, graduating first class, and published his writing in literary magazines *The Classic*, *Contrast* and *The Purple Renoster*.

There was, of course, no way Ndebele was not going to be noticed, as outspoken and bright as he was, and so South African security agents paid his parents a visit back home in Charterston Location, east of Johannesburg, which meant that Ndebele did not return home until 1990. He elected to remain in Lesotho, but also lived in Cambridge, England, where he did his MA, and Denver, Colorado, where he did his PhD.

Later he became head of the department of African literature at Wits, a deputy vice-chancellor at UWC and then vice-chancellor of Turfloop before joining the Ford Foundation in New York and then returning to become the vice-chancellor and principal of UCT. He is now the chancellor of UJ.

Ndebele describes his commitment to BC in a rousing analysis: 'The BCM gave my political instincts strong psychological moorings. I experienced it as an authentic existential base from which to imagine a future democracy in South Africa in which the Black experience was taken for granted as the normative base of a national identity, and which did not need to justify itself in an endless protest mode.

'I first entered the BCM when, as president of the SRC at the UBLS, I was invited by SASO to deliver a keynote address at their historic council at Hammanskraal in 1972.

'The letter of invitation was signed by the general secretary of SASO, Barney Nyameko Pityana. My address was published in the first edition of *Black Viewpoint*, edited by Biko.

'The culmination of the period for me was when BCM activists Jeff Baqwa and Onkgopotse Tiro came to Lesotho in the winter of 1973 to begin to implement a BCM plan to spread the students' movement across Africa.

'SASM was launched at the Roma campus of UBLS with inaugural members from Lesotho, Swaziland, Botswana, Namibia, Zimbabwe and Mozambique. I was elected on to the executive committee, chaired by Tiro.'

Ndebele was emotionally damaged by Tiro's murder by parcel bomb, writing that 'no human being could have survived the power of the destruction that wrecked the house in which Tiro opened the parcel of death'.

The towering collection, *Fools and Other Stories* (1983), which won Ndebele the Noma Award in 1984, is today as arresting as ever it was. It may be his most shining achievement among many publications, and his many honorary doctorates including from Wits, Cambridge, the Wesleyan University in the US and Soka University in Japan.

[www.njabulondebele.co.za]

Lewis Nkosi (1936–2010)

There were few Black writers who captured the anguish of exile with as much eloquence and discomfort as the BC literary theorist and wordsmith, Nkosi.

Writing in Utah State University's 2007 *Ariel: A Review of International English Literature* collection, 'Still Beating the Drum: Critical Perspectives on Lewis Nkosi', Professor Christopher L Wanjala of the University of Nairobi said Nkosi would, in an effort to understand his situation which played out for a total of 30 years, 'consciously balance the literature of the African continent against the literature of the African diaspora'.

Nkosi wrote beautifully about many things but his unending puzzlement and dislocation in exile could not be solved, even through his fascination with those he dubbed 'new Africans': Kwame Nkrumah of Ghana, Kenyan activist Tom Mboya,[88] and Patrice Lumumba of the Congo. Wanjala wrote: 'They expressed the new African spirit and the humanism on which the future of Africa was to be built. So digested was it, that the protest and the vocabulary of racial integration, the passion and grace ... burst out effortlessly in Nkosi.'

The writer's 'personal anguish' in exile was, however, too profound, wrote Professor Annie Gagiano of Stellenbosch University, also in *Still Beating the Drum*. Caught without home's distractions, Gagiano opined, he was lost: 'It may be with more of a feeling for other exiled writers than from any predominance of personal anguish ... that Nkosi acknowledges both the pain and the danger of being cut off from "one's people".

'A writer needs his people', Gagiano wrote, 'in order that they should corroborate his vision or at least ... dispute his statements' about them. In prolonged exile, memory can no longer bear the burden of immediacy; the writer's messages to his people begin to assume a strange unreality, if not features of a lunacy.'

[Gagiano, 2007]

Lesego Rampolokeng and Ingoapele Madingoane
These two South African writers and performance poets are linked together over two fraught generations as they shared so much in influence, weight, complexity – and sheer bloody-mindedness.

---

88   Thomas Joseph Odhiambo Mboya (1930–1969) was a trade unionist, educator, Pan-Africanist, author, independence activist and statesman who was one of the founding fathers of the Republic of Kenya. He was assassinated in 1969.

Rampolokeng was born in 1965 in Orlando West, Soweto. He hit the strange and lyrical mother lode of expression during a renewed height of state repression in the 1980s. Madingoane combined praise-singing and storytelling in what was effectively a form of spoken word, back in early 1970s Soweto. Madingoane's Pan-Africanism was intense. He directed his Black audiences to Zimbabwe, Mozambique and Namibia in his songs of a continent on the verge of its total freedom.

Utterly unafraid to lambast and assault the racist establishment, the unsmiling and aggressively talented Rampolokeng was also dangerous to the system. But that fact allowed him some access to the world's stages where those abroad who were repelled by apartheid's evil and were issuing sanctions at liberty gave him a free space to tell the story of BC.

Rampolokeng collaborated with musicians Julian Bahula, Souleymane Touré, Louis Mhlanga and the Kalahari Surfers, bringing an erudite tone with splashes of Fanon. Always upon his heart was his predecessor of this simmering poetic title: Madingoane, whose magnetic effect has ripened the politics of others, and would continue to do so in the coursing verbal rebellions of Kgafela oa Magogodi, Lebo Mashile and Natalia Molebatsi.

Achmat Dangor (1948–2020)

Banned for six years in South Africa during apartheid, Dangor instead found himself in New York where he taught creative writing. His consciousness was his literary caravan from city to city.

It was his membership of the BC cultural group Black Thought which led to the regime's clampdown on him. A modern equivalent of Dangor's ambit might be the #FeesMustFall movement of 2015 when Black students objected to the cultural values of their institutions being essentially white, allowing white students to retain privilege over Black students.

Dangor would have recognised their cry: Theirs was a fight against 'a widespread dictatorial and militarist attitude meted out against anyone who stands for justice for the Black body'.

He published two poetry collections, *Bulldozer* (1983) and *Private Voices*

(1992), and several novels: *Waiting for Leila* (1981); *The Z Town Trilogy* (1990), a potent novel about Hillbrow; the classic *Kafka's Curse* (1997); *Bitter Fruit* (2003), which was shortlisted for the 2004 Man Booker Prize for Fiction; and *Strange Pilgrimages* (2013), a collection of short stories .

Dangor was later chief executive of the Nelson Mandela Children's Fund, director of UNAIDS in Geneva and managing director of the Nelson Mandela Foundation.

Dangor died in Johannesburg during the Covid-19 pandemic of 2020.

[Black Thought, 2015]

James Matthews (1929–)

A poet, writer and publisher, Matthews is the author of five anthologies, a collection of short stories and a novel, despite having most of his work banned during apartheid. So compelling was Matthews's writing, however, that it was frequently translated and published abroad.

For 13 years he was denied a passport, detained from September to December 1976 at the height of repression after the Soweto massacre. Matthews wrote during this intense period of solitary confinement, determined not to be undermined by attempts at destroying his self-identity. Four years later, he was invited to the Frankfurt Book Fair and then awarded a fellowship to Iowa University.

A founding member of the Vakalisa Arts Association and of COSAW, of which he was also a patron, Matthews didn't stop at writing. He also established the art gallery Gallery Afrique and the BLAC Publishing House in 1974. It ran until 1991, when it finally had to close after relentless harassment.

Matthews won the Woza Afrika Award (1978), was inducted into the Kwanzaa Honours List at the Black Arts Celebration in Chicago in 1979 and made a freeman of Lehrte and Nienburg in Germany in 1982.

In 2010, he was at last honoured by Cape Town city.

[Content drawn from www.badilishapoetry.com]

'Chimurenga' and 'The Chronic'

Cape Town harboured the *Chimurenga* magazine, a platform that roped in a legion of voices from across Africa and the diaspora.

The Pan-African platform of writing, art and politics was born of Cameroonian writer, journalist and DJ, Ntone Edjabe, emerging out of the post-apartheid furnace almost a decade into democracy in 2002. *Chimurenga* was a market of political reflection, encouraging free ideas about Africa by Africans. Published as a journal of politics, art and culture, it also issued a quarterly gazette, *The Chronic*. This gazette first acknowledged newspapers as a preferred medium, appearing in broadsheet print format, but technology is superseding that concept, and *The Chronic* now appears online and as a PDF.

Chimurenga and *The Chronic* were born out of an urgent need to write our world differently, to ask new questions, and even restyle the old ones, with the aim of not just producing knowledge, but expressing the intensities of our society, capturing its forces and taking action.

Other outputs include the Chimurenga Library, an online resource of collected independent Pan-African periodicals and books, and *The African Cities Reader*, a biennual publication that brings together contributors from across the continent and the world to oppose prevailing representations of urban life.

The *African Cities Reader* was a collaboration of *Chimurenga* and the African Centre for Cities at the University of Cape Town.

Chimurenga also founded the periodic pop-up live radio studio, the Pan African Space Station (PASS), in 2008. This saw a collaboration with Soweto-born musician and composer Neo Muyanga, whose jazz dances on the border of the crafted and the improvised. PASS offered space for performance and exhibition. *Chimurenga* described it as a research platform and 'a living archive'.

It transmitted from Johannesburg, London, New York, Paris, Amsterdam, Lagos, Cairo and Helsinki, and featured more than 150 musicians, artists and writers.

Chimurenga thrived on political reflection, culture and the arts of Africa by Africans, engaging with the ingenuity that defines our contemporary life.

[www.chimurenga.co.za]

'BC behaves best if it has its own way – and no other way': The musicians

Therese Owen tells the story of how defiantly Black musicians, producers and DJs took powerful control as soon as apartheid was over. An acclaimed South African music journalist, Owen interviewed the artists reflected in this essay by phone from her rural home in Richmond, KwaZulu-Natal, during early 2017, but had spent much time in conversation and on tour with all of them during her years in active journalism.

The winning rapper runs onto stage to the loud applause of the crowd. As he is handed his award, he smiles broadly and bends down to the mic. 'Yeah, yeah! Wassup, Sun City! Firstly, I would like to thank God Almighty. I would also like to thank my parents, my bae, my manager and my record company, and you, the fans. Couldn't have done it without you. Finally, I would like to thank Sis Letta, Bra Caiphus, Bra Hugh, Bra Jonas and Ma Miriam for having the courage to fight for our freedom. Amandla!'

An excited blogger sitting in the audience turns to her friend: 'Nwah, that's so sweet.' The friend blinks her false eyelashes and briefly looks up from her phone. 'Whatevs,' she replies. 'Like choma, are we definitely on the VIP list for the after party? I wanna meet Cassper[89] and AKA[90] and Nasty C.[91] Maybe Cassper will take me for a ride in one of his Bentleys…'

Let's take it back to 1990. The dancefloor is heaving with writhing

---

[89] South African rapper, songwriter and producer Cassper Nyovest (born Refiloe Maele Phoolo, 1990–) is one of the most successful artists in the country's music history. His debut studio album, *Tsholofelo* (2014), produced the well-loved singles 'Gusheshe' and 'Doc Shebeleza'.

[90] Kiernan Jarryd Forbes (1988–), better-known as AKA, is a South African rapper, songwriter and producer who thundered into public view with his single 'Victory Lap' and his debut album, *Alter Ego*, in 2011.

[91] Nsikayesizwe David Junior Ngcobo (1997–), known professionally as Nasty C, is a South African rapper, songwriter and producer. His 2016 debut album, *Bad Hair*, was critically acclaimed, and was followed by *Strings and Bling* in 2018. He was the youngest recipient at the South African Hip Hop Awards when he was named Best Freshman in 2015. Nasty C signed a joint venture deal with Def Jam Records in 2020.

bodies in a dark Hillbrow[92] nightclub. On stage four, raging hip-hoppers are giving it their all. Spitting out lyrics about the social ills of the time.

The country was burning and their lyrical content could have had them arrested. The theme was BC and the group was Prophets of Da City (POC).

Unlike Johannesburg rappers, Cape Town's POC – as they later became known – followed the five pillars of hip hop: rap, breakdancing (or b-boying), graffiti, DJing and knowledge of self. It was knowledge of self that inspired their BC lyrics, reflected even in their image – from stills to clothing to record covers.

The group consisted of Ready D (Deon Daniels, 1968–) on decks and mic, the militant Shaheen Ariefdien on the mic, with Ramone (Dewet) and Ishmael contributing to the vocals as well as b-boying. Ready D would go on to become South Africa's premier hip-hop DJ with scratching skills of an international standard.

Ishmael (Morabe, 1968–) pursued a very successful career, first with kwaito group Skeem, then as a solo artist, before becoming the melodic voice of the threesome known as Jozi. That group included Bongani Fassie, the only child of South Africa's greatest pop superstar, the late Brenda Fassie. Fassie and Ishmael performed in Jozi with then-newbie rapper, Da Les.

Recalling the controversial days of POC, Ready D – who is based in Cape Town, as he has always been – says: 'We created an awakening among many different demographics in the country. We took the concept of BC and put it on the first recorded hip hop release in South Africa. We didn't know the impact we were going to have. We just rapped about what we felt. We didn't go out with a formula. It was just self-expression about what was going on in those hectic times.'

And he was still optimistic about BC in 2017: 'It exists in many forms nowadays and on many different levels. I think it is awesome

---

92 An inner-city suburb of Johannesburg which became a mecca for Black and white South Africans in the 1970s and 1980s when its appeals included clubs, record shops and bookstores which, despite the laws of the apartheid regime, were effectively open to all. Hillbrow is today a Pan-African hive with refugees, migrants and entrepreneurs living and trading in its multiple apartment blocks and on its teeming pavements.

that it exists in so many realms. People are not happy with the current government and are still feeling the effects of the past. This means a lot more people are embracing BC. They're more active ... more conscious of who they are in the African spirit. Through my work, I'm in the privileged position of engaging with young people from different parts of society, so I'm learning about the Now generation all the time. What I have noticed here in Cape Town is that there's a new uprising. It's not exactly BC, but it is a very strong movement where the youth are trying to find out who they are – whether it be the San, the Khoi or their Malaysian roots, even their European roots.'

Ready D and POC's ideology are way different from that which underpin the 'bragging rights' of South African rappers nowadays.

Yet surely that is part of what POC was fighting for back then: for Blacks and all people to live how they choose and to be allowed access to pursue success in whatever form.

But at a time when politics has become a terrain contested between those who seek the comforts of the neo-liberal free market and those who have never had access to it, is it not the duty of artists to comment on an inadequate economic policy?

Shugasmakx (1983–) of revolutionary rap group Skwatta Kamp has a confident take on the issue: 'I think rappers should be more like Tupac. He was BC but he was also a gangsta ghetto prophet. What he showed us is that there are many sides to him. He wasn't just a party animal; he wrote music that [Black] people could relate to.'

Shugasmakx knows what that means. He and the six other rappers known as Skwatta Kamp were the first in their genre to go gold. They started out in the late 1990s, and by 2002 were household names. Their insanely chaotic shows had thousands of fans screaming for more. They took rap into the mainstream via an aggressive sound with catchy pop choruses. Their videos were creative, unique and meticulously put together, and they had something definite to say.

'We represented the energy of the time,' says Shugasmakx, 'of a vibrant and daring Black youth culture. (The independent youth radio station) Yfm was at its peak. (The hip hop-driven) *Hype* (magazine) had just been launched. (The daring township fashion and style label) Loxion Kulcha was clothing almost every cool young Black kid.

'Through our success we proved to aspiring rappers that if you want to, you can make it. We helped embody that from a BC point of view. We proved that we could boldly go – and do – what we felt.'

One of the ways they did this was not to rap in English. Before Skwatta Kamp, rap was viewed as 'belonging' to 'Model C kids'[93] as it was performed in English, often with an American twang. The township children would choose kwaito – a genre they claimed as their identity. Kwaito exploded with the birth of democracy in South Africa. It was the ultimate celebration of freedom among Black youth, and drew an extraordinary culture with it, including a 'uniform' of 'spotties' (low-slung, soft hats), pantsula dancing, slowed-down House beats and 'kasi-style (township) lyrics. But Skwatta Kamp soon came along, saying: 'Aikona! (No!) We rap in our language, with our accents and about our reality.'

In 2002, however, they were accused within powerful ANC circles of 'taking it too far'. In fact, it was the ANC Youth League, then led by president Malusi Gigaba,[94] which took them to task.

Shugasmakx laughs when he thinks back: 'The song [they particularly disliked] was called "Politiks". We were kinda pissed off because our parents had done well and were able to move us from the 'hood into the suburbs after 1994. The whites all left the area as we moved in. Then we started seeing a drop in service delivery and things took a turn for the worse. It was depressing. Then they [the ANC-led government] built RDP houses[95] right next to where we had bought our houses, our investment.'

---

93 'Model C kids' were the Black children whose parents chose to send them to formerly whites-only public schools in the predominantly white suburbs once public education was slowly desegregated from the late 1980s. **See footnote 105 in Conscious Women for more.**

94 Malusi Gigaba (1971–) became a minister and high-flying politician under the disgraced administration of Jacob Zuma from 2009 to 2018. He was later implicated in corruption and left Parliament and the Cabinet under suspicion.

95 'RDP houses' refers to the Reconstruction and Development Programme which the post-democratic ANC government put into place to find a connection with the working class and landless poor. It was designed to supply state-sponsored low-cost housing to those who couldn't afford it, but later, many houses had collapsed due to poor quality construction sometimes put down to tender manipulation.

'We felt neglected by our government at the time,' says Shugasmakx. 'You know, we were trying to make our lives better, but only those government officials who lived in mansions were okay. [And so] the ANCYL lashed out at us like, how dare we say that? We had a one-hour live debate on Yfm with the Youth League. It was huge. We told them that we were just speaking our truth. It was chaos. Then we kissed and made up – and we all forgot about it.

'The interesting thing is that [former ANC] President Thabo Mbeki[96] heard the whole debate. He said to the Youth League leaders that this was "normal" and our expression should be allowed.

'Nowadays, I don't think BC is there. There is too much champagne-popping and not enough problem-solving. But having said that, Black South Africans are doing great things – even internationally. There's Trevor Noah (superstar host of *The Daily Show* in the US) and (House DJ) Black Coffee.

'I know this generation can take it to the world. But there are still so many problems in this country. A 19-year-old from a child-headed household trying to get a bursary ... heart-breaking problems like that. We need to start being more truthful in our music so that people can relate and help save themselves.'

One artist who stayed truthful within his music from the get-go was kwaito and TV superstar Zola (1977–) who hit the ground running with his ground-breaking debut, *Mdlwembe*. Until then, kwaito lyrics had been somewhat one-dimensional, but as the kwaito revolution expanded and independent, Black-owned record companies started to proliferate, producing greats like Arthur Mafokate, the DJ Oskido and the vocal act Trompies, musicians became not only artists, but thriving entrepreneurs. Later, Zola would be among them.

Oskido (Oscar Sibonginkosi Mdlongwa, 1967–) and his partner, Bruce Dope, joined forces with the members of Trompies to form one of the most successful record companies in South African history: Kalawa Jazmee. They made a definitive change to the shape of the sound of Black music.

Soaring acts of the 1990s and 2000s like Boom Shaka, Bongo Maffin and Mafikizolo would not be the South African icons they

---

96   Thabo Mbeki was recalled by his party in 2008.

became were it not for Kalawa Jazmee and magic-weaving producers like Oskido and his cohorts Spikiri and Mahoota.

When approached by companies like Universal Music and Sony Music, Oskido was somewhat puzzled as to what these multinationals could offer them: 'I used to go to taxi ranks with Boom Shaka, set up a big sound system and get Lebo [Mathosa, one of the twosome, with Thembi Seete] and the rest to mime to their music.

'I would then open my boot and sell their CDs and cassettes to the fans right then and there. I already had the CDs complete with the covers and artwork and I had people all over the country selling my products from their car boot, so why did I need these major labels?'

That's true BC style, with an edge of 'kasi *chutzpah*, which imperialist music moguls from especially the US could not counteract.

Yet there was also expedience in other ways, namely politics. Oskido approached the ANCYL with a suggestion, as radio stations were not playing kwaito even in 1994, as it was considered too extreme and underground, it did not fit the public broadcaster, the SABC's format, and Yfm had not yet been founded.

Yet in 1993, just before the first democratic elections, kwaito was already massive in the taverns and township clubs.

Meanwhile, a resurgent ANCYL was holding rallies around the country to bring young people into the party's camp. Oskido suggested to the League that, for a nominal price, it could hire his artists like Brothers of Peace, Boom Shaka, Alaska and Trompies to perform at these rallies. This would attract larger crowds – a win-win situation.

The then leader of the ANCYL, the fiery and controversial Peter Mokaba, agreed. The rest was history. But that history – between the ANC and kwaito, an essentially BC music form with few inherent links to either the policies of the ruling party or its particular liberation record – does not end there.

Mafokate exploded onto the scene with the big, big song with the incendiary name, 'Kaffir'.[97] The chorus was an instruction: 'Hey baas, don't call me kaffir!'. This was emphasised by melodic female backing

---

97   'Kaffir' remains a racist hate name for Black South Africans and, as of 2018, can earn those who use it in public a prison sentence or a fine under post-apartheid legislation.

vocals: 'Don't call me kaffir-r-r-r.'

Arthur's independent record label 999 discovered major stars like Lira, Queen and Chomee, and through his connections with the ANCYL, Arthur would go on to do massive productions for party rallies and events. Chomee in particular would go on to be one of Zuma's and Malema's favourite stage sweethearts.

By 1998, kwaito was stratospheric – and looked like it was here to stay. The financial independence the genre gave to Black musicians, producers and DJs like Mdu, Spikiri, Brown Dash, TKZee and Mzekezeke was overwhelming. It came with swagger, fame and celebrity. But the lyrics were still rather empty. Some were defiantly crass.

It was the crassness that prevented many kwaito tracks being playlisted on radio. It was also what attracted the attention of Mandela. Being a hands-on leader as he was, he called a meeting with the kwaito leaders, Oskido and the Kalawa Jazmee team among them. Mandela said that, while he 'appreciated' the fact that kwaito was the popular face of a free Black youth, with freedom came responsibility. He said the foul language they used was 'inappropriate', and that the kwaito artists should realise their power and take responsibility.

'We all nodded in agreement, and after that we cut down on the swearing,' says Oskido. 'How could we not? It was, after all, Nelson Mandela.'

Then along came Zola: 'My lyrics are hard-hitting and have always been uncomfortable for the powers that be,' he says. 'As a musician, you have to be brave and be the voice of the people. In the beginning I truly didn't know what to sing about except what I knew [of Black life] and what I witnessed.'

The independent Black-owned record label Ghetto Ruff, which signed Zola, realised he was special, and not 'just another' kwaito artist. Zola had intelligence, passion and the gift of the gab. He could communicate with township people, rural people and even an average white person, given the chance.

He was as comfortable in the boardroom as he was sitting in a shack in Alexandra or in a kraal in deepest KwaZulu-Natal.

Zola had presence on and off the camera. That was how he got his own TV show on the public broadcaster, the SABC, which signed off on *Zola 7*. It centred around Black people turning to him to help them solve their problems and it was an outrageous success. But Zola did not want 'his Black people begging for his help'. He insisted that, before he featured them on the show, they had to show initiative and prove they had already tried to help themselves. That Black self-awareness, Zola hoped, would assist the urgent need for Black South Africans to move out of the victim mentality created by apartheid.

Zola was soon the most powerful TV star in the country. His music complemented that surge.

'I think that kwaito and my music resonated with different souls, with people who grew up in the apartheid times as well as the younger people,' he says. 'In terms of my lyrics and my television show, I warned the youth that they had to go to school and get an education.

'Back then, everybody spoke BC. At some point it became less BC and more South African.'

Zola believes his fans were able to relate to him because 'I never became too bling or Hollywood. People knew I would turn up in a squatter camp. We took people's lives beyond a dream. It became reality.'

He sees contemporary Black-dominated movements like the student uprising #Fees Must Fall as 'the awakening of a new BC'. 'The youth used to read about protests and mass action in textbooks. But in 2015, they inhaled it. They inhaled the teargas and felt the rubber bullets.'

He laughs: 'I can't believe those *buffels* [South African police tanks, first used during apartheid] are still working.'

Zola notes, however, that the Born Frees are genuinely panicked about their future. That South Africa could almost catch fire brought it home.

'Thing is in those days, during apartheid, BC came with a lot of humility and less individuality. Nowadays there are major challenges in our society because of individualism. We as Black people always operated as a unit, whether it be church, street committees, schooling. Now there is a new animal which is equally as ugly as racism. It is classism.

'We must remember that the strength of the wolf is in the pack and the strength of the pack is in the wolf. I do believe that with the students' activities, BC [was] revived. But BC behaves best if it has its own way – and no other way.'

༶

'BC is love, self-love and respect. It is a way of life': Mak and Matsemela Manaka

Rabbie Serumula speaks to Mak, the poet son of the influential BC artist and musician, Matsemela Manaka who was the product of a creative outburst in the 1970s

The clicking sounds of a typewriter would always reassure Maakomele Manaka (1983–) that his father was home. As a child, Mak, as Manaka is known, would also sit next to the late Matsemela Manaka (1956–1998) – BC activist, poet, drummer, painter and playwright – as he painted. His father gave him a paintbrush early on because he could see that his son had an innate interest in art of all kinds: 'There was something about colour that captivated me. The same happened to me with literature. My father realised that his art had a magnetic effect on me and so he let me do what he did,' says Mak.

Matsemela Manaka was born in Alexandra, Johannesburg, in 1956.

He grew to have a critical eye and a philosophy shaped by BC. Most of his life was spent in Soweto, however, where he attended primary and secondary school.

Following the violent deaths of students during the 1976 uprising, some of Manaka's close friends were arrested and tortured. Only 20 years old when he was also detained, Manaka was among the creative outburst of young people from Diepkloof who originated the Creative Youth Association (CYA), which was driven by BC ideology. Manaka would then found the legendary Soyikwa Institute of African Theatre company at the Funda Art Centre in the same township in 1978.

It was during this dark period of our history that many in his generation left the country in pursuit of military training with liberation movements in exile. Peaceful demonstrations were no match for the apartheid regime. But unlike those who went into exile, Manaka left Johannesburg for Pietersburg in Limpopo.

'My grandmother told me that something had changed in my father when he came back,' says Mak. 'He came back a different man, with a bigger purpose.'

Limpopo was the fertile land where the seeds of his artistry were planted. There, away from the inferno streets of Johannesburg, Manaka wrote poems, plays, painted in oils, and made lithographs and woodcuts. He also composed and performed music. Upon his return to Diepkloof, he brought with him hundreds of lines of art that he was burning to publish through Ravan Press. But Manaka was not only to be published; he was to publish as well – and not just any rare volumes.

From 1979 to 1981, he was co-editor of *Staffrider*, the exceptional bi-monthly literary and cultural magazine that was to become one of South Africa's most significant influences.

Manaka, too, published his work in *Staffrider*, a word which was slang for the people who, without a choice, had to hang outside or cling to the roof of overcrowded apartheid trains. Black people were, of course, not allowed to share coaches with white people at that time. Started by Kirkwood and also edited by the beloved late writer Chris van Wyk, the pioneering talent-seeker Mutloatse and artist Kay Hassan, the anti-establishment *Staffrider* provided a space for mostly Black writers, graphic artists and photographers.

Nadine Gordimer – who won the Nobel Prize for Literature in 1991 – was comfortable with having her work appear in its pages alongside aspiring writers, many of whom would later become names with significant literary presence.

Manaka's own body of work included short stories, graphics and photographs from southern Africa. But he didn't stop at the printed word and image. He also wrote and staged plays alongside his wife Nomsa Kupi Manaka, who was a choreographer and actress.

'My mother still teaches dance to your children,' says Mak.

It was, however, his father's political plays, written throughout the 1970s and 1980s, that became renowned for the articulation of the conditions under which Black people lived. He went straight for the jugular of apartheid South Africa.

Manaka's play *Egoli: City of Gold* spoke of the dehumanising work on the mines, and the men who left their homes to live in single-sex hostels. Banned by the apartheid government in 1980, the play was well received in Germany where Manaka was invited to take it to the Erlangen Festival. Other Manaka plays that have entered the hallowed literary halls include *Vuka* (1982), *Children of Asazi* (1984) and *Goree* (1989).

'My father used to say making art is more than just a final product. It is some form of a ritual, a spiritual obsession. Art is an integral part of a people's culture,' said Mak. 'It bears witness to a people's myths and beliefs. Art is meant to articulate the social, agricultural, political, economic, cultural conditions of our people.'

Now also a poet and writer, Mak's lineage has woven its creativity into his blood. Born in 1983, Mak's parents didn't wait long to introduce him to the arts: 'My parents took me to the theatre when I was 18 months old. I grew up knowing art to be life and that my parents produced art for social transformation, as was the norm with BCM-ideologised cultural workers and organisations.'

Mak remembers how his family would go to the Funda Centre every weekend, and it became a place where he spent most of his younger days. And it wasn't only Mak. Funda was a haven for township children, who went there to learn dance, fine art, music, and how to write poetry and plays.

'My father had invested all of his being in the arts. He preached that it teaches you discipline and opens your mind to a world of opportunities. He loved nothing more than sharing the beauty of art with others.

'"We came home one afternoon and found children sitting in our backyard. They had paintbrushes in their hands, and sheets with brushstrokes lay in front of them. My dad had brought the Funda Centre home,' Mak relates.

'My grandmother said my father was a special child and that he didn't want to be born into this world because he knew the hell our people were living in at that time.'

When Manaka was in his mother's womb, he moved closer to her spine. As a result, says Mak, 'when my father was born, he was frail. He grew up with a frail physique, poor eyesight and a squeaky voice. But my grandmother always knew her son would grow up to fulfil his purpose in life.' And so he did.

It was in winter 1998 when Manaka died in a car accident at the age of 42. Mak was only 15 years old.

'My father once told me that you need courage to be an artist. You will say things that people will not agree with.' Yet Mak also needed to find considerable courage inside himself to deal with his father's sudden death.

Fortunately, a year before his father's passing, Mak started writing poetry. This was two years after a near-fatal accident in which he was involved when a wall collapsed on him and his friends. There were six of them, and one died. The accident left Mak in a wheelchair for a year and a half.

He started performing on the anniversary of his father's death, debuting in Lugano, Switzerland, at a tribute to Manaka. Mak has since performed his poetry around the world and maintains that art finds its solace in people's hearts when it is produced for social transformation.

'There has always been BC in our literature, even before the era was so named. BC is love, self-love and respect. It is a way of life. I now understand what my parents did and stood for. I'm putting that in my art. If people look down on art, I feel like they are looking down on my family.'

Art captures people's memories. During the BCM era, people were mobilised through art because nothing is more eternal. Art tells our stories, informs us on where we come from and who we are.

'I don't think my dad would have become the man we all know if it wasn't for my mother. But the more I understand myself, the more I understand the man he was. Not only as an artist, but as a child born of the flames.'

Of all the song, dance, painting, poetry and plays by Manaka, the best sensory experience remains that sound of the rapid clicks from his father's typewriter.

That sounded like home to him.

[*Additional source material:* www.poetryfarm.wordpress.com; www.sahistory.org.za; www.poetrypotion.com; www.poormagazine.org]

Mongane Wally Serote and the national poets

Rabbie Serumula interviewed the national literary jewel and ANC stalwart at his home near Yeoville, a storied suburb of Johannesburg which was once home to a boisterous community of Black and white activists, artists and communists. Serote, who was 76 in 2020, was named South Africa's Poet Laureate in 2018.

'We were not protest poets, we were not Soweto poets. We were revolutionaries, we were national poets,' said Serote. 'The academics are cheating our people when they tell them anything other than this.'

That concept of inclusion under the banner of resistance is important. Where journalists and critics often seek a means of categorising people, Serote's point was that their vitality as writers exceeded – and exceeds – just a concept or just a place. They espoused a consciousness that knows no boundaries.

That approach is what kept Serote alive in the imaginations of three generations of South Africans, and many cultural workers of all ideological persuasions. At the same time, he has a pride in the fact that his work and that of fellow poets (Sipho) Sepamla, Oswald Mtshali and (Mafika) Gwala gained momentum from the SASO of 1968.

'The bravery, the anger, the fighting spirit of our people – these were the core elements of the BCM, which were used to conscientise our people,' said Serote. His view was that the BCM was a reaction to apartheid legislation, which was deepened by the 1976 massacre.

Serote and other revolutionaries' poetry was a mechanism in re-establishing a tradition of Black writing in the country. They produced content uncomfortable, even dangerous, to the apartheid regime.

'It was a time when it was very dangerous to write the kind of poetry that we were writing. But we did write it. We did not only write it, we went to different parts of the country to articulate it,' he explained.

Born in Sophiatown in 1944, his education was in the squalor of Alexandra. He later attended Morris Isaacson High School, Soweto – not knowing that his work would later offer some pivotal knowledge to the 1976 students' uprising.

Serote said he became involved with the BCM through a need

to express Black identity, resistance and revolt. BCM fostered and affirmed his cultural and political values. He and many of his fellow writers and artists homed in on the minds of Black people: to stop them from trying to live up to a 'white' standard; to find their Blackness with pride and beauty.

To alter consciousness, there was another aspect of the arts that needed to change, Serote says. 'When we looked at the plastic arts [painting, sculpture, film and photography], we saw something that had to change, and we discussed it elaborately. Photographers were not articulating the bravery, commitment and courage of our people because they stood on the side of the guns and showed us as victims.'

Once photographers such as Peter Magubane and Alf Kumalo 'stood with the people' and adopted a 'pro-Black' position, theirs would be a much more influential presence. Just that shift in camera angles impacted on the minds of Black people. That, in itself, said Serote, was an act of BC.

BC creates 'a mirror through which people can look at themselves and be happy with the reflection, but now that we have gone through the BCM and are in post-apartheid South Africa, there should be something else we can do to stay creative with the country's diversity.' It's so important that people 'must never forget that the most oppressed are still Black people. They are the ones who are not employed, they are the ones suffering immensely under poverty.' The arts must speak to Black issues.

'When I go to Alexandra, I always hurt badly inside because you see people just standing in the streets.'

One art form that continues to speak to these issues is film, while theatre and other performing art forms need to ensure their attention is not diverted. That, said Serote, could be dangerous.

'When I was in my early 20s, I was forever active with poetry all over the country. That is not happening now. I see, dotted here and there, are places where, say, poetry happens. It is no longer a national art form. I listen to music sometimes and think, shouldn't we be more creative about putting that mirror in front of us?'

Serote's fondest memory of taking poetry to the people during the height of the BCM was that 'the bravery of young writers created a very strong bond'.

Among his many awards are: the 1973 Ingrid Jonker Poetry Prize for the best debut collection in English; the 1993 Noma Award for publishing in Africa; the 2003 English Academy of Southern Africa Medal for contribution to the English language; the 2004 Pablo Neruda Medal for Writing, and his *Third World Express* being selected among the Africa Book Centre's 100 Best Books of the Twentieth Century in 2008.

Serote was awarded the Order of Ikhamanga in Silver for 'excellent contribution to literature, with emphasis on poetry and for putting his artistic talents at the service of democracy in South Africa' in 2007 by then-president Thabo Mbeki.

His anthologies include the acclaimed *Yakhal'inkomo* (1972), *No Baby Must Weep* (1975), *Third World Express* (1992) and *History is the Home Address* (2004), His novels are *To Every Birth Its Blood* (1981), *Gods of Our Time* (1999) and *Scatter the Ashes and Go* (2002).

[Additional sources: www.rosemarieberger.com; wordnsoundwordpress. com; *The Complete S'ketsh Theatre Magazine*, www.michaelchapman.co.za and www.sahistory.org za]

Poetry: Where's thy sting?

It was a decade in 2020 since BC poets and musicians had first sharpened their craft on the South African platform, Word N Sound.

Its positive acts of expression had a following that reached beyond borders, with ties all over the world. It brought some of the best global poets to its space every year after its first annual international youth festival in 2010.

Although those expressions were often simply about beauty or desire, its stage reinforced South Africans' love of public political performance, albeit that the mission for poets after apartheid was somewhat different from what it was at the height of BC. The arch-enemy – that against which we rail and insist, rebel and resist – was not as monstrous then as it was before.

But just as it was for the revolutionary poets of BC, performance is still a direct and challenger art, which keeps its place because it is authentic, it can reflect. If it listens; it is conscious; it is made up of issues. Corruption in government, inequality, poverty, racism, sexism, xenophobia. It talks to where we are, wherever we are.

For some years after 1994, public poetry took a backseat, having once been so effectively used as a protest art under the apartheid regime. Then it was a powerful way to mobilise minds into a single unit of consciousness – the ultimate voice of persistence and a pat on the back for those who needed to hear that being Black means not striving for whiteness. Revolutionary poets would not stand for such gaslighting. Their poetry spoke of identity, resistance and revolt.

The poets of a quarter century after apartheid have their own struggles, however – among them, how the reincarnation of the arts can become a sustainable career. There was always revolution in South African music. But poetry?

It needs a sting. Or, it needs a bite or to be struck on the flesh or in the heart. With Word N Sound showing its mettle, and some potent tongues, South Africans only need to pay more attention to their poetical renaissance – round about now. And in so doing, we show that BC is not only about pain but about the world.

Distinguished contemporary American poet Tracie Morris – who specialises in sound poetry and has studied poetry forms and performance around the world – explains this in *Well+Good*, 'A lot of times, Black poets are put in a little teeny tiny box, and it's like, "Tell us of your people".'

'It's very exoticising and limiting. It's damaging because it reduces us as people. Black people have opinions on everything – just go to a Black barbecue. [This reduction] is a way of saying, "The only thing that we're interested in is the way that you feel about yourself". In other words, you're not a person of the world [...] you're just a Black person in the world. I don't think that that's helpful.'

We accept solidarity from poets like Chicago's Diamond Sharp, a performer who has also been published in *Vice*, *Pitchfork*, the *Wellesley Review* and many others. Listen to her at https://thisisrhymesandreasons.com/diamond-sharp/. Her grasp of conversations about mental health for Black women is especially exquisite and important. It's clever and empathic.

Among her works in this arena which other Black performance

poets may consider is *Exile*, in which Sharp imagines herself discussing her Blackness with playwright Lorraine Hansberry.

Another poet who richly intuits BC as performance for this moment, is Malcolm London, who Cornel West described as 'the Gil Scott Heron of his generation'. At not yet 25, London was an award-winning poet, educator, organiser and international public speaker. See him in narration at https://reelchicago.com/article/strange-loop-conspiracy/

[Brown, 2020: https://www.wellandgood.com/black-poets/; https://www.2009-2019.poetryproject.org/people/diamond-janese-sharp/; Simmons, 2018: https://southsideweekly.com/words-become-witchcraft-breakbeat-poets-black-girl-magic/Johanson, 2018: https://africanah.org/spoken-word-artist-malcolm-london/]

The loudest Black voice: Mzwakhe Mbuli

Arguably the most successful spoken-word and performance poet in South African history. Mzwakhe Mbuli arrived under the auspices of his own BC before he was to move actively onto the anti-apartheid stage in the early 1980s. He'd then expose some of his own wild, personal side once the drawbridge of fame was let down.

Awkward, at times juvenile in the actual quality of verse, Mbuli's poetry was nonetheless indisputably strong in its reach into an audience and the thunder of delivery. Undeniably controversial, the Apostolic Faith Mission pastor and ex-convict, who spent four years behind bars for armed robbery and possession of a hand grenade, coined his own art, 'Mbulism'.

Nicknamed 'the People's Poet', Mbuli was born in Sophiatown in 1958, experiencing the loss of his family home as a very young child when the apartheid regime forcibly removed the suburb's Black residents and bulldozed their histories.

He used considerable oratorical skill to express the human devastation of apartheid and then the disappointed revolutionary ferment of a post-democratic society.

Popular enough to be invited to perform at assassinated SACP leader Chris Hani's funeral in 1993 and at Mandela's inauguration in 1994, Mbuli has been thrown shade as time has gone on, most markedly when he was pilloried for his response to a popular music hero Mandoza's death and his seeming support of a corrupt former head of the national public broadcaster, the SABC.

Yet his inflections, intonations and pitch at a time marked his brilliance as he drew on genres as diverse as freestyle rap and traditional praise-singing.

His 'Change Is Pain', a pure and simple protest poem from 1986, understood Black oppression, with Mbuli himself a victim of the state, repeatedly detained in the 1980s and denied the freedom to travel. But by 1990, when the ANC's exiles were returning and the congress movement was at its height, Mbuli was sharing stages with Miriam Makeba, 'the Lion of Zimbabwe' Thomas Mapfumo, Senegalese superstar Youssou N'Dour and Peter Gabriel.

Among his other well-known works are *Unbroken Spirit*, 1988; *Resistance Is Defence*, 1992; *Mbulism*, 2004; *Thunder (Ladum' Izulu)*, 2008; *Africa Amandla*, 2012, and *Born Free but Always in Chains*, 2015.

Stage left: The theatre of the people

It was leftist, said the critics. Its participatory intention and deep radical education drew attention to the poor and powerless, said the Left. For many South Africans who were denied – or couldn't afford – access to liberation literature and uncensored TV, radio and film, it was the barricade between them and the prejudice of difference.

Many productions staged after 1976 were influential in how fearlessly they responded to apartheid, the writers influenced not only by their circumstances, but also by activist European playwrights like Bertolt Brecht and Augusto Boal.

German poet, playwright and theatre reformer Brecht's eternally popular *Mother Courage* was the kind of writing ripe to be reworked for our revolutionary moment. It was in how Brecht approached the relationship between performers and audience that had an impact on local theatre-makers. As web-log *Theatre Archive* records: 'He didn't want them to sit there numbly watching his play for entertainment purposes alone. He wanted them to have questions and reactions to what they had seen.

'To achieve this he added … direct addresses to the audience, interruptions of the action with ironic songs commenting on the action to create a critical consciousness within his audience.'

The Brazilian playwright Boal was also an inspiration in how he got actors to respond directly to members of the audience to encourage the mutual empowerment.

South African resistance theatre drew on techniques like those to offer audiences of the 1970s a chance to say what they were feeling about living under apartheid. In city theatres like the Market Theatre in Johannesburg and the Baxter in Cape Town, especially Black theatre goers, who were otherwise commonly unable to mix freely in a social setting, could briefly escape apartheid's mind control.

But the theatre of BC was certainly not all about the city. Theatremakers found any space appropriate for forceful, progressive interaction with an audience.

Gibson Kente (1932–2004)

The father of Black theatre was unafraid to tell the truth about what was happening in the townships, using halls, churches and even spaces in his own house.

A centre of many other artists' lives, Kente even penned a farewell song for superstar Miriam Makeba, which she performed in his studio, before she went into exile in the 1960s.

Although that song and many others remained, there were works that were barred from the airwaves. Three of Kente's plays – *How Long*, *I Believe* and *Too Late* – were banned, unbanned and banned again after the West Rand Administration Board, the regime's bureaucratic office in Soweto and surrounds, declared in 1975 that scripts would have to be submitted for review before plays could be performed.

He was jailed in 1976 at the end of filming his play, *How Long*. The film was never released.

Reverend Mzwandile Maqina's popular *Give Us This Day* – which 'took Soweto by storm', according to *The World* newspaper – was another which fell when the sword of censorship was swung. As happened to Kente and many other theatremakers, his work was banned in May 1976.

Children raise their fists during a youth day commemoration held on 16 June 2006 in Soweto. (Photo: Paballo Thekiso)

EFF supporters chant songs and hold up placards during a protest march in Johannesburg city centre on 1 November 2013. (Photo: Paballo Thekiso)

Academic and human rights activist Salim Vally speaks from his office at the University of Johannesburg. Vally has continued to lead the charge for freedom in education, especially for black students. (Photo: Paballo Thekiso)

Struggle icon and a June 16 mastermind, Sello 'Bra Mike' Matsobane, speaks about the events that led up to the day that defined South African history. (Photo: Paballo Thekiso)

Revolutionary poet Mongane Wally Serote speaks about the role the arts played in advancing belief in the power of blackness to overcome racism and hatred. (Photo: Rabbie Serumula)

Writer and poet Mak Manaka's work and imagination was influenced by his celebrated father, artist Matsemela Manaka, and his dance pioneer mother, Nomsa Manaka. (Photo: Rabbie Serumula)

Kwaito legend Bonginkosi Dlamini, popularly known as Zola 7, promotes black people's ability to overcome white supremacy. (Photo: Paballo Thekiso)

One of the most influential musicians in South Africa, Thandiswa Mazwai is a foremost proponent of blackness and African liberation. (Photo: Paballo Thekiso)

American #BlackLivesMatter activist Thenjiwe McHarris has sought to blur the boundaries between young people in South Africa and the United States in pursuit of common goals. (Photo: Paballo Thekiso)

Former BC activist, and now the CEO of the Nelson Mandela Children's Fund, Sibongile Mkhabela, speaks about her Movement days and lessons learnt. (Photo: Paballo Thekiso)

Wits student Tshepiso Modupe joins other women activists for a #FeesMustFall protest against a proposed 10.5% increase at the university in August 2013. A hike in fees affected mostly black students. (Photo: Paballo Thekiso)

#FeesMustFall demonstrators outside the ANC party headquarters, Luthuli House, in central Johannesburg in 2013. Many among them advance a contemporary Black Consciousness. (Photo: Paballo Thekiso)

Former Wits SRC president Nompendulo Mkhatshwa addresses students during a #FeesMustFall protest at the Linder Auditorium on the Wits education campus, 30 August 2013. (Photo: Paballo Thekiso)

Former Wits SRC president Shaeera Kalla addresses students during a #FeesMustFall protest at Linder Auditorium on 30 August 2013. On her left is Nompendulo Mkhatshwa, also a former Wits SRC president, and other women leaders of the movement. (Photo: Paballo Thekiso)

Zulaikha Patel is a South African anti-racism activist, black feminist and revolutionary. She became a symbol of the fight against Pretoria Girls High School's policy regarding black girls' hair in 2016, at the age of 13. (Photo: Paballo Thekiso)

Acting for the masses

The People's Experimental Theatre (PET) in Lenasia took the stage to where the people were. It was an all-Black organisation, like the Theatre Council of Natal (TECON), Mihloti Black Theatre, a BC troupe founded in 1971 by musician and music teacher Molefe Pheto,[98] MDALI (from 'umDali', meaning 'creator' and the acronym for the Music, Drama and Literature Institute) which included a number of cultural groups in Johannesburg townships; and the Soweto Ensemble, an organisation of Black intellectuals who staged plays in the township, including Jean Anouilh's *Antigone*, Sartre's *Huis Clos* and Sam Gorey's *Shaka*.

These collectives deliberately used their art, and particularly theatre, to spread a BC ideology. There was support from other BC-inclined quarters, like the FUBA Gallery, co-founded by artist and art critic David Koloane in the bloody year of 1977. At FUBA, Black artists got preference.

Commercial theatre would battle to achieve the same goal, but as writer and actor Ian Steadman writes in his 1990 Wits History Workshop paper, 'Towards popular theatre in South Africa', a work like *Shanti*, 'a typical BC play', demonstrates 'a conscious didacticism'. *Shanti* – written by a BCM leader, Mthuli ka Shezi – was banned but kept making appearances at BC events.

South African performer, activist and writer Robert Mshengu Kavanagh[99] described in the introduction to *South African People's Plays* (Heinemann, 1981), which he also edited, that *Shanti* 'is possibly the best-known play to emerge from the activities of the BCM, of which it was formally a part'.

'*Shanti* operates on three levels, it seems to me. It is a play about lovers

---

98 See more about Molefe Pheto in Chapter Six: Conscious Women, 'The new wave of BC is only beginning: The story of AZAPO's Manku Noruka'.

99 Robert Mshengu Kavanagh is also the author of *Theatre and Cultural Struggle in South Africa* (Zed Books, London, 1985), in which he 'reveals the ... interplay of class, nation and race ... when theatre itself became a political battleground'. Kavanagh's account spans multi-racial projects created by white liberals, commercial musicals for Black audiences by Black entrepreneurs, and the efforts of the BCM to forge revolutionary theatre [Rakuten kobo, 2020: https://www.kobo.com/hk/en/ebook/theatre-and-cultural-struggle-under-apartheid].

... about a man's struggle against oppression and ... about solidarity among the oppressed ... Shanti, who is Indian, and her boyfriend, Thabo, who is a Black African, try to surmount the barriers', including the fact that different races were separated into different communities by law. 'Government pressure against marriages between African and Indian (were) virtually as severe as between Black and white.'

As Kavanagh writes, the theme was both 'private tragedy' and political oppression.

In South Africa, people were not only 'classified into white, African, Asian, Coloured, Chinese, etc., but even these categories (were) further divided. Thus an African (could) be a Sotho, Tswana, Pedi, Zulu ... etc. A Coloured (could) be a Cape Coloured, a Malay, or simply "Other Coloured".'

Shanti's main character was based on activist Shanthie Naidoo, a South African hero who was among the women who refused to testify in the 'Trial of 22'[100] in 1969 and then underwent a brutal period of detention designed to destroy them. Shezi wrote the play, which is still regarded as one of the most militant pieces of work in the BC period, 'in the real situation of South Africa in 1973–74, (during which) the first political task was to mobilise a united Black front'.

Shezi and Pheto were among the courageous of the original BC theatre creatives, along with [Lewis] Nkosi and [Sipho] Sepamla, who was a member of the BC-aligned Medupe Writers' Association. His fellow writers understood the weight of his satire, with his greatest success the banned 1981 play, *A Ride in the Whirlwind*, set during the Soweto uprising.

Shezi, a former SRC president at the University of Zululand and a vice-president of the BPC, was a cultural guerrilla before his time.

---

100   The '22' were revolutionaries charged with communism. Most had been leading members of the ANC, the South African Congress of the Trade Unions and the Transvaal Indian Congress and included Shanthie Naidoo, Winnie Madikizela-Mandela, Joyce Sikhakhane-Rankin, Rita Ndzanga and Peter Magubane. In the aftermath, activists were driven underground or jailed. The '22' were awarded the Order of Luthuli in Silver in 2017 [The Presidency, 2017: http://www.thepresidency.gov.za/national-orders/recipient/22-anc-political-trialists-1969].

Zakes Mda (1948–)

Another who led that fiery charge was international literary idol, Zanemvula Kizito Gatyeni Mda, better known as 'Zakes', an admired artist, filmmaker, poet, teacher and novelist.

He experienced his family being forced into exile in Lesotho in the 1960s, but Mda's own passage to be reunited with them was dangerous, and by 17 he'd joined the PAC.

Disillusionment with its militancy did not deter his inclination towards BC. In fact, the two concepts – militancy and BC – were not mutually exclusive. Rather, Mda, who studied law but abandoned it for the arts, was far more effective to BC as a writer.

His 1987 MA thesis at UCT, 'The utilisation of theatre as a medium for development communication', reflected the conscious individual who has given much time to the development of others, particularly children, in a developing world context.

When he earned the Olive Schreiner Prize for Drama in 1995 and became dramaturge and writer-in-residence at the Market Theatre – just one of many national, African and international accolades – he was able to leverage his insight for the greater good.

Mda's 1977 drama, *We Shall Sing for the Fatherland*, began his story of radiant, world-class novel-writing and more than 30 plays.

The Market Theatre

Lit by the lustre of Mda and others, (former CEO) Ismail Mahomed would argue that this global landmark was just as effective at endorsing BC as were the Black theatre companies and Black writers.

Mahomed's links to the theatre stretched back three generations, to when his grandfather and great-grandfather were fruit and vegetable merchants on that very site. As a child, Mahomed used to go with them to the Indian Fruit Market, where the Market Theatre now stands in Newtown on the outskirts of the Johannesburg CBD.

The connection between these histories provides Mahomed – who grew up in Lenasia, the area to which Indian people were banished in the 1950s upon the destruction of mixed communities like Sophiatown – with an exquisite sense of his own consciousness. That is knitted into South Africa's Black political, cultural and artistic history.

The Market's collection of plays about Black life, including *You Strike the Woman You Strike a Rock*, *Black Dog – Inj'emnyama*, *Sophiatown*, *Woza Albert*, *Asinamali* and many more, is an indispensable BC archive.

Co-founders Barney Simon and Manny Manim opened the theatre in 1976.

Salisbury Island

Professor Ashwin Desai of the Centre for Sociological Research at the University of Johannesburg gave the world a little-known picture of spatial oppression in a 2013 paper, 'Theatre of Struggle: BC on Salisbury Island'.

It might not be a name known to all South Africans, or indeed, many anti-apartheid activists, but it was the location for a university in which apartheid planners found a 'symbol of their desire for a prison-like geography'.

'In the midst of Durban's harbour, [Salisbury Island] had a history of abandonment,' writes Desai. 'A disused military barracks and naval base, a former leper colony, it was here that authorities decided to establish a university for Indians in 1961. The Island could best be reached [only] by ferry.'

Yet, as Desai's paper also shows, the physical and political repression at University College allowed the passage into public prominence of many powerful and unique individuals within the BCM: Prominent among them were Saths Cooper, Sam Moodley and Strini Moodley – names which are today instantly recognisable to students of BC.

Although they were the ideal intended victims of apartheid's Extension of University Education Act of 1959, they refused to acquiesce in the silence expected of them. (More generally known as the Fort Hare Act, it 'created the legislative underpinning to establish separate universities for different racial groups'.)

Desai cites another former Salisbury Island student and now professor Betty Govinden, an author, as she recalls: 'Yes, there was a certain desolation. The sky was not limitless and seemed to hover just above you. We never learnt to forget that [this] was a discarded military barracks, and we were its "discarded people".'

But University College also 'became an incubator for critical thought, dissent and lifelong radical political commitment', says Desai.

Cooper and the two Moodleys were 'early collaborators of Biko' when he was a student at the Non-European Section of the same university, although not at that location. They had their own histories within the 'Indian' section.

'Sam Moodley (born Pillay) was born in the coal-mining town of Dundee in northern Natal in 1948. She was politicised at an early age as the town had a strong history of politics. At school she was on the same debating team as [other political] heavyweight[s].'

Moodley wanted to study law but settled for a BA degree because her father was afraid she would 'get involved in politics'. She then did speech and drama.

'Saths Cooper was born in 1950 in kwaDabeka just past Clermont township. As there was no school in the area, Saths's (worker) father established a school in the warehouse for children in the area. Students of various ages studied in one class.'

Cooper recalls to Desai how pamphlets could be seen 'raining from the sky' in the area after the Sharpeville massacre, 'because these guys would fly overhead with military planes and drop pamphlets asking people to not obey the boycott and stuff like that'.

He went to high school at Sastri College[101] where he became politicised.

'When South Africa celebrated the fifth anniversary of the Republic in 1966, Saths', records Desai, 'participated actively in anti-Republic Day mobilisations. Students boycotted the singing of the national anthem, *Die Stem/The Call of South Africa*.'

Cooper matriculated in 1967 and 'ended up at University College, much against my will, a serious spirit of resistance to a narrow ethnic

---

101   The first Indian high school and teachers' training college in South Africa. Opened in 1929 by the Governor-General of South Africa, the Earl of Athlone, it was founded by the Honourable VS Srinivasa Sastri, Agent of the Indian government to South Africa in 1927, and designed by Hermann Kallenbach, a friend of Mahatma Gandhi. In 1936, the Natal University College set up a campus for Black students using Sastri College; it, which was declared a monument in March 1989 [https://amandladurban.org.za/sastri-college-winterton-walk/].

institution'. Although he created and was involved in a number of clubs for the creative arts, he always had a vigorous personal political flavour.

Strini Moodley was born in Durban in 1946. His father was already a powerhouse in the trade union movement and, through his father's influence, Moodley became an activist while he, like Cooper, was at Sastri College.

'The first political act that I got involved in', Moodley told Desai, 'was [also] to boycott the declaration of the Republic of South Africa; [I was then] engaged in all kinds of activities in what was then called the [Natal Indian] Youth Congress.

Moodley proceeded to Salisbury Island in 1967 – like Cooper, 'much against his will' – but he was armed with Fanon's *The Wretched of the Earth* and Stokely Carmichael and Charles Hamilton's *Black Power*.

It was after Strini Moodley became a member of SASO and befriended Biko that 'his political thinking [was shaped] in fundamental ways'.

Desai records Moodley: 'I came into contact with Biko in about 1966 and we became very close friends. We would sit around and have parties together and have a lot of political discussions.'

Sam Moodley recalls Salisbury Island as being 'extremely volatile, a time when students were resisting in whatever way they could find'. An important way to mobilise students was to initiate clubs.

Cooper was ultimately expelled, accused of cheating during a music exam. This was likely a means for the university authorities to get rid of him as the rector, SP Olivier, said Cooper could return only 'if he gave up political activism'.

Govinden recalls there was a 'hidden curriculum, with material such as Freire's *Pedagogy of the Oppressed* being circulated amongst the student community'.

While still a student on Salisbury Island, Cooper would extol the virtues of Négritude and produce plays like *Antigone*, 'to prod us to question the immoral state'.

Theatre, explains Desai, was to become 'a key channel for resistance among the students, as they performed skits on campus life, challenged the authorities by staging productions off the Island (which was forbidden) and used drama as a way of mobilising student protests and raising consciousness'.

'It was part of a more widespread movement among writers and BC leaders to expose the iniquities of the system.'

Creativity flourished on Salisbury Island and elsewhere in the ghettos of the 1970s 'in new poetry, plays and stories; in new views of art as community-based people's resistance, [and took on] a distinctly Africanist energy that challenged prevailing Europeanised assumptions'.

Strini Moodley established a now-legendary avant-garde theatre group on Salisbury Island, called 'the Clan'. Members included him and Sam, and friends Asha Rambally, Ben David, Dennis Pather, Kiruba Pillay, Sam Pillay, Kogs Reddy and Roy Thatiah, whose names will resonate within the BC community.

Like TECON, the Shah Academy and the Avon Theatre Group, so-called 'Indic' theatre was true protest through art. TECON was founded by the Moodleys and Cooper, along with comrades Roy Jagesar, Smiley Peters, Rad Thambadoo, Ronnie Govender, Benji Francis and others based at the University of Durban-Westville in 1969.

They were as literary as they were militant, using their theatre groups as vehicles for political mobilisation, and propelling a South African Black Theatre Union to provide unity.

'It was the first time that the administration and all aspects of theatrical production were organised by Black people,' acknowledged a piece in the *Black Review* in 1973. 'The students staged several productions, which played on the inequities and brutality of the apartheid state and its policies and brought them into conflict with the authorities.'

In particular, co-writer Moodley's 1967 political revue *Black on White* 'exposed the problems of racism and ethnicity in South Africa'.

The production was to lead to Moodley's expulsion from the university, too – along with Pather, Reddy, David and another comrade, Nash Naina.

Black on White was then staged at Wits and at the conflicted 1967 NUSAS congress in Grahamstown upon request from Biko.

Strini Moodley said the white students at that congress 'exposed the falsity of white liberal activity in Black politics ... as [they got] quite angry with us'.

Activists Moira Powys, Selma Soni, Kiruba Reddy and Neelan Tharmalingam were all vital to the success of 'the Clan', while Moodley and Cooper were to become two of 'the most visible faces' of the BCM, wrote Desai.

It troubled Strini that 'you had whites like Helen Suzman[102] and Alan Paton[103] and all these liberals speaking on behalf of Black people and we felt, no, Black people can't sit and watch what is happening in this country when they are the victims.

'Black people have to take their future into their own hands and have to fight for their own liberation; other people are not going to be able to give you your liberation. You have to fight for your own liberation.'

[Desai, 2013; Gastrow, 1995; www.ukzn.ac.za]

Conscious pictures
Lefifi Tladi (1949–)

Born in the 'Black spot' of Lady Selborne, Pretoria, Tladi has layered a cascading shimmer upon South Africa's creative life. Intense artistic commitment was always his 'bag', his 'personal style', as Louis Armstrong would have said.

Tladi has been described as a definitive prototype for the BCM, yet that didn't quite capture his wild joy, his smile and the abundant expression that made him one of the country's greatest heroes. Although Tladi's art cannot be separated from a political sensibility, he was always ahead of his time.

Today's young protagonists of BC would do well to get to know the lyrical work he produced with the performance act Dashiki. A mash-

---

[102] Helen Suzman (1917–2009) was a prominent white liberal politician who used her position in the apartheid Parliament to push for some discriminatory legislation to be reconsidered, and to draw international attention to oppression. But she was criticised for not doing enough, and for positioning her values within whiteness rather than for total Black liberation.

[103] Alan Paton (1903–1988) was the author of *Cry, the Beloved Country* and *Too Late the Phalarope*.

up of music and poems, their work as Black creative activists easily travelled into southern Africa when the apartheid regime tried to shut them down. Few artists can earn a crowd's collective Black Power salute.

Tladi could do that from the 1970s when, as has been documented many times, he was nicknamed 'Jomo' after the charismatic Kenyan anti-colonialist, Jomo Kenyatta. The men looked somewhat alike, but also, to the incipient BC crowd, Tladi too was an African revolutionary, an anti-imperialist – unique and undaunted.

Among his achievements were setting up community art projects, which stored the essence of BC's desire for Blacks to develop themselves in their own, Black way. Tladi worked hard within the BCM's CulCom (culture committee), because apartheid had not 'exposed us as a nation to our own creative genius'. He showed this by, for example, opening a small art museum in the bantustan of Bophuthatswana's Ga-Rankuwa area west of Pretoria in 1970. The security police harassed him and troubled his artists, then arrested him after the Soweto massacre.

But Tladi continued to develop his skills in exile in Gaborone, and went to Nigeria in 1977 as part of the ANC contingent for the major cultural festival, FESTAC (also known as the Second World Black and African Festival of Arts and Culture, the first having been in Dakar, Senegal, in 1966).

Even after moving to Stockholm, Sweden, Tladi concentrated on how art could conscientise Europeans about apartheid.

He spent his life as a role model for BC's rejection of a dominant white value system, urging the oppressed, as have all the great BC philosophers, to positively relocate their Blackness within their own minds.

Paul Stopforth (1945–)

The momentous *The Biko Series*, which Stopforth completed in 1980, is as much a depiction of the vulnerability of a man in his sacred silence after his terrible murder, as it is of a political figure in all his superlative strength.

The artist's life was changed when he was 'given privileged access to autopsy photographs of Biko's poor body'. As the *Hermetic Philosophy* advises: 'The lips of wisdom are closed, except to the ears of understanding.'

Using mixed media on paper, his series of 20 pieces pay direct witness to the agonies of the apartheid system. These are testimony, alternately quivering and swirling like a heavy wind in the dust. These are intimate: body parts, right down to the bottom of Biko's feet.

Raised during apartheid, Stopforth says it was only after he graduated that he began to create 'images that have since become icons of the struggle against apartheid'. He elaborates on his website paulstopforth.com as to how this unfolded: '[These were] assemblages that contain photographic evidence of police brutality, alongside fragments of the real world gathered from the streets. [These] are the first constructions I made with direct reference to the nature of what was taking place.

'The subsequent installation of life-size plaster figures representing the ongoing torture and deaths of political prisoners while in detention took place a week after ... Biko had been murdered by the security police.'

Stopforth tells how his works 'reflect[ed] on the brutality of the apartheid system, and the ongoing damage done to the lives of human beings everywhere who take a stand against authoritarian states, systems and regimes'.

He spent a postgraduate year at the Royal College of Art in London, and it was upon his return to South Africa that Stopforth 'utilised a more expressionistic and distorted pictorial means' to focus then on the perpetrators of the system.

His triptych, *The Interrogators*, is about the security police who interrogated Biko; Stopforth says it's about the 'banality of evil'.

'I want to bring the facts home to those willing to look,' he writes. 'My figures parallel something that we can't be witness to. We can't refuse to accept that these things happen.'

There is a despair there that makes you flinch. In their quietness, they are crude and noisy. Such is the confident *glissando* with which Stopforth proceeds as he confronts us. Of all his work – and it is tremendous – it is *The Biko Series* which clatters to the front of our consciousness.

The multiple award-winning artist taught at Harvard and was a full-time visiting faculty member at the School of the Museum of Fine

Arts in Boston.

[www.paulstopforth.com; www.sahistory.org.za; www.davidkrutprojects.com]

Durant Sihlahi (1935–2004)

Influenced as a child by the dazzling murals and floors painted by the Xhosa women in his paternal grandparents' village, Cala, in the Eastern Cape, Sihlali was a precocious talent who started art lessons when he moved to his parents' home in Moroka, Soweto.

Tutored by artist Alpheus Kubeka at the acclaimed Polly Street Recreation Centre in the Johannesburg CBD, Sihlali showed high promise even as a teenager. The artist Cecil Skotnes, who also taught him, encouraged Sihlali to find an aesthetic within the realities of Black urban life. This was not unlike the master Gerard Sekoto, whose painterly stories of street and township life in the 1930s and 1940s still garner millions in sale prices on international auction.

Sihlali was offended by the categorisation of his work as 'township art'. He insisted that he was instead capturing the textures of the anti-apartheid resistance. Social destruction is the nuance of his later work, although Sihlali customarily returned to murals and graffiti.

He ran the fine arts department at FUBA in the early to mid-1980s and taught students at the Wits Technikon and Funda Art Centre.

Omar Badsha (1945–)

Many words could be orchestrated about this guru, whose photography, resistance art, activism and writing made an incalculable contribution to the meaning of 'South African' over 70 years. Yet Badsha didn't stop at developing those individual powers. In creating first Afrapix and then www.sahistory.org, an invaluable resource used by everyone, Badsha shines among South Africa's many historians.

Thus, a praise poem by Neelika Jayawardane seems the most valid means of capturing him: 'Immanuel Kant would have been distraught if he were to see Omar Badsha's work. Neither great beauties nor scenic vistas meant to evoke sublime pleasure were the focus of Badsha's camera.

'His eye – sharp and contentious as his tongue is known to be – cuts through the cultural baggage that trains us to look at the beautiful and the acceptably pretty.

'He is known for having fashioned a new visual vocabulary for translating the lives of those that apartheid excluded out of South Africa's consciousness; often, the public whom he photographed may not have even realised that they were excised into the periphery of the nation's vision of itself, nor have had the luxury of imagining themselves as part of the national narrative.'

Detailing Badsha's photographic erudition, Jayawardane tells another side: 'Though [Badsha] is the go-to person that international scholars and curators seek out when looking for information about the history of political documentary photography, he is not one of the big names with which South African photography is associated internationally.

'The reasons are obvious: few commercial galleries were open to exhibiting the works of Black photographers, and no agents came forward to promote Black photographers' work unless it had commercial appeal or spoke to the stereotypes that apartheid – and white supremacy in general – supported.

'Badsha refused to exhibit in segregated studios, or state-sponsored shows, marginalising him already as a "difficult" character who didn't play the game of supplication properly. And during the late '60s and '70s, unless Black photographers took a specific kind of photograph documenting spectacular violence, press agencies didn't come calling, either.'

She then tells how, 'in response to these disparities, in 1982, Badsha and a collective of photographers founded Afrapix, an independent photographic agency that not only helped promote Black photographers on the international circuit, but played a significant role in documenting South Africa's political climate during the 1980s, and shaped the tropes of social documentary photography in the country.

'Perhaps because Badsha's interest was in collective organising and not personal fame, his own work was not as well recognised. Rather than following violent flares between Black South Africans and the apartheid regime's police forces, he recorded the dynamics of daily life under apartheid.

'At the core of the conversations I've had with Badsha is his tenacious grip on political integrity; this wilful desire – to record and be witness to subsumed histories, to walk in with his unapologetically political lens – maintained his integrity as a narrator of South African history.'

[Jayawardane, 2015]

Ralph Ndawo

BC publisher Mutloatse affectionately referred to the admired lensman by calling him the 's'bali who photographed poetry'. The Ralph Ndawo Foundation has gone further, saying he was 'a dedicated professional, stoic under suffering and harassment, and a credit to Black journalism and all it stands for.

'He came from a generation which created excellence out of nothing and his readiness to impart and share his talent and experience with those around him will forever endear his memory to us.

'He died when his dreams were yet to be fulfilled and those who come after him must pick up his spear and go forward.'

Ndawo – like his BC contemporaries Bob Gosani, Alf Kumalo, Jürgen Schadeberg, Peter Magubane and Omar Badsha – gave especially young Black people a reason to persevere with little more than a camera.

His foundation says he was always 'a man of Johannesburg, born in a backyard at the corner of Commissioner and End streets in Doornfontein in 1932'.

Ndawo became 'one of the country's leading news photographers by buying a cheap box camera in 1957. One of the pictures taken with the camera won him a more modern camera in a photographic competition – and he began to take his photography seriously.'

His vision came when he was in the shadows, processing film as a darkroom assistant. Then Ndawo got work at the *Golden City Post*, *Drum* and the *Rand Daily Mail* as a 'proper' photographer, his imagery blessedly stark in black-and-white.

[www.ralphndawofoundation.co.za]

Jahmil XT Qubeka and other reels

It was unusual to be banned in 2013, but that's what happened to young Black director Qubeka's film, *Of Good Report*. That act of the Film and Publications Board (FPB) in the end drew grand sensation to

Qubeka's work, which had been scheduled as the 34th edition of the Durban International Film Festival's opening night attraction.

The FPB was uncomfortable with *Of Good Report*'s portrayal of a high school teacher's obsession with a teenage pupil. It felt 34-year-old Qubeka (1979–), who felt defamed as a self-described 'proud son of Africa', had made child pornography as defined in the Act.

Yet the other side of the story offered a warmer grasp of what Qubeka was about. He told *Variety* magazine that, despite growing up in the bantustan of Ciskei, he 'doesn't have the weight of apartheid on his shoulders', that he was 'cocooned from it because I grew up in a system that was subsidised by the apartheid government'.

The interpretation was that, through this 'engineered marginalisation', Qubeka had grown up in a more privileged social class, despite being Black. But for Qubeka himself, this was less a comment on the so-called validity of his 'Blackness' than on the unusual opportunity he was given from childhood, through this irony of his more elite upbringing, to focus on his Black self-development.

His earlier 2010 film, *A Small Town Called Descent*, had quickly celebrated his arrival.

Now the challenge for Qubeka – and his righteous peers like filmmaker Charlie Vundla (*Friends in Need*, 2008, *How to Steal 2 Million*, 2011 and *Cuckold*, 2015) – was to quicken the Black South African stride in the steps of the world's great directors.

Qubeka pursued that at the 2017 Cannes Cinefondation's *L'Atelier* where he was one of 16 directors selected to participate. That resulted in his film *Sew the Winter to My Skin*, the story of John Kepe, 'the Samson of the Boschberg'. This 'poetic chronicling' of the escapades, arrest and trial of a Robin Hood of the mountains pieced a legend together from multiple perspectives, including that of white farmers, a town militia, a torn journalist covering Kepe's trial, farm labourers and a local community.

'[It] explores the futility of the white settlers' preoccupation with the preservation and protection of their ideals and physical possessions [in its] search for a hero amongst victimised Black people.' Interviewed on shadowandact.com at Cannes, Qubeka called the film 'a passion project'.

His Xhosa-language film, *Stillborn*, was screened at the international BRICS[104] Film Festival in China also in 2017, telling of a robot which obsesses itself with human ancestry. Qubeka told *MTV News* that his inspiration for *Stillborn* came out of a childhood of watching sci-fi.

The movie was shot on location in Johannesburg inside and outside refineries and mine shafts and features dazzling footage of the quintessential Soweto attraction, the Orlando Towers.

Vundla's work, *The Tribe*, an explicitly sexual film about a troubled university professor, also drew attention that year. Screened at the Toronto International Film Festival, the Pan African Film Festival in Los Angeles, the Atlanta Film Festival, the New York African Film Festival and the Sydney Film Festival, it showcased Vundla as writer, director and producer.

Other inspiring works are now being made under less onerous conditions, by South Africans in South Africa from a BC perspective.

The predominantly Sesotho Western, *Five Fingers for Marseilles*, directed by Michael Matthews, competed at the Toronto Film Festival in late 2017. Telling the story of 'Five Fingers', a legendary individual who fought against police oppression before fleeing the rural Eastern Cape town of Marseilles, it was bought by streaming networks to air across Africa.

The Xhosa drama, *Inxeba (The Wound)*, a queer love story drawn around initiation rituals from director John Trengove, starred top South African musician Nakhane (Touré) and was chosen as South Africa's entry for the 2018 Academy Awards. But *Inxeba* faced a fast attack from some within the houses of traditional Xhosa leadership for what they perceived as an assault on their way of living. This, however, only added to its allure within critical, writerly, art, youth and global LGBTQI networks.

African mentors of cinematic greatness include Mali's Cheick Oumar Sissoko (1945–), who later turned to politics but whose film, *The Garbage Boys*, is a profound examination of Black children's lives; Ousmane Sembène (1923–2007), who pioneers independent post-colonial African cinema with his work out of Senegal; the experimental

---

104   BRICS is the acronym for an association of five major emerging national economies: Brazil, Russia, India, China and South Africa.

Senegalese filmmaker Djibril Diop Mambéty (1945–1998) whose 1973 film *Touki Bouki* won prizes at Cannes and at the Moscow Film Festival and tells the story in English and Wolof of a charismatic cow-herd; esteemed photographer and filmmaker Gordon Parks (1912–2006), who reworked an entire Black generation's view of itself with *Shaft*, and the award-winning film and TV director, writer and documentarian, Ava DuVernay.

[Rorich, 2015; Obenson, 2017]

Six

The Conscious Women

Compiled and written by Masego Panyane and Janet Smith

B lack Consciousness has largely been drawn through the eyes of men. Many have been strong, influential and unforgettable; others of dubious personal character and suspected of misogyny or the deliberate undermining of the role women played in their movement. Yet women were also protagonists and heroes of BC, and refuse to be written out of history. Nomzamo Winnie Mandela remains an icon within the Black Power movements for her revolutionary strength. Young activist Zuleikha Patel is only at the beginning of raising her flag. Nina Simone and Thandiswa Mazwai have ideologies and gifts in common. A dedication to history and the promotion of a positive Black life billow the sails of their movement, even as they face some of the most violent, gendered challenges the world has seen.

'I was part of something that was so massive': The story of Zuleikha Patel

Masego Panyane conducted two interviews with the South African teenage activist whose young Black Feminism first brought a nation to a new consciousness in 2016. In 2020, Patel is one of the most important figures in BC and the shifting world culture towards Black girl- and women-centred sustainable life

---

'My hair matters'
2016

The opening refrain of American musician Solange Knowles's song 'Don't touch my hair' (*A Seat at the Table*, 2016) is the anthem for all women who have had to withstand unwanted attention on their coiled crowns.

Hair is an integral part of identity. As Ramphele notes in her autobiography, *A Life*, when she became initiated into the BCM, she began keeping herself as 'natural' as she could be. This included taking off her wig, which had been a companion for years. She instead began rocking her short, 'boyish' hair and her Black femininity, accepting that she had simply been 'captured' before being conscientised.

'I shed the wig I used to wear whenever I felt I needed to look more respectable than my [real] hair suggested. The "Black is Beautiful" slogan of the time had its desired impact on all of us.'

The BCM inculcated into Black people that their looks and, importantly, their natural hair, were beautiful and perfect. But this is a continuing revolution, as was recognised when pupils at Pretoria High School for Girls (Pretoria Girls, PHSG), a 'reputable' former Model C school,[105] came out guns blazing in a protest against a discriminatory school code that policed Black students' hair.

The girl at the centre of that protest was 15-year-old Zulaikha Patel. She stunned the country with her bravery in standing up against the institutionalised racism at her school. But for Patel, the decision

---

[105] Model C schools refers to the defunct structure of formerly whites-only schools. Segregated education officially ended in 1996, but a 'whiteness ethos' prevailed. The 2016 protests were a peak point in struggles against discrimination around dress, hair, headscarves and religious practices. Model C schools exemplify 'the entangled power matrix that characterises coloniality' in post-apartheid South Africa (Christie & McKinney 2017: University of Cape Town, South Africa and University of Queensland, Australia).

to protest was not one that she took lightly. It was the culmination of years of having to explain her identity, which is closely linked to her Indian-Ndebele and Muslim heritage.

'For most of my life, I have been treated as an experiment of a child. I'm mixed race. My parents are both people of colour, but of different ethnic backgrounds, and people have always asked me what I am. They'd touch my hair because it's always been this curly texture, and people would ask me if I'm sure I'm Black.'

It's this repeated experience that led to Patel's powerful defence.

As Professor Hlonipha Mokoena points out in her essay, 'From slavery to colonialism and school rules: A history of myths about Black hair', Patel's school is an index of this form of anti-Black repression.

'Pretoria Girls is not the first institution to try and police Black people's hair. In an article titled "When Black hair is against the rules", *The New York Times* responded to hair regulations that had been published by the US Army in 2014. These prohibited twists, "matted" hair and multiple braids – all of which were read as references to natural African hair and hairstyles.'

This was the experience of Patel and others at PHSG. The styles they believed would enhance the beauty of their hair, while keeping it neat, were seen to be 'too much', and not in keeping with the school uniform. Yet ironically, Patel's hair had privately led to her being called 'exotic', and beautiful – for a Black girl.

'I have been required to consistently explain what and who I am. If I tell people I'm Indian, they go: "Hmm, you're Indian?" Then I tell them I'm Black and then they ask to touch my hair again. I have always wondered why my hair has to always be something to use to prove my identity.'

An explanation for some people's fascination with her hair is that, in apartheid South Africa, one of the ways to determine the race of a person with 'ambiguous' features was to perform the so-called 'pencil test' on them.

The 'test' would determine, by if and how the pencil remained in the hair as the person shook their head, their race, but a general rule of thumb was that if hair showed even a slight kink, the person would be unable to 'pass for white'.

The simple action of deciding how to wear your hair each morning is a luxury that Patel does not have. Her hair – in the Afro state – is in a form of protest against being told that her fluffy, loosely curled, brown cloud of gorgeousness is inadequate, 'inappropriate'.

'I went to schools where I have been racially discriminated against. I am exposed to hair rules that work against African [Black] hair, like "hair must be tied at the nape of your neck". If you have an Afro, you can't really do that.

'I got to Girls High and I was told I needed to cut my hair – that it didn't fit well with the school uniform. When I asked what kind of hair "fits", I didn't get an answer.'

It is this that led to Patel developing a strong sense of self that allowed her to stand up even when many advised against it. For her, the embrace of BC gives her hope because it cements the belief that she, too, in her 'racial ambiguity', belongs in South Africa.

'I am Black and I am proud of it.'

Her favourite phrase is, 'White feminism was built on the backs of women of colour', which is her WhatsApp status. As for the 'Rainbow Nation' project, Patel – born in 2002 – is a 'Born Free'[106] expected to move through a hyper-racialised South Africa.

The protest by the students at Girls High, says Patel, 'had been coming'. She traces back the history of oppression at the school to 'the day that Black students were "allowed" to enter it'. In her view, the department of education has, in part, failed the Black girls because its investigation into the events at the school yielded 'no results'.

Investigators indicated they weren't provided with enough 'evidence' of oppressive action by educators, even though Black girls said they had experienced open racism. Efforts at repairing the broken trust seemingly failed.

'All of us at school who were on the front of the protest are still victimised. I am referred to as a terrorist. Once, a teacher ran out of a classroom crying because she did not want to be seated in front of "a terrorist" anymore.'

What the 2016 protest at Girls High by 50-odd Black girls aimed

---

106 South African youth born after the fall of apartheid, who make up almost 40% of the population.

to do was claim their sense of self and dignity from an institutional culture that is present not only at their school, but at other Model C schools – one which denies them comfort in their Blackness through accepting what comes with it: the darker skin tone; the broader nose; the languages, and the nappy, *kroes*[107] hair.

When asked to complete the sentence 'My hair is', Patel said: 'My hair is my identity/ my hair is not a weapon/ my hair is a trigger for white supremacy/ my hair matters/ my hair is beautiful.'

[Ramphele, 1996; Mokoena, 2016; Byrd & Tharps, 2014]

'We cannot have our futures dictated by those who won't be part of them'

2020

The 2016 protests snowballed, and Patel and other Black South African children and teenagers, especially girls, were recognised around the world for fighting discriminatory policies that still haunt many democratic, 'free', institutions. Masego Panyane found a now 18-year-old Patel more committed to BC than ever, calling it 'an ideology that was her guiding light through difficult times'. She believes it can be used to tackle some of the major challenges facing young Black people in South Africa today.

MP: Almost three years after that protest, where are you now in your head?

ZP: Where I am currently in terms of issues of identity and decolonisation, I feel like the fire is burning even more, given the issues that we are facing currently as Black people in South Africa. Also given what I have been through over the last few years, I have seen these issues intensify, but I have also seen the response I get for my resistance, which has been vicious victimisation and targeting. It has made the fire in me burn even more.

---

107   From the Dutch word, 'kroes', meaning 'kinky hair; with lots of small curls'. Used as an insult by whites during colonial times and apartheid to refer to the 'tightly-curled' hair of Black and Coloured people [Pettman, 1913: Via https://dsae.co.za/entry/kroes/e04120].

MP: Was the protest that happened in 2016 resolved?

ZP: It wasn't. The first problem is that we seem to have a problem holding a white minority to account for their actions towards Black people, and for the actions of their forefathers that they continue to benefit from. There was no accountability.

As my academic career at the school draws to an end, as my matric year comes to an end, I am the only remaining member of that original protesting group. Every other member of the movement has graduated high school because I was the youngest one at the time. And four years down the line, I have not received a single apology from the school authorities.

They were not held accountable for their actions, and what it became defined as, was that Karen (a popular nickname for a racist white woman) did not know what she did wrong, and I'm the one that must be in the position to educate Karen in what she's doing; that it is wrong.

The second problem was that white-owned media houses hijacked the narrative from those that started the movement. When we came out guns blazing, we said this is an issue of addressing identity in this country, and, more than anything, the race politics within the space of education. This isn't merely a hair issue.

We did not want this issue to be watered down because we were addressing the fact that the most fundamental part of society, being basic education, remains heavily colonised and heavily attached to the legacy of apartheid.

No one heard us.

As we know and understand, the government of South Africa continues to fail Black people – in particular, young Black people. They don't hear us out. Young Black people have never been given a chance to speak for themselves.

As I look back, I think I now understand why it is that the government is so hands-on with its agenda of excluding young Black people and not listening to them. We as young people were never part of the negotiations.[108]

---

108   Talks between the National Party government and the ANC (with some representation from other parties) between 1992 and 1993. More than a

We don't know what they negotiated with De Klerk, and therefore all of their actions go with what they signed with De Klerk. They cannot go against what they bargained for with the oppressors at the time.

Power is not something that can be bargained for. Power is supposed to be taken. It cannot be that in a majority Black country, we still don't set the policy, law and how our country will operate. And so what we saw was that the government took this issue, which snowballed globally into a massive movement, shoved it under the rug and moved on as if nothing happened. What then followed is that they became the accomplices of the institution (PGHS) when it came to targeting us.

The targeting really intensified towards the end of 2016. It became so bad that we began to question things as 'Born Frees'. Are we really free? Is freedom really our reality if we are experiencing the same targeting which our forefathers experienced during apartheid?

MP: Why was this intimidation necessary from the school authorities, when you were raising something that needed to be addressed?

ZP: I was part of something that was so massive. We resisted a system that has been around for centuries; that has been thriving for centuries. The system isn't broken. It is operating for those that built it, and it is operating for those it serves.

What we essentially did was target that system and we pushed for its dismantling. When I, as the oppressed, say I want justice and equity (not equality) directly to someone who is privileged and has been privileged their whole lives, they hear that and it sounds like a threat.

You threaten their entire livelihood and existence because that is based on *my* disadvantage. Every single day, white people continue to get rich and thrive off the disadvantage of Black people. They are not prepared to let go.

MP: How has BC served as a guide as you navigated these four years of high school?

ZP: You know, there were times when I really did crumble, and I

---

quarter of a century after the first democratic elections in 1994, it is accepted that white minority rights were prioritised at the expense of the Black majority to safeguard capital. The economy is dominated by white Afrikaner men, racism prevails and there has been little integration at basic education levels.

just felt like the walls were caving in on me. To a certain extent, this then also becomes public humiliation because it raises the question to the people around you: 'Why are you always the one that security is called for, that is escorted by armed security? What have you done?'

When you are a young, Black, outspoken woman who rejects the status quo and conformity, you become an outcast and people refuse to associate with you. So, you take on a lonely path. It became quite an extremely lonely path for me. But one thing that kept me going was BC, and in particular the stories of women who built the BC movement.

During my grade 10 year in 2018 – which, I believe, was one of the hardest years for me, seeing as I faced so many issues at the time – I remember being told that 'my presence incites violence', that I am 'conspiring', and I was then removed off (school) property by security and a white man who's in authority at the school. That was humiliating.

If you are around people and they see you being escorted off by so many men who they see in authoritative positions, they start asking themselves, 'Are you actually a danger to society?'

I held very close to me the story of mam' Ntsiki (Biko), and over the years I grew very fond of her and I began to read about her more. Her story kept me going and it kept the fire burning in me; burning brighter than the fire that was burning around me. It navigated me through.

Also the story of mam' Winnie.

Through the stories of these women, I was able to find parts of myself. They resonated so deeply with me. I idolised these women. I started understanding that my resistance will never be in vain. What we are doing now is we are slowly but surely breaking down this machine of oppression.

This work isn't for myself, but it's for the Black girls who are going to walk these (school) corridors, rightfully, as they should. Far too many times we are told we don't belong in those corridors. But our forefathers built these institutions for free.

MP: There's still a major challenge to access education for Black children in South Africa. This is compounded by issues of youth drug abuse, youth unemployment. How do we use the ideology of BC to confront these? Can this be done?

ZP: Definitely. Black Consciousness is the only solution for us Black people. BC allows us the opportunity to understand that as long as we're not mentally emancipated, there can never be true emancipation. That's what we're currently facing.

A lot of these issues stem from the psychological enslavement of Black people, and BC addressed how (that mental slavery) results in these issues (being compounded). If you address issues of race, you have to also address issues of class, and you can't leave out issues of gender. Oppression is multi-layered. That's why as a young Black woman I find a home in the ideology of BC. It is something I embody as an everyday way of life and as an identity. I don't see myself identifying with anything outside of BC.

MP: What is your message to other young Black women?

ZP: No one will hand power to us. So it's up to us to take that power and use every day of our lives to demand that power. We need to continue the struggle. We have to. We need to stand together because we are the majority and there is power in numbers. If we can stand together, we can overthrow this system of oppression.

As the majority, particularly being young, Black and female, we cannot have our futures dictated to us by a male minority that every day perpetuates sexism and toxic masculinity, and does not stand against GBV in this country. We cannot have our futures dictated by them, and as young people, we cannot have our futures dictated by those who won't be part of them.

'I am not my circumstances': The story of Sibongile Mkhabela

Janet Smith speaks to the former BC activist, who is CEO of the Nelson Mandela Children's Fund and the Nelson Mandela Children's Hospital Trust, an initiative of the Children's Fund. A social worker by profession, Sibongile Mkhabela is a distinguished example of what community leaders achieved with a generation of South African children. She was among the scholars arrested in connection with the 1976 Soweto student uprisings and was detained in 1976 and again in 1977, when she was the only young woman student leader to go on trial with 10 young men. Mkhabela was held at the Old Fort Prison in

Johannesburg, Kroonstad Prison in Free State, Klerksdorp in North West province and at Pretoria's maximum security prison before being banned.

JS: What was the meaning of BC for you when you were growing up? What was 'consciousness' for you at that stage, living as you were in an urban area in a place (Soweto) that reflected a lot of the push and pull of South African politics?

SM: You know, if I say I was 'consciously' political, I probably would not be telling the truth, because you know, you are young. What I got to understand very well is that there were several influences that got me probably to adopt a more BC approach, or what I got to understand to be a more BC approach, and that was the church [in which] I grew up.

It is primarily a protest church that broke away from the Methodists, which is seen as a 'white' church that had no understanding of the rights of the African Black majority, so I grew up in the midst of these conversations being held [about that breakaway] by the elders around me.

And then I got exposed to the Young Women's Christian Association [YWCA] – not so much in terms of BC, but in terms of self-esteem, in terms of dignity, in terms of standing tall even in the midst of very difficult situations. So I learned to appreciate [the message I got]: I am not my circumstances. And, within that, one then gets exposed to books and reading.

The YWCA exposed us to libraries; Saturday mornings, we would have lectures by the likes of Tom Manthata.[109] I also get interested in conversations and reading by following my brother around. I get to love books.

---

109   Thomas Madikwe Manthata (1939–2020) – a former Robben Islander tried for treason in 1984 along with fellow UDF leaders Popo Molefe, Moss Chikane and Mosiuoa Patrick 'Terror' Lekota; he became a commissioner at the South African Human Rights Commission – succumbed to COVID-19 complications at the age of 81 at One Military Hospital outside Pretoria, having left an indelible mark on the search for justice and human rights in South Africa. Manthata, who was part of the TRC, served as a student leader before he became a rigorous, critical educator who encouraged political debates among his pupils, who included the President of South Africa, Cyril Ramaphosa [https://www.sahrc.org.za/].

When I get to high school [Dr BW Vilakazi] , the issue of Afrikaans started there. I [found myself] in a class that was a guinea pig for testing Afrikaans as a medium of instruction. It affected me personally.

I failed a year, which I could not tolerate – nor could my father, because my mother had died that same year – the first year that I was in high school. It was a very traumatic time. But growing up within and amongst people who said, you matter, and you are not your circumstances, you find strength within yourself.

Then, as I went to Naledi High School – having moved away from Dr BW Vilakazi, the laboratory for Afrikaans – I get to a school that appreciates the mind and challenges us. I find I am drawn to public-speaking and debating. I find myself comfortable in the world of words and playing with words, and I love my English master who is very determined to get us to speak English. He keeps saying the best English is simple English – drop the big words.

In debating, you try to show off; you try to read as much as you can and memorise as many big words as you can and our English master is like, 'No, no, no, no, no. There is a simpler way of saying something and I want you to learn to speak simply but speak properly.'

One reason I wanted to go to Naledi High School is that from primary, we were looking at the young people in Naledi High and you admired them – you admired how they speak, how they can engage in conversations. So Naledi, I think, pulls together or concretises all my consciousness about myself and gives me a sense or an ability to analyse the world from a particular perspective.

[In debating] we were looking at the OAU at that time, and whether it was necessary and of course most of it was imagined. We hadn't had the experience of being outside of South Africa, so we had to imagine what it meant to be African.

But it also meant, at a very young age, 15, 16, you are beginning to understand, okay, so this is where Africa started. This was the intention of the colonisers, and I don't want to see myself through the eyes of the colonisers and all that is happening within our history lessons. Our history teachers were the most important to us. We thought they were giving us too much work, but we loved it. We loved the fact that we had two history books: the history book that we must remember for life, which formed my consciousness, and the history book that I had to know for exams what to write in order to tell the white man.

Naledi High was called 'the Wild West', but Mr Mtimkulu, my principal, would talk about 'the jewel in the west', and all of that built our self esteem and made us feel a sense of pride and dignity in who we were. It's only on reflection – probably when I got to university many, many years later – that I realised that, in fact, we were very poor.

I am surprised that a nine-year-old can say, 'I come from a poor community'; and it's not because poverty was disguised [when we were growing up], but poverty was not something that defined us.

It probably helped that we were not in today's world where there is so much exposure to how other people live. Now [children look at themselves] in relation to others.

When Mtimkulu [called us] 'the jewel in the west', he was reflecting the hierarchy because if you were in Dube, you were better off. If you are in Orlando, you know you are one of those who were probably exempted from being Black and African and you can go to more places than other people. You know there were exemptions, but if you are coming from Zola, clearly you are coming from the grassroots of the grassroots.

But he made us to be proud.

I think the consciously political ideology that we were adopting came in later. Probably in the middle of the second year of high school when SASM is introduced, really by SASO. These things are historic. Look at the Frelimo rallies and how high school and university students responded to that, through SASO in particular. Look at the expulsions [from universities] of some SASO activists and how our schools took on some of those activists as 'help' teachers. They were not trained as teachers, but they did a good job as teachers.

Now that, coming into schools ... that kind of SASO influence being presented now as a framework for what it actually means to be Black, what it means to take pride in the person you are and taking responsibility for your own situation, [coupled with] Black Theology, and many of us being organised around debates [that was an influential moment].

The disadvantage young people have today is the absence of

structures, because from an early age, I would be able to say: I am a member of this, I am a member of that, I am part of this, I am part of that.

All these things formed who you were. In particular, there were programmes organising young people around faith: faith as an African child, as a Black child. What does Christianity mean to me? And most afternoons were really spent discussing what it means to be an African and a Black Christian.

We would discuss the scriptures, like, 'I am the God of the oppressed', and then [try and reinterpret it].

I think what influenced me the most was when I began to understand what it meant to be created in God's image and [to see] the God in me. Once I saw the God in me and the God who created me, I understood that if I allowed anybody to have control over me, I was giving up on the God in me. Every time we were in prisons going through torture, I used to remember: you are made in God's image, the centre and the core of your being is godly and it will therefore not subjugate itself.

JS: When did you step up and say, I am now in the BC movement. I am going to be facing the might and the wrath of the state.

SM: Even to this day, the separation of 'political' BC and self-awareness is very difficult. I will tell you why. I think for me what's very important is an approach that talks about a membership of an organisation or faith. I think all of that in my experience starts with an individual. So, no matter what BC leaders did [as such], my resoluteness and understanding and perceptions didn't have to do with what they did or didn't do. It had to be owned by me totally and absolutely, and that ownership is a process.

You can decide, today I am going to be a member of this party or that party or the other party, but the process of consciousness and the development of a consciousness that would stand against anything is totally individual.

Part of politicians' power is to take control of what you call 'the masses', but once you learn through God that the so-called 'masses' are made up of individuals, and that if each individual believes absolutely in something they own, that's more difficult to control.

I knew I had adopted a particular way of looking at the world when, around '74, '75, I was able to say to another person: yes, we can have nice conversations, but don't try to convince me about the rightness of your non-racial approach, because my Blackness has got nothing to do with the whiteness of the other.

I thought BC was the greatest weapon to fight apartheid – that you didn't fight apartheid on tactics, you fought apartheid on belief and values, so long as you believed in and you knew that your argument was correct.

I felt the fight did not start around concrete things such as, what are we are going to do with Bantu Education? That's not what tipped the scales for me. What tipped the scales was what fundamentally took away our ability to continue being ourselves; what took away the dignity of our faith, the freedom that we had, even within the apartheid system, to associate with others, to live wherever we wanted to live, to force us to be a part of something we didn't want to be a part of.

We did not want to be part of the Afrikaans-speaking community. That was not who I was. I didn't want to be that, so making us [effectively do that] was taking me, the person, away from who I was. But it was also taking away our potential as a people – our sense of self and the appreciation of who we are.

You know politicians love to control and to own. The problem with BC [for them] is that it is very difficult for any politician to 'own', [because that would mean] to control human beings.

No leader of BC would make me do something that I felt, from a 'values' point of view, contradicted what I thought was right. [But] if you have a group of people who really just believe in a particular leadership or organisation and all of that, it is easy to sway them and put them into any boxes you want to put them in.

I think the biggest battle I would imagine in South Africa with the ANC as a movement is precisely that: the understanding that BC builds from the individual into the masses. And at its core is time. I reflect back to the people who spent time with me when I was 10 years old – the people who taught me and made me argue, and told me to go and read *It Is Not Yet Uhuru*, who made me read all those books when

I was so young. Who made me ask: Who is Kaunda? Who is Nyerere? What do they stand for?

Those people spent that time to build the individual in us, and when you put all those things together, they created the kind of individual who can stand, even if they have to stand alone and defend a particular perspective or vision of society. [That is] the kind of society we envisioned when we were free when our land would be restored, our dignity, more importantly, would be restored.

If you look at what Biko and the Pityanas and that group did at that time … One, they had the ideology of BC. Then there was the BCP and the BPC and so, via SASM, what were we encouraged to do?

Now we have learnt who we are and that who we are is also related to who our people are, so what do you do? Simple stuff that would be put down to social work and welfare. Guys, but the fence in the school is broken down. Build it up. There was a Zanempilo clinic, which was established by Stephen Biko. Now, there are old ladies who sometimes can't go and get their own medicines. Go and get their medicines for them. Restore their dignity. Look into their eyes.

So, it connected us with people and it made the ideology feel 'lived'. As a SASM kid, you would know that okay, today, guys, we are organising ourselves after school. We are just going to knock on doors and check all the old people who are on their own in their homes, to see if they need anything done. And we would get it done.

You know now, on reflection, I am asking: Why did these guys send us to do all these weird things? But I can see they wanted us to appreciate the dignity of our people, whatever work they did. I so wish we had spent as much time with our young people as time was spent with us.

When you see the school system today, it's difficult to understand it within that with which we grew up, because the school system then allowed the teacher – in fact, forced the teacher – [to endorse the fact] that every kid, from the time they were at primary school, had to read independently and summarise at least six books, independently. That's besides your setwork. Six books so you gain the culture of reading. And I think that had to do with the kind of leaders who were in our communities, and what they wanted to achieve.

Many people are surprised that Bantu Education produced what it produced, but it was [really] communities which produced a lot of the leaders, and part of that was just getting us to read.

As you moved into high school, you moved with that culture of reading, but then we also had people coming from SASO producing and giving us books, and through all of these you begin to see this huge community that believes the same way you believe and that strengthens your own beliefs and the ideologies and approaches you have learnt.

JS: The threat that some people see in BC means that some choose to reduce it to a white versus Black issue.

SM: It is also about a struggle. It is also about a history. But BC is more about your history, your circumstances and making sense out of all that. [That's why] Biko and others said it was 'not skin deep'.

We are not talking about the differences in pigmentation. We're talking about a particular history and circumstance that could be ascribed to African Black people. In fact, not even just African: people who have a particular history. [This] is why, within BC, you did not have Coloured people because Coloured people and Indian people were defined as Black.

Biko, I think, struggles with this question. Is it a pigmentation issue we are talking about? And he struggles to define BC as being an 'awareness' and an intention to change society, such that each one of us feels free in who they are.

I think people remember when they were exposed to BC, and [for many, it was around being called 'non-white', because then] you are defining me in relation to a white person. I am Black and somebody else might be white, but we might share the same understanding of our political, economic and social justice; we might have the same agenda of social justice and the issues of social justice then come into that conversation about awareness, about consciousness as a people, starting with an individual.

JS: Your understanding of Africanism ... was this brought about also by your parents? You've said they provided you with something which was perhaps outside the experience of other children. Who were they to you? Their histories were quite distinct.

SM: Both my father and my mother came out of Mozambique. My mother comes out of the rural [areas], so we are really first-generation South Africans which, whenever there is xenophobic violence, I am, like, uh … Just hold on a bit. We are sounding like Donald Trump. None of us can really say we are 'South African'. In any case, these boundaries are not quite what they need to be.

I told you about my church. We are part of the African Methodist Church and its history of having broken out from the Methodist Church is very important. My father – having left Mozambique at the time of Portuguese [colonialism] and [taking into account] the treatment that he suffered under Portuguese rule – was not a talkative person. But whenever we had an opportunity to hear him, he would talk about what he suffered.

Sometimes he went to prison in Mozambique, but [he and others] never really understood what was going on. So they made a choice to come to South Africa and he brought us up as South Africans, but with a clear link to Mozambique.

I was six years old when he took me to see his home. I remember sitting under a cashew nut tree, but I also remember that I was very difficult. I just wanted to go back home. I didn't understand the place. It was too hot.

But in our home on a day-to-day basis, my mother – being a very open person – ran an open house to the point of ridiculousness (and we met a lot of people that way). I think we grew up in that kind of atmosphere.

Some of my uncles didn't speak the local languages. They spoke Portuguese, they spoke Xitsonga which is really the Maputo dialect. The Mozambique dialect is Xironga. Some of my aunts who helped my father to bring us up when my mother died had married in Zimbabwe and my mother had a strong link to Zimbabwe. Her in-laws were in Zimbabwe, so there was also that traffic that would come through.

I guess in a way one grew up in a home that was full of other influences.

I recognise my mother's cooking today as I travel. I recognise the chilli. I could see the Spanish/Portuguese influence in her cooking, which I have learned to like mixing up nuts in food, cream in food, white rice and all of those things that, as you grow up, you realise, okay, so this is where this came from. These were the kinds of influences that were in my food, in our music in the house, in just the culture of the home.

To an extent, we were brought up in Zulu schools so we spoke in Zulu, but there was another culture when we closed our doors.

We had our relatives in the home, and we would not just be in South Africa.

JS: Your daughter, Ntsako Mkhabela, is a playwright whose acclaimed play *By the Apricot Trees* is really about you. Does it give you a sense of joy that the BC you've practised all your life is – whether by osmosis, talking, books – now part of your children? Does that take intellectual effort and a love of it in what you say and do when you are raising children?

SM: I think when you are raising children, it just takes a lot of work. But if you want them to have enough tools to analyse the world they experience, I think for Ish [her husband, Ishmael Mkhabela] and I, part of it was just the experience.

Our daughter was born in 1983. She was very young, but she experienced the hostel violence because she was living with her grandmother at the time in Meadowlands [Soweto] and she remembers hiding under the bed [while this was going on in the streets around them]. She remembers the experiences of the townships at that time better than the younger one, because the younger one was born in 1986, which was still tense, but by the time she was aware, things were beginning to change.

She's the eldest, and her biggest fear was exposed when my brother-in-law bought a site to build a house in Spruitview [Soweto], so we went to see the site and she was terrified. She was terrified of the open space and she couldn't get out of the car, and I was, like, why? And she said, 'I don't want to go to the open space.' And we remembered she had seen [those kinds of] open spaces as the battlegrounds in the townships. I lived in Moletsane and worked in Zola and most of the time I walked from home to the office. But there were times during those tense 1980s when I had to pick her up, strap her on my back and run.

So she had experienced some of the struggles at a very, very young age.

We also [took] a decision that, on important days, we would talk to them about those days. So we lit a candle at home from the time they were young, from the time they could understand what happened at Sharpeville [for Human Rights Day on 21 March]. We tell them the story of Sharpeville and that candle would be lit the whole day. The same would happen on June 16 and still happens today. I think it's important for children to know their history. It was just a way of trying to create a symbol that the children, young as they were, would remember as a sign of mourning.

My younger daughter [Hlawulani] is a political science student trying to get a doctorate, and she is very interested in the continent. So the work that she does is on the battles of sub-Saharan Africa, and sometimes she scares me. My friend and I were saying to her, 'Remember when you were small and sitting in the back of a car in the 1980s and already then it was the matter of women, Black women and pap smears and so on', and she [would be] saying, 'Mum every time we get into the car, it's women, women, women, women. Can't we talk about anything else?' Now she is the one who is going on about women, women.

I think bringing up children is a conscious effort. It is a conscious job and it is a present job. You are on all the time; you are on mentally, spiritually, physically.

We are not consciously making them believe in BC. We are just telling them our story and the stories of their people and how we see the world. In Ntsako's piece, I see the struggles and sometimes I see some of the overload that I probably put on her, like taking her to see *Sarafina*[110] when she was three.

---

110   *Sarafina!* is a South African musical set at the time of the Soweto uprisings in 1976, adapted into a 1992 film starring Whoopi Goldberg and Leleti Khumalo. The original show enjoyed major success on Broadway in 1988 and 1989, running for nearly 600 performances. The main character, Sarafina, inspires her peers to join the BC movement behind the marches of 16 June.

If you had to listen to our conversation as a family now, we are talking about socialism, social analysis, anarchy and all of those things. They are just regular conversations at the dinner table; I just think it's being present.

[In my past, I remember] members of the community who spent weekends with children they didn't even know, they didn't even recognise ... [to have] an influence for life.

Another issue is language. Go to Germany, live there for five years, you will come back speaking the language. [That's not the case in South Africa.]

White people [should] understand how much it helps them to cross bridges; it creates a different environment, [it gives them] access to things that would not be accessible in the medium of English.

When I am speaking English like I am doing now, you are probably getting 70% of me. If I speak in my language and I can express myself in other ways, you get more of me, both emotionally, mentally, intellectually.

Sibongile Mkhabela is a fellow of both the Rockerfeller Foundation and Duke University, and is on the board of the Global Philanthropy Alliance. Mkhabela is trustee and former chairperson of Black Sash. She is a recipient of the National Order of Luthuli (Silver), awarded by the President of South Africa in recognition of her fight against apartheid, including the role she played in the 1976 student uprising.

'We are igniting each other': The feminism out of South African student protests

#FeesMustFall elicited an unexpectedly Black feminist dissent. Even if students knew that among them were young women whose strength would be magnified over time, they had previously not had the public platform that #FeesMustFall offered. They would step up to a national political spotlight in addition to navigating existing cultural ideas that could have confounded their ability to lead in the moment.

The first openly intersectional struggle in the country's history, #FeesMustFall brought to the fore a ferocious phalanx who were initially physically pushed aside by their male comrades, but showed they were having none of that – not from the generation who ran their institutions; not from the liberal white students who might not have been aware of how NUSAS was repelled by SASO in the late 1960s; and not from the equally young, mostly Black men who sought to dominate the floor.

The young Black feminists of #FeesMustFall were, however, to quickly discover what their elders in the BCM knew:

They are on their own in a country where women are under mortal threat.

Social worker in training Keitumetse Fatimata Moutloatse is a former #FeesMustFall activist and the founder and chairperson of Black Womxn Caucus (BWC), a non-partisan movement established in 2017. A response to the destruction and havoc caused by Gender-Based Violence (GBV) in South Africa, it aims to become the biggest feminist movement on the continent and in the diaspora.

Masego Panyane first interviewed Moutloatse in 2017 when Moutloatse was a prominent Fallist with an overtly BC ideology. Panyane spoke to her again in 2020 about how BC must be utilised in the war against the GBV epidemic where the activist is still fighting in the front ranks for Black liberation.

Moutloatse imagines a movement removed from the public eye: intimate, and built on consolidating and extending specific goals. In her mind, it's 2025 and #FeesMustFall is nearly a decade in the past.

But it's 2017 in a disappointing reality.

A 0% increase has been announced for university fees after negotiations, but for a limited period, and the more prominent, media-savvy student 'faces' have returned to class with the masses. Meanwhile, some at the core of the Fallist leadership are trying to build bonds just as those in the BCM did 40 years before.

Moutloatse captures some of the human history.

'When the "faces" pulled out, all I could think was that we needed to resuscitate #FeesMustFall. We stopped contesting each other and we took more of a nurturing approach. We'd sleep at Solomon Mahlangu House. We knew each other's timetables. While the university operated as normal, we did both: protested and went to class. This was because the struggle had to continue.'

Moutloatse is one of the most radical among the new class of revolutionaries, as she also operates in the international activist arena, for example through participation in the Mumbai Manifesto Against War, Exploitation and Precarious Labour[III] declared on 20 November 2016.

III   Some 350 trade unionists and activists from all 'currents in the workers'

In 2020, we spoke about BCW, and her developing BC as an activist.

MP: What drove the creation of BWC in 2017? It's now three years old and growing.

KFM: BWC came at a time when there was already calamity in the country. For me, I was especially sparked by the brutal murder of Karabo Mokoena – who I knew, by the way. We grew up together but were separated by schooling.

The last thing I anticipated is hearing about her in that context. Her story was literally paraded on social media and mainstream media, as she was, and for me, this really highlighted the plight of women in terms of GBV.

It was a culture shock to the country because it's always been an unspoken secret, a part of how we live. We all know it happens, but we had never seen it in our faces quite like that.

I think that year is when things really took a drastic turn. That year was also the year where it felt like the #FeesMustFall Movement had kind of died off. It felt like it was destabilised; we no longer knew where we were going.

There was fatigue from a lot of activists, people redirecting their energies towards completing their academic years, and some leaving the institutions. So there was a vacuum in terms of activism.

But there had been a spike in gendered movements within the #FMF: the RU Reference list; I Am One in Three; Rhodes War; The Transcollective at UCT … so gender was really becoming a very important part of student movements. Some argued this was why #FMF collapsed, which I don't necessarily agree with. I think it's something that can still be up for debate.

Around the same time there were a lot of kidnappings happening

---

movement' representing 28 countries, including 'South Africa/Azania', gathered in Mumbai at the World Conference Against War, Exploitation and Precarious Labour, after which a manifesto was distributed which directed resistance at 'the imperialist system' [https://buildingtheinternational.wordpress.com/2016/11/24/mumbai-manifesto-against-war-exploitation-and-precarious-labour-20-november-2016/].

in and around Braamfontein [the suburb where Wits is situated]. I remember saying that I cannot understand how we're expected to write through all of this because many of us come to campus to study there, we move around a lot in the late evening for that reason, and sometimes stay in the libraries until the early 'AMs'.

How are we expected to write exams, because there's this huge case of a [Black woman] who was brutally murdered by her partner? What was quite evident around that time, was it felt like the faces of the victims were all Black women. Or, at least, it was their stories which were the ones being paraded. So, BWC came to life.

I think it's important to note that when BWC started, it started as a moment. We were feeling very anxious and unsafe. Our first meeting took place on 18 May 2017, a day before the funeral of Karabo Mokoena. I don't think from that first meeting anyone thought a social movement would be born. But we continued meeting.

For the first year and a half, BWC really grounded itself in the university, and then there was a need for us to move beyond campus. One of the biggest challenges was that feminism was and still is the heart of our ideological and practical work. There was a need for us to universalise feminism.

So the idea that people who are engaging with feminist discourse are only based in the university is problematic. But the shift away from that base was a challenge.

During 2018, BWC started to engage in community-based processes, and that's where the inter-generational organising principle came into effect. The youngest member in our team is 13, the oldest in her seventies. I am absolutely proud of our team and the work we've done thus far.

MP: You mentioned that it seems the faces of GBV in this country are Black womxn. I would like us to zoom into this. Is that why you didn't simply call this movement 'the Womxn Caucus'?

KFM: Because of the past that we come from, I'm just trying to think about apartheid and how narratives around apartheid are framed even today. There has been this removing of the dignity of Black people generally in the face of turmoil and particularly in death. There is a way in which Black pain is paraded and that it's commodifiable.

So the death of Black womxn is at the forefront of social media and television. Not to say womxn of other racial groups are not experiencing the same. They are. But there is so much sensitivity around how their stories are told in comparison to when it happens to us. The crudeness of it. There is no appreciation for the dignity of the grieving family, especially understanding that death is a very important thing within Black culture. How we mourn for our loved ones who have passed is so important.

So at that time, it felt like we have no dignity in life, and we have no dignity in death. I think there was and there still is a need for the provocation of a BWC. By us saying 'BLACK', we are provoking and elevating a conversation.

I do think it's also important that we understand that when we say 'Black' Womxn Caucus, at no point do we seek to erase the experiences of other womxn, other racial groups and other genders. No. We are purely saying that the framework or tool of analysis, if we look at the livelihood of Black womxn in this country currently, is not looking good for us specifically.

Also, the 'Black' in BWC transcends identity in the sense of skin colour. It looks at 'Black' as a political tool. I think when we think about BC, we understand that 'Black' transcends the colour of your skin and it speaks to a socio-economic, political environment that enforces the subjugation of people.

When we think about oppression, when we think about subjugation, about death, about people who are being screwed over by a system, we think of Blackness. And so the 'Black' in BWC also speaks to the socio-political and economic conditions.

Even our definition of GBV is beyond sexual and physical harassment. We are saying that we cannot separate the fact that we are in the most unequal society in the world from high rates of GBV. We cannot separate that we have an increasing unemployment crisis in this country from GBV. We cannot separate that, even in the discourse and conversation on land redistribution without compensation, that womxn are excluded from that conversation. We cannot separate that from GBV.

We can't separate the fact that we have a gendered divide in how much we get paid from GBV. We can't separate that precarious work, work that is unvalued or referred to as unskilled labour, is still dominated by womxn, and they are not receiving full legal and labour rights. We cannot separate that from GBV. So BWC takes a deliberate position that GBV is political, it's social, it's economical, it's environmental and it's spiritual.

So our interventions need to be elevated. Our interventions need to be intergenerational. We are ultimately calling for a reconfiguration of society.

MP: You helped take the GBV fightback to sectors of society that had been rather silent on this with the #SandtonShutdown[112] protest in 2019. What has the wider response from capital been, considering the visceral link between capital and politics in South Africa? Both are dominated by men. President Cyril Ramaphosa signed the Gender-Based Violence Declaration in 2019 when he called GBV 'a national crisis'. But this doesn't appear to have stemmed one of the biggest social ills in South Africa, remembering that the country – like so many others – has agreed to the United Nations Global Goal 5 for gender equality, including ending all GBV?

KFM: When you are building a system or process, the first thing you do is identify what works and what doesn't. I think because for the past 26 years [since the first democratic elections], we have been sold this very 'kumbaya',[113] with emphasis placed on this 'togetherness' in South Africa.

Unfortunately, the socio-economic, material conditions don't match to what we're being. The contradictions are rife. They play

---

112   Hundreds of womxn and allies gathered at the Johannesburg Securities Exchange (JSE) in Sandton, the wealthy business and residential area of Johannesburg, to protest GBV in the ambit of corporations.

113   'Kumbaya' is the African-American or Native American spiritual sung in groups at protests, marches or church events as an anthem of togetherness, which is today a mocking reference to performative togetherness. When it appeared in the 1920s, it was a soulful plea for heavenly help against oppression.

themselves out, and the pushback then becomes: What does the alternative look like?

That's the biggest uncertainty we are facing. When we make radical demands such as shutting down the JSE, demanding that the private sector help fund the fight against GBV, their first response is that 'we are always giving money out through the CSI' [corporate social investment].

We are saying that is not enough. CSI is not the money we are interested in.

We are also making a demand that the gender payment gap, which corporates perpetuate, is problematic.

When we make these demands, it's with the understanding that there will be pushback, because for that [sector of] society it means there are parts of their privilege that they need to let go of.

When we speak about reconfiguration, we are saying we want to assess what power looks like, to see how these privileges – given at birth, apparently – are manifested.

I think the biggest pushback, not only with GBV but the broader liberation project of Black folk in Africa and the world, is that in order for us to achieve what we need, it does require that the oppressor relinquishes those. The issue is not that we don't agree in principle that change needs to happen, but to get to that violence-free society, those with privilege have to do a lot of work.

Part of what BWC aims to do too is assess a false consciousness that exists in South Africa around the normalisation and acceptance of violence. We can no longer separate what are considered 'women's issues' and those of national importance. All of it is 'of national importance'.

We also advocate for the socially castrated and those who exist on the margins of society.

MP: How can we use the BC lens to contribute to ending GBV?

KFM: We must look at some of the biggest critiques of BC, that it felt like it excluded gender; that the 'consciousness' was for men. So men must adjust their thinking in order to find solutions for everyone in the fight against GBV. We say: Open up our understanding of BC to also be inclusive of gender.

By profession, I am a social worker in training. One of my observations and a challenge facing the movement is that until we believe we are worthy of this liberation, we will never be compelled to fight for it. When we look and think in the frame of BC, people must have the tools to empower themselves, to be able to identify the pitfalls of their lives and to believe they are worthy of the lives they speak of (and tweet about).

I see a lot of people say they want a changed society, they see the crisis of youth unemployment, they identify the land issue, but are not believing of it. As a result, we are almost complicit. We even have the language to diagnose the problem, and speak about what the solution could possibly be, but until we believe it is for us, we will never implement.

South Africa has a femicide rate five times the world average. Johannesburg is the most unequal city in the world. South Africa has one of the highest alcohol consumption rates in the world. We have a huge dependency on substances. We are one of the most stressed countries in the world. We have increased suicide rates.

The evidence is there. It suggests that the kind of lives we lead are not working out for us. We need to do the work of inspiring our communities to believe they can change.

One of the principles of the BWC is empowerment, and not in this very superficial way where we do skills trainings for a month and then we leave these communities after a month as if all is well. The empowerment we speak of is about the dignity of our people, who must believe that they are the experts of their realities.

Until our people believe this, that they are the change agents they so desperately need, we cannot effect meaningful change. We remain committed. We must capacitate communities. As bleak as it sounds, we believe the alternative society will come.

Keitumetse Fatimata Moutloatse is a Wits University BA Social Work triple major: Psychology and Sociology. She was in the Fallist and End Outsourcing movements and mobilised from within the Pan Africanist Congress of Azania Student Movement.

'The new wave of BC is only beginning': The story of AZAPO's Manku Noruka

The only woman to hold office in the highest body of BC political formation, AZAPO, 20 years into democracy, Manku Noruka has lived the struggle in various roles within the movement. She talks to Masego Panyane in Johannesburg about the state of the country, the role of women in activism and the shape of BC today.

Formed two years after the Soweto uprising, AZAPO held aloft the banner of BC in the wake of the mass bannings of 1977. Focused on propagating BC in its programmes, AZAPO was considered racist by whites and even some Black 'Charterists', with its detractors fearing it didn't believe white South Africans had a role to play in liberating Black people from oppression.

Its membership was open to Black, Coloured and Indian South Africans.

Yet while there has long been talk of AZAPO descending into political obscurity, the organisation is alive, and members like Noruka believe important work is being done on the ground among the people.

Noruka, who served as AZAPO's general secretary, says her introduction to politics was by way of Molefe Pheto's acclaimed 1983 banned book *And Night Fell – Memoirs of a Political Prisoner in South Africa* (Allison & Busby, now Virgin Publishing), the story of a Black music teacher.

BCM activist Pheto – a musician and music teacher himself, who was imprisoned by the apartheid regime and banned – founded BC theatre, poetry and music company Mhloti with luminaries including Mongane Wally Serote and Thamsanqa 'Thami' Mnyele. Among other bold events, he organised Black arts festivals under the banner of MDALI, of which he was a co-founder.

After Biko was murdered, Pheto left South Africa for 20 years in exile in the UK, returning in the 1990s to settle on a farm outside Johannesburg and later publish his second book, *The Bull from Moruleng: Vistas of Home and Exile*, in 2014.

And Night Fell offered Noruka 'a mixture of fascination and [a sense of] mischief' because of the engaging manner in which it tackled topics of BC, the arts and the struggle for liberation.

'The way [Pheto] was addressing BC and the arts in such a humorous way, and about the time that he spent in jail, it wanted me to inquire more. That's how I got introduced. From there it was never-ending – even at school, things were happening. It's either you belonged to the UDF or the BC bloc. The BC resonated more with me.'

Noruka's primary concern with the UDF was its alignment to ANC politics. On the face of it, the UDF sought a united political movement, one that would go beyond specific political affiliations. At its peak, it certainly had dozens of community movements, student movements, trade unions, women's groups and civic groups within its frame. But the UDF's adoption of the Freedom Charter of 1955 left Noruka uncertain about its project.

'The Freedom Charter was saying that the land belongs to all of us. I asked myself, and believed that cannot be right. The BC bloc said this is actually our [Black people's] land, and yet other people were saying BC was racist. It wasn't. If you come into my space, I have rules. And you must respect those rules. This is the land of Black people. I believe that.'

Noruka says the definition of Azania as 'the promised land for Africans, much like that of biblical Canaan' further deepens her faith in the BC way of life.

Her active involvement with AZAPO began after she attended a couple of meetings and saw women activists like Mam' Joyce Kalaote, one of the organisation's leaders, in action against the apartheid government. Noruka found her inspiring.

'I saw her protecting children against the apartheid government and I knew that this was a woman I aspired to become. I have never looked back. See, BC will teach you to know yourself. You become a self-respecting individual and your respect extends to your fellow Black person.'

After a six-week training spell in Botswana in 1989 with AZAPO's military wing, AZANLA, Noruka returned to South Africa ready to fight for the liberation of the country. Her specific task in this respect was to educate the next generation about BC, and to encourage more women to participate actively in the struggle.

Noruka found 'the acceptance and respect' afforded to women activists in the BC bloc 'increasingly attractive'. She says she felt, and still believes, that 'the very nature of BC' allowed for woman activists to be recognised equally. She says there has been 'a deliberate attempt' to acknowledge space for women in the movement:

'It became clear to us that gender-specifics were not important. Men in the BC culture are taught to respect women as their mothers, their sisters. It stems from their own self-respect as people. We acknowledged that we were brought together because we must liberate the country. But before we could do that, we had to understand that for this country to be truly liberated, people must be liberated in their minds. Nothing will hold you back if you will not be defined by anything but yourself.'

This doesn't mean she hasn't experienced a patriarchy common to liberation movements. 'Every now and again I have to squash it. [Even] with my own colleagues, I have to remind them that I am the secretary-general of the organisation, not anyone's PA. I understand that for most of them, it's been a matter of conditioning behaviour from their homes. So I acknowledge that, but I will always call it out.

'There have been challenges, but the support of my female comrades also makes this journey easier.'

The contemporary political scene in South Africa holds its challenges. It's archly mainstream and Noruka says she doesn't buy into the neo-liberal Black expectations.

'I look at people today who speak of AZAPO not being active in elections. [But] truly speaking, people within the AZAPO bloc don't care that we are not doing well [on that front].

'It's a problem in itself that we end up electing people who will not, at the end of the day, help other people to empower themselves.'

What is, however, always important, Noruka says, is that Black people 'must protect' each other.

'I had a cousin of mine who was more of my sister because we grew up together. She was a UDF supporter and I was BC. Because of this, our arguments wouldn't end. But when she died in 2013, she died in my arms. This reminded me that Blacks must protect each other, because other races do the same.'

Noruka's activism with AZAPO has embraced political education and civic engagement, for example in bus boycotts, rent protests and campaigning in strikes. It also showed allegiance to the large-scale organised activism of the Fallist movement – #FeesMustFall, #OutsourcingMustFall, #RhodesMustFall – as it featured young Black activists in the vanguard.

Although there were gender issues within the Fallist organisations, young Black women, in particular, refused to be side-lined. This, says Noruka, is a reflection of their fresh generation, which sees a future for themselves in the forefront of continuing struggles for liberation. She says the Fallist women remind her of herself some 30 years ago.

'I love them. What I love specifically about them is what they are saying resonates with what I stood for. Their struggle is not only for free education, they are also fighting for free decolonised education, something that the BCM has been saying all along. This education they are campaigning for is one that will not just prepare people to be employed. My mother told me she was taught that English is purely for communicating with the *baas*.

'When we came along, they tried to teach us the same thing. Today, it's not like that.'

Noruka aims to teach Black girls to grapple with the ideas of BC in their own languages through poetry, storytelling and other mediums in her work in her Soweto community. She says BC must again be experienced through people understanding the need to take ownership of land, the rise of civic movements which aim to restore the dignity of the Black poor, students and workers, and the questioning of the contested CODESA agreement of the early 1990s which, to the pain of many Black South Africans, contained the Sunset Clauses. All of these have created fertile ground for a re-emergence and re-imagining of BC.

'In some instances the interpretation is not really BC. For instance, the EFF would like to say they are BC. But they are not really. You cannot have BC and the Freedom Charter in the same room.

'If you say you want to push for the acknowledgement of the

Charter, the first step is to go back and think about who wrote it. Why was it written? Who will stand to benefit from it? Once you answer those three questions, you will then see that is not a paper we look at for our liberation.

'Moving ahead, BC is our only answer. The philosophy does not limit us to strictly politics, but it allows us to find ourselves, how Black people can be self-sufficient and for life to go on.'

Noruka identifies with feminism, but within the space of BC. She insists that Black women 'need not be endorsed by anyone'.

On cultivating white allies, Noruka believes white South Africans, particularly women, can be allies – if they internalise and adopt a BC. For her, the new wave is only the beginning. And the magic of it lies in the awakening of the masses who are at an increasing rate refusing to be dictated to. This, she believes, will only grow the nation.

A tale of two Winnies

Winnie Motlalepula Kgware (1917–1998)

The first president of the BPC, Kgware [born Smith] was an educator by profession and a mentor to young people in the BCM from the time she was at Turfloop where she was initially based. Kgware came up against the university's management there when she protested with BC students against apartheid government restrictions.

The background was that the regime had appointed Professor JL Boshoff, a civil servant, as rector in 1969. Dr WW Eiselen, key to the creation of the Bantu Education system, was made chancellor. These appointments considerably strengthened the hand of SASO on campus, and Kgware was witness to the growth of a vocal militant young Black intelligentsia.

Perhaps it's incidental that she was married to academic William Kgware, who would become the first Black principal at Turfloop, but she did use her unique access to at first help students organise a Methodist prayer group in defiance of an order that banned them from worshipping on campus. Once a SASO branch had been established at the university in 1968, Kgware gave its members the sustenance of an elder, also facilitating secret meetings of the organisation's political partner – the UCM, which was banned at Turfloop.

Her husband, who became a professor, was later appointed as rector after the university adopted a principle of Africanisation in 1977, but it was an unhappy decision as he was regarded as a sell-out. Kgware did, however, regain some of his reputation when he again allowed an SRC on campus, which his predecessor Boshoff had prohibited. This did not satisfy the increasingly conscious student body, though, and their resistance activities drew police onto campus. This created significant stress for him and he suffered ill health, before collapsing and dying in 1980.

It was symbolic perhaps that Winnie Kgware would gain her powerful position in BC out of Turfloop, an institution started by traditional leaders in the 1950s in the hope that young Black people would become more self-reliant through higher education. The apartheid authorities then subverted that with the Extension of University Education Act of 1959. It would take intellectual and political guts to achieve.

And mentoring. An example of this would be from 1977 'when security police stopped a bus, in which mourners including Kgware, from proceeding to Steve Biko's funeral in Ginsberg, Eastern Cape'. Johannesburg's *Sunday World* writes about how 'the then 66-year-old got out of the bus and hitchhiked to the funeral'.

Among those Kgware mentored was Peter Mokaba, who would later become an ANC apparatchik, and who is today credited as an influence by EFF leader Malema. (Although controversial for his contrary stance on HIV and Aids, and rumoured to have been an apartheid-era spy, Mokaba gained influence among young Black South Africans in the 1990s for his use of the slogan 'Kill the farmer, kill the Boer' – a chant ruled as hate speech by the South African Human Rights Commission in 2003. Opponents of the song argue that it incites racial violence against whites, while defenders claim the *boer* aspect refers to white apartheid policemen.)

Kgware identified Mokaba when he was at Hwiti High School in Mankweng in what is now Polokwane, where he became president of an SRC whose establishment Kgware had encouraged. As SASO extended its activities to schools, Hwiti became a centre of activity, and Mokaba was quickly expelled.

He eventually matriculated with Kgware's help, and she also assisted him in gaining finance to enrol for a BSc.

Kgware attended the first national conference of the BPC in Hammanskraal in December 1972 and was elected president at age 62 in front of 1 400 delegates representing 145 Black interest groups. The rest of the executive committee comprised Madibeng Mokoditoa (vice-president), Sipho Buthelezi (secretary-general), Mosibudi Mangena (national organiser) and Saths Cooper (public relations officer).

Not many aspirant young Black revolutionaries may remember Kgware today, as all too many BC leaders were side-lined by the ANC's domination of struggle history. She was, however, honoured by the Motheo FET College in her hometown of Thaba Nchu, Free State, where the Winnie Kgware Branch of SASCO was established.

Kgware was also given the Steve Biko Award for her role in the liberation struggle by the Umtapo Centre in Durban in 1998. In 2003, [the president Thabo] Mbeki conferred the Order of Luthuli in Silver on her 'for outstanding leadership and lifelong commitment to the ideals of democracy, non-racialism, peace and justice'.

[www.sahistory.org; www.azapo.org; www.thepresidency.gov.za]

Nomzamo Winnie Mandela (1936–2018)

Still easily recognisable, Mandela's consistent role over 60 years in South African liberation politics was to mentor political youth across ideological lines. Despite the many dangerous and conflicting issues that she traversed in eight decades, and notwithstanding her loyalty to the ANC, she remained a mother figure among young people who chose BC.

Emboldened with a devotion to struggle, Mandela would, for example, take her empathy direct to source in the weeks ahead of the Soweto massacre in 1976 when, together with Nthato Motlana and others, she helped form the Soweto Parents' Association.

It was inevitable she would play a defiant role for children and their parents in the wake of the state-sanctioned violence before she was banished to the Free State, having endured horrific periods of detention and torture, the most destructive being nearly two years of solitary confinement in 1969 and 1970 at the time of the 'Trial of 22'.

Influenced by apartheid forces, Black South Africans understood that Mandela was a scapegoat for uprisings and 'unrest', yet white people were encouraged to fear her, which they did. They saw her raised fist as a threat and she was widely condemned as 'evil' when she was seen to be advocating 'necklacing'[114] informers in the townships.

Her defiant Black Power was the real threat, though, representing more of an intention even than her then-husband, Nelson, who was imprisoned on Robben Island and banned from sight. When Mandela was ultimately banished to the despairing rural Free State town of Brandfort, she was physically disconnected from a supremacist world, but that too was a form of imprisonment.

Nonetheless, Mandela demonstrated what BC was about. She started a gardening collective, ran a soup kitchen, and managed a mobile health unit, day-care centre and a sewing club.

Although she was the banned ANC's most prominent member, her actions fitted with the BCP of which Motlana – whose activist wife, Sally, was detained – was also a supporter.

It was when Mandela returned to Orlando, Soweto, in the mid-1980s and later formed the shadowy Mandela United Football Club, that a murderous period was introduced into the fraught internal politics of the ANC, and she was made out to be at the centre of it.

This was unfortunate as the Mandela United FC could itself have played the kind of role of which the BCP would have been proud. It could have been used to develop and inspire young Black people. It did not. Instead, its activities left young Stompie Seipei dead after Mandela's 'driver', Jerry Richardson, slit the boy's throat. (Seipei had been an activist since the age of 10 and was South Africa's youngest political detainee when he spent his 12th birthday behind bars.)

Mandela was in the sights of the regime's 'Stratcom' unit which

---

114   Necklacing was a form of extrajudicial summary execution and torture in which a rubber tyre filled with petrol was forced around a victim's chest and arms before being set alight.

sought to destroy her reputation and recreate her as an amoral, violent figure within liberation politics. It almost succeeded, and even when she died in 2018, Mandela was still somewhat shrouded in the pain of that time.

Her entire narrative, and her internal agonies, may never be completely known. Her beloved daughter, Zindzi, was said to have not recovered from her mother's death when she succumbed to illness and the symptoms of COVID-19 in 2020.

Mandela's complicated allure rose strong among young Black revolutionaries at the time of her death. An orator, a militant, a mother, an intellectual, a political prisoner and a torture survivor, she remains the most complex Black figure of the South African struggle.

The mother of BC: Dr Vuyelwa Mashalaba

Biko's biographer Mangcu described Mashalaba – who served as general secretary of SASO from 1970 to 1971 – as 'the mother of BC'. Her friend and fellow BC activist, Ramphele, records in the book *Across Boundaries* that Mashalaba was a most accomplished woman when they met in the late 1960s. An admiring Ramphele said Mashalaba emerged out of a family of four equally high-achieving sisters whose widowed mother set a fine example for them in their home in Maclear, Eastern Cape.

Mashalaba, records Ramphele, spoke with a 'distinctive, polished English accent', could play tennis and was a classical music fundi. She introduced Ramphele to her wide circle of politically conscious friends, including Biko and intellectuals Charles Sibisi, Chapman Palweni and Goolam Abram.

Mashalaba was involved in conceptualising SASO together with Biko, Pityana and others, and was an asset to it from the start, for example being selected to persuade the powerful Interdenominational African Ministers Association in South Africa (IDAMASA) to give its support to the organisation in 1971. Her leadership qualities were assured.

Mashalaba later married BC stalwart Justice Moloto. Their children described them as 'simply parents who toiled like any other, wanting to give their three daughters everything of the best, wanting to teach them respect, self-love, self-confidence and BC'.

[Ramphele, 1996a]

'They do not know how much you have been shattered and broken in the past': Nikiwe Deborah 'Debs' Matshoba

Born in Krugersdorp in 1950, Matshoba became politically active after she joined the YWCA, which had a strong presence in townships around Johannesburg. She started studying radiography at the University of Zululand, and her activism through SASO led to her expulsion and arrests, first under the Suppression of Communism Act, then under the Terrorism Act.

Matshoba worked first for the YWCA, which recognised her talents and sent her to its World Congress in Ghana in 1971. But it was as a radiographer, when she was witness to the racist treatment meted out by some of her white colleagues to Black patients, that she was motivated to play a more active role in the struggle.

Mentored by Ellen Khuzwayo, who was working for the ANC underground, Matshoba got involved in BCM youth and literacy initiatives. She worked closely with fellow BC revolutionaries Willie Nhlapo, [Strini] Moodley and [Mosibudi] Mangena. Once they had been arrested, Matshoba was left to continue with BCP work on her own, becoming the national literacy director of SASO in 1974. Yet, it is her harrowing experience of extreme torture in detention that should reward Matshoba's memory with a particular and profound place in our collective history.

Battling the scars of that time, she gave compelling testimony to the TRC's Women's Hearing[115] in July 1997, opening by saying that 'one is to be very strong'.

Her first experience of torture was at the notorious John Vorster police station in central Johannesburg after the Soweto massacre.

---

115   Semantics and legal scholar Ayumi Kusafuka examined issues of truth commissions and gender using South Africa as a case study, explaining how 'South Africa's gendered past was never substantially addressed by the TRC' whose treatment of gender was in part constrained by its 'gender-blind' mandate which ignored the different experiences and interests of men and women [Kusafuka, 2010: https://www.accord.org.za/ajcr-issues/truth-commissions-and-gender/].

'When people look at you walking up and down the streets or associating with them in social circles, they see strength in some of us,' she told the TRC in her opening remarks. 'They do not know how much you have been shattered and broken in the past.'

Matshoba first went to prison in 1976, incarcerated at the Johannesburg Fort where she said she was 'very fortunate [to have] a veteran among us in the person of Winnie Mandela, who had been to the Fort before and, having been familiar with the place, we drew a lot of knowledge and courage from her'.

Matshoba told the story of how Winnie woke them up one night, saying, 'women, we are not going to sleep'.

'We started banging doors, banging doors and calling until the "adjutant" [supervisor] came and wanted to know what was happening. We said we want to see the Security Police.

'Our concern was that there were young children being held in the Fort with their mothers. The next day, the children were released.'

Although she was released in December that year, Matshoba was held again six weeks later under the more onerous Section 6 of the Terrorism Act in the maximum-security section of Pietermaritzburg Prison known as 'the Gulag'. Matshoba was placed in isolation and attended to only by white prison wardresses who would allow Security Police 'to come and fetch you at any odd time of the night for torture purposes'.

'It would never be recorded in the books that you have been taken to the torture chambers.

'The first time when they took me from the prison was a week later. Actually after I had demanded that I wanted to see them. I still came with a Fort mentality. I demanded to see them, because they had just dumped me there after taking me to the female prison and never came to me.

'I just sat there stewing, you know, and thinking what could it be. I remember the wardress, actually, the senior wardress there, saying to me, "How can you, how dare you call the Security Police. Do you not know what these people are going to do to you when they take you? You are better off sitting here not knowing what it is that, why, the reason why you are here"…

'I said, "No, I have work to do, I have a child at home, I need to attend to so many things, I have studies to do, I cannot come and sit here and rot here and not knowing why I am here".'

Matshoba then related how members of the Security Branch arrived 'drunk'.

'The security policeman's name is Roy Otto. They held a braai outside; it was at night. They handcuffed me and manacled my ankle on a big iron ball. They made me stand the whole night.

'There was no chair, but I was given a pen to write a statement, tell them everything about myself and my involvement in SASO. I was an executive member of SASO at that stage. I wrote a brief history of myself. It was Saturday.

'Sunday, I continued the same thing. They kept on tearing the papers and telling me to write. The third night, I started becoming delirious and my legs were swelling. I think that was on a Monday.

'By Thursday, no, Tuesday, by the Tuesday, I was counting nights and this man started beating me up. He held a towel, strangled me with a towel and started bashing my head against the wall.

'Obviously I was very, very weak. I was being given food but I was not made to sit down. I could not sit down and when I collapsed, they kicked me. Eventually I must have passed out. I was bleeding.

'When I came to, I was lying on the floor, all wet. They must have poured water over me. He threw a packet of sanitary pads at me. I got to the bathroom and I could see that I was menstruating and I was just wondering how he realised that.

'The beatings lasted for a week. I was asthmatic and they refused to give me medication. Ultimately, when they realised that they could not get anything out of me and, perhaps, not mainly because of strength as much as it was actually because of weakness, the way I was physically weak and I could not speak anymore.'

Thereafter, Matshoba was moved to a 'filthy' police station, 'swarming with lice, and the blankets stinking and reeking of urine, and I was thrown in there. Actually the worst was that I did not even know where I was, and I was screaming and shouting.

'I did not even have strength, because I was running short of breath.

'I remember somewhere along the line, I was very fortunate that this uniformed policeman came – an Afrikaner. I will never forget his name: Taljaard. He told me that he thought I was mad. I was just a mad person.

'I tried to explain to him, and he listened carefully and understood that, no, I was actually a political prisoner and I had just been tortured.'

'Taljaard' then smuggled in an asthma inhaler and medication for Matshoba, 'and helped me hide them in the cell. We hid them behind the toilets.' 'Taljaard' then also smuggled her out to see a doctor.

'There was a Van Rooyen who kept on coming and saying to me, "We are waiting for you to die. We have realised your weak point and we do not have to torture you anymore. With your asthma, you will go naturally and we cannot be held liable for that."

'Taljaard must have spoken strongly to the doctor. In fact, he even said to the doctor, "We do not want her dying here".'

On the doctor's instructions, Matshoba was taken back to the Pietermaritzburg Prison where she was given a wash rag and carbolic soap, which she had to use for her teeth too. At the police station, the only access she had to washing facilities was an outside cold tap. At the prison, there was a basin in the cell and a toilet, although the white wardresses tormented Matshoba.

'[But] I knew why I was there and the reason why I was there. I always tried to draw a lot of courage and tell myself I am in the struggle and we are in the struggle, because we are assured of victory and I always used to draw courage from those words.'

As the wardresses never properly spoke to her, she was desperately lonely and isolated in addition to being regularly physically harmed. Matshoba said she then, out of despair, 'one day grabbed a wardress's hair, threw down the bars [in the cell door] and started bashing her head against the bars'.

That wardress's job had been to kick Matshoba's plate of food into her cell on a nightly basis: 'I really gave it to her. I beat her up thoroughly and I could not let loose. The prisoners were locked in and it was quiet and it was just time for her to come and feed this animal and she was all by herself. She was screaming, and there was nobody.

'Ultimately, she fell down. I do not know how they saw her, but then they came, they picked her up. I was expecting anything from the

Security Police, anything from being charged, but the best that I was hoping for was that I would be charged just to be able to go to court, [just to] be able to talk to somebody.'

But that didn't happen, although a magistrate allowed her to get a Bible and she was given permission to write a letter home. That letter carried the Pietermaritzburg Prison stamp, which is how her father was able to trace her.

When her family arrived at the prison to see her, that was the first time in 10 months that Matshoba had had any meaningful human contact. After that, she was transferred to Bethal Prison where, because of her asthma, she was placed in the hospital section.

Miraculously, it would disappear.

'For some strange reason, I had overcome [it],' she told the TRC. 'Up to this day, it just left me ... Never had an attack again. I mean, it was amazing how those cosmic powers, whatever it was, worked on me and removed my shortcoming and I started becoming very strong, because I knew that I did not have that weak point that they capitalised on.'

A magistrate later enquired as to her needs, and she said she would like to see her son and her parents.

'Two days later, my sister Thembi and my dad came, but they did not bring Sechaba [her son] inside. I had gone to the police station to meet them there. They were given a 30-minute visit and the Security Police were around for the first time. Actually, what was strange, I was very tough, I was not crying or anything. [But] I cried that day.

'Thembi left very worried because I had shown a sign of weakness, and the only reason I cried was because I had hugged somebody. I had talked to people, I had seen real people.'

Matshoba's hardships continued after she was transferred two more times to other prisons, and then back to the Fort. She weighed 43 kilograms when she arrived at the Fort, and she said the other women political prisoners 'really cried when they saw me'. She had not seen herself in the mirror for 18 months.

Six months after her reincarceration, Matshoba was released and then immediately slapped with a five-year banning order, restricting her to Krugersdorp. Her marriage failed.

'Invariably,' Matshoba told the TRC, 'the only thing that followed one after that was the victimisation, the white victimisation each time you get a job and the system would still follow you and intimidate your employers.

'But ultimately one is proud to say that there are success stories, there have been strengths that we drew from the past.'

Matshoba died in September 2014.

Hamba kahle, qhawe lamaqhawe.

[www.justice.gov.za]

An unstinting hero of the oppressed: Fatima Meer (1928–2010)

The activist, academic and writer was a founding delegate of the Black Women's Federation (BWF) in 1973, although her fight for human rights was by that time already 30 years old.

Meer's activism gained traction within the South African Indian Congress during the Passive Resistance Campaign of the 1940s. She was also a founding member of the fearless Durban and District Women's League in 1949. First banned in 1952, she nonetheless was part of the organisational capacity for the 1956 Women's March on the Union Buildings in Pretoria.

An activist throughout, especially in the impoverished Phoenix informal settlement outside Durban, she was also the author of *Portrait of Indian South Africans* in 1969. All the money Meer made from her book she gave to the Gandhi Museum and Clinic.

An example of what can be achieved when you determine to be self-reliant and set an example, Meer founded and headed the Natal Education Trust, which raised funds to build schools in the Black areas of Umlazi, Port Shepstone and Inanda. She also rallied funding to build the Chief Albert Luthuli and Dr Dube Administration Block and Library and the Mohamed Ali Student Centre at Ohlange High School in Inanda. Among Meer's other inspiring campaigns were the Tembalishe Tutorial College, where students were trained in secretarial practice, organising scholarships for students to the US and India, founding the Co-ordinating Committee of Black ratepayers' organisations and starting the Khanyisa School Project, a bridging programme for Black children from informal settlements.

Later becoming a professor of sociology at the University of Natal, Meer was banned again in 1976 shortly after the Soweto massacre, and detained without trial. Before that, she had drawn nearer to the BCM and found a compatriot in Biko. Her links to BC were also believed to have been behind an attempt on her life at her home in Durban. She was banned for a third time in 1981.

Meer died a hero of the struggle at 81 in the St Augustine's Hospital in Durban after a stroke.

The exception to the rule: Mamphela Ramphele

Born in 1947 in the Bochum District of Limpopo, Mamphela Ramphele was conscientised when she was a child, her older sister Mashadi expelled from high school after she demonstrated against South Africa becoming a Republic in 1961. An uncle of hers had also been detained under the regime's 90-day clause, and Ramphele remembers her parents discussing this and its implications. She was encouraged into student activism by [Vuyelwa] Mashalaba.

Once SASO was established, Ramphele would become a chairperson of its local committee and this opened opportunities to participate extensively in the BCP. A philosophy was that university students enjoyed a relative degree of privilege compared to other Black people, and so they should share whatever skills they had.

Ramphele – who later became Chief Medical Officer at the BCP Zanempilo Community Health Centre in Zinyoka outside King William's Town – is undoubtedly one of the most well-known of the BCM leaders. Among other BCP projects with which she was involved was managing the Eastern Cape branch of the Black Community Health Programme and directing the BCP in that province after Biko was banned.

But her controversial relationship with Biko – out of which two children were born while he was still married to Ntsiki Biko, with whom he also had children – has left her with an ambiguous history. (Her children with Biko were Lerato, born in 1974, and Hlumelo, born in 1978. Lerato contracted fatal pneumonia when she was two months old, while Hlumelo Biko was born after Biko's murder.)

Champions of Ramphele who reject the assertion that she got

'mileage' out of her links to Biko assert her independence as a political figure in her own right throughout the period of the BCM in the 1970s. A qualified doctor, she suffered greatly – with or without Biko.

Ramphele was charged under the Suppression of Communism Act for being in possession of banned literature and then detained in 1976 under Section 10 of the Terrorism Act. By April 1977, she had been banished to Tzaneen where she was to remain until 1984.

Ramphele lived for a while with two Black nuns in a local village called Tickeyline, and there established the Isutheng Community Health Programme with assistance from the BCP. It was designed to empower Black women in the area.

Ramphele further educated herself during her banning, travelling abroad illicitly, and would ultimately be appointed to UCT's South African Labour and Development Research Unit as a research fellow at the end of apartheid. She had by then earned a PhD in Social Anthropology from UCT.

In 1991, she became one of the deputy vice-chancellors and then vice-chancellor of UCT in 1996 – the first Black woman to hold such a position. She had already been a visiting scholar at Harvard's Kennedy School of Government.

In 2000, Ramphele was made one of the four managing directors of the World Bank, attracting controversy, again, for what some believed was an ideological, social and political betrayal of her BC roots.

The World Bank is regarded by Black revolutionary theorists as anathema. This is best summarised in a 2016 piece in *The Conversation* written by Patrick Bond. Under the headline, 'The harsh realities about South Africa that the World Bank dare not speak', Bond – who was also affiliated to the National Union of Metalworkers Research and Policy Institute as a volunteer advisory board member – described its perils for the poor. In agreement with French philosopher Michel Foucault's discourse theory, Bond examined the bank's 'South African poverty and inequality assessment discussion note', saying that its staff and consultants were 'resorting to extreme evasion tactics worthy of Harry, Ron and Hermione' (in JK Rowling's *Harry Potter* series about young wizards).

Although the Bank credited South Africa with spending more than other countries on its social programmes, Bond said that 'of the world's 40 largest countries, only four – South Korea, China, Mexico and India – had lower social spending than South Africa'. He criticised South Africa's neo-liberal policies under the ANC, which had included 'the failed 1996–2001 Growth, Employment and Distribution plan co-authored by two [World] Bank economists'. Bond said 'this made South Africa far more vulnerable to global capitalist crises'.

Meanwhile, calculations showed that the percentage of South Africans actually living below the Bank's own declared poverty line was between 53 and 63%. In addition, Bond said it's believed 'the number of poor people has soared by around 10 million given the 15 million population rise since 1994'.

At the same time he noted the 'wealth accruing through rising corporate share prices' – a situation the Bank 'ignored' as 'radically lower corporate taxes mainly benefit the rich in the same way. South Africa's after-tax profits have been among the world's highest, according to the IMF in 2013.'

Bond further took issue with the ANC's bold proclamations of success around its socio-economic programmes, which affected water, sanitation, electricity and refuse removal provision; social protection in the form of grants, primary health care, education, housing and land, and job creation through the Expanded Public Works Programme.

Although Bond's writing is completely separate from any reference made here to Ramphele, with his subject having nothing to do with her or any other individual, the World Bank's policies towards South Africa may have been influenced during the time that she was an executive there.

Her name is still associated with the Bank, to her reputational detriment within the Left. Bond says in his analysis that 'to truly tackle poverty and inequality, only one force in society has unequivocally succeeded since 1994'.

That force is the social activist.

Many South Africans might have believed that a former BCM

activist like Ramphele should have found her natural home after the end of apartheid in activism, too. Bond, for example, has identified the Treatment Action Campaign and the Anti-Privatisation Forum as activists – and those are certainly among organisations that tend to operate like the BCP of old. But Ramphele had, perhaps unwittingly, set herself up for criticism.

So her decisions to join the board of the BCP's old funders, the Anglo American Corporation, and become a non-executive director of both Mediclinic Holdings and Transnet, and chairperson of Gold Fields, did not always go down especially well in the broader BC community. Thus it is perhaps not so much Ramphele's extramarital relationship with Biko that matters today, but her seeming detachment from the activism of her youth, which could instead have been utilised for the public good.

She hasn't shied away from some topics within BC, though. In particular, she's made a contribution to discussions about women's roles in liberation, most notably in 'The dynamics of gender within BC organisations: A personal view', which was published in *Bounds of Possibility: The Legacy of Steve Biko and Black Consciousness*.

Her fellow writers were Pityana, Lindy Wilson and another great BCM leader, Malusi Mpumlwana. (Malusi Mpumlwana is now the general secretary of the South African Council of Churches and bishop of the Ethiopian Episcopal Church. He and his wife, Thoko Mbanjwa, were, together with activists Mxolisi Mvovo – who was married to Nobandile, Biko's younger sister – and Nohle and Mapetla Mohapi, regarded as Biko's closest friends.)

[Bond, 2016; Pityana, Ramphele, Mpumlwana & Wilson, 1991]

Exposing the torture: Florence Ribeiro

Born in Natal in November 1933, Florence Ribeiro grew up in White City, Jabavu, Soweto. Her father died when she was seven years old, leaving her mother, a domestic worker, to raise her and her three sisters single-handedly.

This was very difficult, but her mother instilled a love and respect for education in her children. Three of her sisters would later become nurses and Florence trained to become a domestic science teacher. She met her future husband, Fabian, when she was in Standard 8. He was at the time a Catholic seminarian intent on joining the priesthood. But the relationship with Florence changed the course of their lives as he went on to study medicine instead.

During his fourth year, the couple got married and moved to Lady Selborne in the Eastern Cape where Fabian served his internship. But the family was forced to leave their home there during the Group Areas Act removals and then settled in Mamelodi, outside Pretoria, where Fabian opened a medical practice and Florence a butchery.

The couple's political activism began in the 1960s through their support of Florence's sister Veronica, who was married to Robert Sobukwe, who was, at that time, imprisoned on Robben Island. By the late 1970s, Florence and Fabian were actively documenting and publicising the brutality of the apartheid security police towards child activists by videotaping the children's injuries. They also provided shelter to young activists, as well as supplying money and transport for those wishing to leave the country.

A danger to the apartheid state, their house was gutted by fire in February 1986. They had already survived several attempts on their lives during 1985 and 1986. Finally, in December 1986, Florence and Fabian Ribeiro were gunned down in the courtyard of their home.

In 1997, the TRC found that the Ribeiros had been assassinated by agents of the apartheid state. But in 1999, the Amnesty Committee of the TRC granted amnesty to their killers.

[SABC, 2010: This website has a press release about *Flowers of the Revolution*, an SABC documentary series which included an episode about Florence Ribeiro]

A stubborn fighter: Shamima Shaikh (1960–1998)

Known to many as the 'Muslim Joan of Arc', Shaikh is probably the most recognisable feminist activist of the 1980s. Her strong relationship with her religion, as well as her desire to seek equity for women in Islam, saw her lead a now-famous protest to attend the *tarawih* prayers (at night in the Islamic month of Ramadan) at the 23rd Street Mosque in Fietas, Johannesburg .

She eloquently wrote: 'For those men and women who view each other only as sexual beings, the mosque precinct – a holy precinct

– can be therapeutic. On seeing women in the holy precinct, the depraved soul has to recognise that women are not just sexy beings but spiritual beings, members of the *ummah*, their sisters in faith. If women are invisible in this holy precinct, his perception of women as just sexy beings will not be challenged and he will never be able to reclaim his full humanity, his Islam.'

Born in 1960 in Louis Trichardt, Shaikh's journey with the politics of liberation began at the University of Durban-Westville, where she was part of AZAPO from 1984. She was also an elected member of the Islamic Society.

A strong advocate of a consumer boycott of white-owned businesses during campaigns against apartheid, Shaikh was active in mobilising Black communities and was soon arrested and detained.

Later a key member of the team behind *al-Qalam*, a Muslim community paper run by the Muslim Youth Movement of South Africa, Shaikh became a mentor for students hoping to help bring down the regime.

She was deeply involved in demonstrations against the apartheid government's Tricameral Parliament and worked tirelessly within Muslim and other communities as a defender of human rights.

Shaikh was involved in the establishment of the Muslim Personal Law Board of South Africa after 1994, but ideological differences with the United Ulama Council of South Africa eventually shut it down.

Shaikh died of breast cancer in 1998 after a relapse in 1996, leaving her two beloved young sons and her husband, activist and academic Na'eem Jeenah.

[www.shams.za.org]

Called woman: Nnoseng Ellen Kuzwayo

Born in 1914 in Lesotho, Kuzwayo grew up on her grandfather's farm in Thaba Nchu, inheriting it in 1930 but then losing it when the apartheid government declared her land to be in a 'white area'. She graduated from Lovedale, Eastern Cape, as a teacher, but returned to her studies at the age of 39 and completed a degree in social work from Wits. Her abusive marriage had broken down by this time, and she was raising her two sons alone.

By 1964 the general secretary of the YWCA in the Transvaal, Kuzwayo was a great champion of Black self-help. After the Soweto massacre, she was the only woman invited into the Soweto-based Committee of 10, but all were quickly held without trial, in Kuzwayo's case for five months, at the Fort.

Her most well-known book is *Call Me Woman* (1985).

Kuzwayo was awarded honorary degrees from the universities of Natal, Port Elizabeth and Wits. She died in 2006 aged 91.

Restoring the family: The Black Women's Federation

Formed in 1975, the short-lived Black Women's Federation (BWF) was located within the BCM, although it always argued expressly for autonomy from the patriarchy. The federation's only concern was for Black women and their liberation, and mobilising to restore the Black family.

Exclusive to Black women members, it first found support in Natal after its inaugural conference, in particular reaching out to Indian women. But African women in the province were especially affected by the colonialist Natal Code of Black Law, commonly referred to as the Natal Code, which dated back to the late 1800s and had not been repealed by the 1970s.

This Code made decisions around traditional culture and continued to relegate Black women to the control and authority of men, especially when it came to property and other assets. Thus, the Natal dominance within the BWF was also due to the fact that Black women there were fighting a peculiarly parochial law, which affected them deeply. Theirs was a subordination that made them perpetual minors. The Code was only scrapped in the 1980s.

The BWF was inspired by the more experienced Federation of South African Women (FSAW), which had perfected the art of mass mobilisation during protests against the pass. The BWF was also drawn to aspects of FSAW's Women's Charter adopted in 1954. But where the FSAW was in favour of non-violence and non-racialism, the BWF was more inclined towards Black civil disobedience and social resistance.

It had seen how the state cracked down on women in the same way as it did on men, banning, placing under house arrest or jailing FSAW leaders including Ray Alexander, Lilian Ngoyi and Helen Joseph in the early 1960s. If anything, the BWF could learn from what happened to the FSAW even as it pressed for greater Black unity. An effective way of doing this was to become part of the BCP's health, education and literacy projects with what Biko called 'a pragmatic Africanism'.

Significant support came from the YWCA, from whose ranks many BC activists emerged, including Matshoba and Mkhabela.

Among the leading lights of the BWF were Meer, president of the African Housewives League in Soweto Sally Motlana, Margaret Naidoo, Jane Chabaku, Joyce Siwane, Nomathemba Sithole, Ursula David, Merina Nyembezi, Virginia Gcabashe, Jeannie Noel, Joyce Seroka, Vivienne Josie and Zubie Seedat.

[Winnie] Mandela would also join and champion the BWF in the Transvaal, despite being associated with the ANC, and the federation got support from SASO leader Mashalaba, writer Kuzwayo, businesswoman Deborah Mabiletsa and church leader Constance Khoza.

Not long after the BWF was launched, the Soweto massacre happened, Meer and Mandela were banned, and Noel and Motlana were detained, along with other leading members Jane Phakathi, Vesta Smith and Seroka. When the BWF was banned in October 1977 along with 17 other organisations, there was no way forward. It had to end its short life.

'A vanguard of women': The Imbeleko Women's Movement of AZAPO

In Xhosa, '*Imbeleko*' means a ceremony to symbolically detach an infant's umbilical cord from its mother and to formally introduce the child to the family's ancestors. The term may also refer to the act of giving birth or the cloth or skin a woman used to carry her child on her back.

In politics, however, the term was applied to the AZAPO women's wing formed in 1987 with inspiration from the Black Domestic Workers Association and Black Women Unite. Using the identity of a mother's body, it is unashamedly socialist. The movement has therefore also always been supportive of workers' rights.

Throughout, Imbeleko has promoted Black self-reliance

and women's self-reliance, driving self-help projects including bricklaying, carpentry and upholstery. Imbeleko has also run health and education-related projects, with the aim of helping Black women earn their own money and run their own lives and families.

Imbeleko was formed at a time when so-called 'Black-on-Black' violence – or, the proxy war between the ANC and the IFP – was high, and Black women were still on the lowest rung of apartheid society. Imbeleko's staying power is attributed to its relevance for Black women from all walks of life, and its willingness to confront their particular conflicts.

In an interview in August 2015, Imbeleko president Kamohelo Motloung said the primary difference between Imbeleko and other women's organisations is that it 'does not exist to be patriarchy-preserving'. She said: 'Many of these organisations are nothing but "women's wings" of patriarchal organisations. In other words, these "women's wings" are extensions of the patriarchy. Their role is to whip women into line in accordance with patriarchal interests.

'That is why it was a "women's wing" [the ANC Women's League] that not so long ago declared to the whole world that no woman in South Africa was ready to lead as the President of the country.

'[That serves] a male chauvinist agenda that has nothing to do with women.

'That is why Imbeleko has positioned itself as a true vanguard of women that is independent and holds the interests of women as paramount.'

'A platform to be heard': The story of *Speak*

By 1982, there were regular efforts to commemorate the historic 1956 Women's March that had so magnificently demonstrated the power of a united South African womanhood. But there was a continuing void for women to be organised outside of political structures. It was after a commemorative event that a newsletter aimed at giving voice to the issues faced by women was launched.

Appropriately titled *Speak*, it intended to see that the liberation of women would happen with the same dedication as liberation would happen for other parts of society.

The magazine started off as a newsletter, a project of the Durban Women's Group, which was focused mainly on housing at the time. As a wider community of conscious women grew, so did the reach of the magazine from Durban to the whole of Natal and then further afield. The first 400 copies were produced in English and Zulu.

The initial sub-committee of the Durban Women's Group responsible for producing the newsletter comprised Karen Hurt, Sandy Africa, Pregs Govender, Jane Quinn, Shamim Meer, Vanessa Taylor, Sheila Jalobe and Gugu Mji.

Speak was bravely published from 1982 to 1994 at the height of the revolt against apartheid, and sold widely at factories, meetings, rallies and other mass gatherings where women were present. Its contributors crossed gender and racial lines.

[Meer, 1998; www.sahistory org.za]

The women who sing BC

Zenzi Miriam Makeba

Born in 1932 in Prospect, an inner-city ghetto in Johannesburg, Makeba grew up in poverty. She gave birth to her daughter, Angela Sibongile,[116] when she was 17 and already showing significant musical promise of a stage career.

She performed with the Manhattan Brothers[117] before being a founding member of the quartet The Skylarks and a star of the *African Jazz and Variety* show, the first Black showcase playing white venues, including the Johannesburg City Hall.

She was then cast in the hit, *King Kong*,[118] which starred two of

---

116   Songs by Angela 'Bongi' Makeba (1950-1985) can be heard in her mother's repertoire, with 'Malcolm X' (1965, 1972) and 'Lumumba' (1970) honouring assassinated Black leaders.

117   The Manhattan Brothers was a popular South African singing group of the 1940s and '50s, performing ragtime, jive, swing, doo-wop, jazz and African choral and Zulu harmonies. Their hit, 'Lovely Lies', made the *Billboard* chart in the US in 1956.

118   *King Kong*, the Black jazz opera, opened at the Wits Great Hall in Johannesburg in 1959. The retelling of the life of South African heavyweight boxing champion

the Manhattan Brothers, Nathan Mdlhedlhe and Joe Mogotsi, as the lead character and his best friend. Makeba played Joyce, King Kong's girlfriend and the owner of a bar called Back of the Moon, which prompted one of Makeba's greatest songs (of the same name). Makeba was also cast in Come Back Africa, and presented the film at the Venice International Film Festival – an event from which she only returned to South Africa from living in exile 35 years later.

Makeba lived in the US in the 1960s, where she met and married Black Panthers leader Stokely Carmichael in 1969. She then moved to Guinea, having been identified as an important figure in the fight for Black liberation and Pan-Africanism.

Makeba twice addressed the United Nations with Guinea as her proxy nation. She was named Woman of the Century by the Bedford Stuyvesant Community of New York City and received the Commander of the Order of Arts and Letters and the French Legion of Honour – three of her many accomplishments in recognition of her work as an artist which saw her 32 records realise global success.

Makeba returned to South Africa in 1990 after the ANC and other liberation movements were unbanned and Nelson Mandela released from Victor Verster Prison.

She died in Naples in 2008.

[Cagnolari, 2018: https://pan-african-music.com/en/miriam-makeba-come-back-africa-2/]

Letta Mbulu (1942–)

A member of the cast of the acclaimed *African Jazz and Variety Show* and *King Kong*, Mbulu began her career as a teenage music star beloved of and mentored by Makeba. Her shine was abruptly dimmed in her home country when Mbulu was driven into exile in the US by the regime at the end of 1964.

It didn't take long for her to find herself in the spotlight again, touring with greats Cannonball Adderley and Harry Belafonte while

---

Ezekiel Dhlamini – who was barred from fighting abroad, turned to alcohol and ended up dying mysteriously behind bars after he killed a gang leader and his girlfriend – went on a sold-out South African tour for two years before it played in London in 1961.

also releasing hits with her legendary musician husband, Caiphus Semenya,[119] whom she met on tour with *King Kong*.

Mbulu won an Emmy Award for her role in the classic film *Roots* and also appeared in *A Warm December* with Sidney Poitier and *The Color Purple* with Oprah Winfrey.

She recorded more than 20 albums, including *Not Yet Uhuru* (1992), the first to be recorded in South Africa after the unbanning of the ANC and other liberation movements, and was always an activist under the skin, joining the Union of South African Artists and being a founding member of the South African Artists United which was behind Semenya's anti-apartheid musical, *Buwa!*, in which she starred.

Mbulu and Semenya – who returned to South Africa from exile in 1991 – were awarded the national Order of iKhamanga 'in recognition of their excellent contribution to music and the struggle against apartheid' in 2009.

Thandiswa Mazwai (1976–)

Black Power movements have been both a solemn and audacious source for women musicians since the late 1960s. They've conscientised a sisterhood and motherhood, and chastised and praised Black brothers.

Their art has reflected alternately dark and powerful Black political times, and the rhythms, shifts and grace in Black society.

South African women flourished within BC music from the late 1990s, yet the stage was most dominated by Mazwai. Others, like Simphiwe Dana and Capetonian all-women rap outfit Godessa, whose beats were made to a strident BC in the early 2000s, also covered themes of identity and gender.

Mazwai, however, brought forth echoes of the BCP and its activities – musical and beyond – as she invigorated South Africa within Africa. Her fearlessness has since seen her address many issues from sex to Black globalisation through kwaito and so-called 'traditional' music styles, as well as mbaqanga, jazz and funk.

---

119   Caiphus Semenya (1939–) is an acclaimed musical director and composer whose compositions were performed by Cannonball Adderley, Harry Belafonte, The Crusaders, Lou Rawls and Nina Simone. Semenya also composed music for *Roots* and *The Color Purple*, which earned him an Emmy Award and Grammy nomination.

Influenced by Biko, Fanon, Achebe and Nkrumah early on, Mazwai has throughout refused to submit to anything but her own mind and her own ritual.

Also known as King Tha, Red and Gunzah Blaze, she performed around the world from 1998 with the conscious kwaito band, Bongo Maffin – which had six award-winning albums – and icons Stevie Wonder, Cesaria Evora, Salif Keita, Skunk Anansie, Hugh Masekela and others. Among other prizes, Mazwai was a two-time recipient of a Kora All Africa Music Award, first with Bongo Maffin and again in 2004 when she went solo with her first album, *Zabalaza*. That album was followed by two other solo works: *Ibokwe* and *Belede* [named for her mother, who died young at 36 when Mazwai was 15]. Mazwai collaborated on two songs with American musician and composer Meshell N'degeoCello on N'degeoCello's album *The World Has Made Me the Man of My Dreams*, which was nominated for a Grammy Award in 2007.

When Mazwai's album *Belede* came out in 2017, journalist Lerato Tshabalala contextualised its references for *The Afropolitan* (the companion website with Kaya fm 95.9): 'The first single, "Jikijela", is a Letta Mbulu ... struggle song, recorded during [apartheid], where Mbulu refers to Black South Africans throwing stones against the tyranny of the regime.'

Mazwai explained to Tshabalala: '"When I saw the images and news clippings of the #FeesMustFall movement, I knew I had to record that song, because of how relevant it was to the student uprisings we were experiencing in 2015."' The artist told *griot.de* (an agency based in Germany which has promoted artists including Makeba, Hugh Masekela and Ladysmith Black Mambazo): 'My music is for those of us who fight to decolonise our minds, and remember it's about memory. Remembering what my mother taught me and also remembering what my ancestors knew.

'That's where the soul of my creativity lives: inside that collective memory of pain and pride, oppression and freedom, mysticism and faith.'

Simphiwe Dana (1980–)

A singer, composer and producer who has woven the broadest loves of African music into the blues and church sounds of its diaspora, Dana, like Mazwai, is unforgivingly political. Yet there is a dance in her fist, raised in her contemporary Black classics like 'Troubled Soldier', 'Bantu Biko Street', 'Uzobuya Nini' and 'Naphakade'.

Her biographer, Professor Dineo Pumla Gqola, described the 'Simphiwe phenomenon' – a woman who defined and reinvented culture – in her unconventional memoir, *A Renegade Called Simphiwe* (2013).

Writing in *The Conversation* about Dana's fifth album, *Bamako*, Phuti Sepuru, a lecturer at the University of Pretoria, reflected on her [fearless engagement], 'often through her social media accounts, on issues around social ills, politics and her personal struggles, such as domestic abuse'.

Co-produced by Salif Keita and named for the capital city of his country, Mali, the album has a powerful sense of 'home' even when the 'place' may change. It is important then, as Sepuru notes, that 'the largest part of [Dana's] musical output is sung in her home language – isiXhosa'.

'An activist who sang': Nina Simone (1933–2003)

One of the most influential Black feminist anthems of all time is Nina Simone's 'Four Women' (1966, on the album, *Wild Is the Wind*), in which, atribecallednews.com writes, she 'portrays four different women of colour and illustrates the struggle of Black identity among women'.

With the unforgettable opening lyrics, 'My skin is black/ My arms are long/ My hair is woolly/ My back is strong/ Strong enough to take the pain/ inflicted again and again', the song holds power five decades later. *The New Yorker* writes: 'If Simone's song suggests a history of Black women in America, it is also a history of long-suppressed and finally uncontainable anger.'

That 'Four Women' was 'charged with being insulting to black women and was banned on a couple of radio stations in New York and Philadelphia soon after the recording was released', is notable in how the establishment feared Simone's voice, and its racism. 'The ban was lifted, however, when it produced more outrage than the song.'

Another enduring BC theme is Simone's song, 'Young, Gifted and Black' (1958, on the album, *Little Girl Blue*) which atribecallednews says 'showed her tireless efforts for equality among Blacks'.

'When you feel really low,' she sang, 'Yeah, there's a great truth you should know/ When you're young, gifted and black/ Your soul's intact...'

Simone performed and spoke at civil rights meetings, but she gave her support to Black nationalism and was in favour of armed resistance and even the creation of an independent Black state. Maya Angelou is quoted, from an article she wrote in the 1970s, by *The Guardian* in 2015: '[Nina Simone] is an extremist, extremely realised.'

Simone said her friend, the great playwright Lorraine Hansberry, conscientised her, and indeed it was Hansberry's unfinished script, *To Be Young, Gifted and Black*, which became the anthem with which Simone is associated. The song was later picked up by other impeccable performers like Aretha Franklin.

The Guardian's Dorian Lynskey describes the song as having 'the pride and optimism of the cover versions [Simone] had alchemised into civil rights anthems: "Feeling Good", "I Wish I Knew How It Would Feel to Be Free", "Ain't Got No/I Got Life".' Simone related in her autobiography, *I Put A Spell on You*, how she 'felt more alive at that time' (during the Black Power era of the 1960s) because 'I was needed, and I could sing something to help my people'.

Yet it was her outrageous musical brilliance on the song 'Mississippi Goddamn', composed in fury after the 15 September 1963 supremacists' bomb which killed four Black schoolgirls in Birmingham, Alabama, which lives on and on, yet is almost unknown in this era. Lynskey said it '[expressed] Black anger in a way that never had been heard in American music before', which meant it was purposefully side-lined by the music establishment.

Simone, who was close to Malcolm X – who happened to be her neighbour in New York – as well as Martin Luther King, and other luminaries like James Baldwin and Stokely Carmichael, was far too Black for America's white media and white music.

Those industries could tolerate protest, as long as it didn't come from a Black woman who could play Bach on their white stages. As Lynskey says, '[Simone's] music was by, about and for Black people'. Ultimately, she was 'an activist who sang'.

[Cade, 2015: https://www.atribecallednews.com/feministmovement-music/123; Pierpont, 2014: https://www.newyorker.com/magazine/2014/08/11/raised-voice]

Seven

Land: The Continuing Revolution of Black Consciousness

Compiled by Janet Smith

The enduring geography of apartheid undercuts every attempt at political liberation in South Africa. Borders – of all kinds – still break us. Land haunts us. The violent white bias of apartheid, enforced by legislation such as the Group Areas Act and the policy of 'separate development' created clear dividing lines. Those still deeply affect identity, wealth generation, mental health, education, stability, crime and all other social responses to owning or not having land. Meanwhile, the Freedom Charter, a founding document of the ruling party, has assisted the lines to lengthen more than a quarter of a century since South Africa's first democratic elections. Its first clause reads: 'We, the People of South Africa, declare for all our country and the world to know: that South Africa belongs to all who live in it, Black and white.' It may acknowledge that 'our people have been robbed of their birth-right to land', but as other struggles go on it is continued land dispossession and land segregation by class, which drives a new BC.

It's about blood, politics, emotion, family, self-determination. But how far would the landless be prepared to go to reclaim their history? Here, we look at the past and how much of it is threaded into the future for BC.

※

Lives in the dark: A brief history of land

It's not anti-white to say that land in South Africa belongs to Black South Africans. Their birth-right was removed and it must be restored.

CNN's David McKenzie and Brent Swails captured it exactly in 2018, before another dispiriting election in which South African political parties wagered land restitution for the support of investors.

Capital has used politics to frame land revolutionaries in the country as enemies for centuries. It's cut them down like invasive trees, but the roots are always only hidden.

'When Nelson Mandela and the ANC came to power in South Africa in 1994, one of the key dilemmas they faced was the so-called land question,' CNN explained. 'The policy of pushing [Black] South Africans off the land to the benefit of whites officially began with the 1913 Native Lands Act, though in reality the practice stretches back centuries.'

The 2019 election was won by the party which has won every election since 1994, and whose president, Cyril Ramaphosa, called the 1912 Land Act South Africa's 'original sin', explaining that 'the poverty that we have … in part, has been given rise to by people not having assets'.

To understand, it is essential to return to the National Party taking control of South Africa in 1948. Its racism was so ingrained that it immediately set about entrenching colonial divisions with ever-harsher laws to negate public Black humanity. Chief among these was to remove Black people's free rights to land and property, and many pieces of legislation would confirm that denial for the next 40 years.

This began for the National Party with the Group Areas Act passed in 1950, and the release of the 1954 Tomlinson Report – a 'study' to lay the groundwork for the bantustans. When Prime Minister DF Malan appointed Professor Frederick R Tomlinson and a panel from the notorious Stellenbosch University think tank, the South African Bureau for Racial Affairs (SABRA), to be the Commission for the Socio-Economic Development of Bantu Areas, there was more to it than just a political conclusion.

The nationalist apparatchiks were engaging in intra-Afrikaner competition at the expense of Black people. Even Malan and the former *Transvaler* newspaper editor, Hendrik Verwoerd, were at odds over the report. Malan wanted 'a comprehensive scheme for the rehabilitation of the "Native Areas" with a view to developing within them a social structure in keeping with the culture of "the Native" and based upon effective socio-economic planning'. Verwoerd, who was his minister of 'native affairs', wanted a different kind of separation.

The epitome of a 'social democrat' racist who believed Blacks were akin to children and could only evolve through the 'guidance' of a white and according to white rules, he wanted 'tribal nations' within a Republic. And so when he became Prime Minister in 1958, Verwoerd set aside much of the Tomlinson Report.

He wanted South Africa's internal borders redrawn.

Thus, the Group Areas Act – under which the regime steadily and violently removed people from 'Black spots' where it believed white people, only, deserved to be living – was instituted apace. By the 1970s, the bantustans and 'influx control' – which decided where Black labour was needed and where not – had been crafted, and Black people banished from the rest of (white) South Africa.

This was wide-scale violent dispossession, with one of the first communities to stage a rural resistance being in Witsieshoek, on the border between Free State and Lesotho, where arable land was being removed from peasants. It had been a contested area for 100 years, having been 'granted' to the Mopeli community after it was annexed by the Boers in the mid-1800s.

Among the early resisters there were Treaty Mahlouoe Mopeli and her husband, and traditional leader Chief Paulus Howell Mopeli. Treaty Mopeli was issued with an order by the Native Affairs

Department in 1954 that banished her to Uitkyk Farm No. 92 in the Groblersdal district in what is now Limpopo Province, where she was 'generously allowed' to join Paulus, who had been banished there already.

It takes nearly six hours to drive from Witsieshoek to Groblersdal in a car today on a freeway. It could have taken a day or two to do the same distance in the 1950s without a personal car. Thus, the intention was of course to effectively separate the Mopelis from their community and their place of birth.

Nonetheless, opposition to state interventions continued even as Treaty Mopeli was identified as a leader of the 'agitators' and sent away. She and Paulus were not specifically restricted to the Uitkyk farm itself, and it was alleged the couple used this slender freedom of movement to garner support for anti-government activities in Groblersdal too, with 'left-leaning' people arriving at their humble home at night.

It was then argued in the 'general public's interest' that they be removed from Groblersdal to somewhere even more rural where their influence could be further dampened. As so the Mopelis were banished to Frenchdale Native Trust Farm in the Mafeking District in what is now the North West Province in 1957 (another six-and-a-half hour journey by car from Witsieshoek on a freeway today). That, too, failed to dim their activism, and Treaty would finally be banished to Ewbank Farm in the Kuruman district in the Northern Cape, some seven to eight hours from Witsieshoek by car today.

Her banishment order was only withdrawn in July 1972.

The Mopelis' story would be replicated in thousands and millions of cases around the country as people were driven to abandon their physical histories and sent scattering off their land into inhospitable territories often far away.

The apartheid regime would eventually segue Witsieshoek into the bantustan of QwaQwa, a 'territorial authority for the Basotho'.

Outstanding writing on this period is in Professor Salim Badat's book, *The Forgotten People: Political Banishment under Apartheid*.

In 1952, the state's attention was turned to the Bo-Kaap area of Cape Town, which was declared 'Malay' under the Group Areas Act. The people allowed to live there had to be descendants of the slaves brought from Malaysia to service the Dutch in the 17th-century, and would otherwise be classified Coloured. Many former slaves and succeeding generations went on to establish businesses in Cape Town, and there is still a strong Malay influence in the city even as the people's slave roots are muted in a democratic state.

Under the South African Constitution of 1996, everyone who is not white is designated Black.

Forced removals continued as apartheid took hold of every aspect of South African life.

There was a similar assault on Sophiatown, Johannesburg in 1955 to that in other suburbs, towns and cities, although this one seized more of an emotional and political spotlight for the fact that many residents were artists, writers and musicians. More than 60 000 Black people had to concede their property there to their white neighbours, who were then suddenly living in a place cynically renamed Triomf ('triumph').

The same would happen in what is now the Fordsburg area in Johannesburg – a majority Indian and Muslim community. Fietas, as it was popularly known, is one of the city's oldest communities and was one of the first that was 'multi-racial'. Boer leader Paul Kruger gave it that status back in 1893, although some blocks of streets were 'white' and others 'Black'.

So it went on: Sea Point in Cape Town was declared 'whites-only'; Black people classified Coloured living in King William's Town in the Eastern Cape were moved to the township of Schornville, and Black residents of Lady Selborne in the centre of Pretoria were 'relocated' to outlying townships Ga-Rankuwa, Atteridgeville and Mamelodi while Indians were sent to Laudium and Coloureds to Eersterust, both some 30 minutes away by car today from Lady Selborne.

By the early 1960s, the Bantu administration and development ministry had calculated that there were about 350 'Black spots', mostly in Natal, that would still have to be dealt with.

Transkei fell first to the sword of the bantustan policy, three years before District Six in central Cape Town was declared a 'white' area. With the Bantu Homelands Constitution Act in place by 1971, the government could allocate 'self-governing' status and effectively began to strip Blacks of their South African citizenship – a right to live freely in their own country.

The ANC declared war on land dispossession from exile in 1967 where its key National Consultative Conference at Morogoro, Tanzania had raged at 'land barons, absentee landlords, big companies and state capitalist enterprises'. Its view was that 'the land and property stolen' should be 'confiscated' from these agents of the racist state and 'redistributed to small farmers, peasants and landless people of all races'. Yet the ANC of 2020 was still battling to achieve that primary revolutionary objective.

While there is a greater concentration of land and property owned by Blacks today, the devastating impacts of the Land Act of 1913 and apartheid are alive. After 1913, only 7% of arable land was in the hands of so-called 'Africans' as white rulers set in place the territorial segregation envisaged even by the Union – British and Boers governing different pockets of 'conquered' land – in 1910.

By 1977, the year Biko was murdered and BC quelled through a slew of bannings, land dispossession was a fact of South African life.

Bophuthatswana was granted 'self-governing' status and became a dusty scene of disparate lives, most closely compared with how Palestinians are torn apart, living in distinct areas separated by the occupier, Israel. (Some live in the West Bank bordered by Jordan and others in the Gaza Strip, bordered by Egypt, with between 93 and 114km of Israel between them.)

In the same way that Israel has broken international law through its people living as settlers in the West Bank and keeping Gaza in a prison-like grip, the apartheid state would shift and move its own defined borders, for instance 'ceding' 25 hectares of land near Thaba Nchu to the 'self-governing' Bophuthatswana, which in turn 'agreed' to cede 25 000 hectares of land to South Africa in the Northern Cape.

This catastrophic pretence around land destroyed millions of Black families and disintegrated Black children's lives, creating fractures over generations. Ordinary people often had no choice but to be land activists.

Against the backdrop of extreme anti-Black legislation, organisations such as the Black Sash, the Transvaal Rural Action

Committee, the Action Committee to Stop Eviction (ACTSTOP), the National Committee Against Removals, the Rural Women's Movement and the Surplus Peoples Project, formed in Crossroads, Cape Town, saw people risk their lives and their existing homes to protest evictions.

Despairingly, anti-Blackness on land issues continued in democratic South Africa even though the ANC-led government no longer had the legislation to protect it by name.

Pro-poor organisations have carried on the brave work of their predecessors during apartheid.

In terms of sheer will, the Bakwena ba Mogopa in Bethanie, North West, are an example of a community that stood up to power, refusing in 1984 to bow to an order to evacuate their land to make way for the apartheid-era South African Defence Force, and refusing again in 2012 to allow the prodigious greed of capital to steal their income from the riches below their feet.

Its history stretching back to when it was part of the Kwena tribe, which migrated from East Africa to southern Africa (see *Mountains of Spirit: The Story of the Royal Bakwena ba Mogopa of the North West, South Africa*, a book by associate professor Freddy Samuel Khunou of the North West University), the Bakwena ba Mogopa had an institutionalised resilience, which saw it win a court interdict in 1984, finally giving it the right to stay put in 1989.

Yet the community remains embattled over land, with former Public Protector Thuli Madonsela having to investigate claims in the 2000s by the Bakwena ba Mogopa and Bapo ba Mogale that they were denied millions of rand in mining royalties owed long after the ANC took power.

This is another cogent area of land fraud in the democratic era – where poor communities are all but robbed through sweetheart deals between government and mining companies. These may be massaged into place by traditional councils and royal families.

In the case of the Bakwena ba Mogopa and Bapo ba Mogale – who occupy land in the Madibeng district between Hartbeespoort and Brits outside Pretoria – there were allegations of fraud, mismanagement and corruption over the proceeds of vast deposits of platinum, vanadium and other minerals. The land upon which the communities live is estimated to have a yield worth more than R10 billion. But heavily invested multinationals owned mining or prospecting rights, thanks to favourable government 'controls'.

Although the North West Traditional Leadership and Governance Act said there was indeed income due to the 'tribal' communities, and that those dues were to be deposited into a bank account managed by the provincial government, the communities said this had not happened as it should.

In 2012, Hugh Eiser, lawyer for the Bapo ba Mogale Traditional Council, was reported in *City Press* newspaper saying: 'The premier [who is the legal custodian of the income], the Member of the Executive Council [or MEC] and the North West officials have done as they pleased with the community's money, while the community, which owns the money, is kept in the dark.'

This is not a rare occurrence in South Africa today in terms of land and the potential it should reap for its righteous recipients.

We again remember that fateful first clause in the Freedom Charter which, while selectively teased into shape by politicians, is not always followed to the letter where there are untold fortunes to be made.

Champion for land justice during the apartheid era, Judge Richard Goldstone – who later also investigated Israeli incursions into Gaza in 2008 on behalf of the UN – made a ruling in the early 1980s that, just because a person had not 'obeyed' the Group Areas Act, they could not simply be evicted. Instead, the onus lay on government to present those threatened by eviction with alternative accommodation.

That ruling around property and land dogged the ANC-led government, which – even if it might prefer to do so in the interests of capital – cannot throw people onto the streets or to the elements without presenting them with a viable housing option. (Private citizens are not subject to the same ruling.)

ACTSTOP was still representing the landless poor in the 1990s when it fought for fair settlements between robber landlords, the authorities and both itinerant and settled tenants in inner cities, particularly in Johannesburg.

Where the battle for land had once been mostly isolated in the rural areas, it intensified in urban areas in the democratic era, particularly in informal settlements and slums on the periphery of business districts and suburbs.

The ANC held its ground on land in the days when it was negotiating a power deal with the National Party. For instance, it wouldn't agree to the terms of the White Paper on Land drafted by the National Party in 1991, insisting it would accept nothing less than the 'restoration of land' for any policy 'to be credible'.

While acknowledging seizure of property 'for public purposes', subject to compensation, the National Party argued that the restoration of land was 'not feasible'. So the ANC's Land Commission held a national conference to develop guidelines itself.

That conference rejected the constitutional protection of property rights, and proposed a 'wealth tax' as a way of financing land redistribution. But in 1992 the World Bank published its *Options for Land Reform and Rural Structuring* and pushed for the 'willing buyer, willing seller' framework. The Bank was firmly against expropriation or nationalisation and, gradually, the political environment of land – which had once seemed so conducive to supporting the peasantry, the poor and a future in which the land 'belonged to all who live in it' – started to shift.

A Land Charter was launched in 1993 at a Community Land Conference. It demanded expropriation at the same time as the PAC was releasing its policy proposing to abolish the existing system of private ownership and the transfer through private transactions.

The heady early days of democracy saw delighted events, such as the contested farm of Doornkop outside the coal-mining town of Middelburg in Mpumalanga being handed back to the community dispossessed of it in 1974.

But decades later, that joy had been transformed into an unhappy saga involving the ANC's political rival, the DA, as 284 families – whose land was given back to them in a ceremony by Nelson Mandela 20 years before – were battling land invasions.

Sowetan newspaper reported that these had already cost the community a desperate 90% of their 850-hectare land as more than 3 000 people invaded.

The local DA ward councillor, invaders and a traditional leader were drawn into allegations of a conspiracy to sell plots, which had led to the mushrooming of shacks in the area.

And so, there is yet another punishing twist in the unending story of the struggle for the land.

[McKenzie, 2018; Khunou, 2016; Badat, 2012; www.documents.worldbank.org, 1992; Gerhart & Glaser, 2010; www.gov.za, 2012; NA, 2012: This site traces the origins of the case involving the Bakwena ba Mogopa and Bapo ba Mogale communities' claims against government officials involving their mining royalties; Government of South Africa, 2012; Sifile, 2014; www.nelsonmandela.org; www.sahistory.org.za]

The South African laws on land

Section 25 of the Constitution: Property

No one can have their property taken away unless this is done according to law. Government must take other steps to help people or communities to get land to live on, and to claim back land if they lost it after 1913 because of an apartheid law.

If a person has been living on land, which they were not allowed to own because of apartheid laws, they will be able to own this land or paid compensation for it.

[www.gov.za/constitution, 1996]

Section 26 of the Constitution: Housing

Everyone has the right of access to adequate housing. The government must take reasonable steps to provide people with this access 'within its available resources'. In other words, government has a duty to provide what it can afford. No one can be evicted from their home or have their home demolished unless a court has heard their case.

[www.gov.za/constitution, 1996]

Confiscation of land without reimbursement

South Africa's government laid out conditions on 11 October 2020, saying a new law submitted to Parliament would pass Constitutional muster allowing land to be confiscated without reimbursement in certain cases if it is unused, abandoned or poses a safety risk.

Compensation would also be possible, and final decisions would be in the hands of the courts.

The bill did not outline circumstances when it may be just and equitable for nil compensation to be paid. It did not prescribe that nil compensation would be paid in all circumstances.

The ANC started a parliamentary process in 2019 to amend the Constitution to make it clear that land could be expropriated without compensation.

Reuters reported that 'Critics on the Left say the ANC has been too timid in redistributing land, while opponents on the right worry that measures seen as confiscatory might frighten away investors'.

'Under the new law, the authorities would be required to negotiate with the owners of land to try to reach an agreement on the acquisition of the property, before it can be seized.'

[Reuters, 2020: https://www.moneyweb.co.za/news-fast-news/sa-lays-out-conditions-to-seize-land]

'They don't know the pain of being landless': Julius Malema and the EFF

Commander-in-Chief (CIC) of the EFF Malema is the most dominant voice in South African politics calling for the amendment of the Constitution to allow the expropriation of land without compensation. Land has been the most incendiary cause of the revolutionary young political party, which practises an ideological hybrid of scientific socialism and BC.

The ANC was once the mother party for its militants, including Malema and deputy president Floyd Shivambu, who were leaders of the ANCYL before being expelled. The ruling party has consistently rejected the EFF's position as 'unconstitutional'. But Malema is unrelenting.

He calls on Blacks to 'unite' on this issue. He says the Constitution has to be amended as it has not been able to serve all the needs of a 'conquered nation', particularly in terms of land.

The founding provisions on property and housing in the Constitution can only be amended with the support of 75% of the members of the National Assembly, while the rest of the Constitution can be amended with the support of two thirds of the members of the National Assembly. The Constitution has been amended more than a dozen times, mostly on technicalities, since 1996.

The EFF's unflagging view on land is that Black people's rights were 'sold out' during the Convention for a Democratic South Africa (CODESA). Malema says the EFF regards the land issue as 'a fundamental principle, which constituted the struggle against colonialism'.

'So those who claim to be radical enough and who want radical change today should actually be in the forefront of agreeing that this Constitution must be changed to make it possible for our people to own the land,' he told *The Citizen* newspaper in February 2017.

'Those people who own the land happen to be in an acceptable language ... private people like individuals, trusts and companies. But when you search deep as to who are these people, these are white people who are still owning our land.

'We remain a conquered nation even when we claim to have democracy. We remain a conquered nation because white monopoly capital still owns the means of production, and at the centre of that is the land question.

'Black people ... all of us,' he says, 'need to unite and amend the Constitution so that we can expropriate land without compensation. There's no white person who will understand that clarion call because they don't know the pain of being landless.'

The ANC claimed in response in 2017 that the EFF – which advances radical economic theory – 'used' the issue of the expropriation of land for its own 'purpose and interest'.

Malema's determination to see the Constitution amended extended to his offering the ANC the EFF's 6% representation in Parliament to add to the ruling party's 62% to acquire the required two-thirds.

He raised the gambit in the National Assembly in February 2017. 'If you vote against this,' he said, wearing the customary red garb of his 'Fighters' [supporters of the EFF] while those around him rocked the signature red beret of Thomas Sankara, 'it's a waste of time.'

'We are already giving our people the land and we are not ashamed. People of South Africa, where you see a beautiful land, take it, it belongs to you.'

The following month, Malema and the EFF were interdicted by the High Court in Pretoria from inciting people to illegally occupy land. Afrikaner lobbyists AfriSake and AfriForum brought the interdict. Malema and the EFF were ordered 'not to incite, instigate, command or procure any individuals to commit the crime of trespassing or to enter any land without the permission of the owners or lawful occupiers of the land'.

The party – which had, indeed, publicly called upon its members to occupy land illegally – had been issuing warnings since 2016 that it would redistribute land – and the ANC had only one apartheid-era law left on its books to try to counteract the *enfant terrible* of South African politics: the Riotous Assemblies Act. So it exercised its right to use that in both the town of Newcastle in KwaZulu-Natal and the city of Bloemfontein, Free State, where Malema had made the calls.

But the charges would take time as the CIC – who declared the land 'was taken by white people through genocide' – made an application to the court himself to have the apartheid act declared unconstitutional and unlawful. And indeed in November 2020, the Constitutional Court found it was inconsistent with freedom of expression, and invalid insofar as it criminalised the incitement of a person to commit an offence.

Meanwhile, the EFF has been relentless in its care to situate it within its supporters' mandate. It entered South African politics in 2014 on an antiracism Black ticket, despite it not declaring an ideology which fitted squarely within the BCM tradition.

It also remains supportive of the Freedom Charter, and therefore potentially holds contrary positions to BC in orientation. Nonetheless, the EFF has used the acceptance of BC within Black communities to criticise the ANC's inability to overcome its neo-liberalism. The

ANC's economic position has indeed led to inertia – strategic or not – in pro-poor policymaking.

The party has stated that 'the EFF believes anti-Black racism must be condemned in all its manifestations, even on the picket lines and marches. Anti-Black racism has no place in our country... That white racists still exist 23 years into democracy, brave enough to publicise their racism on social media platforms or picket lines of protests and marches, is itself a sign of the failure of this government to deal with white superiority and the privilege that sustains it'.

'The ANC, as a liberation movement, should have transformed all the socio-economic conditions that sustain the imagination white people have that they are superior to Blacks. However, they spend more time protecting and promoting corruption and lawbreakers than delivering on the mandate of decolonisation.'

[Mathebula, 2017; www.economicfreedomfighters.org]

'The poorest of the poor will gather once again': Abahlali baseMjondolo (AbM)

The AbM movement convened for its annual Unfreedom Day event on 27 April 2017. While the privileged few within the country celebrated the day as National Freedom Day, it wrote a letter online, explaining why it does not.

'We, the impoverished, the marginalised and the oppressed, will [today] be mourning the absence of this freedom that our mothers and fathers fought for so hard.

'We say that as long as we are still landless, homeless and impoverished, we cannot say we are free. As long as we are subjected to floods and shack fires, we cannot say that we are free.

'As long we are not recognised as human beings, and for as long as our lives do not matter to the politicians and the government, we cannot say that we are free.

'As long as we face assault and eviction when we occupy land and arrest, assault, torture, imprisonment and assassination when we organise independently, we cannot say that we are free.'

A contemporary symbol of the ongoing struggle for land in South Africa, AbM represents mainly Black workers, impoverished Black communities and African migrants – a population 'that freed political prisoners and allowed exiles to return home'. It cites disturbing figures, that 'more than 50% of unemployed people are living in shacks. The politicians are free. We remain in a state of deep unfreedom.'

Using the mottos 'Land. Housing. Dignity' and 'Occupy. Resist. Develop', the movement has been a target of what appears to be state-sanctioned violence, with dozens of its members living in fear or brutally attacked, often through police action, and increasing numbers have been murdered under mysterious circumstances.

Among the dead is Thuli Ndlovu, the AbM chairperson in KwaNdengezi, a township in Durban. She was assassinated in September 2014 when an armed man burst into her home while she was watching TV and shot her seven times. She died on the scene.

Also partial to the Sankara-style red beret, the movement's army of activists have stated their commitment to 'putting the social value of land before its commercial value'.

'We are committed to land reform from below. It needed courage. It needed the ability to move from the land, into the streets and the courts. We are proud that we have been able to occupy land and build our own homes and develop our own communities for our own families.'

[www.abahlali.org]

The bird that tweeted: Corruption flies

The Sankofa bird is an enchantment. The word itself is taken from the Twi language of Ghana, translated as 'go back and get it'. The creature itself is always pictured with its head turned backwards, taking an egg off its back. The bird image is often associated with the Ghanaian proverb, 'It is not wrong to go back for that which you have forgotten'.

The Black First Land First (BLF) movement has made use of the charmed Sankofa bird in its own symbology. To its champions, this would be a positive stance. Never give up. Be honest about your failings. Pick up the pieces. To its detractors, the bird would be a cawing reminder of persistent errors in judgement. Certainly, you can return to your mistakes. But so many?

In the febrile rush of South African politics two decades into ANC rule, land for the Black majority was a sure lance with which to pierce the mettle of the ruling party.

Land and housing have been the slowest aspect of South African 'transformation', and the most problematic, underscored by massive corruption in the construction and land allocation sectors, under-delivery of dwellings for the poor, low-quality building materials, long waits punctuated by illegal invasions, fraudulent tenders and a nagging doubt that the former liberation movement will ever be able to properly accommodate all its Black citizens, never mind the increasing numbers of asylum-seekers and migrants who arrive mostly from other African countries in their numbers every day .

Landless communities require their issues to reverberate across the floor of government, and it seemed for a short time after BLF made a revolutionary call in 2015 that it might indeed establish a radical agenda that could shake up a dormant politics around the subject.

Its leader, former columnist, analyst and left-wing activist Mngxitama, had just left the EFF with which he had been associated since 2013. It was an acrimonious split, and Mngxitama had had to give up his lucrative job as a party MP.

But there were those within the National Assembly who would have been quietly relieved that the fatal fight was had inside the EFF, and that they no longer had to contend with Mngxitama's 'revolutionary socialism', particularly in the Parliamentary Committee on Rural Development and Land Reform, upon which he served.

The rumours fell fierce. Some said Malema had been encouraged to 'get rid' of Mngxitama by allies within the ANC, who felt Mngxitama was a liability. This was denied, although Mngxitama sought support for the claim that the EFF was still 'too close' to, or even a revolutionary proxy for, the ANC, and would not be able to live up to its own radical politics around land.

As the mire deepened, actual land issues were receiving scant press. Mngxitama was, however, drawing the spotlight for individual acts of 'resistance', including occupying the Public Protector's office over the CIEX Report, commissioned by the post-democracy South African government of a British company which specialised in high-level 'recoveries'.

The aim was to see the South African fiscus refunded monies due to it that were lost during illicit apartheid-era looting – but 'the aim' was not necessarily as benevolent as it might have sounded on paper. There were political and finance players from all sides all over its show.

The 52-page document was drawn up in 1999 by Michael Oatley, a former British operative and founder of CIEX.

The report would keep Mngxitama seen and heard for some time, predominantly on the ANN7 TV news channel – a tool of the controversial immigrant Gupta business family which, it is alleged, were actors behind the scenes of massive corruption during nearly two successive Jacob Zuma administrations (lasting from 2009 to 2018).

In mid-2017, a spurious company named Lodidox – owned by a former ANC government spin-doctor and Mngxitama's fellow ANN7 political 'pundit', Mzwanele (formerly 'Jimmy') Manyi – bought shares in the Gupta brothers' media companies from Oakbay, the holding company for the Gupta family's businesses in South Africa. This sale was widely reported on, with *Times Live* writing: 'The Gupta family's Oakbay sold its shares in the media companies to Lodidox in a vendor-financed deal – it lent Lodidox the purchase price'.

'Lodidox appears to be a shelf company. It was inactive from its establishment in 2012 until Manyi became its sole director in June [2017].'

The CIEX Report – which sought to lay bare a 'quantity of theft' by white Afrikaner capital, and state collusion during the dying days of the apartheid regime – at first caught on like petrol to a flame. It would form the basis for 'state capture' counter-allegations, which conjured a front-of-centre place for the BLF even as fury grew around the country towards the Gupta family and its seemingly kleptocratic association with Zuma.

Mngxitama was quickly linked to the 'paid Twitter' scandal that would soon explode around conservative London public relations machine, the Bell Pottinger agency, which was paid by the Guptas to stoke racism and create a miasma of confusion in South Africa around 'hegemonic white capital'. Yet it later became clear this was a red herring – likely sought as a distraction for the Guptas from their own excesses. Bell Pottinger was stripped of its membership of the UK's Public Relations and Communications Association after a disciplinary committee upheld a complaint lodged against it by South African opposition party, the Democratic Alliance. It has since collapsed, with serious consequences for its partners.

Throughout the Gupta scandal – which helped destroy the South African economy – the BLF did its damnedest to get headlines for anti-Black racism through street protests, brawls and perilous warnings to white journalists who investigated or commented on the Guptas.

BC was a persistent veil. The authentic landless poor were meanwhile largely excluded from those demonstrations and statements.

The BLF's detractors wondered when it would properly dig its shovels into the soil of the people. Would these agents of seeming corruption ever live out the profound values of BC which they so robustly proffered? In what appeared a denial of the values of their esteemed intellectual and political foremothers and fathers in the BCM, that manifestation was not to be.

The BLF registered as a political party to contest elections on a Black ticket, but in early 2019, the conservative, predominantly white Freedom Front Plus party appealed to see the BLF deregistered by the Electoral Commission of South Africa (IEC). The IEC then officially annulled the party's registration for its violation of the Electoral Act which prohibits limiting membership on the basis of race.

An Electoral Court dismissed the BLF's appeal and upheld an earlier ruling that the organisation could not be regarded as a political party.

By the end of 2019, the BLF had decided to amend its constitution to allow whites to be members, stating this was to facilitate its re-admittance by the IEC.

Mngxitama, who supports expropriation without compensation of white-owned land, which he says was stolen from Africans, penned the organisation's Revolutionary Call of 2015 in which it stated that 'without land, there is no freedom or dignity. We want "Land First" because it is the basis of our freedom, our identity, our spiritual well-being, our economic development and culture.'

'The land of Africans was stolen and this theft has rendered us landless in our own land. We want all the land with all of its endowments on its surface together with all the fortunes underground as well as the sky. All of it belongs to us! We are a people crying for our stolen land! Now we have decided to get it back by any means necessary [without regard to famine, bloodshed or deteriorating as Zimbabwe did] as our spiritual well-being demands it.'

The BLF's 'code of dealing with house negroes and sell outs' was a guide for members to 'defend Black people they differ with who come under attack from white supremacy'.

In 2018, Mngxitama's Twitter account was suspended for seven days over 'kill whites' threats he tweeted, with some calling for him to be prosecuted for hate speech. He soon deleted a video he had posted on Twitter saying he would 'kill five white people for every Black person killed in the taxi industry'.

Mngxitama told *The Citizen* newspaper he had been 'speaking in the context of "self-defence"'.

'White people have convinced themselves that they can unleash violence upon Blacks and Blacks have no right to fight back. Fighting back is considered a violation of the sanctity of whiteness… Whites believe we have no right to self defence.'

[Quintal & Child 2017; www.parliament.gov.za; Hosken, 2017; www.blf.org.za; citizen.co.za]

Black Lives Matter, the NDN Collective and the LANDBACK campaign

The global network of Black Lives Matter used the occasion of Indigenous Peoples Day on 12 October 2020 to call for justice for Indigenous communities in the US, saying previous cries had 'been ignored by the voices at the top who refuse to acknowledge [their] value and beauty, as well as [their] pain and concerns'.

It released a statement in solidarity with its Indigenous allies, saying, 'We must reject any efforts of those who fight to erase the true history of Indigenous communities', and urging its own supporters to 'begin with educating ourselves'.

'This country's monuments are built on stolen land. The national tourist destination known as Mount Rushmore was originally known as Paha Sapa[120] by the Lakota people and is in their sacred lands, the Black Hills.

'This is unceded, sacred territory of the Oceti Sakowin – Seven Council Fires[121] – that the Lakota belong to. In 1868, the US government signed the Fort Laramie Treaty[122] with the Oceti Sakowin, but stole it just eight years later to satisfy the greed of miners and European settlers.

'In 1941, Paha Sapa was further vandalised by a Ku Klux Klan member who sculpted the faces of four presidents into the side of Paha Sapa. Presidents who were racists, slave owners and colonisers who, while ushering in improvements for the white majority, brought grave harm to Black and Indigenous people.

'This nation, by tearing apart Indigenous land, promoted white supremacy in its highest form which continues to this day. We must all recognise that in our fight to achieve Black liberation, we must be in solidarity with Indigenous communities... When we fight for justice, we must fight for justice for all BIPOC [Black, Indigenous and People of Color] communities.'

Black Lives Matter is a supporter of the NDN Collective, an 'Indigenous-led organisation dedicated to building Indigenous power through ... activism, philanthropy ... narrative change, decolonisation ... [and] Indigenous self-determination'.

The NDN Collective[123] also launched the LANDBACK Campaign,

---

120   The Lakota Sioux consider the Black Hills ('Hesapa' or 'Paha Sapa' in the Lakota language) the centre of their universe where their culture began.

121   The Oceti Sakowin, known to some as the Sioux Nation, is a confederacy of Native Nations that speak three dialects of the same language: the Dakota, Nakota and Lakota.

122   The Treaty of Fort Laramie (or the Sioux Treaty) of 1868 was an agreement between bands of the Lakota people, Yanktonai Dakota and the Arapaho Nation, establishing the Great Sioux Reservation and additional lands as 'unceded Indian territory' in South Dakota, Wyoming, Nebraska and possibly Montana. The US government unilaterally annexed native land protected under the treaty in 1877. In 1980, the US Supreme Court ruled for compensation plus interest, but the Sioux refused the payment, demanding the return of their land.

123   NDN is the abbreviation for Native Indian.

'a multi-pronged effort to dismantle white supremacy and achieve justice for Indigenous people through the restoration of ecological health to Indigenous lands and the ... recovery of Indigenous land ownership' on 12 October 2020.

'We are on the verge of what could be a revolutionary moment,' said Krystal Two Bulls, LANDBACK Campaign director. 'As systems of colonisation, oppression and white supremacy start to become dismantled, getting Indigenous lands back into Indigenous hands is necessary.

'Truth is, that all systems and institutions of oppression that uphold white supremacy were built on top of stolen land by stolen people; so to truly achieve racial justice and move into a revolutionary moment, we have to talk about how racial injustice on this continent began with settler colonialism, the theft of Indigenous lands, and the genocide of Indigenous people.'

The NDN Collective announced the development of the LANDBACK campaign on social media in August 2020, its activism 'catalysed by the powerful stand taken by Land Defenders[124] on 3 July 2020 as Donald Trump made his way to Mount Rushmore in Hesapa, the sacred Black Hills, for his highly controversial Fourth of July event'.

Land Defenders blocked the road to Mount Rushmore and stopped traffic for nearly three hours in the lead up to the event, with 21 ultimately arrested, including Two Bulls and NDN Collective President and CEO, Nick Tilsen.

'Mount Rushmore is an international symbol of white supremacy, and as people across America rightfully pull down statues of white supremacy, we have to look long and hard at how this national monument in the Black Hills upholds and maintains white supremacy on Indigenous lands,' Tilsen said.

Among other land campaigns were calls to change Columbus Day to Indigenous Peoples' Day and to plan continued LANDBACK

---

124   A Land Defender is an activist usually belonging to an Indigenous community in North America. Land Defenders do not consider themselves protesters, but as performing a sacred duty through non-violent resistance to activities that endanger land considered sacred. It is a duty to honour ancestors, current people and future generations.

actions to support Indigenous struggles around the world.

Conor Varela Handley, LANDBACK Campaign organiser, explained: 'We are living in an era of unprecedented environmental change and destruction, where Indigenous Peoples worldwide continue to caretake a large portion of the Earth's remaining biodiversity and carbon sinks. Returning land to Indigenous hands is the quickest, most effective form of environmental protection and climate action.'

In December 2020, US president-elect Joe Biden chose congresswoman Deb Haaland as the first Indigenous person to be interior secretary – a key role in terms of Native Indian affairs. Haaland, a member of the Laguna Pueblo, was quoted by the BBC as saying to the *New York Times*, 'It would be an honour to ... help repair the government-to-government relationship with Tribes that the Trump Administration has ruined'.

[blacklivesmatter.com; www.landback.org; www.ndncollective.org; www.bbc.com]

Appendix

'Sure. There are a few good whites, just as much as there are a few bad Blacks.'

A paper produced by Steve Biko for a SASO Leadership Training Course December 1971

We have defined Blacks as those who are by law or tradition politically, economically and socially discriminated against as a group in the South African society and identifying themselves as a unit in the struggle towards the realisation of their aspirations.

This definition illustrates to us a number of things:

Being Black is not a matter of pigmentation – being Black is a reflection of a mental attitude. Merely by describing yourself as Black, you have started on a road towards emancipation, you have committed yourself to fight against all forces that seek to use your Blackness as a stamp that marks you out as a subservient being.

From the above observations therefore, we can see that the term Black is not necessarily all-inclusive, in other words, the fact that we are all not white does not necessarily mean that we are all Black. Non-whites do exist and will continue to exist for quite a long time. If one's aspiration is whiteness but his pigmentation makes attainment of this impossible, then that person is a non-white.

Any man who calls a white man *baas*, any man who serves in the police force or security branch is *ipso facto* a non-white. Black people – real Black people – are those who can manage to hold their heads high in defiance rather than willingly surrender their souls to the white man.

Briefly defined therefore, BC is in essence the realisation by the Black man of the need to rally together with his brothers around the cause of their oppression – the Blackness of their skin – and to operate as a group in order to rid themselves of the shackles that bind them to perpetual servitude.

It seeks to demonstrate the lie that Black is an aberration from the 'normal' which is white. It is a manifestation of a new realisation that, by seeking to run away from themselves and to emulate the white man, Blacks are insulting the intelligence of whoever created them Black. BC, therefore, takes cognisance of the deliberateness of God's plan in creating Black people Black. It seeks to infuse the Black community with a new-found pride in themselves, their efforts, their value systems, their culture, their religion and their outlook to life.

The interrelationship between the consciousness of the self and the emancipatory programme is of a paramount importance. Blacks no longer seek to reform the system because so doing implies acceptance of the major points around which the system revolves. Blacks are out to completely transform the system and to make of it what they wish.

Such a major undertaking can only be realised in an atmosphere where people are convinced of the truth inherent in their stand. Liberation, therefore, is of paramount importance in the concept of BC, for we cannot be conscious of ourselves and yet remain in bondage.

We want to attain the envisioned self, which is a free self.

The surge towards BC is a phenomenon that has manifested itself throughout the so-called Third World. There is no doubt that discrimination against the Black man the world over fetches its origin from the exploitative attitude of the white man. Colonisation of white countries by whites has throughout history resulted in nothing more sinister than mere cultural or geographical fusion at worst, or language bastardisation at best.

It is true that the history of weaker nations is shaped by bigger nations, but nowhere in the world today do we see whites exploiting whites on a scale even remotely similar to what is happening in South Africa. Hence, one is forced to conclude that it is not coincidence that Black people are exploited. It was a deliberate plan, which has culminated in even so-called Black independent countries not attaining any real independence.

With this background in mind we are forced, therefore, to believe that it is a case of haves against have-nots where whites have been deliberately made haves and Blacks have-nots. There is, for instance, no worker in the classical sense among whites in South Africa, for even the most downtrodden white worker still has a lot to lose if the system is change. He is protected against competition at work from the majority.

He has a vote and he uses it to return the Nationalist government to power because he sees them as the only people who, through job reservation laws, are bent on looking after his interests against competition with the 'Natives'.

It should therefore be accepted that analysis of our situation in terms of one's colour at once takes care of the greatest single determinant for political action – colour – while also validly describing the Blacks as the only real workers in South Africa.

It immediately kills all suggestions that there could ever be effective rapport between the real workers, Blacks, and the privileged white workers, since we have shown that the latter are the greatest supporters of the system.

True enough, the system has allowed so dangerous an anti-Black attitude to build up amongst whites who are economically nearest to the Blacks, that they demonstrate the distance between themselves and the Blacks by an exaggerated reactionary attitude towards Blacks.

Hence the greatest anti-Black feeling is to be found amongst the very poor whites whom Class Theory calls upon to be with Black workers in the struggle for emancipation. This is the kind of twisted logic that the BC approach seeks to eradicate.

In terms of the BC approach, we recognise the existence of one major force in South Africa: this is White Racism. It is the one force against which all of us are pitted. It works with unnerving totality, featuring both on the offensive and in our defence. Its greatest ally to date has been the refusal by us to progressively lose ourselves in a world of colourlessness and amorphous common humanity. Whites are deriving pleasure and security in entrenching white racism and further exploiting the minds and bodies of the unsuspecting Black masses.

Their agents are ever present amongst us, telling us that it is immoral to withdraw into a cocoon, that dialogue is the answer to our problem and that it is unfortunate that there is white racism in some quarters but you must see that things are changing .

These in fact are the greatest racists for they refuse to credit us any intelligence to know what we want.

Their intentions are obvious; they want to be barometers by which the rest of the white society can measure feelings in the Black world. This then is what makes us believe that white power presents itself as a totality, not only provoking us, but also controlling our response to the provocation. This is an important point to note because it is often missed by those who believe that there are a few good whites. Sure there are a few good whites just as much as there are a few bad Blacks.

However, what we are concerned with here is group attitudes and group politics. The exception does not make a lie of a rule – it merely substantiates it.

The overall analysis therefore, based on the Hegelian theory of dialectic materialism, is as follows. Since the thesis is white racism, there can only be one valid antithesis: a solid Black unity, to counterbalance the scale.

If South Africa is to be a land where Black and white live together in harmony without fear of group exploitation – that can only be when these two opposites have interplayed and produced a viable synthesis of ideas and *modus vivendi*. We can never wage any struggle without offering a strong counterpoint to the white racism that permeates our society so effectively.

One must immediately dispel the thought that BC is merely a methodology or a means towards an end. What BC seeks to do is to produce at the output end of the process real Black people who do not regard themselves as the appendages to white society.

This truth cannot be reserved.

We do not need to apologise for this because it is true that the white systems have produced throughout the world a number of people who are not aware that they too are people. Our adherence to values that we set for ourselves can also not be reversed because it will always be a lie to accept white values as necessarily the best.

The fact that a synthesis may be attained only relates to adherence to power politics. Someone, somewhere, along the line, will be forced to accept the truth, and here we believe that ours is the truth.

The future of South Africa in the case where Blacks adopt BC is the subject for concern especially among initiates. What do we do when we have attained our Consciousness? Do we propose to kick whites out?

I believe personally that the answers to these questions ought to be found in the SASO Policy Manifesto and in our analysis of the situation in South Africa. We have defined what we mean by true integration and the very fact that such a definition exists illustrates what our standpoint is.

In any case, we are much more concerned about what is happening now than with what will happen in the future. The future will always be shaped by the sequence of present-day events.

The importance of Black solidarity to the various segments of the Black community must not be understated. There have been in the past a lot of suggestions that there can be no viable unity amongst Blacks because they hold each other in contempt.

Coloureds despise Africans because, by their proximity to the Africans, they may lose the chances of assimilation into the white world. Africans despise the coloureds and Indians for a variety of reasons. Indians not only despise Africans, but in many instances also exploit the Africans in job and shop situations. All these stereotyped attitudes have led to mountainous inter-group suspicions amongst the Blacks.

What we should at all times look at is the fact that: We are all oppressed by the same system; and we are oppressed to varying degrees is a deliberate design to stratify us not only socially but also in terms of the enemy's aspirations. Therefore it is to be expected that in terms of the enemy's plan there must be this suspicion, and that if we are committed to the problem of emancipation to the same degree, it is part of our duty to bring to the Black people the deliberateness of the enemy's subjugation scheme.

That we should go on with our programme, attracting to it only committed people and not just those eager to see an equitable distribution of groups amongst our ranks. This is a game common amongst liberals.

The one criterion that must govern all our action is commitment.

Further implications of BC are to do with correcting false images of ourselves in terms of culture, education, religion, economics. The importance of this also must not be understated.

There is always an interplay between the history of people – the past, their faith in themselves and hopes for their future. We are aware of the terrible role played by our education and religion in creating amongst us a false understanding of ourselves. We must therefore work out schemes not only to correct this, but further to be our own authorities rather than wait to be interpreted by others.

Whites can only see us from the outside and, as such, can never extract and analyse the ethos in the Black community. In summary therefore, one need only refer this house to the SASO Policy Manifesto, which carries most of the salient points in the definition of the BC.

I wish to stress again the need for us to know very clearly what we mean by certain terms and what our understanding is when we talk of BC.

This speech was reproduced by AZAPO in 2001.

'The white Black men':
Onkgopotse Abram Tiro's graduation speech Turfloop, April 1972

Mr Chancellor, Mr Vice-Chancellor and gentlemen, allow me to start off by borrowing language from our Prime Minister, Mr Vorster.

Addressing the Afrikaanse Studentebond congress in June last year, Mr Vorster said: 'No Black man has landed in trouble for fighting for what is legally his.'

Although I don't know how far true this is, I make this statement my launch pad.

RD Brinsmead, an American lay preacher, says: 'He who withholds the truth or debars men from motives of its expediency is either a coward, a criminal or both.'

Therefore, Mr Chancellor, I will try as much as possible to say nothing else but the truth. And to me 'truth' means 'practical reality'. Addressing us on the occasion of the formal opening of this university Mr [Cedric] Phatudi, a Lebowa territorial authority officer, said that in as much as there is American education, there had to be Bantu Education.

Ladies and gentlemen, I am conscientiously bound to differ with him.

In America, there is nothing like Negro education, Red Indian education and white American education. They have American education common to all Americans. But in South Africa, we have Bantu Education, Indian education, Coloured education and European education. We do not have a system of education common to all South Africans. What is there in European education which is not good for the African? We want a system of education which is common to all South Africans.

In theory, Bantu Education gives our parents a say in our education but in practice the opposite is true. At this university [University Education Diploma], students are forced to study philosophy of education through the medium of Afrikaans.

When we want to know why, we are told that the senate has decided so. Apparently this senate is our parents.

Time and again I ask myself: How do Black lecturers contribute to the administration of this university? For if you look at all the committees, they are predominantly white if not completely white. Here and there one finds two or three Africans who, in the opinion of students, are white Black men.

We have a students' dean without duties. We feel that if it is in any way necessary to have a students' dean, we must elect our own dean. We know people who can represent us.

The Advisory Council is said to be representing our parents. How can it represent them when they have not elected it?

These people must of necessity please the man who appointed them.

This council consists of chiefs who have never been to university. How can they know the needs of students when they have not been subjected to the same conditions?

Those who have been to university have never studied Bantu Education. What authentic opinion can they express when they don't know how painful it is to study under a repugnant system of education? I wonder if this Advisory knows that a Black man has been most unceremoniously kicked out of the bookshop. Apparently, this is reserved for whites. According to this policy, Van Schaiks has no right to run a bookshop here.

A white member of the administration has been given the meat contract to supply the university – a Black university. Those who amorphously support the policy may say that there are no Black people to supply it. My answer to them is: Why are they not able to supply the university? What is the cause? Is it not conveniently done that they are not in a position to supply these commodities?

White students are given vacation jobs at this university when there are students who could not get their results due to outstanding fees. Why does the administration not give these jobs to these students? These white students have 11 universities where they can get vacation jobs. Does the administration expect me to get a vacation job at the University of Pretoria?

Right now, our parents have come all the way from their homes only to be locked outside. We are told that the hall is full. I do not accept the argument that there is no accommodation for them.

In 1970, when the administration wanted to accommodate everybody, a tent was put up and closed-circuit television was installed.

Front seats are given to people who cannot even cheer us. My father is seated there at the back.

My dear people, shall we ever get a fair deal in this land? The land of our fathers. The system is failing. It is failing because even those who recommended it strongly, as the only solution to racial problems in South Africa, fail to adhere to the letter and the spirit of the policy. According to the policy we expected Dr Eiselen to decline chancellorship in favour of a Black man. My dear parents, these are injustices no normal student can tolerate – no matter who he is and where he comes from.

In the light of what has been said above, the challenge to every Black graduate in this country lies in the fact that the guilt of all wrongful actions in South Africa, restriction without trial, repugnant legislation, expulsions from schools, rests on all those who do not actively dissociate themselves from and work for the eradication of the system breeding such evils.

To those who wholeheartedly support the policy of apartheid, I say: Do you think that the white minority can willingly commit political suicide by creating numerous states which might turn out to be hostile in the future?

We Black graduates, by virtue of our age and academic standing, are being called upon to bear greater responsibilities in the liberation of our people.

Our so-called leaders have become the bolts of the same machine which is crushing us as a nation. We have to go back to them and educate them. Times are changing and we should change with them.

The magic story of human achievement gives irrefutable proof that as soon as nationalism is awakened among the intelligentsia, it becomes the vanguard in the struggle against alien rule. Of what use will be your education; if it is not linked with the entire continent of Africa it is meaningless.

Remember that Mrs Suzman said, 'There is one thing which the minister cannot do: He cannot ban ideas from men's minds.'

In conclusion, Mr Chancellor, I say: Let the Lord be praised, for the day shall come when all shall be free to breathe the air of freedom which is theirs to breathe and, when the day shall have come, no man, no matter how many tanks he has, will reverse the course of events.

God bless you all.

About the Authors

Baldwin Ndaba is a political journalist for Independent Newspapers. He started working as a journalist in 1996 at the *Diamond Fields Advertiser* in Kimberley, where he won a special commendation in the annual Nat Nakasa Awards for courageous journalism. He earlier found his place in student liberation struggles, particularly as an actor and dramatist in youth productions in the Northern Cape.

Therese Owen misspent her youth in the Durban music scene, which consisted of punks, rastas, goths and rebels without a clue. She studied journalism at Durban Technikon and her love of music saw her become a music columnist for the *Sunday Tribune* and *Daily News*, and later, a national music writer for Independent Newspapers. She is now a full-time writer living in the rural area of KwaZulu-Natal.

Masego Panyane is a journalist but regards herself as a storyteller first. Passionate about the development of Black communities, her interests include the politics of race and gender. She was selected as a Hazelhurst Fellow by Independent Newspapers, where she worked as a national culture writer. She is now a communications specialist at the University of Pretoria.

Rabbie Serumula was the online editor at *Saturday Star* and *Sunday Independent*. The BA Communication Science graduate is a columnist, an award-winning spoken word artist and founding member of poetry trio Magnum Opus. He was a finalist in the Standard Bank Sikuvile Awards for Young Journalist, for story of the year and feature writing.

About the Authors

Janet Smith has been an editor and journalist, and won her first book-writing prize while at university. A Wits graduate, she's the award-winning writer of three young adult books, as well as co-author of *Hani: A Life Too Short*, *The Coming Revolution: Julius Malema and the Fight for Economic Freedom*, *The A to Z of South African Politics* and a contributor to *Not Your Weekend Special*, a collected volume on Brenda Fassie.

Paballo Thekiso, a photojournalist and videographer, worked for Independent Newspapers and was also published by Agence France Press, Africa Interactive, UNAIDS and the FAO, among other organisations. His pictures, which have won accolades, have been exhibited in Italy and Mozambique, as well as in South Africa. He is now also a church leader and involved in many initiatives that aim at uplifting the marginalised.

References

Adenekan, S (2008) 'Eskia Mphahlele', *The Guardian*, London, www.theguardian.com/theguardian/2008/nov/24/obituary-eskia-mphahlele-uncle-zeke

Akyeampong, EK & Gates, HL (eds) (2012) *Dictionary of African Biography*, Oxford University Press, London

Alexander, N (2012) 'The centrality of the language question in post- apartheid South Africa: Revisiting a perennial issue', *South African Journal of Science*, 108(9)

Ally N & Ally S (2008) 'Critical intellectualism: The role of Black Consciousness in reconfiguring the race-class problematic in South Africa', *Biko Lives!*, Palgrave Macmillan, New York, https://doi.org/10.1057/9780230613379_10

Amato, C (2020) 'Bishop Emeritus Rubin Phillip: The guerilla priest', https://mg.co.za/article/2020-02-23-bishop-emeritus-rubin-phillip-the-guerilla-priest/

Associated Press (2003) 'No trial of police in Biko case', https://www.latimes.com/archives/la-xpm-2003-oct-08-fg-safrica8-story.html

Athreya, A (2020) '"Enough is enough": When LeBron James and Dwayne Wade addressed racial injustice with a powerful speech', https://www.essentiallysports.com/nba-news-enough-is-enough-when-lebron-james-and-dwyane-wade-addressed-racial-injustice-with-a-powerful-speech-carmelo-anthony-chris-paul-los-angeles-lakers-miami-heat/

Badat, S (2012) *The Forgotten People: Political Banishment under Apartheid*, Jacana Media, Johannesburg

Baldwin-Ragaven, L, London, L & De Gruchy, J (1999) *An Ambulance of the Wrong Colour: Health Professionals, Human Rights and Ethics in South Africa*, Juta & Company Ltd, Pretoria

Balibar, É (2002a) *Three Concepts of Politics*, Verso Books, London/New York

Balibar, É (2002b) *Politics and the Other Scene*, Verso Books, London/New York

Baskin, J (1991) *Striking Back: A History of Cosatu*, Ravan Press, Johannesburg

BBC.com (2017) 'Civil rights activist Darcus Howe dies aged 74', www.bbc.com/news/uk-39473698'

BBC.com (2020) 'BTS Black Lives Matter: Fans match band's $1m donation', https://www.bbc.com/news/world-asia-52960617

Bessie Head Heritage Trust (2006) 'A brief sketch of the life of Bessie Head', www.thuto.org/bhead/html/biography/brief_biography .htm

Biko, S (1978) *I Write What I Like*, Pan Macmillan, Johannesburg

Bizos, G (1998) *No One to Blame? In Pursuit of Justice in South Africa*, David Philip/Mayibuye, Cape Town

Black Lives Matter (2020), 'Our co-founders', https://blacklivesmatter.com/our-co-founders/

Blake, J (2010) 'Why Sunday morning remains America's most segregated hour', https://religion.blogs.cnn.com/2010/10/06/why-sunday-morning-remains-americas-most-segregated-hour/

Blanchet, B (2020) 'Princeton professor talks about best-selling book on James Baldwin', https://www.dailygazette.com/2020/09/20/princeton-professor-talks-about-best-selling-book-on-james-baldwin/

BLF (2015) 'Black First Land First movement's preliminary report on apartheid-era corruption and other economic crimes', www.BlackIstlandIst.files.wordpress .com/2015/09/blf-report-on-white-corruption.pdf

Bloodaxe Books (2020) 'Notebook of a return to my native land', https://www.bloodaxebooks.com/ecs/product/notebook-of-a-return-to-my-native-land-392

Bond, P (2016) 'The harsh realities about South Africa that the World Bank dare not speak', *The Conversation*, www.theconversation.com/the-harsh-realities-about-south-africa-that-the-world-bank-dare-not-speak-54349

Bonner, P (2004) *The Soweto Uprisings of June 1976*, STE Publishers, Johannesburg

Boso, O (2016) 'Wits alumni tackles university fees', *Wits Vuvuzela*, www.witsvuvuzela.com/2016/04/07/wits-alumni-tackles-university-fees/

BotlokwaFM (ND) www.botlokwafm.co.za/history.php

Brown, KJ (2020) '10 Black poets of past and present who deserve unending recognition for their work', https://www.wellandgood.com/black-poets/

Brown, M (2013) 'Britain's Black power movement is at risk of being forgotten, say historians', *The Guardian*, www.theguardian.com/ world/2013/dec/27/britain-Black-power-movement-risk-forgotten- historians

Business Tech (2016) 'Rand vs the dollar: 1978–2016', https://businesstech.co.za/news/finance/116372/rand-vs-the-dollar-1978-2016/

Byrd, A & Tharps, LL (2014) 'When Black hair is against the rules', *The New York Times*, www.nytimes.com/2014/05/01/opinion/when-Black-hair-is-against-the-rules.html

Cabrita, J & Erland, N (2018) 'New histories of Christianity in South Africa: Review and introduction', University of Johannesburg, University of Cambridge, London, https://www.tandfonline.com/doi/full/10.1080/02582473.2018.1495753

Cade, M (2015) 'The Black feminist movement through music', https://www.atribecallednews.com/feministmovement-music/123

Cagnolari, V (2018) 'Miriam Makeba: "Come Back Africa"', https://pan-african-music.com/en/miriam-makeba-come-back-africa-2/

Chan, EY (2020) 'Why companies were so quick to endorse Black Lives Matter', https://theconversation.com/why-companies-were-so-quick-to-endorse-black-lives-matter-142532

Chaudhry, A (2020) 'Black K-Pop fans continue to face racism online', https://www.theverge.com/2020/7/24/21335831/kpop-racism-fans-black-lives-matter-harassment

Cloete, M (2016) 'Allan Boesak: Innocence and the struggle for humanity', *Scielo*, *Acta Theologica*, www.scielo.org.za/scielo.php?script=sci_arttext&pid=S1015-87582016000400003

Collins, C (1979) 'The birth of the Black Consciousness Movement in South Africa', *World Student Christian Federation Journal*, www.psimg.jstor.org/fsi/img/pdf/to/10.5555/al.sff.document.joa19790000.032.009.762_final.pdf

Collins, C (2012) 'Memoirs of a seeker', www.colincollins.com.au

Crosley Coker H (2014) 'What bell hooks really means when she calls Beyonce a "terrorist"', www.jezebel.com/what-bell-hooks-really-means-when-she-calls-beyonce-a-t-1573991834

Cutler, J (2020) 'Rev. Al Sharpton looks back, forward and at a nation at a crossroads', https://www.nydailynews.com/entertainment/ny-sharpton-crossroads-country-book-20200918-wn5gfhtgozbptpnuwmi7cqwnc4-story.html

Daily Sun (2017) www.dailysun.co.za/News/National/1976-interview-with-tsietsi-mashinini-20170614, [This website for *Daily Sun* newspaper, a News24 title, carried an excerpt from the now-famous interviews published when 1976 student hero Tsietsi Mashinini was still a 'fugitive' from apartheid 'justice' in 1976 and 1978. *Intercontinental Press*, a weekly news magazine produced on behalf of the Fourth International, a global grouping of Trotskyists that existed between 1963 and 1986, published the interviews. The magazine was founded as *World Outlook* in 1963 under the editorial direction of American Trotskyists Joseph Hansen, Pierre Frank and Reba Hansen, and *Intercontinental Press* held the transcripts of the conversations with Mashinini in its archives without a byline for the interviewer]

Daley, S (1997) 'The standards bearer', *The New York Times*, www.nytimes.com/1997/04/13/magazine/the-standards-bearer.html

De Gruchy, J & De Gruchy, S (2005) *The Church Struggle in South Africa*, Fortress Press, Minneapolis

Democracy Now! (2015) 'Vanguard of the revolution: The rise of the Black Panthers and the FBI's war against them', www.democracynow.org/2015/1/30/

vanguard_of_the_revolution_new_film

Desai, A (2013) 'Theatre of struggle: BC on Salisbury Island', *Journal of Natal and Zulu History*, 31(1): 101–16

Diamond Fields Advertiser (2011) 'A great voice for the liberation', www.pressreader.com/south-africa/diamond-fields-advertiser/20110506/281668251547032

Diome, F (2008) *The Belly of the Atlantic*, Profile Books, London http://disa.ukzn.ac.za/sites/default/files/pdf_files/Br1972.0376.4354.000.000.1972.7.pdf, [Digital Innovation South Africa (Disa) established this freely accessible online scholarly resource focusing on the socio-political history of South Africa, which was then purchased by Nzondelelo, an African organisation within the Methodist Church in KwaZulu-Natal. This site bears reference to Black Consciousness organisations within the Christian church during the 1960s and 1970s, in particular the Lay Ecumenical Centre]

Dixon, V (2014) 'Garveyism more relevant today than ever', *Jamaica Observer*, www.jamaicaobserver.com/columns/Garveyism-more-relevant-today-than-ever_17372084

Du Bois, WEB (originally 1899) *The Philadelphia Negro*, University of Pennsylvania Press, Philadelphia

Du Toit, D (1981) *Capital and Labour in South Africa: Class Struggles in the 1970s*, Routledge, London

EFF (2014) Media Release, www.economicfreedomfighters.org/eff-candidates-list-for-2014-general-elections/

Eide, M (2014) 'Stephen Biko and the torture aesthetic', *Ufahamu: A Journal of African Studies*, 38(1): 9–27, www.escholarship.org/uc/item/1854j3hz

Eilersen, GS (2007) *Bessie Head: Thunder Behind Her Ears: Her Life and Writing*, Wits University Press, Johannesburg

Epstein, J (1969) 'A special supplement: The trial of Bobby Seale', *The New York Review of Books*, www.nybooks.com/articles/1969/12/04/a-special-supplement-the-trial-of-bobby-seale/

Epstein, J (1971, now published online) 'The Panthers and the police: A pattern of genocide', *The New Yorker*, www.newyorker.com/magazine/1971/02/13/the-panthers-and-the-police-a-pattern-of- genocide

Essa, A (2020) 'Cornel West: Black Lives Matter and the fight against US empire are one and the same', https://www.middleeasteye.net/news/cornel-west-black-lives-matter-fight-us-empire

Fanon, F (1963) *The Wretched of the Earth*, Grove Press, New York

Fanon, F (1952) *Black Skin, White Masks*, Grove Press, New York

Fatton, R (1986) *Black Consciousness in South Africa: The Dialectics of Ideological Resistance to White Supremacy*, State University of New York Press, New York

Frederikse, J (1985) 'The most I can do is to be the least obstruction', transcript of interview with Gerhard Maré, South African History Archive, www.saha.org.za/nonracialism/transcript_of_ interview_with_gerhard_mar .htm [This is part 1 of 2 transcripts of an interview with Gerhard Maré conducted by Julie Frederikse in 1985 in Durban for her book *The Unbreakable Thread: Non-Racialism in South Africa*, originally published by Ravan Press in 1990. Maré was a founder member of the periodical *Work in Progress* in 1977 which was devoted to analysing South African political developments]

Frederikse, J (2015) *The Unbreakable Thread: Non-Racialism in South Africa*, South African History Archive, www.saha.org.za/publications/the_unbreakable_thread_non_racialism_in_south_africa .htm

Gagiano, A (2003), 'Lewis Nkosi as literary critic', in Stiebel, L & Gunner, L, eds, *Still Beating the Drum: Critical Perspectives on Lewis Nkosi*', www.sahistory.org.za/sites/default/files/file%20uploads%20/lindy_stiebel_editor_liz_gunner_editor_stilbook4me.org_.pdf

Gastrow, S (1985) *Who's Who in South African Politics*, Ravan Press, Johannesburg

Gerhart, GM & Glaser, CL (2010) *From Protest to Challenge: A Documentary History of African Politics in South Africa, 1882–1990, Challenge and Victory, 1980–1990*, Indiana University Press, Bloomington

Gqola, P (2009) 'Black women's bodies as battleground: Wayward sex and interracial rape as tropes', in Jackson, S, Demissie, F & Goodwin, M, eds, *Imagining, Writing, (Re)reading the Black Body*, Unisa Press, Pretoria

Gqola, P (2010) *What is Slavery to Me? Postcolonial/Slave Memory in Post-apartheid South Africa*, Wits University Press, Johannesburg

Gqola, P (2013) *A Renegade Called Simphiwe*, MF Books Joburg, Johannesburg

Gqola P (2013) 'Contradictory locations: Black women and the discourse of the Black Consciousness Movement in South Africa', *Frank Talk*, Steve Biko Foundation, Johannesburg

Gqola, P (2015) *Rape: A South African Nightmare*, MF Books Joburg, Johannesburg

Gqola, P (2017) *Reflecting Rogue*, MF Books Joburg, Johannesburg

Government of South Africa (2012) press release, 23 February, www.gov.za/department-sets-record-straight-bapo-ba-mogale, 2012

griot.de (2018) 'Thandiswa Mazwai', https://www.griot.de/thandiswabio.pdf

Grundy, S (2020) 'The False Promise of Anti-racism Books', https://www.theatlantic.com/culture/archive/2020/07/your-anti-racism-books-are-means-not-end/614281/?utm_source=newsletter&utm_medium=email&utm_campaign=atlantic-daily-newsletter&utm_content=20200722&silverid-ref=MzM5NDc2MTQ5NDM4So

Harris, RA (2016) 'A true Blackman', www.web.archive.org/web/20090629075530/http://www.bnvillage.co.uk/Black-roots-village

Hevesi, D (1989) 'Huey Newton symbolized the rising Black anger of a generation', *The New York Times*, www.nytimes.com/1989/08/23/obituaries/huey-newton-symbolized-the-rising-Black-anger-of-a-generation .html?pagewanted=all

Hewson, LA (ed, 1961) 'The Cottesloe Consultation: The report of the consultation among South African member-churches of the World Council of Churches', World Council of Churches Programme to Combat Racism, World Council of Churches, Zurich, www.worldcat.org/title/cottesloe-consultation-the-report-of-the-consultation- among-south-african-member-churches-of-the-world-council-of-churches-7-14-december-1960-at-cottesloe-johannesburg/oclc/733065743

Hip Hop Archive (2018) 'Artist profiles: The Last Poets', http://hiphoparchive.org/blog/4724-the-last-poets-the-hiphop-forefathers-who-gave-black-america-its-voice

Jayawardane, N (2015) 'Praise poem for the photographer Omar Badsha', www.omarbadsha.co.za/archives/praise-poem-photographer-omar-badsha-neelika-jayawardane

Johanson, C (2018) 'Spoken word artist Malcolm London', https://africanah.org/spoken-word-artist-malcolm-london/

Gerhart, G & Glaser, CL, eds (1993) *From Protest to Challenge: A Documentary History of African Politics in South Africa 1882–1990: Challenge and Victory, 1980–1990*, Indiana University Press, Bloomington

Karis, T & Gerhart, G, eds (1997) *From Protest to Challenge: A Documentary History of African Politics in South Africa, 1882–1990: Nadir and Resurgence, 1964–1979*, Indiana University Press, Bloomington

Kalley, JA, Schoeman, E & Andor, LE (1999) *Southern African Political History: A Chronology of Key Political Events from Independence to Mid-1997*, Greenwood Publishing Group, Westport

Kendi, IX (2016) 'Reclaiming MLK's Unspeakable Nightmare: The Progression of Racism in America', https://www.aaihs.org/reclaiming-mlks-unspeakable/

Khumalo-Seegelken, B (2014) 'The Christian Institute of Southern Africa in interaction with the churches and civil society', www.benkhumalo-seegelken.de, www.benkhumalo-seegelken.de/suedafrika-texte/690-the-christian-institute/

Khunou, FS (2016) *Mountains of Spirit: The Story of the Royal Bakwena ba Mogopa of the North West, South Africa*, Rainbird, Johannesburg

King, M (2011) 'Gladys Thomas of Ocean View, Esteemed Poet', *The Scenic South*, www.scenicsouth.co.za/gladys-thomas-of-ocean-view-esteemed-poet-2/

Kleinschmidt, H (2013) 'Roots and journeys linking the Christian Institute and wider community to the re-ignition of resistance to Apartheid in the early 70s', personal reflection, www.sahistory.org.za/ sites/default/files/Paper_Horst_Kleinschmidt.pdf

Klinkenberg, B (2019) 'Black Lives Matter Petitions Against Deportation of 21 Savage', https://www.rollingstone.com/music/music-news/black-lives-matter-deportation-21-savage-789730/

Lacom & Sached (1986) *Freedom from Below: The Struggle for Trade Unions in South Africa*, Skotaville, Johannesburg

Le Blanc, P (no date) 'The Marxism of CLR James', www.solidarity-us.org/node/775

Levin, S (2018) 'Hundreds dead, no one charged: the uphill battle against Los Angeles police killings', https://www.theguardian.com/us-news/2018/aug/24/los-angeles-police-violence-shootings-african-american

Lingaas, C (2015) 'The Crime against Humanity of Apartheid in a Post-Apartheid World', https://www.idunn.no/oslo_law_review/2015/02/the_crime_against_humanity_of_apartheid_in_a_post-apartheid

Lutheran World (2016) 'LWF mourns South Africa Bishop Buthelezi', www.lutheranworld.org/news/lwf-mourns-south-africa-bishop-buthelezi

Lynskey, D (2015) 'Are you ready to burn buildings?', https://www.theguardian.com/music/2015/jun/22/nina-simone-documentary-what-happened-miss-simone; https://www.youtube.com/watch?v=LJ25-U3jNWM

Macqueen, I (1999) 'Steve Biko, Richard Turner and the politics of Black Consciousness, 1970–1974', Society, Work and Development Institute, University of the Witwatersrand, www.sahistory.org.za/sites/default/files/file%20uploads%20/collaboration_and_debate_in_the_durban_moment_steve_biko_richard_turner_and_the_politics_of_Black_consciousness_1970_-_1974_by_ian_macqueen.pdf

Magaziner, D (2010) *The Law and the Prophets: Black Consciousness in South Africa*, New African Histories, Ohio University, Athens

Malcolm X & Haley, A (1965), *The Autobiography of Malcolm X*, recorded autobiography, www.genius.com/albums/Malcolm-x/The-autobiography-of-malcolm-x

Malefane, M (2016) 'Icon goes solo in polls', *Sowetan*, www.sowetanlive.co.za/news/2016/07/18/1976-icon-goes-solo-in-polls

Mangcu, X (2012) *Biko: A Biography*, Tafelberg, Cape Town

Mathebula, A (2017) 'ANC "totally" rejects Malema's 6% offer for land expropriation', *The Citizen*, www.citizen.co.za/news/south-africa/1442435/anc-totally-rejects-malemas-6-offer-for-land-expropriation/

Manhattan, S (2020) 'Angela Davis calls for justice, not just diversity and inclusion, at virtual AU event', https://www.theeagleonline.com/article/2020/09/angela-davis-calls-for-justice-not-just-diversity-and-inclusion-at-virtual-au-event

Martin, KL (2015) 'Tackling the Question of Legitimacy in Transitional Justice: Steve Biko and the Post-Apartheid Reconciliation Process in South Africa', CUREJ: College Undergraduate Research Electronic Journal, University of Pennsylvania, http://repository.upenn.edu/curej/191

Matlhaku, R (2017) 'Communities should celebrate great teachers', *Sunday World*,

References

www.sundayworld.co.za/talk/2017/01/12/communities-should-celebrate-great-teachers

Maylam, P (2011), 'Basil Moore citation', www.ru.ac.za/media/rhodesuniversity/content/ruhome/documents/CITATION%20FOR%20BASIL%20MOORE.pdf

McFadden, S (2020) 'Black Lives Matter Just Entered Its Next Phase', https://www.theatlantic.com/culture/archive/2020/09/black-lives-matter-just-entered-its-next-phase/615952/

McWhorter, J (2020) 'The Dehumanizing Condescension of *White Fragility*', https://www.theatlantic.com/ideas/archive/2020/07/dehumanizing-condescension-white-fragility/614146/

Meer, S, ed (1998) *Women Speak: Reflections on Our Struggles 1982–1997*, Kwela Books, Johannesburg

Mendoza, G (2015) '13 Young Black Poets You Should Know', https://blavity.com/13-young-black-poets-you-should-know/13-young-black-poets-you-should-know?category1=discover

Millard, A, ed (1978) *The Testimony of Steve Biko: BC in South Africa*, Panther Granada Publishing, New York

Mills, D (1993) 'The Last Poets', https://www.washingtonpost.com/archive/lifestyle/style/1993/12/12/the-last-poets/e31c20d9-a35e-430a-b887-9ae095f65716/

Mngxitama, A, Alexander, A & Gibson, G, eds (2008) *Biko Lives! Contesting the Legacies of Steve Biko*, Palgrave Macmillan, London

Mokoena, H (2016) 'From slavery to colonialism and school rules: A history of myths about Black hair', *The Conversation*, www.theconversation.com/from-slavery-to-colonialism-and-school-rules-a-history-of- myths-about-Black-hair-64676

Moore, B (2011) 'Learning from Black Theology', https://www.ru.ac.za/media/rhodesuniversity/content/ruhome/documents/Basil_Moore_Speech_-_Black_Theology.pdf

Sacramento, L & De Lima, M (2019) 'A literatura de Hamilton Borges entre seus leitores: vozes pretas no "centro do problema"', *contra corrente*, 13: 83

Motshwakae, OM (2015) 'Blackthought', *City Press*, www.news24.com/MyNews24/Black-Thought-20150817

Mphutlane wa Bofelo, M, Shah, A, Moodley, K, Cooper, L & Jones, B (2014) 'Recognition of prior learning as "radical pedagogy": A case study of the Workers' College in South Africa', erudite, https://www.erudit.org/en/journals/mje/1900-v1-n1-mje01117/1021917ar/

MTV (2017), 'Jahmil XT Qubeka premieres his Xhosa sci-fi film in China', www.mtv.co.za/news/jahmil-xt-qubeka-premieres-his-xhosa- sci-fi-film-in-china/baxirp

Murphy, C (1979) 'S Africa pays Biko family $76,700 in compensation', https://www.washingtonpost.com/archive/politics/1979/07/29/s-africa-pays-biko-family-76700-in-compensation/bfbac904-4d31-4bf4-b01b-340cf767692a/

NA (2012) 'Madonsela to probe tribes' lost millions', www.news24.com/Archives/City-Press/Madonsela-to-probe-tribes-lost-millions-20150430

Naidoo, D (2016) 'This is a call for solidarity from South Africa to Palestine', *The Daily Vox*, www.thedailyvox.co.za/derrick-naidoo-call-solidarity-south-africa-palestine

Naidoo, N (2015) 'Obituary: Literature professor Mbulelo Mzamane', *The Witness*, www.news24.com/Archives/Witness/OBITUARY-Literature-professor-Mbulelo-Mzamane-20150430

Natal Society Foundation (1993) www.natalia.org.za/Files/23-24/ Natalia%20v23-24%20obituaries%20Sikhakhane.pdf

National Public Radio (2018) 'Earl Sweatshirt on Resentment, Growth and Giving Yourself A Chance', https://www.npr.org/transcripts/673227162

Naudé, B (1995) My Land van Hoop, Human & Rousseau, Cape Town

Ndaba, B (2013) 'Impasse thwarts AZAPO, Sopa merger', *The Star*, www.iol.co.za/news/politics/impasse-thwarts-azapo-sopa-merger-1617223

Ndebele, NS (1987) 'The Writers Movement in South Africa', https://www.sahistory.org.za/sites/default/files/archive-files/the_writers_movement_in_south_africa_by_njabule_s_ndebele.pdf

Neal, M A (2017) 'Stamped from the Beginning review – a timely history of racist ideas in America', https://www.theguardian.com/books/2017/aug/24/stamped-from-beginning-ibram-x-kendi-review

Nemakonde, V (2019) 'Twitter suspends Mngxitama's account after "kill whites" threats, IEC assessing what to do', https://citizen.co.za/news/south-africa/social-media/2048273/twitter-suspends-mngxitamas-account-after-kill-whites-threats-iec-assessing-what-to-do/

New Nation & The History Workshop (1989) *New Nation, New History*, The New Nation, Johannesburg

Nguyen, T (2020) 'Consumers don't care about corporate solidarity. They want donations.', https://www.vox.com/the-goods/2020/6/3/21279292/blackouttuesday-brands-solidarity-donations

Nkosi, M (2018) 'Pioneering women paved the way', https://www.sowetanlive.co.za/sundayworld/lifestyle/2018-08-30-pioneering-women-paved-the-way/

No Sizwe (Neville Alexander) (1979) *One Azania, One Nation: The National Question in South Africa*, Zed Press, Johannesburg

Nzimande, A (2017) 'Sacrifices of a Different Kind', https://www.iol.co.za/saturday-star/opinion/sacrifices-of-a-different-kind-9831630

Nzongola-Ntalaja, G (2011) 'Patrice Lumumba: The most important assassination of the 20th century', *The Guardian*, www.theguardian.com/global-development/poverty-matters/2011/jan/17/patrice-lumumba-50th-anniversary-assassination

Oliver, R & Fage, JD (1986) *A Short History of Africa*, Penguin, London

Olsson, GH (2011) *Black Power Mixtape, 1967–1975*, Sverige Television AB and Louverture Films, www.youtube.com/watch?v=6bryh0IFMhg.

Obenson, TA (2017) 'Cannes: Jahmil X.T. Qubeka brings epic "Sew the Winter to My Skin" to the Atelier', www.shadowandact.com/cannes-jahmil-x-t-qubeka-brings-epic-sew-the-winter-to-my-skin-to-the-atelier

Obenson, T (2020) '"Small Axe": Why Steve McQueen confronted "Missing Generations" of Black British stories in five new films', https://www.indiewire.com/2020/09/small-axe-steve-mcqueen-interview-1234586832/

Oppel Jr, RA & Taylor, DB (2020) 'Here's what you need to know about Breonna Taylor's death', www.nytimes.com/article/breonna-taylor-police.html

Otten, C (2016) 'The last poets: Americans in poetry – From Black Power to Black Lives Matter', https://www.theguardian.com/books/2016/nov/21/the-last-poets-america-in-poetry-from-black-power-to-black-lives-matter

Pace, E (1984) 'A radical hero: Ahmed Sékou Touré', *The New York Times*, www.nytimes.com/1984/03/28/obituaries/ahmed-sekou-toure-a-radical-hero.html

Packer, ZZ (2020) 'Preacher of the New Antiracist Gospel', https://www.gq.com/story/ibram-x-kendi-antiracism-scholar-profile

Pettman, C (1913) *Africanderisms: A glossary of South African colloquial words and phrases and of place and other names*, Longmans, Green and Co., London, from https://dsae.co.za/entry/kroes/e04120

Pierpont, CR (2014) 'A Raised Voice', https://www.newyorker.com/magazine/2014/08/11/raised-voice

Pityana, B, Ramphele, M, Mpumlwana, M, & Wilson, L, eds (1991) *Bounds of Possibility: The Legacy of Steve Biko and Black Consciousness*, David Philip, Cape Town

Powell, I (2015) 'TRC sheds light on academic's murder', *Weekend Argus*, www.iol.co.za/news/politics/trc-sheds-light-on-academics-murder-1868605

Quintal, G & Child, K (2017), 'Modest Soweto home base of Manyi's new R450m media empire', *The Times*, www.timeslive.co.za/news/south-africa/2017-08-22-modest-soweto-home-base-of-manyis-new-r450m-media-empire/

Ramadiro, B & Duncan, J (2012) 'The revolutionary who changed many lives', *Mail & Guardian*, www.mg.co.za/article/2012-08-30-neville-alexander-revolutionary-who-changed-many-lives

Ramphele, M (1996a) *Across Boundaries: The Journey of a South African Woman Leader*, Feminist Press, New York

Ramphele, M (1996b) *Mamphela Ramphele: A Life*, David Philip, Cape Town

RawStory (2017) www.rawstory.com/2017/05/watch-hbos-bill-maher-gets-into-epic-shouting-match-with-cornel-west-over-hillary-versus-trump/

Reuters (2020) 'TikTok has its Arab Spring moment as teen activism overtakes dance moves', https://www.usnews.com/news/top-news/articles/2020-06-02/tiktok-has-its-arab-spring-moment-as-teen-activism-overtakes-dance-moves

Rorich, D (2013) 'South Africa banned director Jahmil Qubeka speaks out', *Variety*, www.variety.com/2013/film/global/south-africa-banned-film-director-jahmil-qubeka-speaks-out-1200566361/

Russonello, G (2018) 'Keorapetse Kgositsile, 79, South African Poet and Activist, dies', https://www.nytimes.com/2018/01/16/obituaries/keorapetse-kgositsile-79-south-african-poet-and-activist-dies.html

Saad, Layla F (2020) 'Do the work: an anti-racist reading list', https://www.theguardian.com/books/booksblog/2020/jun/03/do-the-work-an-anti-racist-reading-list-layla-f-saad

SABC (2012) 'Press release of *Flowers of the Revolution*', www.sabc.co.za/wps/portal/intsales/pages/documentariesdetail?id=cc9896804614a2078337a796e5573d3a&page_from=documentaries,

Sacks, J (2013) 'Biko would not vote for Ramphele', *Mail & Guardian*, www.mg.co.za/article/2013-03-15-00-biko-would-not-vote-for-ramphele

SAHO (2011) 'Teboho "Tsietsi" Mashinini', www.sahistory.org.za/people/teboho-tsietsi-mashinini

SAHO (2019), 'Dr. Oshadi Maphefo Jane Mangena', https://www.sahistory.org.za/people/dr-oshadi-maphefo-jane-mangena]

Sanneh, K (2011) 'Where's Earl?', https://www.newyorker.com/magazine/2011/05/23/wheres-earl

Scheitle, CP & Dougherty, KD (2010) 'Race, diversity, and membership duration in religious congregations', https://www.baylorisr.org/wp-content/uploads/2019/10/dougherty_race.pdf

Schulz, K (2018) 'The lost giant of American literature', https://www.newyorker.com/magazine/2018/01/29/the-lost-giant-of-american-literature

Schoff, WH, tr & ed (1912) *The Periplus of the Erythraean Sea: Travel and Trade in the Indian Ocean by a Merchant of the First Century*, London, Bombay and Calcutta, www.archive.org/details/cu31924030139236

Seale, B & Newton, H (1995) *Seize the Time: The Story of the Black Panther Party*, Black Classic Press, Baltimore

Seekings, J (2000) *A History of the United Democratic Front in South Africa, 1983 to 1991*, David Philip, Cape Town

Serote, M (1975) *Behold Mama*, Ad Donker, Johannesburg

Seti-Sonamzi, V (2019) 'On Blackness: The role and positionality of Black public intellectuals in post-94 South Africa', https://www.nihss.ac.za/

content/blackness-role-and-positionality-black-public-intellectuals-post-94-south-africa

Shalev, Z & Burnett, C, eds (2012) *Ptolemy's Geography in the Renaissance*, Warburg Institute, London

Shamsian, J (2018) '24 things you may have missed in Childish Gambino's "This is America" music video', https://www.insider.com/this-is-america-music-video-meaning-references-childish-gambino-donald-glover-2018-5

Shringarpure, B (2014) 'Fanon documentary confronts fallacies about anti-colonial philosopher', *The Guardian*, www.theguardian.com/world/2014/jul/21/-sp-frantz-fanon-documentary-concerning-violence

Shropshire, KL (1996) 'Sports agents, role models and race consciousness', *Marquette Sports Law Review*, Milwaukee, 6(2)

Sifile, L (2014) 'DA behind land grabs, say "original" residents', *Sowetan*, www.sowetanlive.co.za/news/2014/12/13/da-behind-land-grabs-say-original-residents

Sifile, L (2016) 'EFF claim in dispute', *Sowetan*, Johannesburg, http://www.sowetanlive.co.za/elections/2016/08/02/eff-claim-in-dispute

Simmons, K (2018) 'When words become witchcraft: A review of *The BreakBeat Poets Volume 2: Black Girl Magic*', https://southsideweekly.com/words-become-witchcraft-breakbeat-poets-black-girl-magic/

Simon & Schuster (2018), 'Taking the arrow out of the heart', https://www.simonandschuster.com/books/Taking-the-Arrow-Out-of-the-Heart/Alice-Walker/9781501179525

Smith, BG, ed (2008) *The Oxford Encyclopaedia of Women in World History*, Oxford University Press, London

Socialist Worker (2020) 'Assata Shakur—a revolutionary who defied US state repression', https://socialistworker.co.uk/art/50364/Assata+Shakur+a+revolutionary+who+defied+US+state+repression

Sosibo, K (2014) 'EFF launches its election manifesto', *Mail & Guardian*, www.mg.co.za/article/2014-02-22-eff-launches-its-party-manifesto

Sosibo, K (2015) 'No country for brilliant thinkers', mg.co.za/article/2015-01-15-no-country-for-brilliant-thinkers/

South African Democracy Education Trust (2004) *The Road to Democracy in South Africa: 1970–1980*, University of South Africa Press, Pretoria

South African Press Association (2014a) 'Family unaware of Biko autopsy report', Independent Online, www.iol.co.za/news/crime-courts/family-unaware-of-biko-autopsy-report-1790344

South African Press Association (2014b) 'Auctioneers retain ownership of Biko documents', News24, www.news24.com/SouthAfrica/News/Auctioneers-retain-ownership-Biko-documents-20141203

Stiebel, L & Gunner, L, eds (2007) 'Still beating the drum: Critical perspectives on Lewis Nkosi', *Ariel: A Review of International English Literature*, 38(4)

Steadman, I (1990) 'Towards popular theatre in South Africa', Wits History Workshop, University of the Witwatersrand, Johannesburg

Stone, BE (2011) 'Prophetic pragmatism and the practices of freedom: On Cornel West's Foucauldian methodology', California, *Foucault Studies*, 11: 92–105

Stubbs, A (1975) 'Martyr of hope: A personal memoir', in Steve Biko, *I Write What I Like*, Pan Macmillan, Johannesburg

Tambo, OR (1987) Speech on behalf of the liberation movements at the 23rd session of the assembly of heads of state and government of the Organisation of African Unity, www.anc.org.za, www.sahistory.org.za/archive/speech-oliver-tambo-behalf-liberation-movements-twenty-third-session-assembly-heads-state-an

Tepper, A (2020) 'How the SoCal coast inspired a legendary author's feminist Kenyan epic', https://www.latimes.com/entertainment-arts/books/story/2020-10-12/ngugi-wa-thiongo-kenyan-epic-the-perfect-nine

The Presidency (2017) Order of Luthuli in Silver, http://www.thepresidency.gov.za/national-orders/recipient/22-anc-political-trialists-1969

Thieme, J (2008) 'Aimé Césaire, founding father of Negritude', *The Independent*, www.independent.co.uk/news/obituaries/aime-cesaire-founding-father-of-negritude-811812.html

Thomas, D (1975) 'A crucial test for the South African Council of Churches', *Pro Veritate*, www.sahistory.org.za/sites/default/files/DC/PVApr75/PVApr75.pdf

Tshabalala, L (2017) 'All Hail, the King!', https://www.afropolitan.co.za/articles/thandiswa-mazwai-5552.html

University of Cape Town (2013), https://www.uct.ac.za/sites/default/files/image_tool/images/328/media/releases/2013/UCTtoconferhonorarydoctoratesonCaiphusSemenyaandLettaMbulu.pdf

University of Missouri-St. Louis Thomas Jefferson Library Reference Department (1997) 'The Slave Consultant's Narrative: The Life of an Urban Myth?', https://web.archive.org/web/20070808080232/http://www.umsl.edu/services/library/blackstudies/narrate.htm

University of the Witwatersrand (2017) 'Robert Sobukwe immortalised at Wits', www.wits.ac.za/news/latest-news/general-news/2017/2017-09/robert-sobukwe-immortalised-at-wits.html

Vally, S (2017) 'Introduction to the special issue in memory of Edward W Said', *Journal of Holy Land and Palestine Studies* 16(1): 1–5, www.euppublishing.com/doi/abs/10.3366/hlps.2017.0149

Walshe, P (1983) *Church versus State in South Africa: The Case of the Christian Institute*, Hurst Publishers, London

Weik, T (2020) 'The history behind "Yellow Peril Supports Black Power" and why some find it problematic', https://www.nbcnews.com/news/asian-america/history-behind-yellow-peril-supports-black-power-why-some-find-n1228776

Winning, A (2020) 'SA lays out conditions to seize land', https://www.moneyweb.co.za/news-fast-news/sa-lays-out-conditions-to-seize-land/

Winter, G (1981) *Inside BOSS*, Penguin, London

Xaba, V (2016) 'Seth Mazibuko out on bail after meter boxes fiasco', *Sowetan*, www.sowetanlive.co.za/news/2016/10/09/seth-mazibuko-out-on-bail-after-meter-boxes-fiasco

Yates, T (2009) 'David Bosch: South African context, ecclesiology in the emerging missionary paradigm', *International Bulletin of Missionary Research*, 33(2): 72–78

Zeilig, L (2015) 'The murder of Thomas Sankara', www.africasacountry.com, http://africasacountry.com/2015/10/the-murder-of-thomas-sankara/

Further reading

www.abahlali.org

www.apartheidmuseum.org

www.azapo.org.za

www.badilishapoetry.com

www.Blackpast.org

www.Blackhistoryheroes.com

www.chimurenga.co.za

www.gov.za/DOCUMENTS/CONSTITUTION/constitution-republic-south-africa-1996-1

www.jstor.org

www.justice.gov.za

www.justice.gov.za/Trc/

www.mandela.gov.za/mandela_speeches

www marxists.org

www.michaelchapman.co.za

www.nelsonmandela.org

www.njabulondebele.co.za

www.omarbadsha.co.za

www.paulstopforth.com

www.populareducation.co.za

www.ralphndawofoundation.co.za

www.sadtu.org.za

www.saha.org.za

www.sahistory.org.za

www.sbf.org.za

www.shams.za.org

QR Codes

Black Consciousness Movement and Capitalism

Black Consciousness Movement philosophy

Black Consciousness Reader authors

Steve Biko's friend Bokwe Mafuna

Black Consciousness and the Christian Church

Steve Biko's friend Harry Nengwekhulu

The role of the arts and the Black Consciousness Movement

We are black and not non-whites

Index

A

Abahlali baseMjondolo 118, 189, 390–1, 423
Abantu-Batho 261
Abe Bailey Institute 6
Abram, Goolam 173, 354
Achebe, Chinua 236
Action Committee to Stop Eviction (ACTSTOP) 383–4
Adams, Eddie 24
Africa, Sandy 370
Africa is a Country 106
African Cities Reader 283
African Housewives League 368
African Independent Churches Association (AICA) 176, 193
African National Congress (ANC) 3, 6, 9–10, 15, 19, 20, 26–9, 31–2, 37–8, 41, 43, 47, 56, 62, 65–7, 70, 73, 76, 80, 84, 88, 90, 102, 119, 121, 169, 193, 196, 210, 212, 217–8, 220, 222–3, 226–34, 237, 240–5, 255, 257, 261, 263, 273, 287, 288–9, 296, 301, 304, 311, 324, 332, 347, 351–3, 363, 368–9, 371–2, 378, 382–5, 387–40, 394–5, 416
    ANC Youth League (ANCYL) 3, 80, 84, 124, 243, 287, 288–90, 387
    Freedom Charter 3, 5, 234, 247, 349, 377, 384, 389
    Kabwe Conference (1975) 10, 227
    Land Commission 385
    Morogoro Conference (1969) 73
    Orlando Task Team (OTT) 212
    Programme of Action (1949) 80
    Strategic Defence Procurement Packages 229
    Umkhonto we Sizwe (MK) 66, 76, 231, 263, 273
    Women's League 360, 369
African Nationalist Legion 93
African Pioneer Movement 95
African Resistance Movement (ARM) 7
African Teachers Association of South Africa (ATASA) 213
Africanist, The 3
Afro-American Association (AAA) 152
Alaska 289
Alexander, Amanda
    Biko Lives! Contesting the Legacies of Steve Biko 118
Alexander, Neville 39, 47, 205, 217, 418–9
    One Azania, One Nation: The National Question in South Africa 221, 418
    South Africa Today 220
Alexander, Ray 368
Alexander Humboldt Foundation 219

Algeria, Algerian 84, 92, 132, 150
 War of Independence (1954–62) 92
All Africa Conference of Churches
 41, 198–9
Allison & Busby 346
Ally, Nurina 122–3
Ally, Shireen 122–3
American Academy of Arts and
 Sciences 97
American Communist Party 157
American Information Centre 30
Amin Dada, Idi 102
Amnesty Committee 365
Anglican Church 26, 191, 195
Anglo American Corporation 364
Anglo-Boer War (1899–1902) 167
 Battle of Isandlwana (1879) 81
Angola 9, 54, 76, 94, 227, 231
ANN7 TV News Channel 393
Apostolic Faith Mission 300
Arab Spring 132, 420
Ariefdien, Shaheen 285
Arnold, Millard *Testimony of Steve Biko:
 BC in South Africa, The* (1978) 90
Assembly of the Zionist and Apostolic
 Association (AZASA) 193
Associated Press 24, 46, 410
Association for the Educational and
 Cultural Advancement of the
African People of South Africa 230
Association of Law Societies of South
 Africa 13
Association of Mineworkers and
 Construction Union (AMCU) 237
Atlanta Film Festival 217
Attenborough, Richard *Cry Freedom*
 (1987) 35
Australia 1, 200–1, 277, 320
Azania 16, 20–1, 226, 234, 236–7,
 274, 276, 340, 347
Azania People's Manifesto 234

Azanian People's Organisation
 (AZAPO) 14–16, 20, 29, 44–6,
 64, 204, 211, 226–9, 230, 233–
 9, 303, 346–9, 352, 368, 404,
 418, 423
Azanian National Liberation Army
 (AZANLA) 16, 227
Azanian Students Movement
 (AZASM) 233
Azanian Students Organisation
 (AZASO) 14, 233
Azanian Youth Organisation 15

B
Baartman, Rev Ernest 195
Badat, Salim
 *Forgotten People: Political Banishment
 under Apartheid, The* 380
Badsha, Omar 55, 215, 313, 315, 415
Bahula, Julian 281
Bahumutsi Drama Group of Soweto 274
Bakwena ba Mogopa 383, 386, 415
Baldwin, James 107, 375, 411
Balibar, Étienne
 Three Concepts of Politics, The 16
Bam, Brigalia 195
Bam, Fikile 218, 223
Bandele, Asha 126, 145
Bandit Queen 161
Bantu Authorities Act (1951) 3
Bantu Education Act (1953) 68, 276
Bantu Homelands Constitution Act
 (1971) 381
Bantu Labour Act 50–1
Baqwa, Jeff 279
Baraka, Amiri 18, 256
BC Party 238
de Beauvoir, Simone 23, 107
de Beer, Cedric 74
Belgium 103, 177, 227
Beese, Barbara 165

Belhar Confession (1982) 177
Belafonte, Harry 148, 371–2
bell hooks 79, 108
Beneke, Jacobus Johannes
 Oosthuysen 57
Bennett, Fred 154
Berlin Congress (1885) 81, 103
Beyoncé 109, 412
Biko, Khaya 187–8
Biko, Nkosinathi 59–61
Biko, Nontsikelelo (Ntsiki) 36, 42,
 43, 45, 361
Biko, Bantu Stephen 4–13, 15, 17–19,
 23, 24, 26–8, 30–46, 48–50,
 52–62, 65–6, 71–3, 75, 90, 108,
 112, 117–8, 120, 140, 146, 171–2,
 174, 180, 182–4, 187–192, 196,
 198, 200, 217, 221–6, 229–30,
 235–37, 241, 248, 262, 271–2,
 279, 307–8, 309, 311–12, 326,
 333–4, 346, 351–2, 354, 361–2,
 364, 368, 373–4, 382, 399, 410–
 11, 413–14, 416–22
 I Write What I Like 18, 112, 184, 187–
 8, 411, 422
Bizos, George 225
 *No One to Blame? In Pursuit of Justice in
 South Africa* 225, 411
BLAC Publishing House 282
Black (Africana) existentialism 109,
 110–1, 114, 122
Black Allied Workers' Union (BAWU)
 8, 10, 39, 230
Black Coffee 288
Black Consciousness Movement
 (BCM) 6, 8–11, 14–15, 18–19, 28,
 37–40, 45–47, 49–50, 63–66,
 70, 73, 90, 117, 209, 226–30,
 233–4, 242, 261, 272, 279, 294–
 7, 303, 306, 310–11, 320, 339,
 346, 349–50, 355, 361–4, 367,

389, 394, 412, 414
Black Consciousness Movement of
 Azania (BCMA) 14–15, 226–9,
 233–4
Black Consciousness Programmes
 (BCP) 6, 8–10, 48–9, 54, 56–7,
 62, 90, 172, 180, 195, 221–2,
 230, 234, 238, 262, 333, 353,
 355, 361–2, 364, 368, 372
Black Domestic Workers Association
 368
Black Economic Empowerment 234
Black feminism 108, 111, 117, 320
Black First Land First (BLF) 93–5,
 391–2, 411
Black Liberation Army 150, 155
Black (Liberation) Theology 6, 29,
 73, 118, 151, 171, 173–4, 181, 185–
 7, 191, 193, 197–8, 330, 417
Black Lives Matter (BLM) 79, 115–6,
 125–9, 131–4, 136, 140–1, 143–5,
 158, 164, 187, 248, 251–2, 260,
 395–6, 410–13, 415, 417, 419
Black nihilism 111
Black Panther, The 146–7, 151
Black Panther Party 146, 150, 152,
 154, 420
(Black) Panthers Free Breakfast for
 School Children Program 148
Black People's Convention (BPC) 8,
 9, 10, 13–14, 29, 32, 40–1, 62,
 120, 195, 210, 226–7, 230, 304,
 333, 350, 352
Black Priests' Manifesto (1970) 6, 176
Black Review 54–5, 271, 309
Black Sash 338, 382
black square 252
Black Star 98
Black Student Union 147
Black Thought 281–2, 417
Black Viewpoint 180, 262, 279

Black Women Unite 368
Black Women's Federation (BWF) 13, 210, 230, 234, 360, 367–8
Black Workers' Council 8
Blair, Tony 160
Blake, Jacob 130
le Blanc, Paul
   CLR James and Revolutionary Marxism: Selected Writings 1939–1949 94
BN Village 93
Boal, Augusto 301
Boesak, Rev Dr Allan 166, 195–8
   Finger of God, The 198
   Pharaohs on Both Sides of the Blood-Red Waters 198
Bolívar, Simón 23
Boko Haram 83
Bolt 263
Bond, Patrick 119, 362
   Against Global Apartheid: South Africa Meets the World Bank, IMF and International Finance 119
   Looting Africa: The Economics of Exploitation 119
   Talk Left, Walk Right: South Africa's Frustrated Global Reforms 119
   Zuma's Own Goal: Losing South Africa's 'War on Poverty' 119
Bongo Maffin 288, 373
Bonner, Phil *Soweto: A History* 214
Boom Shaka 288–9
Bosch, David 177, 423
Boshoff, JL 350–1
Boshoff, Johan 89–90
Botha, MC 213
Botha, PW xv, 175
Botswana 9, 27, 37–41, 50, 63–4, 76, 211, 223, 227, 257, 268–9, 273, 277, 279, 247
Boyce, Rupert 165
Brazil 25, 73, 112–3, 302, 316

Brecht, Bertolt 301
   Mother Courage 301
Bretton Woods 237
Breytenbach, Breyten 75
Brezhnev, Leonid 91
BRICS Film Festival 316
Brinsmead, RD 404
British Anti-Apartheid Movement 91
British Black Panthers 159, 160–1
British Broadcasting Corporation (BBC) 106, 132, 134, 163, 398, 410
Brooks, Gwendolyn 256
Brothers of Peace 289
Brown, Elaine 151
Brown, Gordon 160
Brown Dash 290
Brutus, Dennis 17
BTS 123–3, 410
Buhle, Paul 94
Bunce, Robin *Darcus Howe: A Political Biography* 159
Bunche, Ralph 103
Bureau of State Security (BOSS) 39, 56, 63, 205–6, 270, 423
   Z-Squad 63
Burkina Faso 23, 105–6, 274
Buthelezi, Manas 166, 198–9
Buthelezi, Chief Mangosuthu Gatsha 7, 14–15, 27–8, 41, 53, 169, 225
Buthelezi, Sipho 252

C

Cabral, Amílcar 53
Cairo University 101
Cambridge (University) 160–5, 278–9, 411
Cameroon 84, 97, 283
Canada 197, 200, 227, 278
Cannes 164, 316–17, 419
Cape African Teachers' Union 214

Carl von Ossietzky University 177
Carmichael, Stokely 48, 94, 147, 151, 160, 308, 371, 375
Carter, Gwendolen M
  Nadir and Resurgence, 1964–1979 74
  Protest to Challenge: A Documentary History of African Politics in South Africa 60
Carter, Jimmy 13
Casablanca Group 84
Castro, Fidel 23, 156–7
Catholic, Catholics 4, 6, 12, 26, 31, 47, 64, 167, 170, 173, 176, 188, 189, 191, 200, 365
  Vatican 191, 200
Central African Republic 83
Césaire, Aimé 104–5, 112–13, 217, 422
Chabaku, Jane 368
Chama Cha Mapinduzi 102
Channel 4 162
Charterists 3, 47, 234, 346
Cheadle, Hilton 55
Cherry, Matthew A 255
Chikane, Frank 173, 177, 195
Childish Gambino 250–1, 421
Chimurenga 123, 283
Chimurenga Library 283
Chimurenga War, 261
China, People's Republic of (PRC) 133, 153, 227, 316, 363, 417
Chirwa, Naledi 243
Chomee 290
Christian Institute ix, 6, 29, 72, 169, 264, 415, 422
  Pro Veritate 169, 176, 422
  Study Project for Christianity in Apartheid South Africa (SPRO-CAS) x, 6, 54, 172–3, 180
Christianity 166, 170, 180–5, 188, 197, 261, 331, 411

Baptist 157, 167, 182, 202
Bible 166–8, 183, 198, 359
Congregationalist 167
Episcopal 364
Methodist 40, 79, 167, 171, 192, 194–5, 200, 208, 328, 335, 350, 413
Pentecostal 166, 177, 182, 201
Presbyterian 167
Protestant 189, 200
Chronic, The 283
CIEX Report 393
Cindi, Zithulele 89
Citizen, The 268, 388, 395, 416, 418
City Press 231, 384, 417–8
Clan, the 309
Clark, Dick 222
Clark, Mark 149
Classic, The 262–3, 278
Cleaver, Eldridge 48, 147–51
  Soul on Fire (1968) 151
Clinton, Hillary 114
Clutchette. John 157
Cold War 278
Collins, Colin 170, 200
Coloured Labour Party 53
Columbia University 77, 94, 118, 121, 191, 256
Commission for the Socio-Economic Development of Bantu Areas 379
Committee for Academic Freedom in Africa 118
Community Health Programme 12, 361–2
Community Land Conference Land Charter (1993) 385
Compaoré, Blaise 105–6
Congolese National Army 104
Congress of Black African Writers 91
Congress of South African Students (COSAS) 14–15, 231–2, 242

Congress of South African Writers (COSAW) 263, 272, 282
Conservative Party (UK) 117
Contrast 278
Convention for a Democratic South Africa (Codesa) 15, 227–8, 349, 388
Convention People's Party 100
Cooks, Carlos A 93
Cooper, Anna J 108
Cooper, Saths 7–9, 65, 89, 235, 246, 306, 310, 352
Copelyn, John 55
Cottesloe Consultation 168, 172, 415
Creative Youth Association (CYA) 272, 292
Crichlow, Frank 164
Criminal Procedure Act 60
Cuba 23, 96, 124, 150, 153, 219, 278, 26th of July Movement 23
Cullinan, Patrick 268
Cullors, Patrisse 125, 126, 145
Cultural Struggle 261, 303
Curlewis, DJ 207
Curtis, Neville 54
Czechoslovakia
    Prague Spring (1968) 25

D

Daily Dispatch 13, 28
Daily Vox 216, 418
Damas, Léon-Gontran 104
Dana, Simphiwe 116, 123, 372, 374
Dangor, Achmat 281–2
    Bitter Fruit (2003) 281
    Bulldozer (1983) 281
    Kafka's Curse (1997) 281
    Private Voices (1992) 281
    Strange Pilgrimages (2013) 281
    Waiting for Leila (1981) 281
    Z Town Trilogy, The (1990) 281

Dashiki 310
David, Ben 309
David, Ursula 368
Davis, Angela 157–8, 416
Davis, Miles 23
Democracy Now! 17, 126, 151, 412
Democratic National Convention (1968) 149, 154
Democratic Alliance 32, 394
Democratic Party of Guinea 102
Democratic Republic of Congo (DRC) 104
    Kinshasa 104
Desai, Ashwin 119, 306–8, 310
Development Institute for Training, Support and Education for Labour (DITSELA) 216
Dhondy, Farrukh 79, 161–2, 165
    KBW (Keep Britain White) 165
DiAngelo, Robin 76–7
Dike, Fatima 261
Diome, Fatou 17, 214
    Belly of the Atlantic, The 17
Dixon, Valerie 98
Dlakavu, Simamkele 243
Dlamini, Mcebo 243
Dolinschek, Martin 56
Dominican Republic 93, 177
Donaldson Trust 235
Donga 263
Dope, Bruce 288
Dos Santos, Hamilton Borges 112–3
Dr BW Vilakazi High School 329
Drum 84, 262, 276, 315
Drumgo, Fleeta 157
Du Bois, William Edward Burhardt (WEB) 96–7, 107
    Philadelphia Negro, The 97
    Souls of Black Folks, The 97
Duncan, Jane 219
Durban and District Women's

League 360
Durban International Film Festival 315
Durban Strikes (1973) 52, 180
Durban Women's Group 370
Dutch Reformed Mission Church 177
DuVernay, Ava 318
Dwane, James Mata 261

E
Earl Sweatshirt 246, 255, 257–8
Earle, Chris 56
Economic Freedom Fighters (EFF) 105, 124, 189, 238, 242–3, 351, 387–9, 392
Edjabe, Ntone 283
Egypt 84, 182, 382
    Cairo 78, 283
    Cairo University 101
Eiser, Hugh 384
Elba, Idris 163
Ellison, Ralph 107
Eloff, CF 177
Eloff Commission 177
Ensor, Paula 54
Eriksson, Alison 39
Erwin, Alec 55
Ethiopia 20, 83, 93, 364
Evangelical Lutheran Church 189, 198
Extension of University Education Act (1959) 4, 306, 351

F
Fabian Society 101
Fage, JD
    A Short History of Africa 20
Fanon, Frantz 17, 53, 62, 79, 84, 91–2, 106, 111–12, 118, 120, 124, 152, 217, 258, 281, 308, 373
    Black Skin, White Masks 111
    Wretched of the Earth, The 84, 120, 308

Farrakhan, Louis 151, 159
Fassie, Bongani 285
Fassie, Brenda 285, 409
Federal Republic of Germany (West Germany) 219
Federal Theological Seminary 7, 171, 187
    Alice Declaration (1972) 7
Federation of South African Women (FSAW) 367
    Women's Charter (1954) 367
#FeesMustFall 139, 142, 216, 232, 240–45, 281, 338–40, 349, 373
Ferguson 127
FESTAC 311
Field, Paul
    Darcus Howe: A Political Biography 123–5
Film and Publications Board (FPB) 159
Finland Helsinki 283
Folb, Peter 224–5
Ford Foundation 278
Fort Hare University 5, 9, 26–9, 34, 79–80, 84, 116, 121, 171, 174, 193, 195, 209, 231, 273, 277, 306
    ANC-SMFC Collection Archives 209
Foucault, Michel 115, 362
Fourth International 95, 236–7
France 17, 24, 25, 50, 78, 91, 102, 105, 150, 218, 227, 278, 409
    Paris 53, 180, 217–8, 283
    Revolution (1789–99) 95
Frederikse, Julie 71, 76, 413–4
Freire, Paulo 23, 73, 112, 173, 191, 200, 217, 241, 308
    Pedagogy of the Oppressed 112, 308
Frimpong, Allen Kwabena 128
FUBA Gallery 303
Funda Art Centre 292, 294, 313
    Soyikwa Institute of African Theatre 292

G

Gagiano, Annie 414, 480
Gallery Afrique 282
Garland, Billy 156
Garvey, Marcus Mosiah 93, 98, 260, 413
Garza, Alicia 125–6
Gat, Julien 104
Gbenye, Christophe 104
Gcabashe, Virginia 368
General Law Amendment Act (1963) 235
German Democratic Republic (East Germany) 157
    East Berlin 101
Germany 116, 157, 169, 177, 189, 194, 198, 219, 227, 274, 277, 282, 294, 338, 373
    Lehrte 282
    Nienburg 282
    Oldenburg 177
Ghana 84, 95–101, 208, 355, 391
    Accra 84, 97–8, 100
    Accra Riots (1948) 100
    Gold Coast 99
    Operation Cold Chop (1966) 100
Ghetto Ruff 290
Gibson, Nigel 117–8
    Biko Lives! Contesting the Legacies of Steve Biko 417, 118
Gigaba, Malusi 287
Gluckman, Dr Jonathan 60–2
Goldberg, Denis 73
Golden City Post 267, 315
Goldstone, Judge Richard 218, 384
Goldstone Commission 218
Gordon, Chodon 165
Gordimer, Nadine 293
Gosani, Bob 315
Government of National Unity 16, 228
Govender, Pregs 370
Govinden, Betty 306
Gqola, Pumla Dineo 79, 116–7, 374, 414
    A Renegade called Simphiwe 116, 374
    Rape: A South African Nightmare 116
    Reflecting Rogue 116
    What is Slavery to Me? Postcolonial/Slave Memory in Post-apartheid South Africa 117
Gqubule, Rev Simon 171
Grimshaw, Anna 94
Groenewald, Christoffel Gert 56
Group Areas Act (1950) 83, 365, 377–80, 384
Guardian, The 91, 103, 126, 128, 145, 154, 159, 161–3, 219, 260, 375
Guevara, Ernesto 'Che' 23, 105, 152
Guinea 84, 101–2, 211, 371
Gutiérrez, Gustavo 191
Gwala, Mafika 264, 271, 296
    Jol'iinkomo (1977) 271
    No More Lullabies (1982) 271

H

Haacke, Hans 218
Haiti Revolution (1791–1804) 94, 105
Hamilton, Charles V 94, 308
Hammarskjöld, Dag 103
Hampton, Fred 148–9
Hani, Chris 66, 217, 300
Harare Commonwealth Declaration 15
Harlem Renaissance 96, 104
Harris, Cheryl I 256
Harris, John Frederick 5
Harris, Rev Vivian 192
Harris, Robert Acemendeces 93
Hartman, Grischelda 215
Harvard University 96, 99, 118, 121, 195, 231, 312, 362
    Kennedy School of Government 262

WEB Du Bois Institute for African and African-American Research 96
Hassan Howe, Leila 161, 163
Haysom, Fink 75
Head, Bessie 246, 266, 268–9
   A Bewitched Crossroad: An African Saga 268
   A Question of Power 268
   Collector of Treasures and Other Botswana Village Tales, The 268
   Maru 268
   When Rain Clouds Gather 268
Health, Education and Welfare Society of South Africa 220
Heathcote, George 267
Heathcote, Nellie 267
Hegel, Georg Wilhelm Friedrich 54, 220, 402
Henry, Paget 94
Hill, Robert 94
Hintsa, King 81
Hitler, Adolf 169, 243
Ho Chi Minh 100
Honeker, Erich 157
Hoover, J Edgar 147–8
Howe, Darcus 159, 163
   Bandung File, The (1985–91) 162
   Slave Nation (2001) 162
   White Tribe (2000) 162
Hubbard, L Ron 158
Humboldt University 101
Hungary 273
Hurt, Karen 370
Hutton, Bobby 148
Hype 286

I
Ibrahim, Abdullah 262
Imbeleko 238, 368–9
Independent, The 104–5
Independent Communications Authority 273
Independent Development Corporation 233
Independent Online 59
India 20, 165, 307, 316, 360, 363
Indian Workers' Association 165
Indicopleustes, Cosmas 20
Inkatha Freedom Party (IFP) 15, 27, 169, 228, 369
Innès, Anthony 165
Inside Higher Ed 94
Institute for Race Relations 30
Interdenominational African Ministers' Association (IDAMASA) 176, 193, 354
Interdenominational African Ministers' Federation (IDAMF) 193
Interfaith Community Development Association 435
Internal Security Act 11, 13, 230
International Civil Aviation Organisation 91
International Criminal Tribunal for the former Yugoslavia (ICTY) 174
International Monetary Fund (IMF) 101, 106, 119, 237, 363
International University Exchange Fund (IUEF) 37–8, 40, 63
Isaacs, Henry 8
Isandlwana 81–2
Ishmael 285
Islam 159, 365–6
   Ramadan 365
   Sunni 159
Israel 64, 114, 216, 382, 384
Issel, Johnny 222, 229
Isutheng Community Health Programme 12, 362
Italy 25
   Rome 18

J

Jabavu, Noni 261
Jackson, Jonathan 157
Jalobe, Sheila 370
Jamaica, Jamaican 25, 98, 149, 161–2
    Kingston 25
    Rodney Riots (1968) 25, 162
Jamaican Observer 98
James, Cyril Lionel Robert (CLR) 94, 159, 165, 219
    Black Jacobins (1938) 94
    World Revolution, 1917–1936: The Rise and Fall of the Communist International (1937) 94
James, LeBron 129
Jansen, Jonathan 261
Jarre, Jean-Michel 217
Jayawardane, Neelika 313
J Cole 249–50
Jeenah, Na'eem 366
Jim Crow, Jim Crow Laws 135, 251
Johannesburg Innercity Partnership 235
Johnson, Linton Kwesi 161
Jones, Ellen E 163
Jones, Peter 39, 223
Jones-LeCointe, Altheia 165
Jooma, Ashraf 236
Joseph, Helen 368
Joseph, Peniel 118
Josie, Vivienne 368
Journal for Critical Education Policy Studies 122
Junge, Rev Dr Martin 198

K

Kabila, Laurent-Désiré 104
Kabwe Conference (1975) 10
Kadoma Consultation 233
Kaepernick, Colin 130
Kalahari Surfers 281
Kalaote, Mam' Joyce 347
Kalawa Jazmee 288–90
Kalla, Shaeera 242
Kant, Immanuel 54, 313
Karenga, Maulana Ndabezitha 18, 149
Karis, Thomas
    Nadir and Resurgence, 1964–1979 74
    Protest to Challenge: A Documentary History of African Politics in South Africa 74
Kathrada, Ahmed 4, 73, 263
Kavanagh, Robert Mshengu 303–4
Keegan, Clive 28, 54
Kendi, Ibram X 144–5
Kennedy, Robert F 148, 260
Kente, Gibson 302
    How Long 302
    I Believe 302
    Too Late 302
Kentish, Rothwell 165
Kentridge, Sydney 13
Kenya 68, 79, 93, 204, 257, 276, 280
Kenyatta, Jomo 204, 311
Kgosana, Philip Ata 261, 239
Kgositsile, Keorapetse 255–9
    My Name is Afrika 256
Kgware, Bob 185
Kgware, Winnie 8, 171, 350–2
Khaled, Leila 23
Khanya College 125
Khanyisa School Project 360
Khoapa, Ben 6, 9, 49, 54, 172
Khoza, Constance 368
Khumalo-Seegelken, Dr Ben 177
Khunou, Freddy Samuel
    Mountains of Spirit: The Story of the Royal Bakwena ba Mogopa of the North West, South Africa 383
Kilgore, James 125
King Jr, Martin Luther 68, 96, 114, 182
Kirkwood, Mike 52, 264, 293
Kleinschmidt, Horst 71, 172, 181
    Roots and Journeys Linking the Christian Institute and Wider Community to the

Re-ignition of Resistance to Apartheid in the early 70s 72
de Klerk, FW 15, 41, 89, 228, 325
Knowles, Solange
   'Don't touch my hair' 320
de Kock, Eugene 41
Koka, Kalushi Drake 8, 39, 230
Koloane, David 303
von Kotze, Astrid 215
Kraai, Nomsisi 238
Kruger, Jimmy 13, 30, 57, 58, 225
Kruger, Paul 381
Ku Klux Klan 157, 396
Kubeka, Alpheus 313
Kumalo, Alf 297, 315
Kupe, Prof Tawana 87
Kuzwayo, Ellen 366–7, 368
   Call Me Woman (1985) 367

L

Labour and Community Resource Project (LACOM) 51
Lamont Smith, C 130
Lancaster House Agreement (1979) Internal Settlement 40
LANDBACK Campaign 395–8
Lang, Dr Ivor 58–9, 224–5
Langa, Ben 32, 273
Langa, Mandla 32, 272–4
   Lost Colours of the Chameleon, The 273
   Naked Song and Other Stories, The 273
   Tenderness of Blood 273
Langa, Pius 35, 273
Lapinsky, Sheila 54
Last Poets, The 259–60
Law Society of England 13
Lay Ecumenical Centre 192, 194–5
Le Balai Citoyen 105
Le Grange, Louis 43, 175
Leballo, PK 84
Legassick, Martin 4

Lekota, Mosiuoa 'Terror' 50, 89, 229, 233, 328
Lembede, Anton Muziwakhe 80, 226
Lenin, Vladimir 152
Lennon, John 157
Leopold II, King 103
Lesotho 37, 40, 82, 180, 188, 273, 277, 278, 279, 305, 366, 379
Lessing, Doris 262
Lewin, Hugh 54
Liberal Party 4
Liberia 84, 211
Libya 83, 84, 227
Lil' Baby 248–9
Lincoln University 94, 101
Lira 290
Loan, Nguyen Ngoc 24
London School of Economics and Political Science 101
London, Malcolm 300
Lorde, Audre 99
Losaba, Andrew 195
Louverture, Toussaint 105
Louwfant, John 6
Lovedale College 187, 366
Lumumba, Patrice 83, 103–4, 106, 280
Luruli, Ntshaveni wa 274
Lusaka Summit 89
Lutheran World Federation (LWF) 198
Luthuli, Inkosi Albert 3, 245, 360

M

Mabasa, Tiyani Lybon 14, 15, 235, 236–8
Mabiletsa, Deborah 368
Mabona, Anthony 6
Mabunda, Gonçalo 254
Mabuza, Lindiwe 261
Mabuza-Suttle, Felicia 47
Machaka, Petrus 6
Machel, Graça 91

Machel, Samora 88–9
Macqueen, Ian 52–6
Madagascar 20
Madingoane, Ingoapele 66, 266, 280–1
Madikizela-Mandela, Winnie 12, 30, 319, 352–4, 356, 368
Madonsela, Thuli 383
Mafeje, Archie 5
Mafokate, Arthur 288–9
Mafole, Tomeka 54
Mafikeng Manifesto (1975) 11
Mafikizolo 288
Mafuna, Bokwe 8, 9, 30–2, 46–50
Magogodi, Kgafela oa 281
Magubane, Peter 29, 297, 304, 315
Maharaj, Brij
   Zuma's Own Goal: Losing South Africa's 'War on Poverty' 119
Maher, Bill 114
Mahlangu, George 'Lucky' 231–2
Mahlangu, Solomon Kalushi 231
Mahlasela, F de Waal 195
Mahoota 289
Mail & Guardian 120, 219
Makhoba, Boyd 261
Malan, Daniel François 3, 379
Malcolm X 19, 48, 62, 78, 94, 99, 143, 146, 152, 159, 260, 370, 375
Malema, Julius 105, 189, 190, 238, 242, 243, 387–9, 392
Mali 79, 83, 84, 114, 374
Mall, Hassan 57
Mambéty, Djibril Diop
   Touki Bouki (1973) 317
Manabile, David 88
Manaka, Matsemela 292–5, 265
   Children of Asazi 294
   Egoli: City of Gold 294
   Goree 294
   Vuka 294

Manaka, Nomsa Kupi 293
Mandela, Nelson 1, 4, 15, 19, 34, 41, 45, 46, 47, 73, 86, 90, 108, 228, 236, 261, 263, 274, 277, 290, 300, 371, 378, 385
   Long Walk to Freedom 274
Mandela United Football Club 353
Mangcu, Xolela 188, 223–6, 354
Mangena, Mosibudi 9, 15, 16, 64, 227–8, 233, 235, 352, 355
Mangena, Oshadi Jane 199–200
Mangrove Nine 159–60, 163, 164
Manim, Mannie 306
Manthata, Tom 328
Manuel, Trevor 229
Mao Tse-tung 133, 152, 218
   Little Red Book, The 147, 153
Maoism 146
Maponya, Maishe 274
   Cry, The (1975) 274
   Dirty Work (1984) 274
   Gangsters (1984) 274
   Hungry Earth, The (1979) 274
Maqina, Rev Mzwandile
   Give Us This Day 302
Marable, Manning 118
Maré, Gerhard 75
Margo Commission (1987) 91
Market Theatre 274, 302, 305
Martinique 91, 104
Martin, Trayvon 125
Martin, Shantell 251
Marx, Karl 54, 152, 217
   On the Jewish Question (1844) 16
Marx, Rubin 57
Marxism 53, 94, 95, 100, 115, 146, 150, 191, 219, 239
Mascimento, Abdias do 112–3
Mashalaba, Vuyelwa 354, 36, 3681
Mashile, Lebo 281
Mashinini, Tsietsi 40, 64, 69, 208–11

Matshoba, Deborah 28, 238, 355–60, 368
Matshoba, Mtutuzeli 266, 274
   Call Me Not a Man 274
Matsobane, Dan 207
Matsobane, Mike 205–8
Mattera, Don 246, 274–5
   Azanian Love Song 261, 275
   Memory Is the Weapon 275
Matthews, James 172, 181, 282
Matthews, Michael
   Five Fingers for Marseilles 317
Mayatula, Mashwabanda 7
Maylam, Paul 171–2, 200–1
Mazibuko, Seth 212
Mazrui, Ali Al'amin 68
Mazwai, Thami 231
Mazwai, Thandiswa 372–4
Mbanjwa, Thoko 364
Mbeki, Govan 73
Mbeki, Thabo 15, 16, 37, 189, 197, 242, 263, 288, 298, 352
Mbembe, Achille 96
Mbete, Baleka 257
Mbuli, Mzwakhe 300–301
   Africa Amandla (2012) 301
   Born Free but Always in Chains (2015) 301
   'Change Is Pain' (1986) 301
   Mbulism (2004) 301
   Resistance Is Defence (1992) 301
   Thunder (2008) 301
   Unbroken Spirit (1888) 301
McCarthy, Joseph 157
McFadden, Syreeta 128
McGill Journal of Education 122, 239
McQueen, Steve
   12 Years a Slave 163
McWhorter, John 77
Mda, AP 80
Mda, Prof Zakes 236, 305
   We Shall Sing for the Fatherland 305
Mdu 290
Media Workers Association of South Africa 231
Medical Association of South Africa 225
Medical Rescue International (MRI) 60
Mediclinic Holdings 364
Medupe Writers' Association 13, 230, 264, 271–2, 304
Meer, Fatima 261, 360–1, 368
   Higher than Hope 261
   Portrait of Indian South Africans 360
   Trial of Andrew Zondo, The 261
Meer, Shamim 370
Memela, Sandile 231
Message to the People of South Africa 172
Methodist Wesley Youth Guild 208
Mexico 25, 78, 363
Mexico City Summer Olympics (1968) 25
Mgojo, Khoza Elliot 195
Mhlaba, Raymond 73, 263
Mhlanga, Louis 281
Mhlope, Gcina 193, 270
   Have you Seen Zandile? 193
   My Dear Madam 270
Mihloti Black Theatre 303
Millet, Godfrey 165
Mills, John Atta 101
Minty, Dr Abdul 91
Mji, Diliza 233
Mji, Gugu 370
Mkhabela, Ishmael 14, 205, 234–5, 336
Mkhabela, Ntsako 336
   By the Apricot Trees 336
Mkhathshwa, Nompendulo 242
Mkhathshwa, Smangaliso 6
Mlangeni, Andrew 73
Mngxitama, Andile 118
   Biko Lives! Contesting the Legacies of Steve Biko 118, 122

Mnyayiza, Nkathazo 264
Mnyele, Thamsanqa 'Thami' 346
Mobutu Sese Seko 104
Modisane, Jerry 8, 188
Moetapele, David 6
Mofokeng, Zakes 40
Mohammed, Elijah 159
Mohammed, Warith Deen 159
Mohapi, Mapetla 10, 11, 50, 62–3, 69, 364
Mohapi, Nonhle 62
Mokaba, Peter 289, 351–2
Mokae, Gomolemo 236
Mokoape, Aubrey 89
Mokoape, Nchaupe 235
Mokoditoa, Chris 5, 174
Mokoditoa, Madibeng 352
Mokoena, Hlonipha 321
Mokoena, Karabo 340
Mokoka, Clement 6
Molebatsi, Natalia 281
Molefe, Popo 328
Molekane, Tumi 247
Moloto, Justice 5, 174, 354
Monrovia Group 84
Monthly Review 236
Moodie, Dunbar 52
Moodley, Asha 237
Moodlet, Kessie 239
Moodley, Sam 306–8
Moodley, Strini 6, 7, 8, 30, 33, 50, 89, 188, 229, 235, 237, 246, 306–9, 355
   Black on White (1967) 309
Moore, Basil 5, 6, 171–5, 178, 200–1
Mopeli, Chief Paulu Howell 379
Mopeli, Treaty Mahlouoe 379
More, Mabogo Percy 120–1
Morphet, Tony 552
Morris, Tracie 299
Morrison, Toni 90

Mosala, Itumeleng 235
Moscow Film Festival 318
Moseneke, Dikgang 50, 87–8, 215, 232
   My Own Liberator 215
Moseneke, Tiego 232
Moss, Glenn 71
Motheo FET College 352
Mothle, Billy 60
Mothopeng, Zephania 10, 84, 205
Motlaba, Mokgethi 186
Motlana, Nthato 12, 14, 32, 35, 48, 234, 352–3
Motlana, Sally 234, 353, 368
Motloung, Kamohelo 369
Motloung, Mondy Johannes 231
Motsisi, Casey 262, 276
Moutloatse, Keitumetse Fatimata 339, 345
Moynihan Report, the 109–10
Mozambique 9, 10, 20, 54, 88, 89, 90, 91, 231, 254, 263, 273, 279, 281, 335
   independence of (1975) 10
   Mozambique Liberation Front (Frelimo) 9, 10, 63, 65, 88–90, 102, 229, 330
   Central Committee 88
Mphahlele, Prof Es'kia 79, 236, 261, 262, 275–6
   Down Second Avenue 276
Mpofu-Walsh, Sizwe 249
Mpumalanga Arts Group 264
Mpumlwana, Malusi 10, 54, 364
Mtshali, Oswald 296
Mtshali, Thembi 261
Mtshizana, LL 188
Muhammad, Elijah 159
Muhammad, Wallace Fard 158
Muhammad University of Islam 122
Mulele, Pierre 104
Musi, Hendrick 6, 24, 26, 29

Music, Drama, Arts and Literature Institute (Mdali) 303
Muslim Personal Law Board of South Africa 366
Muslim Youth Movement of South Africa
   al-Qalam 366
Mutloatse, Mothobi 261, 264, 276, 293, 315
   Forced Landing: Africa South: Contemporary Writing (1980) 261
   Mama Ndiyalila (1982) 261
   Reconstruction: 90 Years of Black Historical Literature (1981) 261
   Umhlaba Wethu (1984) 261
Muyanga, Neo 283
Muzorewa, Bishop Abel 40
Mvovo, Mxolisi 364
Mxenge, Griffiths 10, 35, 62
Myeza, Muntu 50, 89–90, 235
Mzamane, Mbulelo Vizikhungo 277–8

N
Naicker, Arun 277
Naidoo, Derrick 216
Naidoo, Leigh-Ann 216
Naidoo, Margaret 368
Naidoo, Shanthie 304
Nakasa, Nat 261, 262–3
Naledi High School 211, 329–30
Namibia 177, 210, 281
Napley, Sir David 13
Natal African Teachers' Union 214
Natal Code of Black Law 367
Natal Education Trust 360
Natal Indian Congress 53
Natal Society Foundation 193, 195
Natal University
   Non-European Section 5, 27, 53
Nation of Islam (NOI) 158–9
National Action Network 202
National Association for the Advancement of Colored People (NAACP) 71, 97
   Crisis 97
National Association of Youth Organisations (NAYO) 230
National Catholic Federation of Students 200
National Committee Against Removals 383
National Council of Trade Unions (Nactu) 237
National Forum 14
National Freedom Day 390
National Institute for the Humanities and Social Sciences (NIHSS) 122, 215
National Intelligence Agency 56
National Liberation Front (NLF) 219, 220
National Party (NP) 3, 13, 15, 27, 32, 48, 58, 167, 175, 205, 227–8
National Planning Commission 231
National Union of Mineworkers (NUM) 117
   Research and Policy Institute 362
National Union of South African Students (NUSAS) 4–6, 8, 26–7, 28, 38, 53, 54, 71–7, 146, 173, 176, 188, 233, 309, 339
National Youth Organisation 9
Natives Land Act (1913) 82
Naudé, Beyers 6, 13, 71, 166–9, 172, 174, 177, 199
Ndawo, Ralph 315
Ndebele, Njabulo 180, 236, 246, 263, 271, 278–9
   Fools and Other Stories (1983) 279
Ndebele, Regina Makhosazana 278
Ndifuna Ukwazi (NU) 216
Ndlovu, Duma ka 271–2
Ndlovu, Hastings 210

Ndlovu, Thuli 391
Ndlozi, Mbuyiseni Quintin 124–5
Ndungane, Njongonkulu 236
Nederduitse Gereformeerde Kerk (NGK) 167, 168, 177
Nefolovhodwe, Pandelani 50, 65, 89, 228, 229, 233, 235
Négritude 17, 79, 104, 105, 111–2, 308
Nelson Mandela Children's Fund 235, 282, 327
Nelson Mandela Foundation 19, 238–9, 282
Nelson Mandela Metropolitan University 121
Nengwekhulu, Ranwedzi 'Harry' 6, 8, 9, 24–41, 46, 47, 50, 65, 173, 188
Netherlands 37, 278
   Amsterdam 199, 271, 283
   Hague, The 174, 199
   Holland 194, 196
New Age 255, 263
New Coin 196
New York African Film Festival 317
New York Times 77, 102, 107, 123, 126, 144, 151, 253, 255, 262, 321, 398
News24 59
Newton, Huey P 147–51, 152–4
NG Mission Church 196
Ngoyi, Lilian 368
Ngwenya, Rose 236, 238
Nhlapo, Welile 54
Nieuwoudt, Gideon 49, 57
Nigeria 81, 83, 84, 211, 276, 277, 311
   Lagos 283
Nkomo, Nkwenkwe Vincent 89
Nkondo, Curtis 14
Nkosi, Lewis 80, 261, 278–80, 304
Nkrumah, Kwame 83, 95, 96, 97, 99–101, 217, 280, 373
Nkruhamist Gospel 100
Noah, Trevor 288

Noel, Jeannie 368
Non-European Unity Movement (NEUM) 4, 47, 218, 219
North Korea 113–14, 118
North Vietnam, Democratic Republic of 100, 153
North West Traditional Leadership and Governance Act 384
North West University 383
Noruka, Manku 303, 346–50
Ntsebeza, Dumisa 79, 236
Ntwasa, Stanley 6, 30, 34, 174–5, 185, 186, 191
Nyembezi, Merina 368
Nyerere, Julius 79, 83, 101–2, 116, 217, 226, 333
Nzimande, Anele 243–5
Nzondelelo 194
Nzongola-Ntalaja, Georges 103–4
   Congo from Leopold to Kabila: A People's History, The 103

O

Obama, Barack 115–6
Oblates of Mary Immaculate 200
Obote, Milton 102
Odd Future 258–9
Olivier, SP 308
Oliver, Roland
   A Short History of Africa 20
Olsson, Göran Hugo
   Concerning Violence: Nine Scenes from the Anti-Imperialistic Self-Defense 91
One for the Road 174
Ono, Yoko 157
openDemocracy 119
Ophir 263
Oppenheimer, Harry 33
Orange Free State African Teachers' Association 214
Organisation of African Unity (OAU)

83, 84, 99, 234, 329
Organisation of Afro-American Unity 159
Oskido, DJ 288–90
Otto, Roy 357
Outlow, Lucius T 107
#OutsourcingMustFall 349

P
Pace, Eric 102
Padmore, George 96
Palestine 158
   Gaza Strip 382, 384
   West Bank 114, 382
Palestinian Liberation Organisation (PLO) 64
Palweni, Chapman 354
Pambo, Vuyani 243
Pan-African Film Festival 274
Pan-African Parliament (PAP) 83
Pan African Space Station (PASS) 283
Pan African Student Movement of Azania (PASMA) 88
Pan Africanist Congress (PAC) 3–4, 9, 10, 11, 20, 26, 32, 35, 37, 47, 50, 65, 66, 70, 73, 79, 83. 84, 85, 102, 124, 172, 187, 205–8, 209, 215, 222, 223, 228, 229, 231, 233, 239, 267, 305, 385
   Poqo 141, 153
Pan-Africanism 3, 74, 81, 93, 96, 98, 99, 281, 371
Pape, John 125
Parks, Gordon 317
   Parliamentary Committee on Rural Development and Land Reform 392
Passive Resistance Campaigns 360
Patel, Zulaikha 319–320
Pather, Dennis 309
Paton, Alan 310

Patriotic Front 228, 234
Peace and Freedom Party of Cleaver 148
Pennsylvania State University 181
People's Experimental Theatre 62, 303
People's Movement for the Liberation of Angola (MPLA) 94
Periplus of the Erythraean Sea 20
Peter's Theological College 187
Phakathi, Oshadi 368
Phatudi, Cedric 405
Pheko, Motsoko 79, 86
Pheto, Molefe 303–4, 346–7
   And Night Fell – Memoirs of a Political Prisoner in South Africa 346–7
   Bull from Moruleng: Vistas of Home and Exile, The 346
Phillip, Rubin 166, 175, 188–9
Pickover, Michele 60
Pieterson, Hector 210, 245
Pillay, Kiruba 309
Pillay, Sam 307, 309
Pinto, Frieda 163
Pityana, Barney 5–6, 8–9, 24, 26–30, 34, 37, 39, 40, 46, 49, 54, 65, 68–70, 171, 173, 174, 188, 279, 333, 354, 364
Pityana, Dimza 34
Pliny the Elder 20
Pokela, Nyathi 84
Poland 25
   Kraków 101
Popular Education Programme (PEP) 216
Portugal 9
Potgieter, Denzil 57
Powell, Enoch 164
Powell, Ivor 56
Powys, Moira 310
Pratt, Elmer 'Geronimo' 156
Press, Karen
   'Priorities' (1990) 1

Press Council 58, 231
Pretoria Girls High 320–323
Pretoria University 200
Pretorius, Paul 54
Princeton University 107–8
Progressive Party 32
Prophets of Da City (POC) 285
Ptolemy
   Geographia 20
Publications and Entertainment Act (1963) 262
Purple Renoster, The 263, 278

Q
Qoboza, Percy 13–14, 230–1
Qubeka, Jahmil XT 315–8
   A Small Town Called Descent 316
   Of Good Report 315–6
   Sew the Winter to My Skin 316
   Stillborn 314
Queen 290
Quinn, Jane 370

R
Race Today Collective 161
Rachidi, Kenneth 5
Ralph Ndawo Foundation 315
Ramadiro, Brian 219
Rambally, Asha 309
Ramone 285
Ramphele, Mamphela 10, 34, 35–6, 56, 361
   Across Boundaries 354
   Bounds of Possibility: The Legacy of Steve Biko and Black Consciousness 364
Rampolokeng, Lesego 280–1
Rand Daily Mail 6, 29, 30, 32, 46, 48, 58, 315
Randall, Peter 54, 172–3, 265
Ravan Press 172, 264–6, 271, 274, 276–7, 293

RawStory 114
Ready D 285–6
Reagan, Ronald 158
Reconstruction and Development Programme (RDP) 119, 287
RDP White Paper 119
Reddy, Kiruba 31
Reformed Independent Churches Association (RICA) 193
Resha, Robert 275
Review of African Political Economy 119
#RhodesMustFall 240, 349
Rhodes University 5, 28, 53, 72, 108, 146, 161, 171, 172, 174, 200–1, 233, 240, 340, 349
   Unit for Humanities 118
Rhodesia 40
Ribeiro, Fabian 365
Ribeiro, Florence 364-5
Riotous Assemblies Act 11, 389
Rivonia Trial (1964) 4, 29, 73
Rodney, Walter 25, 162
Roma University 180, 278
le Roux, Philippe 54
Royal, Ségolène 105
Rotal College of Art 312
Rural Women's Movement 383
Russell, David 192
Rutledge, Christopher 121

S
Saad, Layla 145
Said, Edward 118, 122
Salisbury Island 306–10
San Francisco State University 147, 152
   Strike (1968) 147
Sanders, Bernie 114
Sandi, Ntsiki 57
Sandile's Kop 82
Sankara, Thomas 23, 105–6, 389
Sartre, Jean-Paul 53, 107, 112, 303

Black Orpheus (1948) 112, 276
Sastri College 307-8
Scargill, Arthur 117
Schadeberg, Jürgen 315
Schlebusch, Alwyn 175
Schlebusch Commission (1973) 8, 54, 74, 77, 175, 226
Schlemmer, Lawrence 55
Schomburg, Arturo Alfonso 96
Schoon, Jeanette 76
Schoon, Marius 76
Scientology 158
Scott-Heron, Gil 154, 300
Seale, Bobby 146, 149, 150-4
   A Lonely Rage (1978) 154
   Seize the Time: The Story of Black Panther Party and Huey P Newton 151, 154
Seatlholo, Khotso 211
Second World War (1939-45) 100
   Atomic Bombing of Hiroshima and Nagasaki (1945) 103
Sedeba, Gilbert 89
Seedat, Zubie 368
Segal, Lauren
   Soweto: A History 214
Seipei, Stompie 353
Sejanamane, James 207
Sekoto, Gerard 313
Sen, Mala 161
Senegal
   Dakar 234
Senghor, Léopold 17, 53104, 262
Sepamla, Sipho 261, 296, 304
   A Ride in the Whirlwind 304
September, Dulcie 205, 217-8
Seroka, Joyce 368
Seroke, Jaki 261
Serote, Mongane Wally 18, 30, 246, 296-8, 346
Seti-Sonamzi, Vuyolwethu 123
Sey, Susan Elizabeth 60

Shabazz, Betty 93
Shaft 17
Shaikh, Shamima 365-6
Shakur, Assata Olugbala 65, 120
Shakur, Tupac 156, 250, 286
Sharp, Diamond 299
Sharpeville Massacre (1960) 29, 65, 86, 205, 262, 268, 307
Sharpton, Al 201-3
Shezi, Mthuli ka 8, 28, 50, 62, 69, 303, 304
Shinners, Mark 50
Shivambu, Nyiko Floyd 387
Shringarpure, Bhakti 91-2
Shubane, Khehla 238-9
Shugasmakx 246, 286-8
Sibeko, David 37
Sibisi, Charles 354
Siebert, Daniel Petrus 57
Sihlali, Durant 261, 313
Sikhakhane, Enos Zwelabantu 192-3
Sikhakhane-Rankin, Joyce 231
Simon, Barney 262, 306
Sisulu, Walter 4, 73, 90, 263
Sithole, Nomathemba 368
Siwane, Joyce 368
Sixth War of National Resistance (1834) 81
Skota, Mweli TD 261
Skotaville 261, 263
Skotnes, Cecil 313
Skwatta Kamp 286-7
Skweyiya, Thembile 35
Smith, Harry 81
Smith, Vesta 368
Snyman, Major Harold 57-8
Sobukwe, Robert Mangaliso 3, 10, 13, 73, 79-88, 116, 226, 236, 268, 365
Sobukwe, Veronica 365
Socialist Party (France) 105
Socialist Party of Azania (SOPA) 15,

236–8
Soka University 279
Solzhenitsyn, Aleksandr 157
Somalia 20, 83
Soni, Selma 310
Sony Music 289
Sorbonne, the 53, 180
Soul Students Advisory Council 153
South Africa
   Alexandra 31, 46, 47, 290, 292, 296, 297
   apartheid 3–13, 18, 23, 25, 27, 28, 31, 32, 34, 38, 41, 43, 45, 47, 49, 50, 51, 57, 58, 64, 65, 66, 71–5, 79, 80, 81, 83–9, 91, 112–3, 117, 125, 167–73, 175–8, 181, 187, 189, 191, 192, 194, 195–8, 200–1, 205–8, 209–11, 212, 213, 214, 216, 220, 223, 225, 226–7, 229, 234, 237, 239, 241, 255, 257, 261–4, 268, 269, 270, 274, 275, 281, 282, 285, 291–4, 296, 298–303, 306, 309, 310–6,
   Båstad 25
   Bloemfontein 193, 272, 389
   Boipatong 169
   Bophuthatswana 169, 382
   Braamfontein 41, 60, 212, 242, 244, 341
   Cape Province 193
   Cape Town 6, 7, 28, 39, 51, 123, 125, 220, 222–3, 233, 239, 263, 267, 269–70, 272, 282, 283, 285, 286, 302, 317, 380–1, 383
   Ciskei 169, 316
   Constitution of 3, 19, 44, 67, 82, 85, 197, 256, 381, 386–8
   Diepkloof 7, 272, 292, 293
   Dinokana 50, 63
   Durban 5, 8–10, 31, 42, 50–6, 62, 75, 90, 118, 120, 173, 180, 189, 190, 196, 239, 271, 277, 306, 307, 352, 360–1, 370, 391
   Eastern Cape 3, 5, 7, 9, 10, 23, 26, 58, 62–3, 81, 82, 116, 171, 173, 313, 317, 351, 354, 361, 365, 366, 381,
   Fort Beaufort Prison 188
   Fort Hare 5, 9, 26–9, 34, 74, 116, 171
   Free State 12, 24, 34, 193, 205, 214, 328, 352, 353, 379, 389
   Gazankulu 169
   Ginsberg 23, 222, 223, 235, 236, 351
   Graff-Reinet 14
   Grahamstown 5, 26, 72–3, 169, 170, 173, 274, 309
   Hammanskraal 7, 8, 10, 14, 49, 176, 199, 279, 352
   Johannesburg 3–6, 8, 11, 14, 30, 31, 35, 46–7, 51, 58, 59, 64, 76, 125, 168, 170, 178, 181, 199, 201, 212, 215, 224, 231, 232, 235, 243, 257, 264, 367, 272, 278, 282, 283, 292–3, 296, 302, 303, 305, 313, 315, 317, 328, 343, 345, 346, 355, 356, 365, 370, 381, 384
   Kagiso 206
   Kakamas 196
   KaNgwane 169
   Khale 64
   King William's Town 9, 10, 12, 39, 54, 63, 192, 221, 224, 361, 381
   Kruger National Park 29
   Krugersdorp 205, 355, 359
   KwaZulu-Natal 112, 119, 120, 121,

367, 284, 290, 389
Langa 31, 239
Lebowa 169, 405
Leeuwkop Prison 50
Lenasia 303, 305
Limpopo 5, 8, 24, 120, 173, 275, 292–3, 361, 380
Marabastad 276
Mariannhill 4, 6, 26, 27, 72, 188
Marikana 237
Midrand 83
Mpumalanga 264, 272, 385
Natal 4–5, 10, 47, 52–3, 55, 72, 193, 194–5, 198, 307, 367, 370, 381
National Assembly 16, 233, 388–9, 392
Ngoye 5, 74, 174
Northern Cape 196, 380, 382
Pietermaritzburg 198, 200, 364, 267
Pietermaritzburg Prison 356, 358–9
Polokwane 24, 351
Port Elizabeth 12, 49, 57, 58–9, 121, 224, 367
Pretoria 4, 7, 42, 59, 60, 89, 190, 199, 220, 310–1, 320–1, 328, 360, 381, 389
Queenstown 3, 194
QwaQwa 169, 380
Robben Island 11, 41, 59–60, 69–70, 154, 160, 163, 169, 177, 187, 250, 273, 285
Roodepoort 14, 46, 235
Rosettenville 170, 174, 187
Sharpeville 4, 167, 239, 275, 337
Sophiatown 46–7, 275, 296, 300, 305, 381
Soweto 3, 7, 11–2, 14, 15, 46, 63–4, 75, 179, 204–13, 234–5, 272, 274, 275, 281, 282, 292, 396,

302–3, 313, 317, 328, 336, 349, 352–3, 364, 368
Transkei 27, 42, 169, 221, 223, 381
Transvaal 5, 12, 13, 26, 62, 367, 368
Turfloop 5, 7, 9–10, 24, 26–7, 29, 63, 73, 74, 90, 120, 174, 208, 228, 238, 278, 350–1, 404
Tylden 3
Umlazi 34–5, 360
Umtata 193
Vaal Triangle 125
Venda 26, 169
Verulam 271
Western Cape 39, 177, 229
Zeerust 50
Zinyoka 10, 361
Zululand 5, 7
Zwelitsha 63
South African Black Theatre Union (SABTU) 309
South African Broadcasting Corporation (SABC) 273, 289, 290, 301
South African Bureau for Racial Affairs (SABRA) 379
South African Catholic Bishops Conference 200
South African Communist Party (SACP) 217, 219
South African Council for Higher Education (SACHED) 51, 220
South African Council of Churches (SACC) 6, 67, 172–3, 176–7, 191, 193, 195, 198
   Hammanskraal Resolution (1974) 199
   Study Project on Christianity in Apartheid Society (SPRO-CAS) 6, 54, 172, 175, 180
South African Defence Force (SADF) 190

South African Democratic Teachers
    Union (SADTU) 213
South African History Archive 209
South African Human Rights
    Commission 174, 328, 351
South African Indian Congress 360
South African Institute of Race
    Relations (SAIRR) 6, 8, 11, 172,
    176, 235
South African Medical and Dental
    Council (SAMDC) 225
South African National Students
    Congress (SANSCO) 233
South African Native National
    Congress 261
South African Police
    Security Branch 12, 49, 57, 62,
    185, 188, 209, 357, 399
South African Paulo Freire Institute
    (PFI-SA) 112
South African Press Association
    (SAPA) 59
South African Press Council 58
South African Student Solidarity
    Foundation 232
South African Students Congress
    (SASCO) 124, 233, 242, 352
South African Students' Movement
    (SASM) 7, 27, 40, 64, 208, 210,
    230–1, 279, 330, 333
South African Students' Organisation
    (SASO) 6–11, 13, 24, 26–8, 30–5,
    37, 42, 46–9, 50, 52–5, 63,
    64–5, 66, 73–6, 88–90, 112, 120,
    170, 172, 173, 174, 188, 190, 195,
    210, 226, 229, 230, 233, 236,
    237, 241, 273, 279, 296, 308,
    330, 334, 339, 350, 352, 354–5,
    357, 361, 368, 399, 403–4
    Policy Manifesto 6, 42, 403–4
South Korea 363

South Sudan 83
South Vietnam (Republic of Vietnam)
    153
    Saigon 24
South West Africa People's
    Organisation (Swapo) 94, 172
Southern African Catholic Bishops'
    Conference (1977) 12
Southern Negro Youth Congress 157
Soviet Union (USSR) 91, 227
Sowetan Live 61
Soweto Black Parents' Organisation 11
Soweto Civic Association 238
Soweto Parents' Association 352
Soweto Parents Crisis Committee
    (SPCC) 15
Soweto Students Representative
    Committee (SSRC) 11–12, 208,
    210, 211
Soweto Uprising (1976) 12, 86, 271,
    304, 337, 346
Spain 25, 78
Sparks, Allister 29
Speak 369–70
Spearhead 263
Spikiri 289–90
Spillers, Hortense 109–10
St Francis College 4, 26
Staffrider 117, 263, 264 6, 274, 293
Star, The 61, 208
Steadman, Ian 303
Steele, Clive Anthony 60
Steele, Maureen 60
Steve Biko Foundation 59, 61, 79,
    117, 235–6
    Frank Talk 55, 236
    Robert Sobukwe Memorial Lecture 79
Stone, Brad Elliot 114
Stopforth, Paul 311–2
    Biko Series, The 312
    Interrogators, The 312

Stubbs, Aelred 40, 171, 175, 178, 187–8, 192
Student Non-Violent Coordinating Committee (SNCC) 147–9
Students Christian Association (SCA) 170
Students of Young Azania (SOYA) 233
Students Representative Council (SRC) 5, 9, 26, 63, 74, 76, 88, 200, 229, 241, 242, 243, 279, 304, 351, 352
Sun Myung Moon 151
Sunday Express 58
Suppression of Communism Act (1972) 63, 198, 207, 230, 355, 362
Surplus Peoples Project 383
Suzman, Helen 32–3, 310, 407
Swaziland 27, 89, 231, 277–9
Sweden 25, 254, 311
  Stockholm 311
Switzerland 194
  Geneva 38–9, 44, 174, 199, 282
Sydney Film Festival 317
Symbionese Liberation Army (SLA) 125

T
Tambo, Oliver Reginald 3, 37, 73, 88–91, 223,
Tanganyika African National Union (TANU) 101
Tanzania 73, 101–2, 153, 227, 248, 255, 257, 382
  Dar es Salaam 4, 257
  independence of (1955) 101
  Morogoro 382
Taylor, Breonna 130, 164
Taylor, Charles 106
Taylor, Councill 149
Taylor, Vanessa 370
Teachers League of South Africa 214, 218–9

Tembalishe Tutorial College 360
Temple University 155
Terrorism Act 8, 9, 14, 58, 62–3, 211, 215, 216, 227, 23, 238, 355, 356, 362
Thaba Bosiu 82
Tharmalingam, Neelan 310
Thatcher, Margaret 117
Thatiah, Ror 309
Theatre Archive 301
Theatre Council of Natal (TECON) 8, 10, 303, 309
Themba, Can 262, 277
Thiong'o, Ngugi wa 92–93, 236
  Decolonising the Mind: The Politics of Language in African Literature (1986) 92
Third Reich (1933–45) 169
Third World Liberation Front 133
Thloloe, Joseph Nong 231
Thomas, David 176
Thomas, Gladys 172, 181, 269–70
  Avalon Court (1992) 270
  Wynberg Seven, The (1987) 269
Times Live 393
Timol, Ahmed 60
Tiro, Onkgopotse Abram 6–7, p, 31, 63–4, 69, 120, 208, 279, 404
TKZee 290
Tladi, Lefifi 249, 310–1
Tlali, Miriam 261, 266, 270–1
  Mihloti 261, 271
  Muriel at Metropolitan 266
Tleane, Console 236
du Toit, Darcy 51
Tometi, Opal 125–6
Tomlinson, Prof Frederick R 379
Tomlinson Report (1954) 379
Toronto International Film Festival 317
Touré, Ahmed Sékou 83, 101, 102
Toure, Souleymane 281
Trade Union Council of South Africa

(TUCSA) 48
Transnet 364
Transvaal African Teachers'
    Association 214
Transvaal College of Education 26
Transvaal Rural Action Committee
    382–3
Transvaler 382–3
Trengove, John
    Inxeba 317
Trial of 22 304, 353
Tricameral Parliament 197, 366
Trichardt, Louis 366
Trompies 288–9
Trump, Donald 114, 130, 135, 156,
    202, 335, 397–8
Truth and Reconciliation Commission
    (TRC) 15, 41, 44, 49, 56–8, 60,
    63, 64, 76, 195, 225–6, 273, 328,
    356, 359–60, 365
    Amnesty Committee 57, 365
    Section 29 hearings 56
    Women's Hearing (1997) 355
Tucker, David 201
Tucker, Ken 251
Tucker, Dr Benjamin 15, 58–9, 225
Túpac Amaru II 156, 250
Turfloop 5, 7, 9–10, 24, 26, 27, 29,
    63, 73, 74, 90, 120, 174, 208,
    228, 238, 278, 350–1, 404
Turner, Jann
    My Father, Rick Turner 56
Turner, Rick
    Eye of the Needle, The (1972) 54, 180
Tuskegee Institute 97
Tutu, Desmond 1, 4, 40, 45, 171, 195,
    206, 236, 261, 266, 278
Tutu, Mpho 40
Tyler the Creator 257–8

U

Uganda 102
Umphumulo Theological College 198
Umtapo Centre 277, 352
Unfreedom Day 390
Unification Church 151
Union of African Socialist Republics 99
Union of Black Journalists (UBJ) 9,
    13, 47, 230–1
Union of South Africa Act (1909) 82
United Coloured People's
    Association 160
United Democratic Front (UDF) 173,
    197, 222, 229, 232–3, 235, 347,
    348
United Kingdom (UK) 116, 160–1,
    164, 231, 346
    Black People's Day of Action
        (1981) 160–1
    Brixton Riots (1981) 161–2
    London 14, 102, 104, 118, 159,
        160–4, 185, 209, 226, 274,
        283, 300, 312, 393
    National Theatre 274
    Northern Ireland 25
    Public Relations and
        Communications Association 394
    Troubles, The 25
United Methodist Church 40
United Nations (UN)
    General Assembly 84, 211
    Joint UN Programme on HIV/
        AIDS (UNAIDS) 282
    Security Council 13, 58
    Special Committee Against
        Apartheid 84
United States of America (USA) 1, 12,
    24, 77, 78, 94–7, 113, 115, 126,
    130, 203, 374, 375, 397, 404–5
    Black History Month 138
    Central Intelligence Agency (CIA) 39
    Chicago, IL 94, 135, 148, 154,

256, 282
Civil Rights Act (1964) 98
Civil Rights Movement 24, 68, 136. 148. 157
Civil War (1861–5) 16
Congress 12, 58, 126
Constitution of 16
Denver, CO 138, 276, 278
Detroit, MI 135, 158
Federal Bureau of Investigation (FBI) 147–9, 156–7
government of 24
Jim Crow Laws 135
Kansas City, MO 97
Los Angeles, CA 149, 256–7, 317
National Guard 135
New York 13, 17, 21, 68, 93, 96, 107, 113, 126, 128, 157, 162, 191, 196, 201–3, 218, 251–3, 254–5, 260, 271, 278, 281, 283, 317, 371, 374–5
Oakland, CA 126, 147–8, 150–1, 153
San Francisco, CA 152, 158, 271, 133, 147
US Air Force (USAF) 153
Washington DC 94, 119, 145
United Ulama Council of South Africa 366
Unity Movement (UM) 218, 220
Universal Music 289
Universal Negro Improvement Association and African Communities League (UNIA-ACL) 98
University Christian Movement (UCM) 5–7, 8, 26, 73–4, 112, 146, 167–76, 184–6, 200–1, 226, 241, 351
  Stutterheim Conference (1968) 170–1
University of Ahmadu Bello 81
University of Botswana 269, 277
University of California, Irvine 93
University of California, Los Angeles (UCLA) 94, 149, 157, 257
University of California, San Diego 157
University of California, Santa Cruz 153, 158
University of Cape Town (UCT) 5, 7, 76, 123, 174, 180, 239, 243, 278, 305, 340, 362
  African Centre for Cities 283
  South African Labour and Development Research Unit 362
University of Chicago 94, 195
University of Dar es Salaam 257
University of Durban-Westville 120–1, 309, 366
University of Edinburgh
  Journal of Holy Land and Palestinian Studies 122
University of Fort Hare 5, 9, 26, 27, 28, 29, 34, 74, 79, 80, 84, 116, 121, 174, 193, 195, 209, 231, 273, 277, 306
University of Heidelberg 198
University of Johannesburg (UJ) 121, 122, 180, 279
  Centre for Sociological Research 306
  Education as Change 122
University of KwaZulu-Natal 112, 119–20, 121, 196, 215, 270
  Centre for Adult Education (CAE) 112
  Centre for Civil Society 119
University of Nairobi 280
University of Natal 5, 42, 52–3, 55, 190, 361
  Institute for Industrial Education 55
  South African Labour Bulletin 55

University of North Carolina 103
University of Pennsylvania 119, 276
University of Port Elizabeth 367
University of South Africa (Unisa)
   8, 31, 46, 54, 63, 120, 124, 174,
   199, 276
University of Stellenbosch 167, 240,
   280, 379
University of the Western Cape
   (UWC) 5, 8–9, 174, 215, 231, 278
University of the Witwatersrand
   (Wits) 60, 74, 87–8, 116, 121, 123,
   125, 214, 232, 238, 241–3, 274,
   275, 278, 279, 309, 366–7
   Education Policy Unit 121
   Vuvuzela 232
University of Toronto Robarts
   Collection 20
University of Wisconsin-Madison 123
University of Zululand-Ngoye 27–8,
   62, 174, 304, 355
US (Us Black People) 149
US Social Forum (2007) 17
Utah State University
   *Ariel: A Review of International English
   Literature* 280

V

Vakalisa Arts Association 282
Vally, Salim 121–2, 219
Vanrenen, Maralin
   Have you Seen Zandile? 261
van Zyl, Danie 172
Variety 316
Venezuela
   Admirable Campaign (1813) 23
Verwoerd, HF 167–8, 379
Vietcong 24
Vietnam War (1955–75) 24, 133
   Tet Offensive (1968) 24
Villa-Vicencio, Charles 261

Voice, The 276
Vorster, BJ 57–8, 83, 175, 404
Vundla, Charlie 317
   Tribe, The 317

W

Wade, Dwayne 129
Walters, Shirley 215
Wanjala, Prof Christopher L
   *Still Beating the Drum: Critical Perspectives
   on Lewis Nkosi* 280
Washington, Booker T 97
Washington, Denzel 35
Washington Post 30, 42–3, 123
WEB Du Bois Learning Centre 97
WEB Du Bois Memorial Centre for
   Pan-African Culture 98
Weekend Argus 56
Weekend World 13, 58, 230
Wesleyan University 279
West, Cornel 113–4
West Rand Administration Board 302
Westgate Walding Auctioneers 59–61
de Wet, JM 5, 174
Wietie 263
Williamson, Craig 38–41, 63, 76, 91
'Willie Lynch' 247
Winter, Gordon
   Inside BOSS (1981) 63
Witness, The 196, 277
Wits Black Student Society (BSS) 232
Wits Historical Papers 60
Wits Institute of Social and Economic
   Research (WiSER) 123
de Witte, Ludo 103
   Assassination of Lumumba, The 103
Witwatersrand Network for the
   Homeless 235
Women's Boat to Gaza 216
Women's March (1956) 360, 369
Wood, Chris 54

Woods, Donald 13, 28, 34
Worcester, Kent 94
Workers' College 239
Workers International International Liaison Committee 237
Workers Organisation for Socialist and Action 220-1
Working People's Alliance 162
World, The 13, 32, 46, 58, 230, 269, 271, 302
World Alliance of Reformed Churches (WARC) 197
Declaration on Racism (1982) 197
World Bank 83, 88, 186, 282-3, 362-3, 385
Expanded Public Works Programme 363
Options for Land Reform and Rural Structuring (1992) 385
World Council of Churches (WCC) 168, 173-4, 198
Word N Sound 298-9
World Student Christian Federation (WSCF) 170
World Trade Organization (WTO) 237
Woza Afrika Foundation 272
Wright, Richard 107
Native Son 107
Wun, Connie 133
van Wyk, Chris 293

X
Xarra Books 275

Y
Yale University 110, 123
'Yellow Peril' 133
Yemen 20
Yfm 286, 288, 289
York University 121
Young African Religious Movement (YARM) 206
Young Communist League (YCL) 124
Young Women's Christian Association (YWCA) 328, 355, 367
World Congress (1971) 355
Youth African Christian Movement (YACM) 206
Yu Chin Chan Club (YCCC) 218
Yugoslavia 25, 78, 174

Z
Zaire 104
Zambia 10, 257, 205
Lusaka 88, 199, 273
Zanempilo Community Health Centre 10, 333
Zeilig, Leo 106
Frantz Fanon: Philosopher of Third World Liberation 106
Patrice Lumumba: Africa's Lost Leader 106
Zille, Helen 29, 32
Zimbabwe 17, 26, 40, 152, 189, 210, 227-8, 233, 261, 279, 281, 301, 335
Chimurenga War (1964-79) 261
Harare 227
Zimbabwe African National Liberation Army 102
Zimele Trust Fund 230
Zinn Education Project 96
Zionism 93
Zola 288, 290-1, 330
Mdlwembe 288
Zola 7 291
Zuma, Jacob 67, 135, 241, 244, 287, 290, 393